THE COMMUNISTS OF POLAND

D0141027

HISTORIES OF RULING COMMUNIST PARTIES

Richard F. Staar, editor

THE COMMUNISTS OF POLAND
An Historical Outline, Revised Edition

Jan B. de Weydenthal

 HOOVER INSTITUTION PRESS
Stanford University   Stanford, California

Hoover Press Publication 347

First printing, 1986

Manufactured in the United States of America

90 89 88 87 86   9 8 7 6 5 4 3 2 1

Library of Congress Cataloging in Publication Data

De Weydenthal, Jan B.
  The Communists of Poland.

  (Histories of ruling Communist parties)
  Bibliography: p.
  Includes index.
  1. Polska Zjednoczona Partia Robotnicza—History.
2. Poland—Politics and government—1945–1980.
3. Poland—Politics and government—1980–
I. Title. II. Series.
JN6769.A52D49 1986   324.2438′075′09   86-18615
ISBN 0-8179-8472-0 (alk. paper)

For my mother and my father, in memory

Contents

Editor's Foreword

This is the fourth in our series of histories about ruling communist parties, from their origins to the present. The project encompasses sixteen volumes and, when completed, should fill a gap in modern English-language historiography. Included are histories of the ruling movements in Albania, Bulgaria, Cambodia, China, Cuba, Czechoslovakia, (East) Germany, Hungary, (North) Korea, Laos, Mongolia, Poland, Romania, the Soviet Union, Vietnam, and Yugoslavia.

Dr. Jan B. de Weydenthal's monograph on the Polish United Workers' Party covers the following:

- Historical background, early leadership, and domestic political activities.
- Illegal status during the period between the two great wars until dissolution by the Comintern in 1938 after purges in the USSR had killed many party leaders.
- World War II and reconstruction of the party on an underground basis in Poland and an open one in the Soviet Union.
- Stalinization and ascendancy of the Muscovite faction.
- Return to power of native communists during the "thaw," their fall, and the current leadership.
- Problems in the late 1970s, relations with the CPSU, and future prospects.

As editor of this series, I am pleased to introduce this study of communism in Poland.

RICHARD F. STAAR
Coordinator of International Studies

Hoover Institution
Stanford University

Preface

This is a second edition of the book that initially appeared in 1978 and is now out of print. The original text was revised in some places to account for new information. Moreover, three new chapters have been added to describe subsequent developments.

A number of people have helped in the completion of this new edition, but two above all: Director of International Studies at Hoover Institution, Ambassador Richard F. Staar, whose patience in dealing with my various problems was endless, and Margaret A. Evling, whose formidable editorial skills were invaluable and whose encouragement was crucial. To both of them—my profound gratitude.

Munich   JAN B. DE WEYDENTHAL

List of Abbreviations

AL	Armia Ludowa (People's Army)
CPSU	Communist Party of the Soviet Union
GL	Gwardia Ludowa (People's Guard)
KOR	Komitet Obrony Robotnikow (Committee for Workers' Defense)
KPP	Komunistyczna Partia Polski (Communist Party of Poland)
KPRP	Komunistyczna Partia Robotnicza Polski (Communist Workers' Party of Poland)
PPN	Polskie Porozumienie Niepodleglosciowe (Polish Independence Accord)
PPR	Polska Partia Robotnicza (Polish Workers' Party)
PPS	Polska Partia Socjalistyczna (Polish Socialist Party)
PUWP	Polish United Workers' Party (Polska Zjednoczona Partia Robotnicza)
ROPCO	Ruch Obrony Praw Czlowieka i Obywatela (Movement for the Defense of Human and Civil Rights)
SD	Stronnictwo Demokratyczne (Democratic Party)
SDKPiL	Socjal-Demokracja Krolestwa Polskiego i Litwy (Social Democracy of the Kingdom of Poland and Lithuania)
ZBoWiD	Zwiazek Bojownikow o Wolnosc i Demokracje (Union of Fighters for Freedom and Democracy)
ZSL	Zjednoczone Stronnictwo Ludowe (United Peasant Party)

Introduction

The Communist party in Poland has undergone considerable political and organizational transformation since it emerged on the national scene in the wake of the First World War. Politically, it has grown from a rather insignificant revolutionary movement of antistate opposition into a dominant force within a regime created specifically for the purpose of preserving this domination. Organizationally, it has developed from an underground group with limited membership and little internal cohesion into an established mass party directed by a clearly institutionalized leadership and forged together by effective discipline.

This change has not followed a constant evolutionary pattern. Rather, it has gone through several distinct phases in which preoccupation with specific political tasks was crucial in shaping the nature of the party, its internal organization, and its relationship to society. These tasks included efforts to create a revolutionary situation, conquest of political power, revolutionary transformation of political and social institutions in order to create a lasting framework for a new sociopolitical order, and systemic stabilization marked by an attempt to integrate the entire society into a socialist community permanently directed and managed by the party itself.

The party has also preserved several strong elements of continuity in its organization and patterns of political operation. Foremost among these has been an unbroken commitment to the traditional ideological premises and goals of communism. Throughout the years, all major party political initiatives have been predicated upon the unquestioned acceptance of the original Marxist assumption that profound socioeconomic changes are both inevitable and necessary. This doctrinal background motivated constant efforts at furthering a specific pattern of transformation of society, culture, and economy.

To adopt this perspective of ideological continuity is not to deny that the initial idealism of early communist revolutionaries has faded significantly. Nor is it to deny that specific doctrinal requirements have been sometimes neglected or even abandoned. But whether party leaders and members continue to adhere to the letter of original Marxist doctrines today is of relatively secondary importance. The point is that no communist party can conceive of its political position as separate from revolutionary ideology. The traditional system of values and beliefs continues to contribute to the party's political cohesion by supplying its members with a sense of general direction for action and a mandatory model of correct behavior.

Another element of continuity has been the long-established set of operational principles, which effectively limit participation in political processes to a select group of party members and officials. Such an exclusive orientation has always reflected the party concern with the preservation of its self-assumed role of the leading and directing force in the process of social change. The roots of this assumption go back to the Leninist concept of a revolutionary organization acting as a leader in the proletarian struggle against the bourgeoisie. Its contemporary expression is more practical and revolves around the insistence on a party-directed coordination of all organized social and political activities.

The problem area around which this work is oriented is the interplay between the elements of change and continuity, and the way it affected the party development throughout its history. For purposes of analysis, the primary emphasis is on evolutionary tendencies within the party's internal organization and changes in the direction and scope of its strategies and operational tactics.

The party is viewed as a specific political instrument, purposefully organized to seize and maintain power in the name of an ideologically prescribed goal of a lasting transformation of Polish society. The pattern of organization, without which the goals set by ideology could not be reached, is determined by definite political functions the party must perform. Strategies and tactics reflect the ways through which the attainment of the goals is planned, and are conditioned by the organizational structures.

The main source of party developmental problems is the correspondence between its structural and operational elements. A modification in one area, either internal organization or strategic preferences, would affect the other area and bring pressure toward a more generalized change. Given this state of internal interdependence, the political effectiveness of the party is largely determined by the degree of synchronization between the patterns of its organization and the patterns of its actions.

The party, of course, has not operated in a void. Its performance and functions have always been shaped by specific political situations and social conditions. The most important situational factor which has directly affected both the goal setting and the organization building within the party has been its allegiance to the Soviet-controlled international communist movement. The Soviet model of party organization became a mandatory pattern for all other Communist parties and has emerged as the main "organizational weapon" for destruction of representative forms of government and establishment of political systems based on dictatorial power. The Soviet leaders have always been the primary instigators and coordinators of communist policies, strategies, and reactions. The party in Poland was shaped in accordance with Soviet prescriptions and its activities have remained closely linked to those of the CPSU.

Another factor that in recent years particularly impinged upon the party has been a quasi-permanent legitimacy crisis of its rule. It arose not so much from a political opposition to the party's directing role within the existing system as from the persistent inability of the party to fulfill the indispensable managerial requirements of such a role. Underlying this aspect has been a growing gap between developmental expectations of increasingly diversified social groups, presenting competing claims, and stabilizing concerns of the political elite struggling to preserve existing structures and operational methods. It produced a constant threat of social disruptions, thus severely undermining the effectiveness of the party rule and periodically endangering the stability of its leadership.

Those problems were brought to a head in the 1980s, when, within a mere two years, the party politically collapsed under the pressure of a popular rebellion, only to rebound to life through an extraordinary effort at self-preservation and with the help of other communist parties and forces, whose actions were coordinated and directed by the Soviet party.

In describing the party's history in terms of its organizational and policy development, this book follows a restricted approach. It is not and does not purport to be a comprehensive story of communism in Poland. Thus, no attempt is made here to analyze and discuss the diverse ideological controversies and debates of the party's early years or in its times of subsequent internal crises, unless they were directly related to the questions of its internal organization or the choice of its basic policies. Furthermore, the book is not an account of Poland's politics either before the establishment of communist rule or even within the presently existing system. The general picture is of such complexity and contains so many different, interacting elements that it extends far beyond the scope of the present study.

Rather, as the title of this book emphasizes, it is concerned exclusively with an organized group of Communists who, acting on the basis of long-held ideological convictions and with the support of their international sponsors, succeeded in imposing their power over Polish society. If nothing else, the book should be regarded as merely a preliminary, far from complete, survey of the party's organizational history. While considerable effort was made to use available Polish materials and official party sources, no definitive assessment could be contemplated as long as full documentary records of the party, as well as those of the international communist organizations, are kept from independent scholars and researchers.

In such circumstances, this work attempts only to identify major problems of party development and to indicate their relevance for further exploration and analysis. The author hopes it will serve as a modest contribution toward greater understanding of the evolution of the party in Poland and supply a fragmentary description of some of the major stages of this process.

THE COMMUNISTS OF POLAND

CHAPTER 1

The Revolutionary Temptation

The history of an organized communist movement in Poland dates from the formation on December 16, 1918 in Warsaw of the Communist Workers' Party of Poland. Its emergence marked the culmination of a long process of transformation and unification of several radical socialist groups into a single organization. More important, it heralded the appearance on the Polish political scene of a revolutionary party which, while proclaiming itself a *sui generis* vanguard of the working class and a custodian of its historical destiny, was to arrogate the sole right to lead the struggle toward a fundamental transformation of Polish society. The birth of the party was prompted by two historically related but politically separate developments. One was the revolutionary seizure of power by the Bolsheviks and the establishment of a communist regime in Russia. The other was the restoration of Poland's national independence in the wake of the First World War. The mutually contradictory social and political trends which those developments entailed were to determine the party's evolution and to affect its activities from the very moment of its formation.

In many respects, the rise of the party was a consequence of the trend within the European socialist movement toward an activist involvement in preparing a massive revolutionary upheaval and of the growing belief that an era of integral social transformation was within reach. This conviction of course was derived from the acceptance of the original Marxist revolutionary ideas. But in the existing conditions of economic scarcity and political instability which had resulted from long years of a protracted war, the ideological assumptions suddenly seemed to acquire practical significance. If nothing else, the downfall of the tsarist regime in Russia and the progressing disintegration of the Austrian and German empires appeared to provide a confirmation of such a possibility.

This trend found particularly fertile ground in Poland, where strong tendencies toward revolutionary activism had germinated long before the formation of the Communist Workers' Party of Poland (KPRP). They began in the early 1880s, with several abortive attempts by domestic radical groups to organize a socialist revolutionary movement. Perhaps the best known group was the Proletariat, an underground party of students and workers which was brutally suppressed by Russian police in 1886.[1] A few years later, following the establishment in 1892 in Paris of the Polish Socialist Party (PPS), radical elements reasserted themselves within that organization, instigating a serious conflict over the party political orientation.

The main argument centered on the question of national self-determination for Poland and the role of the socialist party in achieving that objective. For a majority of PPS leaders and activists, the restoration of an independent Polish state and the elimination of foreign oppression were the main goals for political activity. Although they recognized the need for comprehensive social change aimed at the removal of long existing inequalities, they envisaged its implementation only within a framework of an independent and democratic state and through primarily reformist and gradualist means. To prepare the realization of this goal, PPS undertook a major effort to unite all socialist groups in the three sections of partitioned Poland into a single national party.

This attitude contrasted sharply with the position taken by a militant minority of revolutionary activists. Having accepted the Marxist doctrine of economic determinism as the guiding principle for action, they strongly opposed the cause of national independence for Poland as being both ideologically undesirable and economically impractical. For them, nationalism or patriotism were essentially bourgeois-invented diversions from the greater and more important objective of a universal proletarian revolution. Consequently, they considered the task of preparing proletarian masses of Poland for an inevitable and decisive social transformation, to be spearheaded by a workers' revolutionary upheaval in more developed and industrialized countries of Europe, as the primary obligation of a truly socialist organization.

In 1893 the proponents of the revolutionary orientation seceded from the PPS and formed, under the leadership of Rosa Luxemburg, Leon Jogiches (Tyszko), Julian Marchlewski, and Adolf Warszawski (Warski), a new party known as the Social Democracy of the Kingdom of Poland. In 1899 it merged with a group of radical Lithuanian socialists led by Feliks Dzerzhinskiĭ and became the Social Democracy of the Kingdom of Poland and Lithuania (SDKPiL). For the next twenty years the new party was to provide the ideological and organizational backbone of the revolutionary movement in Poland.

Largely under the influence of Rosa Luxemburg, ideological mentor of the party and conceptualist of its policies, the Social Democracy adopted as its primary task to attack and repudiate the patriotic orientation within the Polish socialist movement. The inaugural program of the party, written by Luxemburg herself, asserted that "the patriotic tendency, the ideal of an independent Poland, has no prospect of winning the social-democratic workers to itself." Instead, it called for concerted action of the working masses against the capitalist system, a struggle "which does not reckon for its realization on fortuitous transformation in European politics, does not owe its existence to the wishes and ideals of individuals and dying classes. Rather, it is bred of the objective course of history. . .which simultaneously develops capitalism and thereby has created the political power that will destroy it—the proletariat."[2] To accentuate the rejection of Polish national aspirations, the party's chosen name, geographically limiting its activity to the Russian part of Poland, clearly indicated its intentions to prevent any linkage, political or organizational, with the socialist movement in other parts of the country.

The political and ideological differences between the PPS and the SDKPiL also found a practical expression in distinct approaches to the problem of internal organization of the two groups. To the degree that the PPS maintained the goal of national liberation as its dominant objective, it set out to develop a network of underground, paramilitary units especially trained to prepare an armed uprising and work toward a general insurrection. In time, this effort became a major contributing factor to the establishment of a strong internal discipline within the party as well as to the emergence of a clearly defined leadership maintaining a considerable level of cohesiveness in the organization.[3] As for the SDKPiL, its vision of a revolutionary action revolved around the assertion, formulated by Rosa Luxemburg but shared by many other Marxist theoreticians, that social change would have to result from "the direct, independent action of the masses" and not merely from the activity of the political organization, even if it purported to represent the interests of the masses.[4] As a result, the political activity of the SDKPiL centered mainly on an effort to educate the workers and to propagandize the cause of revolution rather than organizing itself for the purpose of actually making a revolutionary breakthrough. This resulted, in part, from the character of the party leadership, which consisted mainly of theoreticians and intellectuals given more to abstract speculations than organizational work. In addition, most of the influential figures in the party resided permanently abroad, either in Germany, as was the case with Luxemburg, Tyszko, Marchlewski, and Warski, or in Russia. Such physical separation from the rank and file in Poland was hardly conducive to an organizational cohesiveness.

In view of such political and organizational differences between the two socialist organizations, it was not surprising that the gap between them grew with time, and mutual hostility became more pronounced with passing years. And yet, neither of them was able to establish a clear dominance over the worker movement. Insofar as both were forced to operate underground, they remained numerically small—by 1904 the much larger PPS was able to claim only several thousand active members[5]—with limited public appeal and a restricted field of political activity. Their organizational efficiency was clearly determined by a generally hostile political environment controlled by dominant foreign institutions.

In 1906 another split within the PPS contributed to a sudden expansion of the revolutionary movement. Largely under the impact of the 1905 rebellion in Russia, interpreted by many Polish socialists as indicative of the impending dawn of far-reaching democratic and social change, the PPS underwent a severe internal crisis. The long-established patriotic leadership, which had always insisted on the primacy of an insurrectionist action against tsarist Russia over the objective of immediate socially oriented change, suffered a political defeat. At the PPS congress in February 1906, a new majority subordinated the cause of an independent Polish statehood to the goal of a social revolution throughout the Russian empire. The traditional theme of national sovereignty was reduced to a mere demand for the institutional and cultural autonomy of Poland within a reconstituted Russian state. The subsequent congress, held in Vienna in November 1906, only confirmed the new direction for PPS activity and further isolated the patriotic wing from the mainstream of the party. It was later to split from the PPS and to form, under the leadership of a determined insurrectionist and able organizer, Jozef Pilsudski, a separate branch of the socialist movement known as the PPS-Revolutionary Faction. As for the new majority, to underscore the break with past political traditions it adopted a new name, the PPS-Left, as an indication of its new orientation.

The rejection of the patriotic stance constituted a major step toward bridging the political gap between the socialists and the SDKPiL. While both parties seemed to share a similar view as to the need to promote an immediate social revolution, the remaining differences concerned merely a choice of tactics and strategies to be used in the work toward fulfillment of that goal. Perhaps the most important problem separating the two groups was the question of their attitudes toward other social and political organizations and their role in the process of social transformation. The SDKPiL adopted a position of revolutionary exclusivity, rejecting any form of cooperation with other parties or even workers' unions as a matter of ideological principle.[6] By contrast, the PPS-Left was willing to accept tactical cooperation with other leftist groups and gave its explicit support to the activities of a broadly conceived syndicalist movement. In effect, it considered mass social manifestations of protest and dissatisfaction, such as strikes and workers' demonstrations, as the most important stimulants of change toward future revolutionary transformation.[7] In some respects, this position brought the party closer to the Menshevik position in the Russian Social Democracy, while the SDKPiL identified itself more with that of the Leninist wing of the Russian movement.

The outbreak of the First World War brought the two parties even closer together. Both groups took a determined stand opposing proletarian partici-

pation in a war which they considered as basically reflecting imperialist interests of big capitalist countries. This similarity in political outlook led to some
forms of organizational cooperation. After 1914, several interparty committees were created with the explicit purpose of coordinating antiwar activities
of the members and sympathizers of both groups. Increasingly, the prospect
of eventual organizational unification became a subject of serious consideration by the leaderships of both the PPS-Left and the SDKPiL, with the latter
still, however, hesitant to accept the merger with the formerly more patriotic
group.

The triumph of the October 1917 revolution in Russia was a major cata-
lytic event that forced attitudinal and policy change for both parties. For most
Polish revolutionaries, the emergence of the Soviet state constituted the
fulfillment of a long-held dream, the beginning of an egalitarian millennium.
More important, the manner in which the reins of government in Russia had
been seized by the Bolsheviks and the communist regime established provided the Polish revolutionaries with an influential model of a successful
action. It supplied them with a sense of political direction, and suggested
methods of activity as well as ways of consolidating power. The singular
significance of the Russian events for the radical parties in Poland was further
underscored by the active involvement of numerous activists from the Polish
socialist underground in both the revolutionary upheaval and the subsequent
organization of the Soviet state. Some of them, most notably former SDKPiL
luminaries such as Feliks Dzerzhinskiî, Karl Radek, and Jozef Unszlicht, occupied high positions in the new revolutionary government. Others, whose
number was recently estimated at around eight thousand, thus greatly out-
weighing the parent organizations in Poland,[8] were active at different levels
of Soviet administration, in the Russian party, and in the military formations.
Such extensive involvement in Russian affairs had its historical justification,
as the SDKPiL had maintained close organizational ties with the Russian Social Democratic Party since 1905. Following the October Revolution, the
Council of People's Commissars established a special department of Polish
affairs which, under the direction of a long-time SDKPiL activist, Julian
Leszczynski (Lenski), was charged with providing political leadership for the
activities of the Polish revolutionaries.

The unquestioned solidarity with the Russian revolutionary experience
and the political support for the Bolshevik leadership became the major, unifying themes of the rapidly solidifying alliance between the radical socialist
groups in Poland. Although their most prominent leaders, most notably Rosa
Luxemburg, who had been since 1914 imprisoned in Germany, took strong
exception to Lenin's autocratic methods of imposing revolutionary dictatorship upon Russian masses,[9] the radicals' response to Russian developments

was uniformly enthusiastic. They had little doubt that the Bolshevik revolution would provoke a chain reaction of proletarian upheavals in other countries of Europe and were determined to follow its example in Poland.

The prospect of such a revolutionary success was significantly enhanced by an increasingly chaotic political situation in Poland. The final collapse of the Austrian and German empires led to the emergence, in November 1918, of an independent Polish state. But the evolving process of national resurgence began under distinctly inauspicious circumstances. On the one hand, the advent of national independence brought to an end a century and a half of struggle against foreign rule and occupation. It was greeted with widespread patriotic euphoria. The rapid disintegration of alien autocratic institutions and the removal of foreign control over political life paved the way for a rebirth of self-government or at least some forms of rudimentary democracy. This process was accompanied by a rapid proliferation of newly organized groups and movements, each hoping to influence and to shape the policy for the country. On the other hand, economic and social conditions were serious, with all signs pointing to even further deterioration. Having suffered from several years of war waged on her territory, Poland was torn by widespread social dislocations and economic destruction. Inflation and unemployment were rampant. It was clear that social cleavages, produced by long existing strains in political and economic relations, were too deep to be bridged easily by patriotic emotions. The sudden emergence of a new state provided little if any assurance of prompt and lasting relief. The very survival of the country required a rapid sociopolitical reintegration by means of new institutions, new loyalties, and new supportive organizations. Until this could be accomplished, the country appeared ripe for a complete revolutionary transformation.

It was this specter of internal weakness and institutional fragility of the new state that spurred political action of the revolutionary groups in the form of a unification of the SDKPiL and the PPS-Left into a single communist organization. The main objective of the newly formed Communist Workers' Party of Poland, as proclaimed in its inaugural statement, was to become a rallying force for the underprivileged and disaffected to achieve a "proletarian revolution" which would be conducted along the lines of the Bolshevik experience.[10] It therefore called for an immediate transfer of power from the newly constituted government to the working masses, which were to organize themselves into councils of workers, peasants, and soldier delegates. They were to form the basic political structure of a "dictatorship of the proletariat" which would lead the process of social transformation to its socialist conclusion.

Notwithstanding those attempts to incorporate Lenin's successful operational formulas into its program, revolutionary effectiveness of the KPRP was from the very beginning severely impaired by its organizational limitations and the narrowness of its social base. With respect to the organizational character of the party, its distinguishing feature was the absence of an internal machinery capable of directing and synchronizing various aspects of its activity. The entire structure consisted of several separate organizational centers, each maintaining its own network of cells and conducting its own pattern of political work. The internal distribution of power had never been institutionalized, nor were the lines of communication between separate units established. In an effort to introduce some measure of unification into the newly formed organization, the founding congress adopted a provisional charter, envisaging the creation of a territorially based network of party circles to be directed by elected committees subordinated to the Central Committee as the highest policymaking body.[11] But insofar as these regulations were to be implemented in the future, presumably after the revolutionary upheaval itself, their impact on the party internal structure remained negligible. To provide for at least a semblance of organizational coherence, the congress elected a twelve-member Central Committee with the seats divided equally among the former SDKPiL and PPS-Left adherents. Yet is was a collective, a deliberative rather than operational body, functioning on the basis of a majority vote. A first executive organ, a secretariat, appeared only in the spring of 1919, but was given primarily administrative rather than political tasks.[12]

As for the party's social appeal, there is little doubt that it was able to secure support from only a very small segment of the population. The size of its membership was recently estimated by communist scholars as having ranged from about 5,000 at the end of 1918 to 7,000 in mid-1919. Even this relatively small figure could be misleading because of an uneven distribution of the party units. Thus, although it claimed to have established some form of an organizational presence in about 80 localities by the beginning of 1919, the party's political strength was limited to only a few urban centers. These included the Dabrowa mining region in southern Poland as well as Warsaw and Lodz, two large industrial cities in the central part of the country. Those three urban concentrations accounted for more than 75 percent of the entire membership of the party.[13]

Still, the lack of organizational cohesion and the weakness of popular appeal were not the only factors that shaped the political character of the party. Much more important was its continuing commitment to orthodox Marxist revolutionary principles, which had a critical effect on the KPRP's perception of social and political relations. Indicative of this attitude was the party's insistence on the dominant role of the proletariat, in the sense of a primarily urban manual working class, in the revolutionary transformation, and its refusal to even acknowledge the sociopolitical importance of peasants. This view originated from Rosa Luxemburg, who, having fully accepted Marx's analysis of sociohistorical determinants of change, had accused "the peasantry [of] having no political profile"[14] and described the peasants as the most backward and conservative social group. Its acceptance by the party had important symbolic and practical political implications. Symbolically, the very name of the party, through the inclusion of the term "Workers'," conveyed its attachment to the doctrinal identification with a purely worker revolution. In practice, the party rejected the Leninist concept of land distribution among the peasants, opting rather for comprehensive land nationalization aimed at an immediate transformation of peasants into "the rural proletariat."[15] However, under Polish social and political conditions, with the peasants constituting the largest group in society for which the goal of agrarian reform was much more important than revolutionary nationalization, such a proletarian orientation bordered upon a political disaster. It not only enhanced the already existing peasant antagonism toward the party, but also effectively precluded any possibility of creating a potentially revolutionary situation in the countryside.

An even more important issue, which was eventually to determine the political fate of the KPRP, was the party's unconditional refusal to accept the existence of a newly emerging Polish state. Following the traditional Luxemburgist line and in open defiance of Lenin's explicitly stated position,[16] the party declared itself opposed to "every political solution that is to be connected with the evolution of a capitalist world, solutions such as autonomy, independence, and self-determination." The motive force behind this opposition was the conviction that a final disintegration of the capitalist system was imminent and a mounting wave of the international revolution would bring a decisive change in Poland. Such linkage between the domestic and the international processes of change was explicitly asserted in the party's program, which pointed out that "in its difficult struggle toward a final victory, the Polish proletariat shall rely on the social revolution in other countries; just as in the socialist system the social management will be based on close cooperation of all people, so in the very process of revolution, solidarity and mutual help as well as a common front against common enemies become the main principles of the struggle."[17] The obvious corollary of this stand was the party's assertion that any form of cooperation with or even tacit approval of the Polish bourgeois state would be a basically regressive and counterrevolutionary action.

Given this antipatriotic ethos and dominant concern for revolutionary change, the main emphasis in party activities was on efforts to undermine the authority of the state and to sabotage the work of government institutions. This was combined with an attempt to develop alternative centers of political power. In this context, the KPRP devoted particular attention to a rapidly expanding movement of councils of workers and peasants. Although the emergence of the councils preceded the formation of the party, resulting from a largely spontaneous process of local self-organization prompted by a massive political and economic disorder, it provided the Communists with a ready-made forum of political activity.

From the very moment of its creation, the party concentrated a major effort on capturing organizational control over the councils in order to shape them into instruments of political subversion and antistate agitation. Initially, this effort appeared to be quite successful. In the elections to the workers' councils at the end of 1918 and at the beginning of 1919, the party virtually tied the patriotic PPS in Warsaw and received substantial popular support in other industrial centers of Poland. On the average, the KPRP polled between one-third and one-half of the workers' votes in most of the urban localities.[18] Largely under communist influence, some of the councils adopted radical programs of action.

The main result of this activity was a mounting wave of industrial strikes, frequently associated with political antigovernment demonstrations. The unrest was especially strong in the mining districts of southern Poland, where the communist-dominated workers' councils called for an immediate takeover of factories, expressed their solidarity with the Soviet revolution, and succeeded in forming special paramilitary detachments of "Red Guards."[19] Similar efforts at igniting popular manifestations of discontent were mounted in other parts of the country, particularly in the large urban centers of Warsaw and Lodz.[20]

These revolutionary activities brought about a series of counteractions by the government. In late December 1918, regular army troops put down the strike in the mining town of Dabrowa. The Red Guard units were disarmed and the communist-oriented workers' council was dissolved. At the same time, in an effort to diffuse the social tension, the government adopted a comprehensive economic reform program including the introduction of an eight-hour working day in industry as well as several provisions aimed at improving health standards and work conditions. But the most significant development, which effectively destroyed the revolutionary potential of the workers' movement, was a growing divisiveness within the workers' councils themselves. In June 1919, following a series of protracted political disputes, the PPS refused to participate with the Communists in the councils and decided to set up its own workers' organizations. Left on their own, the communist-dominated councils rapidly disintegrated. The socialist organizations gradually shared the same fate. By the end of 1919, the short-lived experiment with the councils of workers and peasants as political institutions separate from the government ceased to exist. Their place as workers' representative organizations was taken over by the rapidly growing trade unions. However, insofar as the primary function of the unions was to achieve economic advancement for the workers rather than to seize political power, they were singularly ill-equipped to serve as a stepping stone for the party toward a revolutionary transformation.

With the downfall of the workers' councils, the party lost its chosen outlet for revolutionary action. More important, however, as a result of its determined refusal to come to terms with the reality of an emerging Polish state, the party was also rapidly losing all other possibilities to influence the flow of political events. The obvious illustration of this point was provided by the KPRP's decision to boycott the first parliamentary elections in January 1919. Commenting two years later on the motivations behind this decision, prominent party leader Maksymilian Horwitz (Henryk Walecki) explained that "above all, the party boycotted the elections because it wanted to clearly juxtapose the idea of democracy to the idea of proletarian dictatorship; the slogan of a Parliament against a slogan of a [Workers'] Council. Furthermore, [the party] assumed that revolutionary developments in the West, and in consequence in Poland, would offer an opportunity to crush and disperse the Parliament. Finally, insofar as the task of turning the electoral and parliamentary activities toward revolutionary goals would have required complicated tactical adjustments in an already difficult situation, it exceeded the political capabilities of the young and not yet fully consolidated party."[21] The net political result of this decision was an absence of a parliamentary representation for the Communists.

A second, and extremely important, consequence of the party's absolute commitment to revolutionary priorities, a stance that radically affected its activities for the years to come, was its failure to maintain a legalized political status. In mid-January 1919, the government issued a decree requiring all social and political organizations operating within the country to register with authorities. This requirement presented the party with a critical choice. On the one hand, compliance with the government ruling would entail formal recognition of the Polish bourgeois state and its political authority. On the other hand, a rejection would inevitably expose the party to official harassment and impose far-reaching restrictions on its activity. To the degree that the party and its leaders had always regarded the existence of a separate Polish state as clearly inimical to the transformation of the entire social system, the resolution of this dilemma was never in doubt. The party refused to comply with the regulations and on February 7, 1919, a deadline set earlier by the government, it voluntarily descended into the political underground. Thus, having experienced barely two months of open activity, the KPRP became a secret, illegal, and subversive organization. It was to remain in this role for the next quarter of a century.

At that juncture, the political fortunes of the party took a decisive, downward trend. Inasmuch as its general operational outlook had been formulated in anticipation of major revolutionary changes abroad and increased socio-economic difficulties at home, the evolving situation on both those fronts pointed to a different direction. The failure of the January 1919 revolution in Germany shattered the hopes for a spontaneous revolutionary sweep across Europe. This development was particularly painful for the revolutionaries in Poland, as two of their former leaders, Rosa Luxemburg, and Leon Jogiches, were murdered in the German prisons. The Russian Communists were engaged in civil war and there was little hope that they could provide immediate and direct help for the KPRP in its political struggle against the Polish state. In addition, a gradual recovery of the Polish economy was progressively eroding the party's initial strength on the domestic front. Increasingly, the party was being confronted with the prospect of the revolution slipping irretrievably away.

Against this background, the outbreak of war between Poland and Russia provided a new hope of regaining lost chances for a revolutionary upheaval. For the Polish government, which launched military operations against Soviet Russia in April 1920, the war was an attempt to impose a lasting solution to the vital problems of national security and independence. Its major objective was to push Russia eastward and to create, on the "liberated territories," a bloc of separate but federated states of Byelorussia, Ukraine, and the Baltic countries.[22] If successful, such a solution not only would arrest the spread of communist influences from the east but, more important, contribute to the creation of an effective buffer zone between Poland's eastern borders and her traditional Russian enemy.

But the Communists in Poland did not see the Polish-Russian war as a conflict between states or nations. To them it was a part of the revolutionary proletarian struggle against the bourgeoisie, in which the former happened to be Russian and the latter Polish. They condemned the Polish attempts at forming a military and political alliance with Ukrainian nationalists and accused the government of an imperialist aggression against the Soviet republic. When the party appeals for a general protest strike against the military offensive in the spring of 1920 proved unsuccessful, the KPRP organized a massive campaign of opposition to the Polish war effort, including widespread sabotage, diversion, and espionage.[23]

After a series of initial Polish military successes, the tide of the battle turned and by the end of May the Soviet armies started to press westward. The rapidly emerging prospect of a decisive Soviet victory created a need for a formulation of the party's policy on the revolutionary strategy at home and the development of future relations between Poland and the Soviet state. This need appeared to be particularly urgent, as there had developed some internal differences in respect to the desirability of direct Soviet participation in the process of a revolutionary transformation in Poland.[24] Whether through a fear that a Russian involvement would trigger a patriotic reaction against communist rule or a belief that native Communists were capable of conducting the revolution themselves, several prominent party activists, including Julian Marchlewski and a former SDKPiL militant, Henryk Stein (Domski), argued against the Soviet invasion of the ethnically Polish lands. Others, such as former PPS-Left leaders Feliks Kon and Pawel Lewinson (Lapinski), supported a direct extension of Soviet-conducted revolutionary war into Poland. Such debates ended abruptly following an instruction issued in June 1920 by the Central Committee of the Russian Communist party for its Polish Bureau to organize a future communist government in Poland to be installed by the Soviet army.[25]

At the end of June 1920, Soviet troops entered Polish territory. Disregarding their earlier apprehensions, all Communist leaders in Poland rallied to the cause of a seemingly inevitable sovietization of the Polish state. On August 2, a Provisional Revolutionary Committee for Poland was established in Bialystok, the first city occupied by the Red Army that was considered truly Polish by the Bolsheviks. Chaired by Julian Marchlewski, its membership was an obvious extension of Soviet officialdom. It included Feliks Dzerzhinskiî, the head of the Soviet political police (Cheka) and member of the Russian Communist party's Central Committee; Jozef Unszlicht, a deputy chairman of the Cheka and former member of the Petrograd Revolutionary Committee in 1917; Feliks Kon, an official in the Communist International; Julian Lenski, the head of the Polish Department of the Russian party; and Edward Prochniak, a member of the Polish Bureau and agent of the Cheka.

Acting as a transistory organ of the prospective communist government in Poland, the committee's major tasks were to assist the Soviet military authorities on Polish matters, organize local revolutionary units, and develop an initial program for the future administration. Its authority, however, proved to be a mere reflection of Soviet power. The conduct of the Red Army in Poland was never effectively influenced by the committee, if in fact it ever sought to restrain all too frequent excesses of pillage and rapine. Similarly, the spread of local revolutionary committees, largely publicized by the party press, was more apparent than real and reflected only a Russian-directed propaganda operation. As admitted later by Julian Marchlewski himself, the Red Army "could not become an instrument of order" and "created a whole apparatus with the purpose of renewing or establishing of [sic] the Soviet system."[26] For the Polish population there was little doubt that the Provisional Revolutionary Committee acted only as a disguising instrument for the Russian aggression against their country.

The only area in which the committee was allowed to display a modicum of autonomy concerned the formulation of a political program for the future. Its most important feature was the definition of communist policies toward land ownership, a crucial position in a society in which small and poor peasants accounted for about 70 percent of the population. More than anything else, the committee's approach toward this critical question gave an illustration of the political orientation of its members. Once again, the old ideological principles of revolutionary purity came to the fore. Disregarding any tactical considerations of political expediency, the committee called for an immediate nationalization of landed estates with a view toward the subsequent introduction of collective agricultural cooperatives.[27] The motivating factor in this insistence was, of course, a firm belief in the necessity of a rapid transition from the semicapitalist Polish socioeconomic system to socialism, in the sense of a complete abolition of private property of all means of production. The sentiments of the peasants, as well as the problem of their attitudes toward the revolution, were simply ignored.

The significance of this program went beyond any political considerations of its practical importance. In retrospect, it appears more than doubtful whether any more cooperative policy toward the peasants, such as free self-appropriation of land for example, could have made a difference in the popular opposition to the Soviet invasion. The long-standing hostility toward the Russians was too deep to be easily overcome by any, even the most appealing, programs. What mattered was what the program revealed about the communist movement of Poland and some of its leaders grouped in the committee. It was a movement motivated and led by intellectual extremists but not practical revolutionaries. Their doctrinaire attachment to ideological dogmas, a complete disregard for tactical flexibility, a sense of revolutionary arrogance, and unrestrained ruthlessness in the choice of means to achieve the final goal only confirmed that assessment.

Meanwhile, the war was being decided on the battlefield. Having swept to the gates of Warsaw in August 1920, the Red Army was eventually defeated and pushed back deep into Russian territory. Even if the initial Polish federalist objectives were never achieved, the final settlement at the negotiations in Riga during March 1921 brought a substantial victory for Poland, giving her control over considerable parts of Byelorussia and the Ukraine.

Paradoxically, the war served also as an important stabilizing factor in the process of social, institutional, and political consolidation of the Polish state. It demonstrated that national loyalties among the Polish people far outweighed the class oriented appeals of the Communists. The common effort at resisting the Soviet onslaught, shared equally by peasants, workers, and all other social strata, virtually contributed to the restoration of social cohesion. The evolving political stability found its practical expression in the process of an institutional development. On March 17, 1921, the Parliament (Sejm) adopted a new constitution, which provided a legal framework for the political system. Three days later, on March 20, 1921, a plebiscite in Upper Silesia gave Poland a major part of that heavily industrialized region. Along with the settlement with the Russians, this act established a final determination of national frontiers and provided a clear definition of a territorially stable national unit.

In light of these developments, the position of the Communist party appeared virtually untenable. In effect, with its reputation tarnished by the stigma of collaboration with a foreign enemy, the KPRP seemed to be on the verge of complete disintegration. Its organizational structure was in disarray. Some of its leaders either broke their ties with the movement in Poland, as was the case with the members of the Provisional Revolutionary Committee who rejoined the Soviet administration, or were in prisons in Poland, or escaped to the Soviet Union and Germany. Most of the local units simply abandoned their activity, and the party at large was rapidly losing whatever public support it had had before. Although there are no precise figures that could illustrate the degree of membership decrease, recently published information related to the developments in the three main centers of the KPRP's activity may furnish a glimpse of the situation in the party. Thus, by the end of 1921 the party lost about 80 percent of its members in the Dabrowa mining district (from 2,500 to 500 members), 40 percent in Warsaw (from 1,000 to 600), and about 60 percent in Lodz (from 600 to 235).[28] There is no reason to assume that similar decreases did not take place in other local organizations.

In order to salvage the remains of the organization, it became imperative for the party to accept some strategic and political concessions and introduce far-reaching changes in its activity. The most important decision was the forced but inevitable acceptance of the Polish state and its political system. The era of revolutionary communism was coming to a close and the party was entering a new period of its existence bereft of old enthusiasm and convictions.

C H A P T E R 2

The Fading Spark

The political and institutional consolidation of the Polish state had a sobering effect on the Communist Workers' party of Poland. Its dream of a rapid revolutionary transformation of society seemed to be vanishing into a distant and uncertain future. A creeping disillusionment gripped the party, producing a growing feeling of drift and lack of direction. Faced with the threat of an imminent collapse of its social and organizational base, the party was forced to rethink its fundamental assumptions and practices.

The crucial problem was the need for an ideological redefinition of the party itself. It was clear that the old concept of the party as a strictly revolutionary organization, advocating a frontal attack against the existing society and aiming at the establishment of a dictatorial regime, was inadequate under conditions of relative political stability. The change in institutional environment called for an adjustment in policies and operational style. At the same time, there was considerable concern within the party that any such adjustment should not be equated with the emergence of some new political frame of reference which could jeopardize the ideologically defined goals of its activity. The inherent incompatibility between those two tendencies created a major source of internal tension.

An additional element shaping the ideological character of the party was its increasingly intimate identification with the Soviet party. There was of course nothing new about a close relationship between the communist movements in both countries. The Russian revolutionary activities had long provided a source of inspiration for the Polish Communists and there had been frequent interaction and cooperation among radical activists of Russian and Polish movements. But, at least until the end of the First World War, both the programs and the activities of Polish revolutionaries had also been strongly influenced by Western, particularly German, ideas on revolutionary change. Following the failure of radical upheavals in the West, however, the KPRP's orientation gradually changed. Since the Soviet Union emerged as the symbol of revolutionary success and its survival became the only source of hope for an eventual expansion of a revolutionary movement to other parts of the world, support for the Soviet state and loyalty to the Soviet party were ac-

cepted by the KPRP leaders as the unique determinants of ideological commitment. In the long run, this position became a cornerstone of the party's
policies, strategies, and programs.

Such close identification with the Soviet state and the Soviet party had a
decisive impact on the character of the KPRP, providing it with distinct political opportunities but also creating important constraints for its activity. As for
the opportunities, the link with the Soviet Union preserved the revolutionary
identity of the party and vitally contributed to its survival as a separate organization. Given the weakness of the party's organizational and social base, its
exceedingly ambitious goals, and the hostile political environment, there was
little chance that the party could maintain itself alone as an independent communist organization. It is more than probable that had the party leaders
adopted their own revolutionary line, they would have been either coopted
by other organizations or deprived of any significant role. Nor does it appear
that a separately formulated ideological prescription for action would have
been successful in swaying the masses toward the party. No ideology has ever
been important without a firm organizational basis behind it and the KPRP
clearly lacked the resources for establishing such a base.

Most of the constraints resulted from the party's dependence on Soviet
guidance in and control over the formulation of its policies. This was due to
the Soviet party's leadership in the revolutionary movement, and particularly
its monopoly over all major policy and ideological initiatives as well as its insistence that all other parties follow these positions. Within this context, the
Soviet leaders arrogated a right not only to determine political issues that the
KPRP could act upon, but also to select the party leaders so those policies
would be properly implemented. Such practices resulted, however, in a near
complete loss of a political and national identity for the KPRP. Gradually the
Polish people came to think of the party as little more than a local appendage
of the Soviet government, an agency created to promote the interests of the
Soviet state and the Soviet party but not those of the local population.

From the very beginning, the basic dilemma for the KPRP was to balance
its ideological and political commitment to the Soviet-led revolutionary cause
with organizational self-preservation. In large measure, this was due to Soviet
ambivalence on crucial issues of international revolutionary policy. The Soviet leadership was prone to adopt sweeping, frequently contradictory,
changes in international policies and to reverse its strategic positions
abruptly. To a great extent, these changes reflected the vicissitudes of internal
Soviet politics, produced by conflicting orientations within the Soviet party.
However, due to the pivotal position of the Soviet party in the communist
movement, those conflicts were rapidly externalized and created widespread
confusion abroad over the direction the revolutionary struggle was to pursue.

Notwithstanding its clear acceptance of Moscow's leadership in the conduct of the world revolutionary struggle, the KPRP and its leaders were slow to recognize and adjust to the new political and organizational unitary imperatives. This process went through several distinct stages. The first period, 1922–1925, was characterized by an effort to preserve a modicum of political autonomy for the party within the communist movement and an attempt to contribute toward formulation of that movement's policy. Initially, this involved adoption of several measures for domestic deradicalization of the party. In a move which clearly indicated the party's reconciliation to the continuing existence of the Polish state, the KPRP decided in early February 1921 to participate in future parliamentary elections and to establish some form of a communist presence in state representative institutions. In April 1922, following the Comintern decision to abandon an activist revolutionary strategy in Western Europe in favor of tactical cooperation with other leftist groups against bourgeois governments, the party called for the establishment of a united front of socialist and communist parties in opposition to the government in place.[1] At the same time, it appealed for the creation of a political alliance between the workers and the peasants in a common struggle against the established system. Although this effort at bringing together those two social groups stopped short of any modification in the traditional party program of full land nationalization, it was indicative of a growing realization among important segments of its membership that without peasant support the party would not be able to achieve any of its political tasks. Taken together, these measures heralded a major departure from the old Luxemburgist radicalism.

The party was clearly taking a turn toward the right but, insofar as it was consistent with the shift in international communist tactics, this change was mainly dictated by political expediency rather than alteration of old ideological convictions. The traditionally held dogmatic tenets were not only difficult to abandon but also, for many a party activist, remained the only rationalization of the party's existence and activities. Thus, even if the new orientation was reluctantly accepted as only a temporary necessity, there were sharply conflicting opinions within the party as to its impact on revolutionary developments in general and the Polish political situation in particular. Such conflicts were perhaps inevitable in a party which had grown from a loosely formed conglomeration of politically different groups persistently attached to their own history, traditions, and ideological preferences. There is little doubt that the formative experiences of those groups continued to exert considerable influence on the general pattern of policy formation and party organization.

In many respects, the political uncertainty surrounding the issue of united front tactics was a catalyst for bringing conflicting tensions within the party into the open. This resulted in a rapidly expanding political fragmentation of the KPRP and the emergence of several distinct groups advocating radically different approaches to the problem of promoting revolutionary change in Polish conditions. The second party congress, which gathered in a suburb of Moscow during September–October 1923, provided a forum for confrontation between those groups.[2]

The right wing of the party, which had been primarily responsible for the adoption of political changes during 1921–1922, was led by former PPS-Left leaders Maria Koszutska (Wera Kostrzewa) and Maksymilian Horwitz (Henryk Walecki) and a veteran of the old SDKPiL, Adolf Warszawski (Warski), or the "Three W's," as they were usually called. Having established themselves as dominant party leaders since the beginning of 1922, they firmly supported the Soviet-sponsored united front orientation and saw the close political alliance between workers and peasants as the only realistic strategy for a future revolutionary transformation of Polish society. Although this strategy had been obviously inspired by the Soviet posture and continued to receive Comintern support, the rightist leaders seemed to perceive this relationship as a possible rather than necessary congruence of interests. In other words, they seemed to have assumed that once the focus of revolutionary activity in Poland was established, the party would be able to develop its own policy of change free from outside pressures and restrictions. This appeared to be the main message of Warski's programmatic statement to the congress, in which he pointed out that "having found an eternal source of the Polish revolution [in the peasant, national, and worker problems, which the bourgeoisie is incapable of solving] we do not need to look for and wait for others, or to seek help from outside forces."[3]

On the other side of the political spectrum was a much smaller but equally determined group of radical leftists. Led by old-line SDKPiL activists such as Henryk Stein (Domski), Stanislaw Martens (Skulski), and Zofia Unszlicht (Osinska), this group represented a policy of refusal: it rejected the united front orientation in its entirety, opposed the prospect of a worker-peasant alliance, and negated the gradualist strategy of revolutionary change. Indicative of this position was Domski's warning that "the distinguishing feature of the united front tactic is not its external character—rapprochement with other parties—but rather [the fact] that it leads to ideological changes, more specifically, to a regression toward minimal objectives and programs [of change]."[4] The left wing group was inclined to intensify class conflicts at home while waiting for a new revolutionary war from abroad to put an end to the existence of the Polish state.

There was also a third group within the party which, while ready to follow Comintern instructions regarding the revolutionary movement in general, was hesitant to embrace the idea of political cooperation with other parties in Poland. It included several high-ranking Soviet officials who had been active earlier in the Polish revolutionary movement, the most prominent being Julian Leszczynski (Lenski), Julian Marchlewski, and Jozef Unszlicht. They pointed to long-standing animosity between the communist organizations and the patriotically oriented socialist movement and warned that any form of political union under such conditions would be exceedingly difficult if not impossible to achieve for the KPRP. In the words of Julian Lenski, one of the most outspoken critics of the rightist orientation, the only acceptable form of a united front to the party in Poland was a "revolutionary united front" eventually leading to the "dictatorship of the proletariat."[5]

Following two weeks of intense, frequently bitter debates, the congress accepted the views of the right wing group as the official party orientation. The reins of power were firmly in hands of the rightist triumvirate of Kostrzewa, Walecki, and Warski, who were able to bring several of their supporters into positions of leadership while relegating opponents to politically insignificant functions. But their victory was more apparent than real. The congress' approval of the rightist stance was far from unanimous and it was clear that a substantial minority of the delegates remained highly critical of new party policies. As for the majority, a motive force behind its political consolidation was not to renounce the revolutionary role of the party but to revitalize its activity so it could influence political events in Poland. This feeling was significantly enhanced by the growing hope, bolstered by repeated assurances from the Comintern, that a revolution was again brewing in Germany and, consequently, that the situation in Poland could rapidly change in favor of the Communists.

However, political events both in Germany and Poland were to shatter those hopes. The abortive communist attempt at a revolutionary uprising in Germany precluded any possibility of an expansion of the proletarian struggle on an international scale. In Poland, in spite of a massive wave of industrial strikes during November 1923, the KPRP failed to establish any form of a cooperative political action with either the PPS, which supported the strikes, or the workers themselves. It was clear that the united front strategy, both at the larger international level and in Poland, was on the verge of collapse. In effect, at its fifth congress in July 1924 the Comintern adopted a new direction for communist activity, shifting its emphasis from cooperation with other leftist parties to mass-oriented revolutionary activism. As for the KPRP, this shift implied a political defeat for the rightist leadership, which suddenly found itself exposed to attacks from its leftist enemies.

The political situation within the party was even further complicated by a direct involvement of some of its top leaders in the internal Soviet conflicts, and particularly in the growing feud between Trotsky and Stalin. While the animosity between those two Soviet leaders had predated the October Revolution of 1917, its intensity greatly increased following the death of Lenin in

January 1924. With power over the Russian party and, therefore, over the entire communist movement hanging on the solution of these conflicts, the attitude of foreign communist leaders toward rival Soviet groups became the main criterion of political and ideological orthodoxy. Almost from the outset, the KPRP's leadership aligned itself with Trotsky. In December 1923, the Central Committee of the party sent a letter to the Russian party refusing to even "admit the possibility that Comrade Trotsky could be put outside the ranks of the leaders of the Russian Communist Party and those of the Communist International."[6] It reiterated this endorsement, in spite of a personal rebuke from Stalin, in another letter in March 1924.

There were several reasons for this open display of KPRP support for Leon Trotsky. To begin with, many Communists in Poland credited the success of the Russian revolution in October 1917 to his skillful leadership and tactical brilliance. Subsequently, as a nearly victorious commander of the Red Army during the Polish-Russian war of 1920, Trotsky earned their admiration and respect. To some of the party leaders, Trotsky appeared as the only Russian Communist capable of taking over the helm of the Soviet party and state after Lenin's death. Indicative of this attitude was Kostrzewa's letter to the party in January 1924, in which she stressed that "Trotsky is the only man in Russia today who could become an object of mass 'veneration.' Now that Lenin is dead, there could be a need to find such a man—it corresponds to Russian tradition and the spirit of the times. Masses will look up to Trotsky. Yet he cannot become what Lenin was within the party [and] here is the conflict."[7] Furthermore, Trotsky's internationalist outlook strongly appealed to the Communists in Poland, while they were increasingly apprehensive of Stalin's parochial or Russia-first orientation. Last but not least, the KPRP leaders were concerned that any further intensification of the internal Russian squabbles might have a profoundly destructive effect on the revolutionary movement itself by changing the focus of communist policy away from issues and toward personalities.

From Moscow's viewpoint, however, the KPRP's avowal of its fears and preferences was seen as an unwarranted interference in Soviet domestic affairs. It amounted to an attempt at weakening the Soviet revolutionary leadership and, above all, it earned the party the enduring enmity and suspicion of Joseph Stalin. At the fifth Comintern congress in July 1924, the KPRP's leadership became the target of severe criticism for its allegedly disruptive activities in the international communist movement. To investigate those charges, the congress set up a special commission headed by Stalin himself. During a three-day investigatory session, the main attack was launched by Julian Lenski, who accused the KPRP's leadership of espousing reformatory opportunism rather than revolutionary vigilance and charged the rightist triumvirate with complete responsibility for the party's political weakness.[8] Some of the party leaders, especially Wera Kostrzewa, mounted a spirited defense arguing that the internal crisis of the KPRP was rooted in long traditional differences between the Luxemburgist wing of the party and its more moderate majority, which she vainly tried to link with Leninist orientation.[9] But at the end, the confrontation boiled down to the question of the KPRP's interference into Russian affairs. As pointed out by Stalin in his concluding speech, "the Russian question has the decisive importance for the whole revolutionary movement in the West as well as in the East. . .[T]he Soviet power in Russia is the foundation, the mainstay, the refuge for the revolutionary movement of the entire world. Thus, upsetting this power would mean upsetting the revolutionary movement throughout the world."[10] In light of this interpretation, there was nothing that the rightist leaders could do or say. Following Stalin's instruction, the commission dissolved the existing leadership of the KPRP and ordered its key members to refrain from political work. Subsequently, a new Central Committee of the KPRP was constituted by a decree of the Comintern with the specific purpose of a thorough restructuring of the party and adoption of new policies.[11]

These decisions were duly approved by the third congress of the party, which met in the Soviet city of Minsk in March 1925. At that time, the party committed itself to an intensive programmatic and organizational "bolshevization."[12] This involved a break with the united front tactics and adoption of a new course of revolutionary militancy against the state and society in Poland. The Soviet party's organizational model was accepted as a guiding principle of party internal work. Furthermore, to eliminate even a semblance of potential political differentiation among communist organizations in Poland and in Russia, the name of the party was changed to that of Communist Party of Poland (KPP). This change had an important symbolic meaning as the dropping of the word *worker* meant a loss of the traditional ideological identity.

Notwithstanding this imposition of an organizational, Moscow-oriented uniformity, the political profile of the KPP still remained at variance with Soviet expectations. This was largely due to the ascendance of the radical leftist group to the leadership positions. While they owed their newly found prominence to the Soviet backlash against the right wing orientation, they soon showed a considerable degree of independence from the Comintern's line. Once in power, they rapidly developed their own program of revolutionary vigilance in Poland, which included massive use of violence and widespread terrorist tactics. This merely resulted, however, in the intensification of an anticommunist campaign by the government and far-reaching restrictions on communist activity. Furthermore, the new leftist leaders did not hesitate to expand their militancy into the international arena. While careful not to address themselves to purely Soviet matters, they sharply criticized other parties within the movement for a lack of revolutionary decisiveness and activist determination. Yet, insofar as such activities proved to be dysfunctional for communist work in Poland and were judged as diversionary for international communist unity, they soon became a subject of critical scrutiny by the Comintern. By mid-1925 a new Polish commission of the Comintern severely condemned the left wing orientation and the party leadership was summarily dismissed.

Paradoxically, following the downfall of the leftist group the organizational control over the party fell again to Adolf Warski, the former leader of the right. But his authority was severely restricted and his policy making functions strictly limited. The party was deeply affected by internal political malaise and crippled by organizational weakness. This was fully acknowledged by Warski himself when he sadly remarked at the December 1925 party conference that "the rightist leadership, having lost its authority within the party, was defeated at the fifth congress of the Comintern, disintegrated and ceased to exist. The leftist leadership went bankrupt soon after the third congress [of the KPP] and fell apart. . .The party was left without any leadership. But without a leadership there is no party."[13]

In retrospect, this statement might have indicated that already by the mid-1920s there was little doubt in the minds of many a Communist in Poland that their party was in a state of irreversible decline and that they themselves were to be blamed for this debacle. From then on, the KPP became only a weak reflection of its Soviet sponsor. Increasingly, the party's dependence on the Soviet Union was to engender far-reaching, self-imposed as well as Moscow-imposed, restrictions on its ideology, behavior, and policy positions.

Thus ended the first, semiautonomous stage in the party's development. The next period, 1926–1929, was characterized by a continuing factional fragmentation within the party which, produced by long years of political frustrations, only tended to crystallize around current events and issues. This process of internal disintegration was accompanied by a steady increase in Soviet influence over the party's activities and the establishment of a direct pattern of Moscow's control over the party organizational structure.

A major event profoundly affecting the internal situation within the party and exposing it to a new wave of Soviet criticism of its policies was the military coup-d'état staged in May 1926 by Marshal Jozef Pilsudski. Prompted by the economic and political ineffectiveness of the rightist government in place, but also instigated by a real threat of the emergence of a rightist dictatorship, the coup brought a shift in the parliamentary system toward a more authoritarian regime.[14]

Whether through expectation that Pilsudski's intervention would lead to a revolutionary situation similar to that in Russia in 1917, or hope that by supporting a likely victor the party could improve its political position in the country, or assumption that anything would be better than a rightist dictatorship, the KPP decided to give its full support to the rebellious forces. Even before the outbreak of military revolt, the party propaganda gave a blessing to the impending action. During the coup, the KPP cooperated with the PPS and the trade unions, which also supported the coup, in organizing a timely railroad strike that effectively obstructed the deployment of anti-Pilsudski loyalist military units.

The coup succeeded within a few days of its inception. The rapidity with which the political conflict was resolved caught the party by surprise, shattering its possible hopes for a major and prolonged internal conflagration. Order and tranquility were restored by Pilsudski so quickly and fully that no opportunities for exploiting a potentially revolutionary situation ever really developed. Furthermore, it soon became obvious that Pilsudski refused even to acknowledge the KPP's support. In fact, several hundred communist activists were arrested even before the end of military operations; they were to be released only after the pacification of the country was fully completed. Finally, the political course which Pilsudski had set for Poland soon proved to be different from the initial communist expectations. Not only did he not follow a leftist line but "declared that he was in favor of neither Left nor Right, but of social equilibrium."[15] It gradually became possible that the party's decision might have been a serious tactical miscalculation.

The Soviet reaction was prompt and devoid of any ambiguities. In a speech delivered on June 8, 1926, in Tiflis, Stalin accused the KPP of being "weak, exceedingly weak" and incapable, because of its "incorrect attitude toward Pilsudski's troops. . .[of taking] its place at the head of the revolutionary minded masses. . .I must confess that our Polish comrades have, in this case, committed a very grave error."[16] To the extent that this statement was an obvious political indictment of the KPP strategy in Poland, its message was to have strong implications for its organizational and political cohesiveness.

Following a formal condemnation of party tactics by the Comintern, which accused the KPP leadership of political immaturity as well as gross negligence of Soviet and international revolutionary interests,[17] the level of internal conflicts within the party reached a rapid crescendo. Centered on the question of how to interpret the nature of Pilsudski's coup and how to assess its long-range implications for the party and for Poland, the conflicts created the threat of permanent organizational and political disintegration for the party as a whole.

The KPP split into two distinct groups, the so-called *majority* and *minority* factions. The former saw the evolving situation in Poland in terms of growing military dictatorship with fascist inclinations and called for a broad unification of all leftist forces to oppose the government. The latter regarded the regime as an already full-fledged, fascist dictatorship and accused the majority of opportunistic and quasi-collaborationist tendencies in its call for leftist political unity. The fourth KPP congress, which gathered in Moscow during September 1927, provided a forum for a massive display of internal dissention.

The marathon debates—the congress lasted for about four months—were replete with mutual recriminations and contradictory accusations, punctuated at times by occasional fist fights.[18] Their results remained, however, highly inconclusive. No new strategies or policies were adopted. The newly elected leadership consisted, in almost equal proportions, of the representatives of both factions. The final resolution made the defense of the Soviet Union and its policies the only objective with which all the delegates could fully agree. No other proposal or goal could obtain sufficient support and approval. The party remained deeply divided, with the lines of organizational authority muddled by ideological and political differences.

Under those circumstances, the Comintern took upon itself the task of bringing the party to order. At its sixth congress in 1928, two experienced Soviet officials, Dmitriĭ Manuilskiĭ and Otto Kuusinen, were appointed by the Comintern as supervisors for KPP activities. Finally, in April 1929, following the consolidation of Stalin's control over the Soviet party and the Comintern arbitrators, the reins of power within the party were taken over political responsibility within the organization. With the explicit help of two special Soviet delegates, Wilhelm Knorin and Nikolai Popow, who acted as Comintern arbitrators, the reigns of power within the party were taken over by the leaders of the minority group.[19] They included Julian Lenski as the party first secretary, as well as Saul Amsterdam (Henryk Henrykowski), Alfred Lampe, and Jerzy Heryng (Ryng) as his most influential associates. The final confirmation of the victory for the minority faction was made at the fifth congress of the KPP which, meeting in September 1930 near Leningrad, called for an intensification of the revolutionary struggle against the fascist regime in Poland.[20]

In many respects, this development brought to an end the long-standing ideological and political schism within the party. While it did not prevent sporadic and periodic flare-ups of factional dissensions, the most important of which was the emergence of a Trotskyist opposition within the KPP during early 1930s led by Isaac Deutscher, Paul Minc, and Abe Flug, the minority leadership remained firmly in the saddle until the party's dissolution in 1938. During the last period of party existence, 1930–1938, characterized by unquestioned ideological obedience to Soviet dictates and a complete organizational subservience to Stalin's commands, the same group of seemingly committed revolutionaries was forced to champion the dreaded cause of united front strategy that was imposed by the Comintern.[21] It seems that, after having been simple and obedient soldiers in the Russian-sponsored revolutionary movement, they developed such a devotion to duty that it finally overshadowed their concept of the revolution itself.

Notwithstanding its ideological and political dependence on Soviet guidance, and despite the illegality of its activities in Poland, the Communist party succeeded in maintaining a relatively stable, albeit small, following in the population. Operating in a society which included a substantial proportion of ethnic minorities, the party skillfully exploited a sense of grievance, oppression, and estrangement among those elements. It also established itself as a party of the radical alternative to the system in place, an ideological attraction to the intellectuals who dreamed about large-scale social transformations, and a political ally for impoverished artisans and unemployed workers who saw little if any remedy to their problems in the government-sponsored programs and official institutions. Only a few of them could be considered as conscious revolutionaries, but their support contributed to the party's political strength.

The exact size of party membership has remained obscure. As a secret, conspiratorial organization, constantly exposed to the danger of government persecution, the party did not maintain systematically prepared data of its social composition. Estimates must, therefore, rely on sporadic and far from complete official and semiofficial information and reports.

During the first period of its activity, the party membership hovered around 2,000, exceeding 3,000 only in 1924 (see Appendix 1). Subsequently, it increased to about 6,000 in 1927 and then stabilized at the level of 3,000 members. During the 1930s, the size of the party grew to 9,300 in 1933, the highest number in the party's history. In the following years, however, it steadily declined and by 1937, the last year of regular political activity, descended to about 4,000.

In light of these figures, the party emerges as a minuscule organization, suffering from considerable fluctuation in its membership levels. The sporadic periods of growth in recruitment seemed to have been prompted by waves of economic crises which plagued Poland in the early 1920s and the 1930s, rather than any sudden changes in its otherwise very low ideological appeal.

While it had always presented itself as a political vanguard and representative of the working class, the party was never able to establish a significant following among the workers. Their proportion among party members remained negligible throughout the years, reaching a high of only 17 percent during the years 1931–1933 and then gradually declining. In contrast, the party enjoyed much greater popularity among poor artisans and impoverished rural workers and peasants, whose share of the total membership ranged during the 1930s from 50 to 60 percent.[22]

Another important feature of the party's social composition was a high proportion of ethnic minorities among its members. Given the existence of very substantial alien populations in the post-First World War Polish state—

primarily Ukrainian and Byelorussian but also German, Lithuanian, and others—and their cultural, economic, and political separateness from the native Polish community, the communist internationalist orientation always constituted a powerful attraction to those groups. The party not only developed an active program of recruitment among those groupings but also set up distinct communist parties in the Polish-controlled parts of Byelorussia and the Ukraine. These two organizations, the Communist Party of Western Byelorussia and the Communist Party of Western Ukraine, were formed in 1923 as semiautonomous units with their own central organs, congresses, and administrative staffs, but remained subordinate to general directives of the Polish party's Central Committee and its congresses.[23]

Perhaps the most significant characteristic of the party's social composition, however, was the great percentage of Jews among its members and officials. As with other statistical aspects of the party organization, the Jewish share in the KPP membership remains difficult to establish. Current communist and Western estimates put the number of Jews in the party at about 22 to 26 percent throughout the 1930s with a particularly strong concentration— exceeding 50 percent of the membership—in the urban areas of central Poland.[24] Yet, if a precise proportion of Jews within the party remains clouded in uncertainty, there has never been any doubt as to their political and organizational importance. The Jewish revolutionaries had played a very important role both in the creation and the development of radical movements in Poland. They provided the intellectual leadership to the SDKPiL and the PPS-Left. Subsequently, the Jewish communists assumed a pivotal position in the leadership of the KPRP and the KPP, occupying most of the seats in their Central Committees.[25] Suffice it to say that with the exception of Kostrzewa all principal leaders of the party, such as Warski, Walecki, Domski, Lenski, and Henrykowski, were of Jewish origin.

Such numerical and organizational Jewish presence in the party did not imply, however, any identification of its activity with the political interests of Polish Jews. There is little doubt that an overwhelming majority of the Jewish population was unaffected by party appeals and a considerable proportion was openly anti-communist.[26] Throughout the 1920s and 1930s the party competed for influence among the Jews with other left-wing Jewish organizations, such as the popular General Jewish Labor Bund (the Bund) or the Zionist Poale Zion, but those efforts were largely unsuccessful. While it had been able to attract into its ranks several small groups of disaffected radicals in the early 1920s, the KPP's revolutionary orientation found little support in the Jewish community at large.

The multiethnic character of the party had its considerable social and political drawbacks. Socially, it condemned the party to a position of marginality and exposed it to numerous anti-Semitic attacks as well as restrictions imposed by the government. Politically, it almost precluded an expansion of party appeal to a larger native population.

Another factor which greatly undermined the operational effectiveness of the communist work was a persistent inability of the party leadership to develop and maintain a cohesive organizational structure. The task of internal institutionalization of the party was not really confronted until the second congress of the KPRP in 1923. At that time, the party adopted its first organizational statute.[27] It established a basic party structural framework of territorially based circles (*kolo*), which were administratively and politically subordinated to regional organs. The motive force behind this organizational development was a desire to tighten discipline and strengthen the authority of central leadership. The congress established two mutually interlocked central executive organs: the Politburo and the Orgburo, both of which were to be elected by the Central Committee to maintain political and organizational control over the party at large. Activities of all local party units were to be totally subordinated to the top leadership. The Leninist concept of democratic centralism became officially accepted as the guiding principle of party organization.

Further efforts at imposing operational centralization and discipline were undertaken at the third congress in 1925. Just as it turned politically to the left, the party also committed itself to organizational "bolshevization."[28] This involved dissolution of old territorially based circles and adoption of the Soviet revolutionary model with work-place cells as basic units of the party. It also meant statutory emphasis on mandatory activism of all members, professionalization of political and administrative staff, and rejection of all factional divisiveness through strict obedience to the central leadership's directives. The Orgburo was replaced by the Secretariat of the Central Committee. Gradually, this organ became the mainstay of party work, controlling by the end of 1935 about 150–190 full- or part-time paid functionaries and up to 500 voluntary activists.[29]

Despite these elaborate efforts to establish a centralist command structure, the party leadership was never able to secure effective control over the membership. In part, this resulted from constant factional infighting. But it also reflected the inherent difficulty of running a secret organization under the conditions of perpetual outside pressure and official hostility. In those circumstances, discipline could not be enforced as it might have been within an openly operating organization. To maintain the political loyalty and ideological commitment of the membership, efficient means of instant communication were absolutely indispensable.

Yet it was here, in the vital area of intraparty exchanges and contacts, that central leadership organs failed to establish themselves as sources of prompt decision making and tactical judgment. Throughout the two decades of party existence, most of the Politburo members permanently resided abroad—in Moscow, Gdansk, Berlin, or Paris—and only a section of the Secretariat operated in Poland. Time-consuming exchanges of information between local units and central organs contributed to organizational inefficiency, at times even providing grounds for contradictory decisions and confusing hesitations. In many cases, the choice of tactics and strategies was made at the lowest level and the party leadership was simply faced with a *fait accompli*. Writing in the 1950s about the nature of early communist work, prominent KPP activist Roman Zambrowski pointed out that "the conditions of illegal activity required a great deal of independence for local party activists. . .Often it was necessary to take a position immediately, without waiting for the decision of the Politburo, or the Secretariat in Poland, or even of a district committee of the party."[30] The gap in communication within the party was further compounded by the fact that all communist press organs, as distinct from sporadic leaflets and *ad hoc* printed appeals, were published abroad, particularly in Germany, thus significantly affecting the flow of vital political and ideological information. As a result, the membership's understanding of the general problems of party strategy and tactics was vague and its responses frequently slow in coming.

As if to compensate for its internal social and organizational weakness, the party achieved some success in developing a relatively large pool of potential sympathizers and supporters. In 1922 the KPRP set up its own organization of youth, the Communist Union of Polish Youth. Although it remained formally separate from the party itself, with its own network of circles and committees, the union's activities were closely supervised by the adult organization. Its membership, which according to official KPP sources reached about 16,000 young people in 1933,[31] was considered the main source of prospective recruitment into the party. Many of the union's adherents were drawn from university students and some of its leaders, most notably Alfred Lampe and Roman Zambrowski, rose in time to high positions in the KPP as well as in its subsequent mutations. The party also maintained close links with various radical groups which periodically appeared on the Polish political scene, such as several peasant organizations—the Independent Peasant Party or Self-Help—or ethnic associations—Byelorussian Hromada or Ukrainian Selrob.

However, the party's greatest political success was not found in revolutionary work. Rather, it was achieved within the framework of a democratic parliamentary system which offered to the illegal communist group an opportunity to spread their ideas, present their goals, and attack their enemies with total impunity and freedom.

Having overcome its initial distaste for bourgeois parliamentary politics, the party presented itself to the electorate in 1922 under the name of Union of the Urban and Rural Proletariat, a legally registered electoral body fully entitled to present its list of candidates throughout the country. It polled about 1.5 percent of the vote (132,000 out of almost ten million) and won two seats in the Sejm (parliament). The communist deputies were soon joined by four Ukrainian representatives and established an openly operating communist parliamentary group, which rapidly emerged as an important official channel for party propaganda.

In the subsequent Sejm elections in 1928 the Communists, using several separate lists under a general heading of Worker-Peasant Unity, greatly increased their popular appeal. Including invalidated ballots, they polled more than 900,000 votes, or about 8 percent of the total, and elected seven deputies to the 444-member chamber. The official Communist Parliamentary Faction was headed by the top party leader, Adolf Warski.

The communist electoral success was due in great measure to the mechanics of proportional representation. In 1922 the party did not win a plurality in any of 64 electoral districts in which it presented itself. In 1928 it won a plurality in just one district where it drew 34.6 percent of 191,176 votes cast.[32] In the elections of 1930, following a modification of electoral rules, the party polled only 232,000 votes. The number of communist delegates was cut to four. Subsequently, in the aftermath of a constitutional change in 1935, the KPP decided to withdraw from parliamentary and electoral activities.

The fifteen-year period of communist participation in parliamentary activities provided the party with considerable political benefits. It offered the party an important, officially publicized forum for airing its views on the subjects of both domestic and international politics. The communist deputies delivered close to 500 speeches, an equal number of interpellations, and made some 80 parliamentary interventions; most of these actions were widely discussed in the press. The party, through the political cover of its electoral formations, gained an important opportunity to act as a semilegal organization, free to organize public meetings, discussions, and manifestations.[33] And yet its involvement in democratic politics was always considered by the party as a momentarily convenient instrument of propaganda rather than a goal in itself. Their main objective was always to prepare the ground for a future revolutionary political and social transformation. The specific operational tasks were spelled out in the early 1920s and there was no indication that the party ever wavered from its original positions. They were to include:

[F]irst, to intensify the revolutionary ferment among the working masses in face of the increasing offensive of the capital and the government which, together, are resolved to shift over all the costs of the capitalist and state reconstruction on the shoulders of the working masses;

second, to intensify the revolutionary sentiments of the broad masses of landless and small peasantry, resulting from the failure of the agrarian reform as well as the sharpening of class antagonisms in the struggle for the land;

[third] to intensify the revolutionary tensions in the eastern territories, which result from the colonial and exterminatory policy of the Polish government as well as from the unceasing national and religious persecution.[34]

But, it is within this framework of a revolutionary commitment that the party activities produced a record of a conspicuous failure.

In the area of industrial relations, the party proved to be unable to capitalize on recurrent waves of worker unrest and dissatisfaction. This was particularly apparent during a dramatic proletarian revolt in November 1923 when, following a violent clash in Krakow between striking workers and military units, the workers were in control of Poland's third largest city and the country reached the brink of a civil war. Yet the party did nothing to contribute to the emergence of a possible revolutionary situation. In the words of a prominent leftist KPP activist, the party seemed to have "gotten frightened by the very goal [the revolution], the reaching of which it preached."[35] Similarly, the party did not succeed in politicizing worker protest movements in the 1930s, in spite of widespread unemployment and frequent strikes.[36] The essence of industrial conflicts remained strictly economic and not revolutionary.

With respect to the peasants, party efforts were severely hampered by its traditional identification with the urban proletariat. Only in the 1930s, when constantly rising disparity between the prices of industrial products and agricultural commodities brought the farm operators and rural workers to desperate protests, did the Communists gain a modicum of political influence. But inasmuch as this might have facilitated a recruitment drive for party membership in villages, the Communists were never able to establish control over the peasant protest movements.

Thus, notwithstanding the KPP's involvement in strikes, disorders, and protests against government economic policies, it won little political influence, domination of the proletarian movement, or any other tangible revolutionary gains. Control of worker and peasant political activities was firmly in the hands of other parties, the Polish Socialist Party and the Peasant Party, respectively. All communist attempts at forging political and/or operational links with those organizations proved futile. The party was simply regarded as too compromised and tainted by its Soviet associations for such alliances to work.

In effect, the national issue continued to be a primary factor in the party's inability to gain even a semblance of popular acceptance as well as a main source of its political weakness. Even if the Communists had grudgingly accepted Poland's independent existence, they never recognized her sovereignty over the territories she had won during the Polish-Russian war of 1920 and constantly wavered in their attitudes toward the legal status of lands restored to Poland from German occupation. This disregard for Polish national sensibilities reached its highwater mark in the early 1930s when, in response to Moscow's prodding, the party came out in support of German revisionist claims to Silesia and Pomerania. At its last congress, which gathered in November 1932 near Mohylev in the Soviet Byelorussia, the KPP approved a program attacking the Versailles Treaty.[37] Shortly afterward, the KPP Central Committee's message to a "Polish-German Workers' Committee" in the then-German town of Gliwice proclaimed that "after eleven years of Polish occupation of Upper Silesia. . .the KPP declares that the victorious Polish proletariat. . .will annul all the rulings contained in the Treaty of Versailles with regard to the Pomeranian corridor, and Upper Silesia, and will ensure the populations of these lands the right to self-determination even as far as secession from Poland."[38]

The subsequent change of heart, prompted by a change in Soviet policy in the aftermath of Hitler's coming to power, did little to repair the damage that had been inflicted on the party's standing at home. During the next few years, all communist efforts to create a joint anti-fascist front with the socialists, the Jewish Bund, and other smaller left-wing groups were rejected. The party stood alone as an ideologically and politically alien organization.

A much more important danger to KPP's political and organizational viability, which was eventually to determine its very existence, was an increasingly negative assessment of its role by Soviet authorities. During 1933–1934 several KPP activists, including two Central Committee members, Jerzy Czeszejko-Sochacki and Tadeusz Zarski, as well as long-time communist agent Sylwester Wojewodzki, were arrested in Moscow. They were subsequently accused of collaboration with Polish police, a charge that was never proved but became obediently accepted by the KPP leadership.[39]

The process of arrests and purges accelerated during 1936–1938, when hundreds of KPP activists disappeared in Soviet prisons and labor camps. They included all members of the Politburo and the Secretariat. At least 30 out of 37 members and deputy members of the KPP Central Committee elected at the sixth congress in 1932 were eliminated, as well as scores of former top leaders of the party.[40] The few survivors seemed to have owed their lives to the fact that they had already been imprisoned in Poland and, therefore, were beyond the reach of the Soviet terror apparatus.[41]

Sometime in 1938, the exact date still unknown, the Communist Party of Poland was dissolved by a decision of the Comintern. No official explanation of this verdict was provided and the only public condemnation of KPP activities was a semi-official article published in the Comintern's journal in which the party was accused of having been infiltrated by Polish police.[42] The decision entailed a wide-ranging Comintern-directed campaign aimed at eradicating all organizational vestiges of communist activity in Poland.

This campaign was remarkable in its thoroughness. A special group was set up by the Comintern in Paris to conduct the complete destruction of the KPP's units both at home and abroad.[43] Headed by a Bulgarian Communist, Anton Ivanov Kozinarov (Bogdanov), it consisted of several low-ranking KPP members recruited from among volunteer soldiers of the Spanish international brigades led by a former activist of the Communist Union of Polish Youth, Boleslaw Molojec. Presented as a special "initiative group," its official task was to prepare the ground for creation of a new Communist party in Poland in place of the KPP. In reality, however, its purpose was to suppress all existing KPP cells, isolate the remaining officials of the party, and investigate their activities to determine a possible link between them and Polish or foreign police. By the beginning of 1939, all traces of an organizational existence of the KPP had been eliminated.

The sudden and dramatic end of the Communist Party of Poland subsequently provided fertile ground for numerous speculations as to the real reasons for the Comintern's decision, the choice of methods used in its execution, and its political timing. Particularly important seems to be an argument that the dissolution resulted from the Soviet contention that, inasmuch as the prospect of a KPP-instigated revolutionary change in Poland remained nonexistent while the power of Hitler's Germany was rapidly rising, it would be politically wiser and tactically more effective to end the communist movement in Poland so it would not obstruct possible rapprochement between Soviet Russia and Nazi Germany.[44] However, in face of a continuing Soviet silence on this subject and in a situation when even the essential facts of the case cannot be fully determined, no satisfactory explanation has been provided as yet.

Nonetheless, it might be argued that the party dissolution was an inevitable consequence of the earlier elimination of its leadership. In a small and conspiratorial organization in which personal ties with and loyalty to the leaders had been maintained as the main criterion of ideological orthodoxy and political cohesion, an unexplained removal of all top officials had to stir disintegrative tension and considerable resentment. There is also little doubt that the Soviet and Comintern leaders had fully realized the potential political repercussions of their actions in the KPP membership and had anticipated negative reactions. Yet, their determination to purge the KPP leadership seemed to have been rooted in strategic imperatives of such importance that they superseded any consideration for or interest in the KPP's continuing existence. The Comintern's decision appeared to have reflected two separate concerns: first, an organizational concern of establishing a monolithic international communist movement under Stalin's leadership; second, political concern that the KPP had been infiltrated by enemy agents.

As for the first concern, the KPP leaders had always displayed a remarkable and constant tendency to quarrelsome rifts, factional struggles, and ideological turmoil. In the era of Stalin-centered obedience and discipline, they were suspect either of preserving some traces of past deviations or even developing new ones in the present. Therefore, they had to go. With respect to the second concern, there is little doubt that the Soviet leaders really believed that "[among communist parties] the most contaminated by hostile elements was the Communist Party of Poland where agents of Polish fascism managed to gain positions of leadership."[45] In effect, current communist sources revealed the existence of a police agent within the Central Committee in the early 1930s, an agent who was only discovered after the Second World War.[46] The persistent inability of the Soviet agents to find the true culprit might explain in part the systematic elimination of all possible suspects. After all, from Stalin's point of view, the primacy of a revolutionary cause, or his personal unrestricted dominance over the entire communist movement, made humanitarian considerations relatively insignificant.

Last but not least, the party itself had always been perceived in Moscow as a weak and inefficient instrument of its own revolutionary policy. If the change in Soviet strategies of action required a sacrifice of the KPP's very existence, it did not seem to Stalin and his associates a serious price to pay. In any case, the party in Poland was to reappear under different political conditions, with different personnel, and with new tasks to fulfill.

Rites of Passage

In September 1939 the independent Polish state ceased to exist. Invaded from the west by the Nazis on September 1 and from the east by Soviet troops on September 17, the country put up a heroic but futile five-week defensive struggle. On September 17 the government was evacuated to Romania and less than three weeks later, on October 5, the last Polish military units surrendered to the Germans.

In fulfillment of an agreement reached in late August 1939 by the representatives of the Nazi and Soviet governments, Poland's territory was partitioned between those two states.[1] The area seized by Germany was divided into two parts: the western section was incorporated into the Reich and the rest was turned into a German colony under the name of *General Government.* The territories occupied by the Soviet army were promptly absorbed into the Soviet Ukrainian and Byelorussian republics.

These rapidly unfolding developments brought about widespread panic among the population. Masses of people were roaming the country in search of a safe place. Among them were many Polish Communists who had been previously imprisoned by the government but now, under the conditions of almost total chaos and disorder, were able to escape. Some of them joined the Polish armed resistance to the Germans and participated in the defense of Warsaw as well as in other military actions. Most of them moved to the Soviet-occupied territories. In time they established two main centers of Polish communist emigration in the cities of Bialystok and Lvov. During 1940 and 1941 their activity centered on the publication of several Polish-language Soviet journals such as *Czerwony sztandar (Red Banner)* and *Nowe horyzonty (New Horizons)* in Lvov and *Sztandar wolnosci (Banner of Freedom)* in Minsk. There was no attempt, however, to reconstitute the defunct Communist Party of Poland or to establish any kind of a specific, Polish communist orientation. This resulted partly from the Comintern's continuing refusal to permit any form of organized activity by Polish Communists. But the primary reason seems to have reflected their acceptance of a seemingly permanent disappearance of Poland as a separate political entity.

The main thrust of Moscow policies in the newly acquired areas was to eradicate all social and political groups which might have been hostile to Soviet rule. This involved mass deportations of Poles to Soviet Asia and Siberia and selective liquidations of Polish military personnel and political figures.[2] The wave of repressions affected the Communists as well, and ". . .some of them even underwent a crisis in their relationship with the Soviet Union. Some moved themselves deeply into the Soviet Union of their own free will, while others tried to move to the territories occupied by the Nazis."[3] Those Polish Communists who were judged by the Soviet authorities as sufficiently loyal were given jobs in local industry and administration and a few even succeeded in entering Soviet politics as citizens of their new country of choice.[4]

Communist activities in the German-occupied areas appear to have taken a similar turn: all forms of organized or semiorganized political work came to a complete standstill. The task of creating and conducting resistance to the Nazi invaders became the exclusive domain of various non-communist patriotic movements.[5]

This absence of any involvement in the anti-Nazi opposition could only be explained by the Communists' obedience to general Comintern directives. Spelled out in a policy-setting article by the nominal head of the international communist organization, Georgi Dimitrov, they defined the war between Germany and the West as a basically imperialist conflict and appealed to the workers to refrain from any participation in the military activities. Instead, the workers were encouraged to intensify their domestic struggle against bourgeois governments in place, force them to end the war, and then turn their efforts toward the creation of a class-based revolutionary solution.[6]

In this situation, the main preoccupation of the Communists in Poland was discussion of various future alternatives regarding prospective revolutionary change rather than immediate action. This led to a proliferation of groups advocating different views and opinions. One was the relatively moderate, so-called "Krakow group," which saw the future Poland as ". . .a socialist republic with full political and economic democracy. . .encompassing all unquestionably ethnically Polish territories" and called for a new form of the united front of all ". . .socialist and democratic elements" to provide a stable government.[7] Another was the extremely radical "Revolutionary Worker-Peasant Councils," which linked national liberation with international proletarian revolution and conceived its culmination with the. . .[entrance of Poland] into the International Soviet Republic."[8] Finally, there were the "Associations of Friends of the USSR," which sought a complete identification with Soviet interests and policies and simply concentrated on providing help and support to the Soviet government.[9] All those discussions did not provide, however, for any organizational activity. Even the names of particular groups were coined much later, when changes in the international situation turned the struggle against the Germans into the main source of communist revolutionary virtue.[10]

The crucial event prompting this political transition from passivity to action was the German attack on the Soviet Union on June 22, 1941. In Poland, it brought about a rapid emergence of the first Communist-led organizations, of which the most prominent was the Union for Liberation Struggle founded in September 1941. The main thrust of its initial activity was to serve as a distribution network for Soviet propaganda appeals intended to encourage Polish anti-German resistance movements. To this end, the Soviet government set up in August 1941 a so-called "Kosciuszko" radio station in the USSR. Its broadcasts were transcribed by the Poles and distributed among the population. Their political message, which became the *ipso facto* platform of the union itself, was a call for the unification of all patriotic forces in the anti-German struggle with the ideologically revolutionary content reduced to bare minimum. This apparent departure from revolutionary principles met some opposition in the more traditional communist groupings, particularly among the adherents of the "Revolutionary Worker-Peasant Councils" and the "Association of Friends of the USSR." Their attempts at establishing a more radical orientation for the movement and at developing specific Communist-based forms of active resistance to the Germans rapidly failed. During the summer months of 1941 their leadership fell victim to mass arrests by the Germans and by October both organizations ceased to exist as separate bodies.[11]

While these developments were taking place in Poland, first steps toward the reactivation of a separate Polish Communist party were taken by Comintern leaders. During July and August 1941 several former KPP activists were recruited to the Comintern School in Pushkino near Moscow. Subsequently, Comintern head Georgi Dimitrov selected from among them a special "initiative group," charged with preparing a program and defining the shape of a future Communist party in Poland. Its leaders were former low-ranking KPP activists Marceli Nowotko, Boleslaw Molojec, and Pawel Finder. In September the group presented a draft program for Dimitrov's approval.[12] It envisaged adoption by the party of a goal of comprehensive socioeconomic transformation in Poland, to be achieved, however, through a basically evolutionary and gradual program of internal reforms. The immediate political strategy focused not only on insurrectionist struggle against the Nazis in cooperation with Soviet forces but also on solidarity with non-communist movements and organizations already operating in Poland. Special recognition was also given to the efforts of Great Britain, France, and other Western nations for their fight against Germany.

As for the nature of the new party, the authors of the program proposed to preserve a strong link to the working classes and to identify the nascent organization with the cause of national liberation. Under direct orders of Dimitrov, who personally gave the name Polish Workers' Party to the future organization, its activity was to be formally separated from that of the international communist movement. This reflected of course a purely tactical consideration for dispelling the traditional image of communist foreign allegiance and providing the new party with a semblance of national identity. In reality, the Polish Workers' Party was to be strictly controlled and directed by the Comintern. This was clearly acknowledged in an official instruction prepared by a Comintern official and future party leader Jakub Berman for students in political training schools in the Soviet Union. Dealing with the motives for changing the name of the party, it stressed that

> the party was not called communist for the following reasons: (1) So the enemies would not be able to use the scarecrow of communism; (2) There are still numerous elements, even in the working class, which do not trust the communists as a result of past mistakes and erroneous policies of the former KPP; (3) After what happened [with the KPP] the party, as was pointed out by Dimitrov, must earn the right to call itself communist; (4) It is necessary that the masses look at our party as an organization closely linked with the Polish nation and its vital interests; in this way, the enemies will not be able to call it an agency of a foreign country; (5) *Under this name it will be easier to attract to the party large masses of workers, peasants, and the intelligentsia, and then to organize, under the leadership of the party, a united national front for the struggle against the German-fascist occupiers.* . . .Although our party will not be called communist and will not formally belong to the Comintern, it will be a truly revolutionary party of the Polish proletariat. . .It will conduct propaganda in the spirit of communism and will follow the line of the Comintern.[13]

Having secured the Comintern's approval for their program, the members of the "initiative group" were parachuted to Poland on December 28, 1941, to establish the party in the country itself. In the course of the next seven years, this party was to evolve into a powerful instrument of profound political, social, and economic change.

This process of development went through several distinct stages, in which the preoccupation with certain basic tasks was crucial in shaping the nature of the party and its strategies and tactics. Chronologically, these tasks included establishment of the party organizational and political presence in Polish society, seizure of institutional control over Poland's political and economic order, and setting the stage for the final revolutionary transformation of the country at large. The successful completion of any of these tasks provided a major determinant of change in the party's organizational and operational characteristics.

The Polish Workers' Party (PPR) was officially founded in Poland on January 5, 1942, at a meeting of Pawel Finder and four representatives of different communist groupings existing in Poland. The main purpose of the meeting was to inform local activists about the Comintern's decision to revive the Communist party. Consequently, all other communist organizations were to be immediately dissolved and their members were to join the PPR, whose program was to become the sole basis of their activity. There was little discussion at the meeting.[14] The local activists were simply presented with the program and informed about the formation of a party leadership which, as it had been already determined in Moscow, consisted of Marceli Nowotko as secretary in charge of political matters, Boleslaw Molojec as commander of the prospective party's military organization, and Pawel Finder as coordinator of internal recruitment and organization.

Following these initial formalities, the leadership set about the creation of the party. The entire organization was built from the top down, under strict supervision of the Comintern, and on the basis of rigid centralization in decision making. The task of preparing grass root formations of the party was assigned to special organizing agents, most of whom were sent directly from the Soviet Union and the rest appointed by the leadership. Each of these agents was given a section of the country (*okreg*) as an exclusive area of operation.[15] They were in charge of setting up local committees which, in turn, controlled the work of an evolving network of occupationally centered cells, preferably consisting of only five members. All committee members had to be approved by the central directing group, the Central Committee, whose membership could be expanded only by cooptation.

From the outset, considerable efforts were also made to develop a separate para-military (partisan) section of the party with specific tasks of launching immediate guerrilla attacks against the Germans. In March 1942 this section received a distinct name, the "Peoples' Guard" (GL), and, so as to underscore its political and organizational links with the party at large, all PPR members automatically became soldiers of the Peoples' Guard. Its first armed detachments were rushed into action in the summer months of the same year. But inasmuch as these organizational travails corresponded to the basic outline of a communist strategy which had been set in the Moscow conversations between Dimitrov and the Poles, their effective realization encountered serious difficulties in Poland.

To expand its numerical base, the party had to define its political positions in such a way as to attract both the old KPP faithfuls and the less radical leftist elements who had refused to identify themselves with the old communist line before but could be persuaded to support the new orientation. Yet here was the crucial problem: many traditional KPP activists became critical of the new party. They felt ideologically betrayed by the sudden change of its name and were suspicious of the seemingly nationalistic and insurrectionist trends in the party political appeals. As Nowotko reported to Dimitrov after six months of the recruiting efforts: ". . .the greatest difficulty is in breaking down the factional feelings, particularly among the former KPP members for whom everybody who is not a communist is an enemy."[16] On the other hand, to acquiesce to their demands for greater ideological zeal would mean the loss of many other prospective sympathizers. Taking into consideration the existing proliferation of various non-communist underground organizations, this could bring to an end the party as a viable political entity.

In the area of military planning and organization, a major source of PPR's weakness was the lack of a qualified and trained officer staff. With the singular exception of Molojec, all top commanders of the GL—such as the first chief of staff, Marian Spychalski, and his successor, Franciszek Jozwiak, who had been brought to Poland from the Soviet Union in mid-1942 and promptly coopted by the Central Committee—were politicians rather than military experts. To overcome this shortage of military leadership, Molojec brought from France a group of his former comrades, veterans of the Spanish war.[17] In the years ahead, they were to become, along with several Soviet officers, the backbone of the communist underground military forces.

Despite this military weakness, the party leadership insisted on immediate commencement of armed operations against the Germans. Thus, in May 1942 the GL troops initiated the first limited combat actions and in October they scored perhaps their most spectacular success, the bombing of a fashionable German coffee house in Warsaw. The strictly military value of these activities was very small and they proved to be costly to the GL organization, as several of its units were destroyed by German police and military forces. Their significance should be seen rather in the political aspects of the entire program; they put the party on the map of active political organizations and served as catalysts of the burgeoning non-communist movement toward more decisive armed struggle against the German occupiers.

The crucial factor in PPR's initial political fragility, however, was the ineffectiveness of its top leadership. Nowotko, Molojec, and Finder were unable to establish themselves as popular figures capable of attracting a larger following to the party ranks. Their past activities in the old KPP had been little known and basically insignificant, thus preventing them from building on the respect and loyalty of the old guard. This was particularly true of Molojec who, after having presided over the KPP's dissolution, could hardly be suspected of personal popularity. Furthermore, in their common task of enforcing the difficult process of the centralistic consolidation of the party, all three leaders were bound to make bitter enemies of many a local activist. To make matters even worse, personal relations among them were from the beginning marked by mutual hostility, as functional rivalries and distrust precluded any form of cooperation. The main conflict was between Nowotko and Molojec, with the former putting a primary emphasis on political organization and the latter pushing for military action.[18]

In late November 1942 both Nowotko and Molojec died under rather mysterious circumstances. Reportedly, Nowotko was killed on Molojec's orders after it was discovered that he had collaborated with the Nazis. Molojec, in turn, allegedly was tried and executed by the party for an unauthorized assassination.[19] Whatever the true reason behind this still unexplained elimination of two original PPR leaders, the result was an injection of new life into party activity. The locus of power shifted to a new leadership, in which Pawel Finder became the secretary and his main assistants were Franciszek Jozwiak (Witold) and Wladyslaw Gomulka (Wieslaw). This change entailed a corresponding attempt to redefine the party's tasks in light of different experiences of the new leaders and their concern for political self-maintenance.

On the political level, particularly important was the appointment of Gomulka to the leadership group. In contrast to a preponderant majority of the organizing agents and leaders of the party, who had gone through special training in the Soviet Union and were thoroughly sovietized, Gomulka might have been considered as an essentially home-grown and locally oriented Communist. He was a low-level activist of the KPP before the war, with particular interest in trade union work. He was imprisoned in Poland just before the war and, following the German invasion, escaped to the Soviet Union where he spent two years, 1939–1941, without any significant involvement in communist politics. Having returned to Poland in late 1941, apparently at his own volition, Gomulka subsequently became active in the party work in southern Poland. In mid-1942 he was coopted to the PPR's Central Committee. His appointment to a top executive position in December 1942 was seen by many local party activists as a sign of recognition of their potential importance for the political operation of the party. In time, this attitude was to become a crucial factor in the PPR's future and organizational evolution.

The immediate effect of these developments on the party's policy formulations as well as its internal political strategy was an intensified effort to come to terms with non-communist, anti-German resistance groupings. It was not to be an acknowledgement of weakness, however, but rather an attempt to project the PPR's assertion that, after having proved itself in a direct fight against the Germans, it "earned its due place in the front of struggle against the hitlerite occupiers [and]. . .became a force. . .which everybody must take into account."[20] This assertion paved the way for a series of steps aimed at establishing a cooperative relationship with political and military groups associated with the pro-Western Polish government in London.

In January 1943, the PPR's Central Committee issued an open letter to the

London government's representatives in Poland calling for joint action on the front of struggle against the Germans. At the end of February, direct talks between the party, represented by Gomulka, and delegates of the government took place. However, they quickly bogged down as both sides demanded a drastic reversal of each other's priorities. The Communists wanted to preserve their political and organizational autonomy while pushing for a place in a new, reconstructed, and home-based government. The London delegates insisted on a full recognition of their government's legitimacy and required that the PPR sever its ties with the Soviet Union.[21] By April, the contacts were finally terminated in the aura of mutual hostility and distrust.

In many respects, the failure to forge an operational link-up between these two separate resistance movements was determined by a sudden deterioration in official Soviet relations with the Polish government in London. Established in June 1942 on the basis of mutual recognition and cooperation, these relations were ruptured in April 1943 when the Polish government demanded an open investigation of a Soviet-perpetrated slaughter of several thousand Polish military officers in the Byelorussian forests near the small village of Katyn.[22] The Soviet government refused to accept the responsibility for the mass murder, which had taken place in the aftermath of the Soviet invasion of Poland in 1939, and withdrew its recognition of the London government and adopted a rigidly antagonistic attitude toward all non-communist forces and movements operating in Poland. The communist formations in Poland followed the lead.

To bolster communist activities in Poland and insure greater control over their political direction, the Soviet government set up in June 1943 a Union of Polish Patriots in Moscow with a view to eventually transforming it into a quasi-governmental institutionalized body. Its formation had been preceded by several months of recruiting activities and political training for future officials. The union was headed by a known left-wing socialist and wife of a high-ranking Soviet official, Wanda Wasilewska, and among its directing group were many former members of the defunct Communist Party of Poland, such as Alfred Lampe, Jakub Berman, and Stefan Jedrychowski. A hastily formulated program called for close cooperation between the future independent Poland and the Soviet Union and appealed for the immediate formation of a separate Polish military force in the Soviet Union operating within the organizational framework of the Soviet Army.[23]

The work on the creation of such a force began in May 1943. Paradoxically, it followed by only a few months the departure from the Soviet Union of a large Polish military corps, headed by General Wladyslaw Anders and consisting of those soldiers and officers who had been imprisoned after the initial Soviet invasion of Poland and after their release refused to join the Soviet army, opting rather for combat on the Western front. As for the new communist-oriented military force, the task of preparing it for military duty was performed by regular Soviet officers but the function of political training was fulfilled by former KPP militants and low-level Comintern officials of Polish origin. Among them were several future leaders of the Communist party and government in Poland, including Edward Ochab, Piotr Jarosze-wicz, Roman Zambrowski, and Aleksander Zawadzki. After a relatively short preparatory period, the new Polish corps was moved to the front in Sep-tember and fought its first major battle in October 1943 at Lenino.

Inasmuch as this expansion of political and organizational activity of Polish Communists in the Soviet Union reflected a reorientation of Moscow's poli-cies toward Poland and her government, it became necessary to establish more direct lines of communication between the Soviet-based groups and the organization operating in the country itself. This need was partially fulfilled by the arrival in Poland of Boleslaw Bierut, an old-time Comintern official with close ties to Soviet police, during the summer of 1943. He was immedi-ately coopted by the Central Committee of the PPR. After the arrest by the Germans of Pawel Finder in November 1943 and his subsequent replacement as secretary of the party by Wladyslaw Gomulka, Bierut became, along with Jozwiak, a member of the three-man PPR leadership.

Soon after, encouraged by Soviet military advancement, the leaders of the party decided that the time had come to challenge the non-communist forces on the issue of political power over Poland. Following a series of negotiations with several left-wing groups which until then had supported the London gov-ernment, the party came out in mid-December 1943 with a programmatic declaration calling for ". . .the foundation of a National Council of the Homeland as a factual political representation of the Polish nation, entitled to act in its name and to direct its destiny until the time of Poland's liberation from [German] occupation."[24] On the night of December 31, 1943, the coun-cil came into being as a quasilegislative organ consisting of the representatives of communist, leftwing socialist, and radical peasant groups. It was chaired by Boleslaw Bierut.

The circumstances surrounding the creation of the National Council of the Homeland, in particular the real origin of its sponsorship and the related question of its political role vis-à-vis the Soviet-based Union of Polish Patri-ots, have never been fully explained. On the one hand, Gomulka has always insisted that the council was founded on his suggestion and represented a purely domestic, as distinguished from a Soviet or Sovietized, contribution to the eventual establishment of communist rule. On the other hand, even if we accept his claim to exclusive sponsorship of the council, there is also little doubt that Moscow and its emissaries maintained a close control over the council's program and activities from the very beginning. The fact that it came under the direct supervision of Bierut, who had acted as a Moscow trustee with regard to communist activities in Poland, provides strong support to that conclusion.

Yet, whether or not the council originated from domestic pressures was politically beside the point. What mattered was that its emergence amounted to a *sui generis* coup d'état, to use Gomulka's recent expression,[25] aimed at destroying the very legitimacy of non-communist political structures and institutions and replacing them with a new governmental framework, within which the Polish Workers' Party was to play a dominant role.

Despite these measures aimed at eventual seizure of political power, the Communists remained completely unprepared to lead the nation. They constituted a politically insignificant and numerically minuscule group, situated on the fringes of an anti-German resistance movement. The first indications as to the numerical weakness of the party were given in Nowotko's report to Dimitrov, in which he assessed the PPR's size in mid-1942 at four thousand members and that of GL at three thousand.[26] These figures were, however, obviously inflated if not totally misleading. This becomes particularly apparent when we consider the fact that all party members belonged *ipso facto* to the GL, while one could be a soldier in the GL without belonging to the party. In effect, it seems more than likely that Nowotko's message represented an intentional exaggeration designed either to impress the Comintern leaders with his performance or to be used for propaganda broadcasts to Poland. More realistic figures were recently furnished in the memoirs of the first chief of staff of the GL, Marian Spychalski, who, while stressing that "membership in the Guard was larger than in the party," gave the size of the military organization in mid-1942 at merely 1,500 to 2,000 members.[27] By contrast, the size of non-communist military units operating at that time in Poland was assessed, even in recent studies by communist historians, as ranging from 250,000 to 350,000 soldiers of which some 30,000 to 40,000 were fairly well armed.[28]

Equally important was the absence of a clearly established political leadership of the communist movement itself. There were two separate centers, one in occupied Poland and another in the Soviet Union. While both groups insisted on the commonality of their ultimate purpose, the seizure of power in Poland, they differed in their political and social characteristics. The Soviet-based group was reminiscent of the old KPP, with its heavy stress on complete reliance upon Moscow's directives. It was dominated by experienced activists, including many Jewish Communists,[29] who now took important positions in the Union of Polish Patriots. The domestic group was politically more heterogeneous, with a considerable proportion of its members recruited from among radical leftists rather than from traditional Communists of the KPP mold.[30] Furthermore, the PPR's social composition was almost uniformly ethnically Polish, resulting partly from a conscious limitation of party activities to traditionally Polish areas and from a German-imposed isolation of the Jewish population from the Poles. Its political tactics were dictated by imperatives of the situation at home: in order to survive in a hostile environment, the party was forced to develop considerable ideological and operational flexibility in dealing with both the Germans and the non-communist resistance movements. In the long run, the inherent incompatibilities between the two groups were to become a source of serious friction in internal party relationships.

Meanwhile, the National Council of the Homeland went about formation of new institutional structures for the incipient Polish state. In its first decree it set up a new mass-oriented military corps, the Peoples' Army (AL), which replaced the communist Peoples' Guard, and declared it to be a national armed force open to all volunteers regardless of their political views. The job of its supreme commander went to a leftist but non-party officer, General Michal Zymierski, with the PPR's Franciszek Jozwiak as his chief of staff. The task of civilian administration was to be given to a network of local councils, to be endowed with extensive executive prerogatives but subjected to the centralized direction of the National Council of the Homeland itself.[31]

In May 1944 a delegation of the council went to Moscow to present its program to Soviet authorities and leaders of the Union of Polish Patriots. Following Stalin's personal approval and encouragement,[32] the delegation of the council merged with the union's leadership on July 18, furnishing the grounds for the establishment of the Polish Committee of National Liberation. It was to act as a provisional government responsible to the National Council of the Homeland. The committee, which eventually located its office in Lublin, the largest Polish city on territories controlled by Soviet armies, was headed by left-wing socialist Edward Osobka-Morawski, but remained clearly dominated by Soviet-based Communists. The former members of the Union of Polish patriots held ten out of fifteen ministerial seats.

On July 22, 1944, the Polish Committee of National Liberation issued a programmatic manifesto to the nation outlining its basic policies.[33] It constituted an appeal to the population to rise against the German occupation and cooperate with the Soviet armies. In the area of domestic policy, it called for broad agricultural reform based on land distribution without compensation to former owners of large estates but stopped short of demanding any nationalization of industry. It also promised to reestablish a democratic parliamentary political system and the practice of free elections.

Notwithstanding this success in establishing a political center for a future regime, the Communists still faced a difficult task of consolidation of power through the elimination of existing non-communist movements and organizations. This task appeared particularly important as there were in Poland powerful anti-communist military and political forces which, having provided the bulk of anti-German resistance, commanded considerable popular following in the population at large. Once again, the Soviet Union came to the rescue.

A major development which was to determine the outcome of the struggle for power between the communist and non-communist movements and through it the political fate of the country was the Soviet refusal to provide even a modicum of military support to the non-communist insurgents in their fight against the Germans. On August 1, 1944, encouraged by rapid westward advances of the Soviet armies, the London-oriented Home Army staged an armed uprising against the Germans in Warsaw. The motives for the uprising were both military and political.[34] From the military point of view, the Home Army wanted to contribute to the defeat of the German invaders. Much more important, however, was a political rationale for this action, which was based on an assumption that an independently organized liberation of Warsaw would necessarily entail some form of recognition by the Soviet government of the right of the non-communist organizations to establish themselves as future leaders of a sovereign Polish state.

Yet, it was in the political arena that the efforts of the Home Army leaders met defeat. On orders from Moscow, the Soviet armies abruptly stopped their forward march. The insurgents found themselves besieged by the Germans and isolated from Western Allies. After nine weeks of heroic fighting, the uprising was brutally suppressed. Its social and political costs were staggering: about 200,000 had died and the city was almost completely destroyed. The top Polish military commanders were taken prisoner by the Germans, as were many thousands of their followers. After the military debacle, the non-communist resistance movement was destroyed as an organized political force and rendered ineffective as a potential competitor for power against the Soviet-sponsored Communists.

In September 1944 Boleslaw Bierut as a head of the National Council of the Homeland was declared the new president of the Polish republic. Three months later, on December 31, the Polish Committee of National Liberation officially declared itself the provisional government of Poland and was recognized as such by the Soviet Union. In July 1945, following a long process of international negotiations at the Yalta conference between the major world powers and then in Moscow between representatives of the London and the Lublin governments, a reconstituted provisional government secured recognition by the Western states.

The new administration was based on a coalition of five separate parties: Polish Workers' Party, Polish Socialist Party, Peasant Party, Democratic Party, and Labor Party. The government was headed again by Edward Osobka-Morawski with two deputy premierships going to PPR's secretary Wladyslaw Gomulka and former head of the London government Stanislaw Mikolajczyk. Boleslaw Bierut remained as president and head of state. More important, however, than the distribution of formal positions was the fact that the Communists, fully relying on firm support and help from the Soviet Union, were in control of both formulation and implementation of all policies of the government. No other group or movement could effectively compete for power with the PPR.

This shift in the status of the party, from an underground movement against German occupation to a dominant force in the newly liberated state, had a dramatic effect on its political position. While in July 1944 the PPR membership was officially assessed at about 20,000, by the end of December 1945 it reached 235,000 (see Appendix I). Its main social base was furnished by impoverished proletarian masses, with workers and peasants accounting for 61 and 28 percent, respectively, while the white-collar share of the entire membership was only at 11 percent. In order to broaden its social appeal, the party immediately made a major effort to attract white-collar groups into the party ranks. The officially proclaimed goal of its activities became the creation of a mass, million-member organization of a national rather than class orientation.[35]

Concurrently, a strong effort was directed at consolidating the PPR's internal organizational structure and building an effective system of relationships between party and governmental institutions which would allow it to exercise constant control over the working of state machinery. Although initially presented as a temporary means for running the country under the conditions of war-inflicted institutional and administrative disorder, it became the foundation for a permanent system of political management in which direction of the processes of social, economic, and institutional development became the exclusive domain of the party officialdom. Since its establishment, this system has dominated and shaped the political life of the country, the party, and the government.

The impetus for streamlining the internal organization came from the top, and new forms adopted there were subsequently imposed upon the party at large. The main features of this process were political centralization and functional specialization in decision making. The locus of power shifted from the Central Committee, which had grown to 23 members following the cooptation of the Soviet-based communist leaders in July 1944, to a newly formed Politburo. Initially, the eight-member organ included Gomulka as the party secretary, five newcomers from the Soviet Union—Jakub Berman, Boleslaw Bierut, Hilary Minc, Roman Zambrowski, and Aleksander Zawadzki—and two representatives of the home-based PPR, Zenon Kliszko and Marian Spychalski. In December 1945, Kliszko was replaced by another Muscovite, Stanislaw Radkiewicz.

The first PPR congress, which met from December 6 to 13, 1945, officially changed the role of the Central Committee from an executive to a deliberative body meeting only a few times each year and institutionalized the Politburo as the key decision-making organ. At the same time, the congress adopted the rules of democratic centralism as the main principles of party organization. Although this created a formal elective requirement for all party officeholders, it also imposed a strict observance of internal discipline and an unquestioned subordination of lower party organs to directions coming from the top.[36]

To coordinate the entire party work, the Politburo set up a Secretariat of the Central Committee. Formed at the beginning of 1945, it initially included the heads of six newly established administrative departments—organizational, trade union, propaganda, personnel, military, and agriculture—under the general supervision of the party secretary. At the First Congress, the Secretariat became an elective organ in charge of "directing the current work of the party."[37] From then on, all members of the Secretariat—secretaries—have been elected by plenary meetings of the party's Central Committee from among its members.

This organizational pattern was repeated throughout the network of local party units. The PPR rapidly developed a pyramidal structure in which the primary, occupationally centered organizations were politically and administratively subordinated to the territorially based town and district *(powiat)* committees. These, in turn, were responsible to the provincial *(wojewodztwo)* committees which were controlled by the central organs of the party. All units had their own secretaries, and the directive functions, comparable to those of the Politburo at the central level, were exercised by executive groups within particular committees.

Along with stress on the centrally directed organizational institutionalization, the party leadership began a deliberate drive to recruit reliable personnel to carry out political work. Having grown from a socially marginal radical group with strongly antigovernmental traditions, the party was singularly ill-equipped to take over the management of the entire country. From the beginning it had suffered from an acute shortage of qualified manpower capable of generating popular support for the party directives and positive cooperation from various social strata and interests. The bulk of its activist group came either from among former partisans who were more attuned to coercive and arbitrary means of solving problems than to rational and systematic efforts at implementing party policies, or from among simple opportunists who saw the party as a convenient vehicle for enhancing their social position and material well-being. The recruiting difficulties were compounded by continuing and widespread public opposition to the party's systemic role, its ideology, and its social and economic policies. Concern over authority produced among the party leaders a kind of siege mentality, which led to the adoption of ideological orthodoxy and long-time adherence to the party as the basic criteria of organizational and political advancement.

These factors seem to have played a crucial role in shaping the PPR's apparatus, which grew from only 24 functionaries of the Central Committee in September 1944 to some 1,500 full-time, paid political employees by the end of 1945. According to available data, more than 50 percent of its membership was drawn from among the former members of the Communist Party of Poland and the Communist Union of Polish Youth, while new adherents to the PPR, people without any clearly defined radical political past, were limited to about 23 percent.[38]

The quality of the PPR's leading *actif,* which included all key party office holders as well as its main appointees in the state and economic administration, was strikingly low. By the end of 1945, only 18 percent of them had higher education and the entire group appeared to be dominated by trusted political loyalists, of whom more than 34 percent belonged to the pre-war communist organizations and about 32 percent joined the party during the occupation.[39]

To counteract and contain any possible challenges to communist rule, the PPR took severe measures to increase its political control over the state and economic administrative machinery and to tighten its internal system of security. On a general level, the party set up a network of organizational cells in all state institutions with explicit tasks of ". . .ensuring the prompt implementation of governmental directives, streamlining of work procedures, watching over the correct distribution of personnel, and enforcing work discipline."[40] They rapidly developed into effective instruments of party vigilance, particularly active in administrative units not directly controlled by the Communists. In these they became an alternative center of decision making and political authority.

More specifically, the party established an elaborate system of political safeguards centered around the Ministry of Public Security but directly supervised by the PPR Politburo. Its prerogatives were unusually extensive and included a whole gamut of tasks ranging from supervision of all forms of political and social activities of groups and individuals to strictly military operations in defense of the regime. The Ministry of Public Security maintained its own paramilitary corps, separate from regular armed forces, and employed a considerable body of agents in its numerous regional and district offices. Initially, membership in the party was a prerequisite for acceptance into the system, with former communist partisans and Soviet-trained officers constituting a substantial majority of the operational staff. In time, the entrance requirements were gradually relaxed, but even at the end of 1945 about 50 percent of all employees of the Ministry of Public Security were PPR members. The party organs within the security system were separated from the general PPR organization, held their own regional conferences, and elected their own representatives to party gatherings at the central level.[41]

The establishment and maintenance of a loyal security force was closely related to the leadership's concern over the continuing presence of politically hostile groups within the population. Although the anti-communist resistance was far from unified and comprised rather a wide variety of separate centers of aggregation, with its own political character and specific patterns of activity, it was a constant threat to the party and government. In these circumstances, the success of communist policies clearly hinged on the party's ability to selectively destroy the bases of resistance support and then to suppress their political activities.

The anti-communist resistance developed in two distinct directions. One was a secret military movement which aimed at removing the government by force. Another was an open attempt to organize political opposition, which would appeal to the public at large and try to change the make-up of state leadership through the use of electoral processes.

In dealing with the first, the party mounted a widespread and violent campaign against numerous "forest detachments" operating throughout the country. It was conducted primarily by internal security forces, but also had considerable direct Soviet support. Thus the Soviet police arrested sixteen top Polish military and political underground leaders in March 1945 in Warsaw and took them to Moscow for trial. Subsequently, the Soviet security organs provided the Poles with significant logistic help and supplied them with a large number of command personnel to assist in the struggle against the anti-communist elements. The fight against military opposition rapidly developed into a virtual civil war which lasted until the beginning of 1947. The magnitude of this effort might be discerned from an official assessment that during 1944–1949 more than 434 separate "gangs" of anti-communist partisans, each numbering over 300 members, were operating in the country.[42] The last mopping-up operations continued until 1952. These struggles brought death to thousands of people, destroyed large parts of the country, and served as witness to the popular determination of resisting the communist rule. Although the communist authorities tried subsequently to assuage the conflict through several programs of selective amnesties for the insurgents and other actions designed to attract them to the party's side, the lingering bitterness and desire for revenge were to affect the political climate in Poland for years to come.

The party response to the challenge of a legally organized political opposition was much more subtle. Anxious not to antagonize further the already hostile population, it accepted the emergence of several political parties with generally left-wing orientation. At the same time, however, it exerted considerable effort to infiltrate their leaderships, subvert their policies, and restrict their recruiting and organizational activities. Some of the traditional leftist but non-communist parties, such as the PPS and the Peasant Party, were completely taken over by new leaders, who openly accepted close cooperation with the PPR. The old leaders were forced to set up their own organizations, with different names and under very restrictive conditions. This was particularly important in the case of Stanislaw Mikolajczyk, a popular pre-war leader of the Peasant Party who, after having been a prime minister in the London government, returned to Poland in 1945 and organized a Polish Peasant Party, as his old group had been turned into a bogus outfit of the Communists.[43]

Furthermore, as a consequence of its controlling position in the government, the PPR was able to preempt programmatic initiatives of all potential competitors by coming out with popular socioeconomic reforms of its own. They included a program of land distribution among poor peasants, implemented during 1944–1945, as well as the nationalization of industry in January 1946. While clearly aimed at the elimination of existing social inequalities, these decisions could hardly be regarded as revolutionary. With regard to land distribution, the reform was limited to merely a portion of the estates—many were turned into state farms—and the bulk of the land offered to the peasants was located in the already abandoned formerly German territories. No collectivization programs were proposed. The main thrust of this policy was toward the elimination of landed gentry as a distinct social group, with its own life style and cultural specificity.[44]

Similar limitations characterized the program of industrial nationalization. It formalized the already existing situation rather than creating anything new. The act itself was restricted to an immediate nationalization of only very large or abandoned plants and did not include any definitive regulations as far as the expropriation of middle-size industry and foreign investments was concerned.[45] Seen from a political perspective, these reforms did not raise any protests from existing political parties, as all were firmly in support of their adoption.

The final battle for power took place during the lengthy process of preparing the country for parliamentary elections. The decisive step was taken at a mass referendum, called in June 1946 to determine the form and the nature of the evolving Polish state. The electorate was asked to approve, first, the change in the parliamentary structure from two- to one-chamber arrangement; second, the land reform and the nationalization of industry; third, the inclusion of the newly acquired western territories into the Polish state.

While all parties already had been openly supportive of both the economic and territorial changes, the seemingly innocuous problem of parliamentary reforms rapidly developed into the main issue of political contention. The opposition groups appealed for its rejection; the Communists and their allies called for the uniform approval of all questions asked. After a heated campaign, the opposition lost. According to the official results, subsequently protested by the non-communist forces, only about 32 percent of the voters rejected the first proposition, with the approval rate of 77 and 94 percent for the second and the third questions respectively.[46] This outcome determined the fate of the opposition groups.

The parliamentary elections took place in January 1947. Six separate political parties presented themselves to the voters but only two, the Polish Peasant Party and the Labor Party, could be considered as opposition groups. The remaining four—the Polish Workers' Party, the Polish Socialist Party, the Democratic Party, and the Peasant Party—were united in an electoral coalition which settled in advance the number of seats to be allocated to each. The PPR was clearly the main force behind this process of coalition formation. It conducted separate negotiations with particular parties and imposed upon them its own conditions of electoral action—an attempt by the then prime minister and top socialist leader, Edward Osobka-Morawski, to take a more independent position led to his prompt dismissal from the government and a termination of his political career.

The party also acted as a *spiritus rector* in the electoral campaign. It mounted a frontal attack against the opposition groups replete with false accusations, distortions, and frequent use of brutal force to suppress their activities. The newly adopted electoral rules disfranchised about a million potential voters, thus serving as a tool of intimidation of the electorate rather than a device to regulate political participation. All protests of the opposition parties were simply disregarded.[47]

The election brought inevitable defeat to the opposition groups. Its official results gave more than 80 percent of the vote to the PPR-led coalition, with the anti-communist forces able to obtain less than 15 percent. Out of 444 available seats, the communist-led coalition won 384—PPR, 119; socialists, 119; Democratic Party, 43; Peasant Party, 103—with only 43 going to the opposition groups and the rest allocated among various small organizations (see Appendix 2). The era of limited political pluralization was coming to a close; the country was gradually being pushed toward a new form of communist-controlled political unanimity.

In its first act, the newly elected Sejm adopted a series of constitutional changes. Among the most important were the limitation of parliamentary activities to only two short sessions per year and the establishment of the Council of State, a small organ which was to serve as a collective head of state with extensive legislative decree powers. On February 19, 1947, the Sejm elected Boleslaw Bierut as the council's chairman and the next day he appointed a socialist leader, Jozef Cyrankiewicz, as prime minister of a new government.

The campaign to eliminate the opposition further intensified. The government ordered mass arrests of members of the opposition groups and a wholesale closing of their offices and branches. In November 1947 Stanislaw Mikolajczyk, fearing for his life, escaped from Poland. The remnants of his party were forced to join the communist-approved Peasant Party, giving birth in 1949 to a new political organization, which, under the name of United Peasant Party, has been active ever since as a self-acknowledged supporter of the Communists. All traces of the overt anti-communist organized political opposition ended, and the PPR was ready to take final steps to consolidate its hegemony over other public organizations to ensure their unswerving obedience to its policies.

The main objective of this drive was the neutralization of the Polish Socialist Party. Since the end of the war, the Socialists were closely allied with the PPR. They participated in the government and formed part of the electoral coalition that had crushed anti-communist opposition groups in 1947. Yet they also constituted the only political organization that could conceivably provide a future obstacle to communist rule. The Socialists had substantial representation in state institutions and enjoyed a considerable following in the population, particularly among the workers and urban lower classes. Furthermore, as an old Polish proletarian party, the PPS had long traditions of defending the interests of the poor as well as a strong patriotic orientation. Last but not least, its numerical strength almost matched that of the PPR, with nearly 700,000 members at the end of 1947 to about 820,000 for the communist group.[48] The two other parties, the Democratic Party and the Peasant Party, were politically discredited and too small ever to be able to mount any significant challenge.

To impose its political control over the PPS, the Communists had adopted a strategy of gradual organizational penetration and absorption of socialist groups. From the outset, the PPR concentrated its pressure on socialist leaders by offering them top government appointments as an inducement to close political cooperation. Gradually, this extended to a deliberate effort to capture control of the trade-union movement, a traditional stronghold of the Socialists, which came under communist supervision by the end of 1946. It culminated with the call for a complete "organic unification" of the two parties made in mid-1947 by PPR general secretary Wladyslaw Gomulka.[49]

In the face of continuing communist pressure and despite considerable opposition from the socialist rank and file—more than 100,000 Socialists were purged from their own party for ideological insubordination during 1948 alone—the fusion of both proletarian organizations became unavoidable. The Communists, having secured full control over administrative and economic institutions, were clearly striving toward a comprehensive transformation of the society as a whole.

To a large extent, the momentum toward change—its direction, scope, and timing—had become determined by a series of important developments in the international arena. The fragile state of limited cooperation among the wartime allies was rapidly coming to an end. It was replaced by an increasingly antagonistic competition between the democratic West and the communist East with two main protagonists, the United States and the Soviet Union, demanding loyalty and support from their client states.

To secure a concerted communist strategy toward the rest of the world, the Soviet Union set up an international organization under the name of Communist Information Bureau (Cominform). It came into being at a meeting of the representatives of all ruling Communist parties as well as those of Italy and France, held on September 22–27, 1947, in Szklarska Poreba in Poland, with a clear purpose of providing an institutional forum of policy coordination among separate parties. However, this effort at international communist solidarity soon encountered serious difficulties. They centered on the growing conflict between the Soviet Union and Yugoslavia. The dispute arose on the issue of political autonomy of individual parties, with the Yugoslavs claiming the right to formulate their own foreign and domestic policies within a general communist framework, and the Russians insisting on complete subordination of all parties to their leadership and guidance in policy formulation. It culminated in mid-1948 with the expulsion of Yugoslavia from the communist family of nations but the controversy itself produced a lasting imprint on Soviet relations with other communist parties and states.[50]

For the Soviet leaders, the inherent danger of a nationally oriented diversity in the patterns of communist rule extended beyond any specific interparty conflicts. Rather, it carried the constant threat of undermining their control over the entire movement, made important joint international actions more difficult, and could severely endanger systemic stability in the Soviet Union itself. Determined to prevent this from happening, they began a decisive integrative drive by imposing their own institutional and operational processes on an emerging interstate communist system.

The Polish Workers' Party had always been closely linked with the Soviet party and its policy toward the West explicitly followed the Moscow line. In the summer of 1947, Poland refused to take part in a European conference on the Marshall Plan and then joined in a Soviet-run campaign of vilification against the American initiative. However, on the issue of institutional unification of the communist movement around the Soviet party, and in particular with respect to the applicability of Soviet sociopolitical experience under Polish conditions, the PPR showed signs of wavering in its commitment to Moscow-defined orthodoxy. Some of its leaders became openly resentful of the creation of the Cominform, seeing in it an instrument for imposing internal political and organizational uniformity among all communist states. The motive force behind this opposition was not the rejection of common communist objectives or even the Soviet leadership for the movement as a whole, which all PPR leaders recognized and supported. Rather, it reflected the conviction that a successful introduction of communism into Poland required specific policies and tactics which would correspond to Polish national and social traditions as well as political peculiarities, even if they might differ from those of other countries, including the Soviet Union.

The main proponent of this view was Wladyslaw Gomulka. As chief of the PPR delegation to the founding meeting of the Cominform, he was the only prominent communist leader critical of the nascent organization, defending, instead, the principle of political autonomy for his own party.[51] Gomulka's policy on domestic change in Poland was essentially reformist. He saw the process of internal development as going through gradual and partial stages of reconstructing political, economic, and social systems. Hesitant to introduce sweeping changes lest a faulty move intensify internal opposition to communist rule, Gomulka advocated temporary cooperation with non-communists in the management of the country and rejected collectivization of agriculture in favor of continued private cultivation of land with some form of piecemeal transition to future rural cooperatives.[52] Most important of all, he actively defended the virtues of Poland's independence, attacking old communist anti-patriotic traditions and trying to identify the PPR with the fight for the country's own national interests. Yet in doing so, he not only antagonized the Soviet party and its leaders, but also offended numerous veterans of the prewar KPP who, after having spent long years dreaming of the advent of communist power, suddenly found themselves criticized for past mistakes and political faults.

The straw that broke the camel's back was Gomulka's speech at the Central Committee meeting on June 3, 1948, dealing with preparations for the merger between the PPR and the PPS. Speaking about the united party's future program, Gomulka said that it should adopt "the PPS's splendid tradition of struggle for [Poland's] independence as one of its founding principles," and he castigated "errors" committed by both the SDKPiL and the KPP on that matter.[53] In particular, Gomulka observed that the SDKPiL, "the Luxemburgist rather than the Marxist party," had underestimated the importance of the issue of national independence for the Poles and as a result "failed to provide the leadership for the working class and proved unable to exert any serious influence on the development of the situation in [pre–World War I] Poland."

Gomulka was equally critical of the KPP's policy to "establish a Polish Soviet Republic as the means to liberate the working class." Declaring it "a mistake matching that of the SDKPiL," he noted that "the experience derived from the KPP's policy confirms that a faulty assessment of the situation, a failure to recognize realities, and, above all, a disregard for the positions taken by the working class inevitably drives any workers' party onto a road toward a revolutionary abstraction expressed in lofty slogans without realistic foundations." He added that "neither the revolutionary abstraction nor the dogmatic Marxism led to a revolution or socialism."

More important still, Gomulka argued that the new party should develop its own methods of attaining socialism without copying the experience of other parties. Saying that "the united party ought to be rooted in the ideological foundations of Marxism expanded by Lenin and Stalin," he stressed, nonetheless, that "the theory of Marxism-Leninism is not a closed science and should be continually developed so it could serve as a means of changing and improving the reality." He went on to say that although "socialism is a common idea for the working class everywhere, the road to socialism is not and cannot be the same in different historical situations." To support this view, Gomulka gave Russia as an example, "where the working class seized power through revolution and the establishment of the proletarian dictatorship as the form of authority" and contrasted that with the recent Polish experience "in which the working class also seized power, but without passing through a revolution and maintained its leading role in sharing power with other working strata." Gomulka admitted that the Polish experience had been made possible thanks to the Soviet military support during the war against the Nazis, but he also insisted that "different historical circumstances determine the roads leading the working class to power, diversify the roads to socialism, and [show] how one can and should develop the Marxist theory."

Turning to operational aspects for the new party's program, Gomulka said that it should serve to facilitate the growth of the party's membership. "Mass workers' parties, containing a high percentage of workers and employees as well as self-employed peasants, are very useful in the system of people's democracy," Gomulka told the Central Committee, adding that "the membership should be expanded primarily through the establishment of [party] organizations in the countryside." He supported this view by saying that the expansion of membership would "constitute an expression of public support for the system and an indication of popular confidence in the party as well as a sign of willingness to participate in building a new life in socialism."

These views came under a strong attack at the Central Committee meeting of August 31–September 3, 1948. Gomulka was accused by a number of speakers of being a "nationalist deviationist" with dictatorial tendencies and a "rightist" opponent of the program of a socialist revolutionary change.[54] After a lengthy debate which culminated with Gomulka's forced recantation of his opinions, the Central Committee dismissed him from the Secretariat and the Politburo of the party. His place was taken by Boleslaw Bierut, Gomulka's chief accuser at the meeting and long-time political competitor.

In many respects, this meeting became a turning point in the history of the Polish Workers' Party. On a general level, it heralded an impending shift in the operational locus of the party's self-perceived task of sociopolitical transformation from developmental reformism to revolutionary assault. Although specific ideological directives were to be issued at a later time, the PPR was on its way to making a determined commitment to impose a radical program of immediate change upon the society. Its distinguishing feature was a conscious rejection of the notion that specific Polish conditions should be taken into consideration in defining the scope and direction of this process. Rather, the Soviet experience would provide a model for the creation of a new social and political system. This decision was clearly indicated in a programmatic speech by Bierut, when he stressed that "the Polish road to socialism, in spite of its certain particularities, does not constitute something qualitatively different, but is rather a specific application of the general rules of socialist development, an application which had been made possible by the previous victory of socialism in the USSR, an application which is based on the experiences in socialist construction in the USSR, and which takes into account possibilities offered by a new stage of history as well as specific conditions of Poland's evolution."[55]

More specifically, the fall of Gomulka marked the beginning of a decisive change within the party's elites. The levers of power were being gradually taken over by new leadership groups whose unquestioned obedience to the imperatives of the Soviet-centered ideological movement effectively precluded the resurgence of a distinctly national deviation from the general rules of policy making and organization.

The formal merger between the PPR and the PPS took place at the Unity Congress of December 15–21, 1948, exactly 30 years after another unity congress between the SDKPiL and the PPS-Left. The new organization adopted the name of the Polish United Workers' Party (PUWP).

The new party was thoroughly dominated by the Communists. They provided the bulk of its membership, 955,900 from the old PPR to about 531,350 from the PPS, and clearly affirmed their ideological and organizational leadership. The accent in future political activities was put on ". . .further intensification of the class struggle against capitalist elements. . .aimed at the complete elimination of all forms and sources of economic exploitation."[56] Among eleven newly elected full members of the Politburo, eight came from the PPR—Boleslaw Bierut, Jakub Berman, Hilary Minc, Franciszek Jozwiak, Stanislaw Radkiewicz, Roman Zambrowski, Aleksander Zawadzki, and Marian Spychalski—and only three from the PPS—Jozef Cyrankiewicz, Adam Rapacki, and Henryk Swiatkowski. Of the four deputy members of the Politburo, three were former PPR officials—Hilary Chelchowski, Franciszek Mazur, Edward Ochab—and only one came from the PPS—Stefan

Matuszewski. Boleslaw Bierut was elected chairman of the party and three secretarial positions were given to Cyrankiewicz, Zambrowski, and Zawadzki.

In some respects, the congress marked the end of a long process of political and organizational maturation for the Communists of Poland. From a numerically small and politically isolated group of Soviet-sponsored revolutionaries they evolved, in the course of seven years, into an institutionalized force with complete control over Polish political life. The congress also signaled the beginning of a new era for the party, in which the task of a complete and lasting transformation of Polish society would become the main issue in its activity. The old revolutionary dream finally appeared close to reality.

CHAPTER 4

The Contrived Revolution

With the establishment of the Polish United Workers' Party, the Communists completed a decisive political breakthrough. All organized forces of actual or potential opposition were gone.[1] The party was firmly in control and attuned to the task of creating a new socialist order which would not be subject to challenge or change. This task was mainly an effort to restructure the entire socioeconomic system in accordance with the ideological premises of Marxism-Leninism. Its distinguishing feature, however, was the determination to apply the Soviet experience to domestic developmental processes with little regard to Poland's cultural, social, and economic particularities.[2]

To a large extent, this resulted from mounting Soviet pressures for operational and organizational uniformity of all communist activities. As dissatisfaction grew among the Soviet leaders over nationalistic obstacles to revolutionary change, Moscow took a more activist and interventionist role in the implementation process. Just as it had vitally contributed to the emergence of an early revolutionary situation making it possible for the Polish communists to seize political power, the Soviet Union now thrust itself into the position of principal instigator and coordinator of the socioeconomic revolutionary transformation.

Against this background, both the character of the Polish United Workers' Party and its role in directing the processes of internal change were given new meaning. The accent was put on identification with the Soviet party. The relationship between the two communist organizations paralleled that between the people's democracy in Poland and the full-fledged dictatorship of the proletariat in the USSR. Just as the former was held to be still at an early stage of socialist development and in need of Soviet support for its revolutionary maturation,[3] the PUWP required the assistance of the Soviet party in its ideological and organizational development. This was authoritatively asserted in the report to the Unity Congress:

> There can be no question of any particular or specific type of party of the people's democracy as against the party of the dictatorship of the proletariat, the CPSU. Quite to the contrary, with due regard for the specificity of our develop-

ment, *the model for a party of the new type is and will continue to be for us the Communist Party of the Soviet Union.*[4]

Under Soviet prodding, the PUWP adopted an explicitly revolutionary orientation. Its main objective became the rapid transition from capitalism to socialism. To achieve this goal, the party developed a comprehensive activist strategy in which intensified efforts to destroy existing social, cultural, and economic obstacles to change were coupled with a simultaneous attempt to create a new, integrative framework of lasting foundations for the socialist order.

On the substantive level, the primary emphasis was on the centrally directed transformation and development of state institutions. In part, this reflected the party concern with the maintenance and enhancement of its self-assumed leadership role in decision making and policy execution. To forestall challenges to its power, the party was determined to consolidate its control and subversion over the entire administrative machinery of the state. But this also was related to the way Communists perceived the problems of socialist change and the means to solve them. They defined socialism as the imposition of equality through intensifying class struggle. Its successful achievement depended on political organization and centrally controlled management. As party leader Boleslaw Bierut firmly proclaimed, "it is political power, the state, which constitutes the deciding factor in systemic transformations."[5] Within this context, all state institutions—including economic, social, and cultural—were conceived as instruments to change society. Socialist revolution thus became largely organization building.

The task of transforming the state administration was completed in two separate steps. In March 1950, a bill to restructure the regional state organs abolished local executive offices and established a unifying system of people's councils as the sole institutions of state power, combining both legislative and executive functions. This was followed by adoption of a new constitution in July 1952, providing final articulation of the whole administrative system of the state.

A crucial feature of these changes was their conformity to the Soviet institutional model. Provisions regulating the work of the people's councils closely resembled those of the Soviets and the new constitution followed the Stalinist charter of 1936 in formal arrangements and even detailed formulations. It defined the basis of political power as an alliance between the working class and the toiling peasantry with the former playing the leading role on the basis of "the revolutionary achievements of the Polish and international workers' movement and on the historical experiences of the victorious socialist construction in the USSR, the first state of workers and peasants." The main function of the state was to organize and conduct the unrelenting class struggle which was to lead to the establishment of a socialist society described in the principle "from each according to his ability, to each according to his work."[6]

Following the Soviet doctrine of "unification of powers,"[7] the constitution rejected traditional Western divisions of authority among the legislative, executive, and judiciary branches of government. The right to govern was to be derived only from the directly expressed people's will. The supreme power was nominally lodged in a parliamentary body, the Sejm, which was to act according to conventional forms of procedure and deliberation. However, its real authority was effectively circumvented by the establishment of a collegial head of state, the Council of State, with extensive legislative powers and the right to review and interpret the laws of the country. The office of the president of the republic was abolished and the Council of Ministers became an administrative body with limited political significance of its own. Similar restrictions were imposed on institutions representing social interests. They had a constitutional right to serve as channels for bringing the viewpoints of separate groups to bear on the making of policy providing, however, that these viewpoints would not interfere with the goals and the nature of the system.

A correlate of the political transformation of the state was an effort to set up new economic institutions to create an appropriate organizational setting for the development of socialism. Its motive force was the commitment to Marxist ideology, mandating the specific direction of economic change to provide the material basis of a socialist society with no private ownership of the means of production and hence no social exploitation. Such an approach made it imperative to impose a strict organization and discipline to implement policy. Yet it also had important political objectives of providing an operational basis for the authority and power of the party. As the process of economic change was shaped by planned production and distribution of goods, party agencies were the driving force behind organization, coordination, and integration of all economic activities.

The decisive steps toward the radical restructuring of Poland's economic system were taken in 1949, following an initial period of postwar reconstruction and gradualist reforms. They included the establishment of an hierarchical and strictly centralized network of planning institutions as well as the adoption of new socialist patterns of organization of production. As for the planning institutions, they were set up in all Polish provinces as parts of a separate branch of state administration, the State Commission for Economic Planning, under the chairmanship of Politburo member Hilary Minc. The commission was charged with establishing the minimum targets of production output as well as setting the limits on material and state inputs into the socialized economy. The new socialist organization of production was conceived of as an administratively organized procedure through which planning directives were issued periodically to economic ministries, industrial units, and individual plants. They were then mandated to respond by committing themselves to produce more than had been planned but with the same inputs as they had already been allocated.[8] This new system was subsequently defined as the "bolshevik approach" to planning, management, and production.[9] Its explicitly formulated goal was to create an economic environment essentially similar to the Soviet situation.

Its practical expression was the launching in 1950 of a "Six-Year Plan of Economic Development and Construction of Socialist Foundations" for the years 1950–1955. Prepared with the openly admitted assistance of Soviet advisors,[10] it aimed at rapid transformation of Poland's economy through extensive industrialization and socialization of agriculture. With respect to industrialization, priority was put on development of heavy industry. To achieve this goal a major investment effort was centered on that area, while other industrial sectors were relatively neglected. As for agriculture, the plan envisaged expansion of the socialist sector within which collective producers' cooperatives were to compromise about 20–25 percent of the total cultivated area by the end of 1955. It also called for the strengthening of state agricultural farms, which had served since 1949 as a centrally directed organization providing the "socialist base in agriculture."[11]

Given this dominant concern for socialist transformation, the objectives behind the policies of planned change, such as industrialization or collectivization, clearly went beyond the goal of economic expansion and development. They focused rather on a deliberate attempt to permanently redefine social structures, ways of thinking, and behavior of the population.

Perhaps the most obvious example of the party's determination to induce social change with little regard to the costs involved or economic rationality was the decision to build the huge Lenin steel works and the town of Nowa Huta near the old historic city of Krakow. While Nowa Huta was officially proclaimed a symbol of the new industrial era and a lasting monument to the socialist order, its location precluded from the outset any chance of its ever becoming economically viable. The costs of construction of a new industrial center in an area devoid of readily available manpower were extremely high. More serious, however, was the fact that Nowa Huta had been placed far from main transportation routes. Since steel production was dependent on a continuing flow of imported Soviet ore, the plant's effectiveness and economic value were permanently hampered. Discussing the factors which influenced the decision to build Nowa Huta, a Polish sociologist recently noted that the primary intention was to "create a large new and strong socialist urban working class society, which would in time influence the development of the social structure and social relations in an old and extraordinarily staid population as existed in Krakow."[12]

Another example of the PUWP's commitment to the goal of social renovation was its policy of infusing a "socialist content"[13] into all aspects of cultural life of the country. Political control extended into all educational institutions through the introduction of ideologically appropriate curricula, appointment of reliable educators and administrators, and the imposition of centrally determined admission standards.[14] Just as in the Soviet Union, after 1951 academic and scientific activities became coordinated by a central institution, the Polish Academy of Sciences, functioning under direct control and supervision of the party.[15]

Similar constraints were placed on other fields of creative endeavor. All forms of artistic and literary expression were purposefully channeled toward the party-defined tasks of political and civic edification. To prevent the possibility of even implied criticism of its policies, the party imposed strict controls over cultural organizations and artistic associations. The fate of the Polish Writers' Association, a traditional literary society with a long history of progressive activities, could well serve as an illustration of this process. At its congress in 1949, the association was transformed into a body controlling the writers and its activities became directed at "shackling critical thought, turning writers into thoughtless executors of the instructions coming from the central office for propaganda."[16]

Inherent in all these efforts at social renovation was the conviction that revolutionary change could only be achieved by drastic administrative means. Centrally controlled manipulation of institutional factors was regarded as the main element which would secure the success of making a socialist society in Poland. Insofar as this process of institutional development and change was instigated and coordinated by the party, it rapidly solidified its pivotal position as the leading and directing force in the country.

The supremacy of the party over other institutions was asserted on both ideological and organizational grounds. The ideological principles underlining its self-assumed authority were clearly stated in the preamble to the PUWP statute, which affirmed that "The Polish United Workers' Party is the advance, organized detachment of the Polish working class—the leading force of the Polish nation. The Polish United Workers' Party is the highest form of working class organization and the exponent of the interests of the urban and rural working people."[17] It followed, therefore, that if the party incorporated the will of the forward section of society, it had to be responsible for the ultimate guidance of its development.

With regard to its operational prerogatives, the party kept major decision-making functions to itself by maintaining a perpetual majority in the elective state institutions and providing directive personnel for state and public offices. No autonomous organization or public institution was able to challenge the authority of the party rule. The Catholic Church was a partial exception since it maintained its institutional and ideological separateness in spite of repeated attacks and constant pressures from the party.[18] The *raison d'être* of numerous recognized interest groups, such as trade unions, women's associations, youth organizations, etc., was little more than to provide a system of "transmission belts" for the party directives.[19]

This emphasis on party supremacy and control was related to the essentially revolutionary character of the socialist transformation. The problems involved in imposing an ideologically defined change, a process which inevitably entailed considerable sacrifice by the population, required firm ideological commitment and organizational discipline. Hence only the loyal Communists could be trusted to perform and coordinate many administrative and managerial tasks associated with making a new socialist society. To the extent, however, that the party monopolized both policy-making and managerial roles, it effectively undermined the very institutional basis to the creation of which it was so deeply committed.

Perhaps the most important consequence of this development was the decline in importance of state institutions. They were restricted to the role of formal appendages to the party, serving as a mere backdrop for political and economic activity. The construction of an impressive institutional façade resulted mainly in a massive expansion of bureaucracy: the number of state administrative officials increased from the prewar figure of 172,000 to 344,000 in 1949 and reached 362,400 in 1955.[20] In the absence of clearly defined autonomous responsibilities, the main duties of state administrative officials were to watch and control each other's performance in fulfilling the party-assigned tasks.

There is also little doubt that the revolutionary imperatives of leading the process of socialist transformation affected the party itself. Centrally imposed requirements of political loyalty and discipline brought massive changes in its composition, internal procedures, and operational practices. The historical experience of the Soviet party was again important here. It provided a major reference point for the Polish Communists in dealing with their own organizational problems, which either they or their Soviet referents identified as requiring action.

A crucial organizational consequence of this process was the transformation of PUWP from a mass organization to a *cadre* party. Whereas until 1949 there had been a tendency to accept as new members all those who declared their approval of party programs or policies, the subsequently adopted requirements for membership put a premium on activist involvement defined in terms of new developmental priorities. Such an adjustment entailed a massive reevaluation of the existing party membership as well as an adoption of drastic restrictions on future admissions into the party.

After the apogee of December 1948, the PUWP underwent a series of purges. Their greatest intensity centered on the period between 1949 and 1951; the net membership loss in these years amounted to nearly 350,000 members. In most cases, "ideological alienation" was the major cause of expulsion while penalties for disciplinary and moral offenses against the party rules were largely limited to warnings and occasional reprimands.[21] Not until 1952 did the PUWP resume membership expansion, and then only at a deliberately slow pace and under strict control by the central leadership. In explaining the membership policy as contributing to further "bolshevization of the party," a Central Committee member pointedly stressed that "when we talk about the need to develop new party cadres, we do not mean by that new people in general but rather such new people who would be capable to carry the party directives into effect, who would consider those directives as their own, and who would be willing to fight for their full implementation."[22]

Coinciding with this concern for ideological conformity and activist vigilance was a determined effort to preserve and strengthen the proletarian character of the party. This found its practical expression in two related by analytically distinct strategies. On the one hand, the PUWP membership policy emphasized the need for an intensified recruitment of workers and peasants while restricting the influx of white-collar elements into the organization. As formulated in November 1949, its goal was to secure that ". . .90 percent of new members should be recruited from among the workers and the poor peasants and ten percent from among the white-collar employees, and at that especially from among the technical intelligentsia, the teachers, and the creative intelligentsia."[23] In this way, the party would be able to maintain its ideologically defined position as the main political organization of the working class. In effect, this goal was never fulfilled; the proportion of workers and peasants was gradually declining after the high level of 1949—61.3 and 14.4 percent respectively—and that of white-collar members was constantly increasing (see Appendix 1).

On the other hand, membership in the party became a prerequisite for social mobility of workers and peasants into white-collar ranks. The practice of appointing the most committed party activists to directing posts in state institutions was begun immediately after the war. Since 1948, however, party membership and working class origin seemed to have replaced almost completely other criteria, such as education or practical experience, for personnel selection to responsible positions in administration and the economy. The avowed aim of this policy was to eradicate all "bourgeois elements" which could threaten the implementation of party decisions and to contribute to the long-range revolutionary purpose of creating a new socialist white-collar class which would owe its allegiance to the party and its leadership.[24] Its immediate practical consequence, however, was a dramatic decline in the quality of administrative and managerial performance which, in turn, made the fulfillment of the party's developmental objectives much more difficult if not entirely impossible.[25]

The adoption of the revolutionary course of action brought about a renewed emphasis on the political and organizational consolidation of the party. This process began with the purge of Wladyslaw Gomulka and his former associates Zenon Kliszko and Marian Spychalski from the PUWP. After being accused of lack of political vigilance as well as fostering a "rightist and nationalist deviation" within the communist organization,[26] they were expelled from the Central Committee in November 1949 and forbidden from holding party office, a move which was tantamount to exclusion from the organization itself. This development opened the way for a prolonged process of ideological and political verification which eventually reached into every segment of the PUWP. It became a systematically executed action aimed at a comprehensive elimination of all potential and real opponents of the revolutionary leadership from positions of influence in political life.[27]

Notwithstanding its massive scope, the distinguishing feature of the purge was its relatively mild character. There were no show trials and no executions such as had taken place in other communist-ruled countries of Eastern Europe. Gomulka himself was arrested only in July 1951 and kept in seclusion until late 1954. But even then, no case was brought against him despite explicit Soviet insistence that purge trials be held and severe methods be used. Several theories have been advanced as to why the purge victims in Poland were not treated as harshly as others in Eastern Europe. According to some accounts, there were personal considerations on the part of top PUWP leaders, such as the fear of anti-Semitic repercussions of widespread purges or simple honesty, which led them to resist Moscow demands for a trial and severe punishment of Gomulka and his associates. According to other speculations, the trials were simply being delayed, with Stalin's death intervening to save the Polish deviationists.[28] In any case, no definite answer can be given at this time due to existing restrictions on access to the party archives and documents.

But purging was only one of several consolidating tactics. In their call for renovation, the revolutionary party leaders wanted to create a loyal and disciplined political cadre that would be ideologically cohesive and effectively socialized in their obedience to commands. Their main effort was directed at expansion of the party professional apparatus, which would be free of external commitments and responsive to orders only from specific office holders within the party structure. In the words of Boleslaw Bierut to the Central Committee plenum in May 1950, "reinforcement and assurance of the numerical growth of the leading cadres must become the most urgent task of the party's Central Committee."[29]

At the beginning of 1950, the estimated size of the apparatus reached close to 6,000 full-time, paid party employees. However, its internal composition left much to be desired from both ideological and organizational points of view. Only a small minority, about 9 percent of the total, could be considered as fully reliable and experienced communist organizers. As the hard core of the party professional staff, they occupied the most important positions on the central and regional levels—political functionaries of the Central Committee, provincial secretaries, department heads and their deputies. Many were former members of the old Communist Party of Poland and more than half of them had worked for the party since 1945 or longer. They were assisted by a larger group, about 25 percent of the entire apparatus, of middle rank staff members who included instructors of the provincial party committees as well as town and district secretaries. Among them, some 21 percent had been involved with prewar communist organizations but more than 43 percent had less than two years' experience in party work. The majority of the remaining group, consisting of district functionaries and paid secretaries in large industrial enterprises, were completely new to the ideologically defined responsibilities of leading the socialist revolution.[30] For this reason they were exposed to intensive pressures from the top not only to fulfill the assigned objectives, but also to conform at all times to a centralist pattern of hierarchical subordination and unquestioned obedience.

After mid-1950, the expansion of recruitment to the middle and lower levels of the apparatus was conducted with great emphasis and determination. By the end of that year 3,000 new members were added to the staff and by 1954 its size increased to 14,100 political employees.[31] They were mostly recruited from among the constantly growing ranks of elected or volunteer activists—the numerical strength of this group increased from about 200,000 in 1949 to more than 300,000 in mid-1952[32]—as well as from the party-controlled Union of Polish Youth, which, after its formation in 1948, became the main base of doctrinal training for future party operatives. To insure their ideological preparedness, a network of party schools expanded throughout the country and all candidates for positions in the apparatus were required to complete a program of political indoctrination.

Despite these efforts at internal consolidation, the problems of organizational incoherence continued to plague the lower levels of the apparatus. As reported at the second congress of the party in 1954, between 25 and 30 percent of the provisional and district political employees had to be removed annually for failing to meet centrally imposed standards of revolutionary behavior.[33] To a certain degree, this resulted from the leadership's determination to prevent any possible deviations from the centrally defined course of action; all lower rank officials who showed signs of independent thinking or initiative were purged indiscriminately. On the general level, however, the high rate of turnover clearly suggested that the efforts to create an effective, revolutionary nucleus within the party were not successful. In fact, there were few political cadres capable and willing to direct the process of decisive socialist transformation in Poland.

In light of these persistent organizational strains, the rigid centralization of decision making within the party became the main factor of internal cohesion. Just as party supremacy over other public institutions was considered vital for imposing revolutionary change on society, the problems involved in coordinating party work required concentration of command within the organization at the elite level. From this perspective, unquestioned compliance with orders coming from above became the primary qualification for party membership and office.

Against this background, problems pertaining to the internal structure and recruitment to the party elite became crucial for both the party and the revolutionary order itself. Here again, the identification with the Soviet experience and the need for Soviet support became the essential elements in the process of elite formation. With regard to the structural characteristics, the PUWP adopted the Stalinist operational formula which gave dictatorial powers within the party to a single leader. This did not, however, bring any changes in the party rules or formal patterns of its organization. Rather, its acceptance reflected the conviction, reinforced by direct Soviet intrusion, that the essence of a revolutionary leadership lay in its identification with Soviet practices and patterns. As Wladyslaw Gomulka was to comment on the political importance of this development in his speech in October 1956,

> this system consisted in the fact that an individual, hierarchical ladder of cults was created. Each such cult comprised a given area in which it functioned. In the bloc of socialist states, it was Stalin who stood at the top of this hierarchical ladder of cults. All those who stood on the lower rungs of the ladder bowed their heads before him. Those who bowed their heads were not only the other leaders of the Communist Party of the Soviet Union, but all the leaders of communist and workers' parties of the countries of the socialist camp. The latter, that is, the first secretaries of the Central Committees of the parties of the various countries who sat on the second rung of the ladder of the cult of personality, in turn donned the robes of infallibility and wisdom. But their cult radiated only on the territory of the countries where they stood at the top of the national cult ladder. This cult could be called only a reflected brilliance, a borrowed light. It shone as the moon does. And yet, in the area of its influence it was omnipotent.[34]

Still, structural imitation of the Soviet operational model was not the only critical factor in shaping the character of the PUWP leadership. Equally important were the conditions that determined recruitment to the party elite. The criteria for selection to important party positions seem to have been defined primarily in terms of personal loyalty toward and interaction with the Soviet party as well as explicit approval by Joseph Stalin. This dependent mode of ascending to power critically undermined the PUWP elite's capacity to develop its own organizational rules and specific national policies. Even the top party leaders remained highly circumscribed in terms of their ability to focus on or act within their national sociopolitical environment. Their authority within the party and the country at large was based on and reflected the power, policy preferences, and personality of the CPSU leader—Joseph Stalin.

This distinctive quality of PUWP leaders was derived from their past involvement in Soviet and Comintern activities. By mid-1950, after the purge of Spychalski in November 1949 and Swiatkowski in May 1950, only four out of fifteen members of the Politburo and the Secretariat did not spend the war in the Soviet Union and had not been active in the organization of the Soviet-based communist groups. They included two former socialist activists, Jozef Cyrankiewicz and Adam Rapacki, who had proved their loyalty by destroying their own party, as well as two long-time collaborators of Boleslaw Bierut, Franciszek Jozwiak and Hilary Chelchowski, whose contribution to the anti-Gomulka campaign earned them a place in the party's highest councils. Confirming the growing reliance on Soviet experience among the party leaders, the places of Spychalski and Swiatkowski on the Politburo were filled in May 1950 by General Konstantin Rokossovskiî, a career Red Army officer who had commanded Soviet troops in the Warsaw campaign of 1944 and in November 1949 became Poland's minister of defense, and Zenon Nowak, a surviving member of the Central Committee of the defunct prewar Communist Party of Poland and long-time resident of Moscow.

The most prominent leader of the PUWP was Boleslaw Bierut, who had acted since 1943 as a trustee of Moscow in Poland and remained, to use Khrushchev's apt expression, "Stalin's number one confidant" in the party.[35] Until the second congress of the PUWP in March 1954, Bierut had been chairman of the Central Committee and then became its first secretary. In addition to his party post, Bierut also had been Poland's president until 1952 when, following the adoption of the new constitution which abolished the presidency, he took the job of prime minister while maintaining an ex officio membership in the Council of State. Thus, in combining the top functions of the head of the party, the government, and the state, Bierut achieved a semi-dictatorial position in the political system as a whole.

His closest collaborators in the Politburo were Jakub Berman and Hilary Minc. Both had been low-level activists in the old KPP and during the war worked in the Polish section of the Comintern. After the communist seizure of power Berman became responsible for both ideological direction of the party work and maintenance of political security, while Minc was entrusted with supervision of the revolutionary transformation of Poland's economy. Along with Bierut they formed a powerful overseer group with firm control of the entire party structure and activities.

The stamp of Soviet influence was equally obvious among the second echelon of the PUWP leaders. Among the Central Committee secretaries, in charge of directing the day-by-day functioning of the organization, only Cyrankiewicz could not claim the benefits of a direct experience of Moscow's training. However, his functions centered primarily on work in the state administration, where he occupied the position of prime minister until November 1952 and then was relegated to that of deputy premier. The remaining group, which included Roman Zambrowski and Aleksander Zawadzki and, since May 1950, Franciszek Mazur, Zenon Nowak, and Edward Ochab as well, had an extensive Moscow background—frequently with experience in Soviet police networks—hence was well equipped to shape the work of the Central Committee political apparatus.

The implicit requirement of a direct personal linkage between the PUWP officialdom and the Soviet political apparatus extended beyond the level of the top party leadership. Soviet advisors and experts were assigned to all sections of the party political administration in order to guide their activities and assist in formulation of specific programs. In addition, PUWP activists and officers were periodically sent to Moscow for training in the Soviet party schools and institutions. The major condition for recruitment to and tenure of important party offices became a demonstrable capacity to adapt to the Stalinist organizational and operational paradigm.[36]

Such an emphasis on internal sovietization of the PUWP was related to the persistent doubt among the Soviet leadership itself as to the ability and effectiveness of Poland's Communists to complete the program of revolutionary change. Yet its objective was not only to secure instrumental control over policy-making processes within the PUWP; it was also indicative of the ongoing Soviet effort to shape the character of the PUWP's leadership, and through it that of the whole organization, into a permanently Stalinist orientation. In practice, however, it made the goal of organizational cohesion more difficult to achieve and severely restricted the party's ability to perform a managerial and political role.

Perhaps the most obvious consequence of this drive toward Stalinist centralization was the decline in importance of elective party organs, including the party's Central Committee. Although it has never been considered as the policy-setting body, since 1948 its tasks were reduced to providing a formal *placet* to the lines of policy already formulated by members of the leading triumvirate of Bierut, Berman, and Minc. Thus it became a semihonorific party institution whose members enjoyed considerable social and economic benefits but had little effective authority or power. As one of the most active members of the Central Committee was to complain later, "plenary meetings of the Central Committee were called too infrequently [there were only nine plenums during the years 1949–1954] and the members of the Central Committee were rarely involved in the preparation of key materials as well as policy projects for the plenums, and in the periods between the plenums [they had no influence] in the important policy projects of the Politburo."[37] Similar restrictions affected the work of local party committees and regional organs.

The same situation existed in the relations between the central party apparatus and its local branches. To the degree that operational directives were uniformly imposed from the top, provincial and district staff members paid little attention to the needs or specificities of their regions while concentrating their efforts on obedient administration of centrally assigned tasks. The dominant pattern of party work at the lower levels was to transmit whatever orders they received from above and to watch over their implementation. Its inevitable result, however, was widespread bureaucratization, pervasive inertia, and an almost total alienation from society at large.[38]

A concomitant development was the increase in importance of political security organs, centrally controlled by the Ministry of Public Security. Although formally a part of the state institutional network, the ministry was in practice removed from governmental control and supervision. It acted rather as a special, paramilitary branch of the party organization, functionally separate from its regular units but fully subordinate to the top leadership. The ministry was headed by Politburo member Stanislaw Radkiewicz and the general lines of its activity were set by a select committee of the Politburo which was chaired by Bierut himself and included merely two other PUWP leaders, Jakub Berman and Hilary Minc. Both its internal organization and operational style were strongly influenced by direct Soviet guidance. The ministry's ranks were thoroughly penetrated by Soviet advisors and agents who controlled the key decision-making positions throughout the institutional structure.[39]

After having played the key role in assuring the initial political breakthrough, the Ministry of Public Security now emerged as the main instrument in enforcing compliant fulfillment of the leadership's socioeconomic policies. This expansion of its operational focus carried important political and organizational implications. Politically, it further solidified the commanding capabilities of the top PUWP leaders while also effectively reinforcing Soviet control over the process of revolutionary socioeconomic transformation in the country. Organizationally, the security sector of the party replaced its regular units as the primary factor in shaping the flow of centrally induced social and economic activities. In this way, the enhancement of the role of security forces in controlling revolutionary change, a process generated by the growing insistence on intensified class struggle, largely determined methods of social transformation and ways of consolidating power. It rapidly became a pervasive element in emergent social relations and a distinguishing feature in the centrally directed attempt to create a new socioeconomic system.

The importance of this development could be demonstrated by reference to a more general question of revolutionary tactics. In a recent work Feliks Gross points out that the crucial ingredients of a successful revolution have always been enthusiasm and fear: ". . .it is enthusiasm which so often moves the party and the masses to action; it is fear which moves the very same masses to obedience and submission to the party and its elites."[40] An obvious implication of this reminder is that the main concern for a revolutionary elite should be to develop a pattern of action which would combine those two elements. A degree of popular support would be necessary for the party of radical and rapid change in order to achieve the fulfillment of its goals. Manipulation of fear alone, however forceful and efficient, could only temporarily affect or modify social behavior, but lasting change requires policies more complex than those based on fear itself.

There is little doubt that the PUWP leadership perceived from the very beginning that popular involvement in the implementation of its policies would be of crucial importance for the success of the socialist revolution and the creation of a new socialist order. As Hilary Minc stressed in explaining the nature of planned economic change, "to plan means first of all to mobilize the masses whose creative energy and enthusiasm are the most important factors in the realization of the plans."[41] The drive toward expanding the mass involvement in socialist construction, though elite-induced and institutionally regulated, at first produced some degree of favorable response in several segments of Polish society. Among them were some disaffected intellectuals who were attracted to the party-created vision of future social justice and egalitarian freedom, numerous workers for whom the party opened avenues of upward mobility, and impoverished peasants who flocked to new industrial sites in search of jobs and new social status. To some, long-established political and social obstacles to necessary social change appeared of such a nature that they considered revolution as the only means to open the roads.[42] To many, the initial image of the party and its leadership became the embodiment of a heroic struggle for a better and more rational world.[43] It produced something akin to what Alex Inkeles termed the "totalitarian mystique,"[44] an acceptance of the ultimate inevitability of revolutionary success that effectively overshadows commitments to other principles and values.

But the practice of the communist revolution rapidly destroyed those early sources of popular support. It became clear that involvement in the process of change would never lead to effecting the practical outcomes. Increasingly, the revolution came to mean the centrally directed disintegration of society, institutions, and values; it became a kind of void that to many spoke only in terms of violence and fear. In this situation pressure and coercion, rather than reliance on popular support, became the order of the day.

To the degree that the goal, policy, and process of revolution became associated in the public mind with coercive and manipulative methods of implementation, the eventual failure of the socioeconomic program of change became inevitable. The high incidence of violence and pressure in the leadership's effort to impose change brought only massive revulsion from the population at large. The party's relationship with society was based on sheer power but not political authority. In the long run, this was bound to have a profoundly negative effect on the PUWP's efforts at political and social legitimation.

CHAPTER 5

Test of Retreat

Writing in the early 1960s, Richard Hiscocks pointed to a series of Soviet developments following the death of Stalin in March 1953 as the main factors of change in the nature and direction of Poland's experiment in socioeconomic revolution. They included the denunciation by the Presidium of the CPSU's Central Committee of one-man rule and adoption of the principle of collective leadership in the party, the elimination of the security service chief Lavrenti Beria and curbing of the police powers through a new emphasis on socialist legality in all party and state activities, reconciliation with Tito's Yugoslavia in 1955, and the violent attack on Stalin and his policies at the CPSU's twentieth congress in February 1956.[1] The first two heralded a new course in Soviet domestic policy which emphasized less coercive methods of rule but within a basically unaltered Stalinist political framework. The remaining two signaled a repudiation of the Stalinist system in its entirety and marked the beginning of political as well as ideological de-Stalinization.

The point that Soviet internal developments served as major stimuli for change in Poland's political and socioeconomic system as obviously well taken. It was congruent with the nature of Soviet-Polish relations which, having been based since the Second World War on Moscow's monopoly over ideology and power, engendered among the PUWP leaders a pattern of emulative behavior with regard to Soviet institutional and policy priorities. Furthermore, the new Moscow initiatives clearly were not designed for Soviet domestic purposes only, but constituted authoritative redefinitions of communist ideology and practice to be incorporated into policy programs of other parties as well. Thus, just as Soviet influence had provided the impetus for the PUWP's revolutionary stance, it became the driving force behind the movement for reevaluation of the party's organization and activities.

In addition, once the Soviet example had been provided, many internal Polish reforms were precipitated by unanticipated domestic crises. The PUWP leaders responded to these on an ad hoc emergency basis. As the initial measures of political relaxation offered to the public a glimpse at the record of past communist practices, they also opened up the possibility of far-reaching criticism of existing conditions. The growing restlessness, both within the party and in society at large, rapidly crystallized around current events and issues as convenient rallying points. In this way, the Soviet-induced process of change triggered a powerful popular movement which developed a momentum of its own, eventually threatening the stability of the established hierarchy of power and with it the political role of the party itself.

Whether through conviction, fear, or plain lack of vision, the top PUWP leaders were unusually slow to realize the full impact of the Soviet developments on the party and society in Poland. Although the CPSU's decision on collective leadership was duly noted by the party,[2] there was no real change in the PUWP organizational style. Bierut remained firmly in control and the requirement of collective direction seemed to have been applied more to middle and lower ranks of the party hierarchy than to its top leaders. As the official statement put it rather ambiguously, "the principle of collective leadership—the main condition of intraparty democracy—should be consequently adhered to by all party organs, and each deviation from it must be severely punished."[3] It left the unanswered question as to who was to punish the judges.

Similar restraint characterized the initial steps toward economic reorientation. At the Central Committee plenum in late October 1953, Bierut announced an impending shift in investment priorities away from heavy industry to consumer goods, agriculture, and housing. He also called for a more diversified approach to peasants in which a certain degree of support would be offered to poor farmers while the main pressure would concentrate on more affluent *kulaks*. To the degree that the plenum decisions corresponded with the unveiling of Malenkov's new course in the Soviet Union, they marked the inauguration of economic change in Poland. Nonetheless, their scope was distinctly insignificant. There was continuing stress on the need for collectivization, even if the purely economic value of this policy was implicitly discarded.[4] Limited economic concessions centered on tax relief and a small decrease in prices accompanied by promises of a future increase in the standard of living.

Perhaps the most important change was the redefinition of the role of security organs within the party. Before the death of Stalin and elimination of Beria, their functions had included control over the work of party officials at all levels; subsequently they became fully subordinated to the regular party apparatus. By December 1953, an entire network of special party units was established with specific tasks of directing and supervising all activities of the security organs. The network was built from the top down. At the central level, a new section of the party apparatus, headed by Politburo member Franciszek Mazur, was put in charge of the work of the Ministry of Public Security, including personnel decisions, political training, and operational scrutiny. This section set up its local branches to which were assigned comparable functions at the local level. Security operations had to be approved beforehand by party officials and the ministry was required to report periodically on all aspects of its work. In short, the security sector of the party was turned into a tool of its regular organization.[5]

Yet these organizational changes brought about little, if any, relief from coercive pressures. In effect, organized violence seemed to have mounted since the death of Stalin. Thus, in May 1953 several former army officers were executed and in September, following a show trial of Bishop Czeslaw Kaczmarek on charges of spying for the United States, the government arrested and put in seclusion the Primate of Poland, Stefan Cardinal Wyszynski. At the end of the year, nine bishops and several hundred priests were locked up in prisons.

In light of these developments, it is safe to conclude that political change was not accorded a prominent place in the party's strategies after the death of Stalin. Rather, the preservation of continuity emerged as its main priority. In part, this might have resulted from the leadership's awareness that "a point of no return had been reached and that a sharp reversal would be dangerous."[6] Consequently, the top party leaders might have deliberately stalled on internal reforms while searching for political alternatives. Furthermore, their inherent uncertainty as to what direction the Soviet party would take could have provided an additional incentive to stand fast and resist any potential challenge to their power. Equally important, however, seems to have been their attachment to establish communist assumptions and practices. Once the pattern of coercive rule had been internalized by individual leaders and institutionalized in the political system, there was a natural tendency to continue. Both the sequence and consistency of party activities during the initial post-Stalinist period seemed to confirm that point.

This tendency to resist change and preserve systemic continuity was fully manifested during the second PUWP congress which met in Warsaw during March 10–17, 1954. The focus of the gathering, which was attended by the CPSU first secretary Nikita Khrushchev and numerous other foreign delegates, was on evaluation of the party's revolutionary experience and definition of its future tasks. With regard to past accomplishments, Bierut set the tone with his report, stressing that the "socialist character of our political and economic achievements is already obvious to everyone" and proclaiming that "the greatest gain, the main instrument of the Polish people's revolution is our state—the state of people's democracy." As far as the future was concerned, Bierut continued to insist that since "the socioeconomic foundation and goal of our people's revolution is the peaceful construction of a socialist economy. . .[the only] means to accomplish this goal are constantly growing industrialization of the country, increase in agricultural production, and gradual socialization of the countryside." In this context, while pointing out that

Poland "already became a strong industrial country," Bierut promised that "in the next two years, special attention will be given to a more regular expansion of producers' cooperatives [collective farms]. . .[and] to the inclusion of more villagers into the newly created cooperatives as well as to the englargement in the membership of the old ones."[7]

A more pessimistic evaluation was made by Hilary Minc. In his report on the state of Poland's economy, Minc complained that both industrial output and consumer goods production were still inadequate, and openly admitted that "an analysis of the present situation shows that fulfillment of the Six-Year Plan will not be an easy task; its very goals are threatened and this threat should be removed as far as possible." Just as if to prepare his listeners for the prospect of an impending failure, Minc pointedly stressed that "the plan is not a dogma and should not be treated as such."[8]

The internal organizational changes were held to a bare minimum. Following the Soviet example, the principle of collective leadership was introduced in an amendment to the party rules. The position of party chairman, until then occupied by Bierut, was abolished.[9] But there was little change in the composition of the newly elected highest organs of the party. The Central Committee was expanded from 75 to 77 full members, of whom 22 were newcomers. The number of deputy members of the Central Committee decreased from 61 to 50. Almost no change took place in the membership of the Politburo, which consisted of Boleslaw Bierut, Jakub Berman, Jozef Cyrankiewicz, Wladyslaw Dworakowski, Franciszek Jozwiak, Franciszek Mazur, Hilary Minc, Zenon Nowak, Edward Ochab, Stanislaw Radkiewicz, Konstantin Rokossovskii, Roman Zambrowski, and Aleksander Zawadzki. There were also two deputy members of the Politburo, Hilary Chelchowski and Adam Rapacki. The leading position within the party again went to Boleslaw Bierut, who became first secretary of the PUWP's Central Committee. Other members of the Secretariat included Wladyslaw Dworakowski, Franciszek Mazur, and Edward Ochab. Finally, Franciszek Jozwiak retained chairmanship of the Central Commission of the Party Control, an agency responsible for cleansing the party ranks of the threat of political, ideological, and moral deviations.

In accord with the Soviet practice of precluding the accumulation of leading posts in the party and the government, Bierut relinquished the office of prime minister. It was given once again to Jozef Cyrankiewicz, while positions of first deputy prime ministers were taken by Hilary Minc and Zenon Nowak. In short, the levers of control within both the party and the state institutional network remained firmly in the hands of the same group of experienced Stalinists who had been responsible for the initial adoption of the revolutionary strategy and now seemed determined to carry it through. The party itself, having gone through the process of extensive purges and verification, seemed to be "more cohesive and unified than ever before"[10] and was viewed by its leaders as fully equipped to act on effective implementation of their goals.

As if to confirm this view, the congress called for further expansion of the "directing and organizing role of the party. In the face of new objectives, the most important point is to continually strengthen the link between the party and the working masses of town and country, to lead their creative efforts, to raise their consciousness, to stimulate their initiative and reinforce their activism."[11] Among the practical measures to achieve these goals, the congress decided to reform the system of rural administration to institutionalize closer party control over local state organs. As explained by Bierut, the reform, which abolished some 3,000 large parish (*gmina*) people's councils and created in their place more than 10,000 smaller commune (*gromada*) units, was to "bring about closer ties between the communes and the district organs of the party, the government, and social organizations, which had been separated from the peasant masses by parishes. This would contribute to the strengthening of the worker-peasant alliance and would solidify the leading role of the working class in that alliance."[12]

Notwithstanding this insistence on continuity in the pursuit of a centrally directed program of revolutionary change, the first signs of organizational erosion and ambivalence toward leadership policies appeared within the party soon after the congress. They resulted in part from a continuing confusion among PUWP's officials and activists as to which direction Soviet internal development would take. The difficulty intensified when it became clear that, despite persistent uncertainties regarding Soviet positions on many ideological and political issues, the main thrust of Moscow's new orientation permanently deviated from the old Stalinist line. This had profound implications for the Polish party, leading to an emerging political ferment within its ranks.[13] The net effect of this development was the loss of prestige and intraparty authority by the top leadership.

The growing gap between the party's elite and its rank and file was drastically enlarged following disclosures about the leadership's life style and political practices made by a former high official in the Ministry of Public Security, Jozef Swiatlo, who had defected to the West in December 1953. In a series of radio broadcasts to Poland in 1954, Swiatlo gave detailed descriptions of the party elite's luxurious living standards in the poverty-ridden country and revealed the almost total corruption of its most illustrious representatives. More important, Swiatlo fully described the role and activity of the security organs in furthering the program of revolutionary change, their domination of regular party organizations, their barbaric methods of operation, and the degree of their infiltration by Soviet police. He then put the total blame for this state of affairs on the shoulders of the top PUWP leaders, particularly

Bierut and Berman, accusing them of consciously persecuting their political opponents within the party and of serving as *sui generis* Soviet agents in Poland.[14]

Swiatlo's revelations not only created widespread consternation within the party at large but also sparked many of its activists to action. This was plainly manifested at the Politburo meeting with the central-level party activists in early December 1954.[15] During the two-day session, the top leadership was exposed to an unprecedented attack from its own staff directed at the centralistic style of rule within the party, the frequent mistakes in policy making, and the exclusion of elected party officials from participation in decisions. Although the full content of the discussions was never revealed, the meeting seems to have marked a turning point in party policies. As was later admitted by then Politburo member Edward Ochab, "the leadership found itself then in factual isolation" and was forced to accept immediate revisions both in the style and the program of its activities.[16]

The immediate consequence of this development was the dissolution of the Ministry of Public Security on December 7, 1954. Its functions were divided between the Ministry of Internal Affairs and a newly created Committee for Public Security accountable to the Council of Ministers. The former chief of the security system, Stanislaw Radkiewicz, was shifted to the Ministry of State Farms. The chairmanship of the committee went to Politburo member Wladyslaw Dworakowski. In this way, the security organs became, at least formally, separated from the party organization; from then on they have continued as part of the state administration.

The matter did not stop here. At the Central Committee plenum in January 1955, past activities of the security organs were thoroughly denounced and violently condemned. In a subsequently published report from the plenum, a newly elected Central Committee secretary, Jerzy Morawski, noted that "with bitterness, with burning pain and shame we learned about facts of brutal violation of the principles of people's legality by some organs of security service. . .there were cases of arrest of innocent people and of keeping them illegally in prison, [there were also] cases when, instead of trying to find the truth, evidence had been changed to suit accusations prepared beforehand. There were also cases of shameful, inadmissible methods of investigation." The report then went on to stress the pervasive control by security agencies over political, social, and economic institutions in the country as well as to attack their "unacceptable interference" in the work of party and state organs. However, there was no attempt to investigate or discuss the political and organizational foundations of the security system. Instead, the whole blame was put on the narrowly defined security officialdom, who were accused of "breaking away from the party and the working masses, of trying to separate from the party and avoid control of its organs, of hiding their activity, and of lying to the party."[17] Thus, by official fiat of the Central Committee, the security system, until then a part and parcel of the party itself, was not only put outside of the organizational structure but also condemned for institutional and political insubordination.

Consequent to this action, several high officials from the security section who had dealt with internal party matters were expelled from the PUWP at the beginning of 1955; subsequently some of these were arrested and tried for abuse of their official responsibilities. At the same time, Wladyslaw Gomulka was secretly released from detention; the process of change within the party was on its way.

To the degree that this development signaled a general weakening of the coercive pattern of rule, it prompted a revival of public interest and more active involvement in politics. This process, marked by an almost incessant chain of literary and press discussions and re-examinations, created an ideological background for the rapidly expanding political ferment. It led to a proliferation of ideas on ways to promote social and economic change, to increase popular participation in public affairs and, finally, to enlarge personal and cultural freedom of expression.

Symptomatic of this new mood of activism was the launching of a movement of discussion clubs for intellectuals and students. The first such group, the Club of the Crooked Circle, was created during the spring of 1955 in Warsaw and rapidly developed into a popular forum for political debate.[18] During subsequent months, the network of discussion clubs quickly expanded and by the end of 1956 reached the astounding number of more than 200.[19] They became a breeding ground for innovative ideas and projects which were gradually spreading among the population at large.

The main proponents of these trends were communist intellectuals and students, most of whom had initially supported the principles behind the party revolutionary strategy but had become disillusioned with its implementation. For them, the unfolding revelations of corrupt and coercive party practices were a rude awakening to reality and forced a radical rethinking of fundamental assumptions and dreams. The most dramatic manifestation of the creeping malaise which gripped the party intellectuals was the publication of the "Poem for Adults" by a well-known communist writer, Adam Wazyk. In his work, Wazyk not only decried the failure of the party's leadership to bring Poland's society closer to the communist ideals, but also bitterly attacked the very foundations of the system in place, pointing to its ideological hypocrisy and political arbitrariness.[20] To the extent that it represented the emotions and feelings of a devoted party activist, the poem became a symbolic expression of the growing conflict between the PUWP's elite and a crucial segment of its membership over the interpretation of the basic principles of communist political rule.

Similar patterns of unrest developed within the communist Union of Polish Youth. Since its creation in 1948, the union had served as a training ground for PUWP professional and activist cadres. This organizational link shaped in great measure the nature of its activities. Its main role had been "to represent the state toward the youth. . .[which, however,] led to the bureaucratization of the union's organs and agencies as well as to the gradual change of the organization into the office for youth affairs."[21] With the growth of political ferment within the party, the attitudes of many youth activists began to change. While not all of them were ready to break with the established operational style—union leadership was still in the hands of authoritarian Bierutists—numerous others became determined to influence party policy making toward reforms and liberalization. The most critical group centered around the union's weekly *Po prostu* which, during the years 1955–1956, developed from an ideologically orthodox youth publication into an outspoken voice for political, social, and cultural renovation.[22]

Insofar as the political ferment was rooted in the activities of selected groups of communist activists, due to party restrictions on other social organizations and its monopoly over means of communication, it remained dependent upon reactions and decisions of the party leadership. But the mood of frustration and discontent, produced by long-existing strains in public life, was already spreading over the country. The dissatisfaction welled up from many sources and the general demand for something new was increasing in strength. In this situation, the intraparty unrest appears to have served as a catalyst for intensifying tensions within the population. Anything that could rally together those two currents of dissent was bound to trigger the momentum needed for comprehensive political change.

The twentieth congress of the CPSU in February 1956 greatly heightened the conflict within the Polish United Workers' Party. Khrushchev's condemnation of Stalin and the system which had taken his name finally led to a complete delegitimization of those PUWP leaders who, like Bierut or Berman or Minc, had been closely identified with the late dictator. More important, implicit in the new Soviet policy of de-Stalinization was the notion that the revolutionary model of change, which had been imposed by Stalin on other communist-ruled societies, was wrong and that the future strategies of socialist construction could take other than revolutionary forms. The immediate relevance of this view for the PUWP was in making old Gomulka's concepts of a more gradualistic and specifically Polish way toward socialist transition once again ideologically acceptable. On a more general plane, however, it signified that the focus of communist politics itself was undergoing drastic change. Revolutionary attempts at large-scale socioeconomic transformations were rapidly losing their viability. The main issues appeared to revolve more and more around the politics of consolidation. Within this context, the success of socialist development would be determined by a process of evolutionary improvement and adaptation rather than a dictum from above.

Given this new accent on strategic transformation, the dominant concern among the PUWP leaders was with finding ways to adjust to the situation. The inevitable pains of a political transition were somewhat relieved by the death of Boleslaw Bierut on March 12, 1956, while he was in Moscow to attend the CPSU congress. Bierut had typified the coercive and dictatorial element of communist rule, and his death removed the most important symbolic obstacle to the introduction of a new party strategy of gradual liberalization. On March 20, the Central Committee plenum elected Edward Ochab as its new first secretary. Two additional secretaries, Jerzy Albrecht and Edward Gierek, were also elected at the same time.

The choice of Ochab was reportedly made under the personal prodding of Nikita Khrushchev, who attended the plenum and vetoed the more popular candidacy of Roman Zambrowski on the ground that his Jewish origin could impede party efforts to maintain control over the population.[23] In addition, since Ochab had been one of the most outspoken critics of Gomulka in 1949, his elevation to the top indicated continuing Soviet opposition to the nationally oriented brand of socialism represented by the former leader of the Polish Workers' Party. As if to confirm this point, Gomulka's concept of the "Polish road to socialism" was strongly attacked in the official party press for its "false class content. . .: holding up the process of revolutionary transformations, freezing the alignment of class forces in the countryside, holding up the process of basic transformations not only in the economy, but also in culture, science, and education. In essence, [Gomulkaism] was not a form of specific application of the Soviet experience, but its negation and, objectively, it represented a rejection of the road to socialism."[24] Similar views were voiced by Ochab when he spoke to the party activists on April 6, although he then conceded that the charge of subversion brought against Gomulka had been wrong and his arrest unjustified.[25]

At the same time, the party moved swiftly to eliminate some of the most drastic aspects of past political practices. Several former high communist officials, including such Gomulka collaborators as Zenon Kliszko, Ignacy Loga-Sowinski, and Marian Spychalski, were released from prisons and readmitted to the party. On April 20 a massive amnesty was declared, freeing some 30,000 people. On the same day, Stanislaw Radkiewicz, the former head of the defunct Ministry of Public Security, was removed from the Ministry of State Farms and the Politburo. Finally, on May 6, Jakub Berman was forced to resign from his post in the Politburo and the government. Simultaneously, the party press reported a widespread purge of the lower ranks of the security organs, with new limitations to be placed on their future role. The entire coercive machinery of the party and government was undergoing a process of rapid disintegration.

Although the main targets of official criticism were Stalinism and the "cult of the individual,"[26] the general demand for change spread to the rest of the society. The most important manifestation of the growing social unrest was a worker revolt in the city of Poznan during the last days of June 1956. It arose from workers announcing specific economic grievances against local management decisions at a large machinery plant, but grew to a series of mass demonstrations after the protesting workers were attacked by police units. Following two days of unrestrained violence, the revolt was finally suppressed with considerable military force.[27] Although the workers' grievances were not immediately satisfied, the brutality of the repressive reaction provided the catalyst for a larger movement toward social reforms and political change.

In many respects the Poznan revolt became the turning point in the process of political change in Poland. It signified that old patterns of party control over society were breaking down and the intensity of popular discontent was rapidly approaching proportions which the leadership would not be able to manage. It also revealed that the capacity and willingness of the party itself, particularly at its lower levels, to cope with social unrest under difficult conditions were most problematical. As a Central Committee staffer later admitted, "at Poznan, within two or three hours, this 'powerful' organization was swept away from behind its desks and played no role whatsoever in those tragic events."[28] It was this specter of mounting social dissent and organizational disarray that ultimately spurred political action to a decisive shift away from the old revolutionary course. However, the change was not to renounce the dominance of the party over society but rather to give it a new meaning so that the party could continue its self-asserted leadership role under different conditions and with a new orientation.

The first steps in this direction were taken at the Central Committee plenum of July 18–28, 1956. The tone for the deliberations was set by Edward Ochab who, in a keynote address, pointed out that the Poznan revolt had provided "a warning signal of a serious deterioration in the relationship between the party and the working class" and frankly admitted that at the roots of these difficulties was "the functioning of the party itself as well as the frequently faulty understanding of its leading role." He then called for a "decisive reorientation in the conceptualization and in the practical implementation of the leading role of the party."[29] This point was further expounded in the final resolution of the plenum, which stressed that "the party ought to concentrate its efforts on strengthening ties with the masses, on rapid improvement of the standard of living, and on greater democratization of life in the party and the country. . .The party ought to devote its full energies to the task of changing the methods and the style of its work. . .in order to secure the fulfillment of this program."[30]

Despite this seemingly general agreement on the need for change, there was still no indication that a comprehensive program of political reforms would be adopted. Instead, the main thrust of the debates, which were never published but subsequently partially leaked out, appears to have centered on criticism of past practices and mutual recriminations of blame for their implementation rather than on formulation of new approaches to the problems at hand. This was due in great measure to internal divisions within the party leadership on the nature, scope, and direction of change. Commenting later on this situation, Gomulka explained that

> political differences in the leadership of the party, that is in the Politburo. . . and in the Central Committee, could be reduced to two basic problems: first, the conception of Poland's sovereignty; and, second, the conception of what should be included in what we call the democratization of our life within the framework of the socialist system. Some members of the Central Committee feared that settling our party and state relations with the CPSU and the Soviet Union [on a more equitable basis]. . .would bring unfavorable consequences. While not questioning the need for carrying out certain changes, they were, however, in favor of preserving the previous state of affairs. This was the main line of division in the leadership of the party. Differences in the understanding of the context of the democratization of our life were not clear. All the same, they existed in the leadership of our party. Irrespective of these basic political differences, there were other problems causing discord in the party leadership. Among these was the problem of appointments to leading party and state posts and the question of approaching this problem from the national point of view. Some comrades approached this problem in a very simplified way which could be taken for anti-Semitism. In addition to that. . .many comrades, irrespective of what views they held on problems discussed earlier, differed among themselves on the question of my return to active party life. It was, in this case, a problem not only of my person but of the right evaluation of all phenomena which in the past had been described as right-wing, nationalist deviation from the party line. . .It is obvious that such a state of affairs paralyzed the leadership's activity which, in turn, had to create internal disorientation within the party with all its consequences.[31]

This process of political fragmentation within the party leadership, which had been growing since the beginning of 1955 and merely crystallized at the July 1956 plenum of the Central Committee, also had an important impact on the organizational cohesiveness of the PUWP. It was clear that the Stalinist pattern of rigid internal centralization, in which the monopoly over all major policy and ideological initiatives had been in the hands of a small group of leaders, or even one leader, was rapidly disintegrating. In its place, there emerged within the Central Committee several separate factions, each advocating its own program of change but primarily formed for the purpose of capturing control over the party organization. Although momentarily confined to the top level of the PUWP's officialdom, this pattern of internal divisiveness could rapidly extend to lower units and through them to the organization at large. Left unchecked, it might have caused a permanent split within the party, not unlike that between the "majority" and "minority" factions in the 1920s, resulting in the party's inability to direct the process of change itself.

In strictly political terms, the plenum provided the forum for a confrontation between two socially, politically, and ideologically distinct factions. Subsequently, they came to be known, after their meeting places, as the Pulawska group and the Natolin group, or, they called each other, the Jews and the Boors, respectively.[32] The latter consisted mainly of those party officials and functionaries, all of them ethnically Polish but with strong Soviet ties, who had not been in the first ranks of the Stalinist heirarchy of power. In light of the Soviet-directed de-Stalinization, they naturally considered themselves primary contenders for posts to be vacated by already discredited, though still active, top rulers. For them, political evolution was largely understood in terms of change within the directing personnel. Therefore, their main attacks concentrated on the most important personalities of the failing system. However, their reformism seemed to end at that point, as they openly advocated a strong-arm policy in restoration of the already considerably weakened order and discipline in both party and society. Realizing that their key source of support could come from backing the new Kremlin leadership, they did not hide pro-Soviet sentiments. At the same time, however, they demanded Gomulka's inclusion into the PUWP's highest councils. This last position might have been dictated by tactical considerations designed to garner popular support as well as to make up for the closeness of the Soviet ties. In the Natolin strategy, the return of Gomulka would constitute a serious blow to his former enemies, such as Edward Ochab and Roman Zambrowski, and ultimately facilitate the seizure of power over the party.

The Pulawska group seemed to be a rather loose coalition of various intraparty groupings temporarily united against the Natolin group. It included a large contingent of former first-rank Stalinists who, motivated by either ideological disillusionment or fear for their own fate, decided to support a platform of reforms and political change. In addition, the group was supported by some of those party activists who saw the future of communism in Poland in terms of extensive economic and institutional changes directed toward greater legality and more effective liberalization. Among the group's members were many Jews who had spent the war in the Soviet Union and returned to Poland in the wake of the communist victory. The Pulawska faction maintained close relations with the majority of former socialists and advocated a relatively more independent stance for the PUWP in its future relationship with the Soviet party. Many of its members were hesitant to support Gomulka's return for fear that it would only antagonize the Soviet leaders and make the process of internal democratization more difficult.

The issue which reportedly triggered the collision of the two groups at the plenum was the suggestion by Soviet premier Nikolai Bulganin, who came to Poland on an official visit during the plenum, that the party prosecute its two most prominent living Stalinists, Jakub Berman and Hilary Minc, as scapegoats responsible for the mistakes and crimes of the revolutionary era.[33] Since both men were Jewish, this proposal furnished the pretext for a violent anti-Semitic attack by the Natolinists against the ruling establishment, the important segment of the Pulawska group.

The assault was led by Politburo member Zenon Nowak, who attempted to lay a heavy responsibility for Stalinist oppression upon Jewish members of the party leadership.[34] He particularly singled out several prominent Stalinist personalities of Jewish origin, implying that these men had been the true culprits of the coercive pattern of rule. Furthermore, Nowak maintained that the smooth functioning of the former system was made possible primarily as a result of the preponderant number of Jews in key party and government agencies connected especially with foreign affairs, central party staff, and security police. Accordingly, he saw a vast regulation of appointments to important political posts as the best tactical way of modifying the Stalinist operational system, better and more effective than any program of democratizing reforms executed by former Stalinists now turned liberals.

Although Nowak's attack failed to swing the party in the direction of an immediate anti-Semitic purge, it effectively precluded formulation of a program of action acceptable to all groups. Changes in the top leadership seemed to confirm this assessment. Among three newly elected Politburo members, former socialist Adam Rapacki was identified as a supporter of the Pulawska group, Roman Nowak represented Natolin, and Edward Gierek, who had supervised the party-directed suppression of the Poznan workers, was viewed as a rising apparatus member of the essentially Bierutist persuasion. Of the two new deputy members of the Politburo, Stefan Jedrychowski was close to Pulawska group, while Eugeniusz Stawinski supported the Natolinists; both had extensive background in Soviet war-time politics. A similar lack of decisiveness was manifested in the plenum resolution regarding Gomulka and his former collaborators, particularly Kliszko and Spychalski. They were officially rehabilitated and their party rights were restored, yet no responsible party positions were offered to them. The entire Central Committee, and through it the party organization, seemed to be almost paralyzed by its inability to integrate diverse views into a common platform.

Meanwhile, the locus of political action appeared to shift rapidly away from party control. Prompted by the Poznan events, social unrest was turning into an avalanche of popular discontent and protest. Particularly important was the emergence of workers' councils, conceived, after the Yugoslav example, as elective organs of self-government separate from other organizations. They sprang to life during the summer as a result of a spontaneous movement of dissatisfaction with the ineffectiveness of the party-controlled trade unions and a growing determination to increase direct worker participation in the management of individual factories and enterprises.[35] Almost simultaneously, there were mounting pressures to change the nature of trade unionism in Poland from that of transmitting party orders to the workers to representing the workers' interests vis-à-vis the party and the government.[36]

Demands for greater political autonomy were also growing within the party-controlled youth organization. Already in April 1956, the youth organ, *Po prostu,* called for a thorough reorganization of the Union of Polish Youth with a view to creation of a new body free from official political control.[37] Since that time, several "revolutionary groups" emerged within the Union and were active in planning its future organizational and operational forms. More and more, the very basis of the party's leading role in the system was becoming the focal point of popular criticism. Thus, an illustrious young philosopher, Leszek Kolakowski, who had been well known for his hard line attacks on religion during Stalinist times, now demanded the removal of "political restrictions on independent thinking."[38] Several prominent communist economists made proposals for immediate economic reforms, including the end to collectivization.[39] Finally, former socialist Julian Hochfeld appealed in late September for a reactivation of parliamentary democracy and stressed that the ultimate objective of true democratization would be "a Sejm [Parliament] supervising the government and a government responsible to Sejm."[40] Given this expansion of popular unrest, it became clear that, short of massive compulsion presumably at the hands of the Soviet leaders, the process of political disintegration of party control could not be abruptly halted by any one leader or group of leaders then in power. The solution necessitated a further change in the party leadership and the adoption of a socially acceptable program in which the pattern of future evolution would be clearly defined and institutionalized.

This realization of the party's rapidly weakening position, combined with its internal authority crisis, furnished the basis for a growing consensus within the top ranks of the PUWP, the Politburo, and the Central Committee, that nothing short of the restoration of Gomulka to power could save their rule. As a communist victim of Stalinist persecution, Gomulka was well suited to the symbolic assertion of a sharp break with an unsavory past. His long-standing commitment to the party's cause guaranteed that Gomulka could be trusted to defend the ideological and operational principles of its rule. In addition, Gomulka was the only prominent personality within the party with a clearly established and well-known record of opposition to Stalinism. Given these qualifications, it was hoped that Gomulka's return would finally create within the party and society a sense that real change was taking place yet without destroying the system at the same time. However, the issue of Gomulka's political comeback also created serious new difficulties. They essentially originated from two sources. The first was the obvious need for an immediate change in the composition of the leading party organs to accommodate Gomulka's personal preferences and wishes. The second was the problem of persuading the Soviet party that Gomulka's ascendancy to power would not be a challenge to its relations with the PUWP and could actually improve the ties between the two communist organizations.

The internal problems of leadership change appear to have been resolved during a series of negotiations which the Politburo initiated with Gomulka soon after the July plenum of the Central Committee. The resulting arrangement prompted Hilary Minc's resignation from the Politburo on October 9. In this way, the last member of the Stalinist triumvirate left politics. The final decisions on the composition of the new party leadership were reached at the Politburo meeting on October 13–15, with Gomulka officially invited to take part in the proceedings. For purposes of their ratification the Politburo convened a plenary session of the Central Committee on October 19.

The issue of Soviet acceptance of Gomulka and his eventual political program was more complex.[41] While there is little doubt that Moscow had been kept informed about political developments within the party in Poland, it is also more than likely that, due to the internal disorganization within the PUWP's leadership, the Soviet leaders received differing interpretations of the meaning and direction of political change. As to confirm this uncertainty, a strong delegation of the CPSU arrived unexpectedly in Warsaw on October 19, at the time of the opening of the Central Committee plenum. It was led by Nikita Khrushchev and included Lazar Kaganovich, Anastas Mikoyan, and Vyacheslav Molotov, as well as a large group of high-ranking military officers. The most fundamental Soviet interests were obviously at stake.

In light of this development, the PUWP plenum was adjourned following the hasty cooptation of Gomulka and his former associates Spychalski, Loga-Sowinski and Kliszko to the Central Committee, as well as the election of Gomulka to the Politburo delegation which was to meet with the Soviet visitors. Although the official record of these dicussions has never been published, it became clear from sporadic comments of the PUWP delegates that the Soviet leaders were seeking to gain the continued adherence of the PUWP to Moscow communist standards rather than to impose any specific variant of the socialist developmental model or to directly interfere with the internal political problems within the PUWP. As one of the participants, Politburo member Aleksander Zawadzki, later assured the Central Committee, "[T]he problems [of change in the leadership composition] were discussed from the beginning as internal matters for our party and the Central Committee."[42]

Notwithstanding this political concession from the Soviet side, discussions were clearly "difficult and bitter."[43] To a large extent, this resulted from Soviet apprehensions of the intensity of the anti-Russian sentiments of the Polish population and fears that the PUWP would not be able to contain the situation. In effect, movements of Soviet troops were reported around Warsaw, a fact Khrushchev later acknowledged when he recounted that "the situation was such that we had to be ready to resort to arms if the threat of an armed struggle in Poland became real and if we were in an imminent danger of being cut off from our army."[44] Still, the Poles were finally able to pacify the Russians. Evidently convinced that they would gain more from letting Gomulka rebuild the party according to his own preferences rather than from an immediate military intervention, the Soviet leaders left on October 20 and called for a continuation of the talks in Moscow at a later date.

Following the drama of the CPSU-PUWP meeting, the resumption of the Central Committee plenum turned into a celebration of Gomulka's victory. Gomulka set the stage in his main address, thoroughly condemning mistakes, faults, and crimes of the past Stalinist era.[45] Although admitting numerous accomplishments of the revolutionary programs of industrialization, Gomulka pointed to equally numerous instances of waste, bureaucratization, and excessive centralization. He then decried the economic folly of the party's agricultural policy but stopped short of a total rejection of collectivization. Instead, Gomulka proposed a program of voluntary socialization of agricultural farms. His basic developmental message was unmistakably clear: no more developmental compulsion and imposition of programs from above.

With respect to intraparty political change, Gomulka condemned the Stalinist system of distribution of power with its emphasis on centralistic leadership and the "cult of personality." Without specifically defining the details of his program, Gomulka called for greater democratization of party structure and operations and promised a return to legality in inner party life. He also appealed for functional separation of the party and the state, according to the principle that the party "must not govern but merely guide" the state machinery.

While calling for limitation of the party's direct involvement in policy administration, however, Gomulka also insisted on maintaining the PUWP's political control over the entire process of change. He stressed that "We shall not allow anyone to use the process of democratization to undermine socialism. Our party leads the process of democratization and only the party, acting in conjunction with other parties of the National Front, can guide this process in a way that will truly lead to the democratization of relations in all spheres of our life, to the strengthening of the foundations of our system and not to their weakening." Gomulka's determination to retain the party's political dominance was confirmed in the plenum final resolution which, after including all major points of his speech, proclaimed that "the Central Committee declares that at the present time the deciding task in the further development of Poland toward socialism is the strengthening of the leading role of our party as the directing political and ideological force of the working class, of the Polish nation, and of the people's state."[46]

Gomulka's speech was followed by a series of supportive declarations by other party leaders. There was very little substantive discussion of a new party program and the major thrust of deliberations centered on varying degrees of criticism of the past. The only controversy arose over the question of whether Konstantin Rokossovskiî, the Minister of Defense and Soviet officer imported in 1949, should be included in the new Politburo or dropped from the party's high councils, as had been proposed by Gomulka's supporters. Even so, after the apparent approval of Gomulka and his program by the Soviet leadership, there was no chance for Rokossovskiî's proponents to persuade the Central Committee to go against Gomulka's wishes. In any case, there was no indication that Rokossovskiî himself was interested in the reelection, as he had actively participated in preparing the list of candidates for party positions before the plenum itself.[47]

On October 21, a new Politburo was elected. It consisted of nine full members: J. Cyrankiewicz, W. Gomulka, S. Jedrychowski, I. Loga-Sowinski, J. Morawski, E. Ochab, A. Rapacki, R. Zambrowski, and A. Zawadzki. There were no deputy members. The seven secretaries of the Central Committee were J. Albrecht, W. Gomulka, E. Gierek, W. Jarosinski, E. Ochab, W. Matwin, and R. Zambrowski. Wladyslaw Gomulka was unanimously elected the party's first secretary.

The October plenum has frequently been considered, by Polish as well as Western observers, as providing a crucial point in the history of communism in Poland. Indeed, there are several important reasons to accept the validity of this judgment. Perhaps the most important long-term consequence of the plenum was its rejection of a revolutionary strategy of socialist change. To be sure, this did not signify the abandonment of the very goal of ultimate transformation of Poland's society into one corresponding with socialist ideas of a defined socioeconomic order. But, to the degree that socialist revolution had become identified with a centrally planned and organized attempt to impose change from above without any consideration for the sacrifice of the population, the plenum's repudiation of Stalinist methods, policies, and patterns of rule effectively precluded its ideological appeal and undermined its practical relevance.

The immediate implication of this decision for party policy, however, was a widespread and rapidly intensifying uncertainty as to what should be done next and a feeling, shared by many party members and large segments of the public alike, that perhaps the party itself, previously a source of developmental dynamism, had become an impediment to progress and change. This point was certainly not lost on many a party leader or activist. Hounded by the specter of political stagnation, some of them hoped to recapture the lost momentum by comprehensive redefinition of the revolutionary meaning and a restructuring of the process of change.

Thus, Gomulka's long-time advisor and his sometime friend, Wladyslaw Bienkowski, argued that "revolution had come to us in a ready-made and seriously bureaucratized form" and, therefore, the October change should be construed as "the continuation of the [political] revolution of eleven years ago, more difficult and painful because [now] it is necessary to eliminate much from what has accumulated since and do what history usually does not accept—return to the point of departure."[48] Others, soon to be identified as political and ideological revisionists, saw the solution to the problem of change as an introduction of massive reformist adaptations into the communist experience to help their party adjust to new social, political, and cultural realities. For them it was not enough to change the scope and timing of developmental policies, they demanded a thorough overhaul of the party's organizational structure, its methods of operation, and its relations to the public at large. Still others, adopting a mantle of doctrinal orthodoxy, stressed the need for continuity, or even radicalization, of basic social and economic policies of the past era, apparently believing that their alteration would inevitably jeopardize the final fulfillment of socialist goals.

The growing controversy within the party over the direction its policies should take provided the basis for a rapidly progressing fragmentation among its membership. In contrast to an earlier pattern of factional divisions among the Natolin and the Pulawska groups, which had been limited to the highest echelons of the party organization, the dispute between the revisionist reformers and the dogmatic radicals extended through the entire organizational structure. Although the objectives of both groups were not so much to affect a change in the party leadership as to influence the process of policy formation, their activity vitally contributed to a persistent political and organizational incoherence within the party itself. As for Gomulka's policy preferences, he gave no immediate indication of his choice of action, a fact which only added fuel to internal controversies.

Another important development, directly related to the October events, was the shift in the locus of party operational support from essentially Soviet sources to domestic constituencies. To a large extent, this shift was determined by the leadership's rejection of a revolutionary orientation. Just as the roots of the initial revolutionary measures had been in the Soviet insistence on developmental communist uniformity, so the repudiation of the centralistic compulsion was perceived by Poland's population as an essentially patriotic act by the new PUWP leaders. In this respect, the unscheduled meeting between the Soviet and Polish leaders on the eve of the Central Committee plenum acquired a special significance. It was seen by the Poles as just another attempt by Moscow to interfere in domestic affairs and they fully identified the position of the PUWP delegation with the defense of national rather than communist interests. Throughout the country demonstrations were staged in support of Gomulka and the rest of the party leaders, furnishing an impressive display of public solidarity with the party itself.

This turn of events created an unprecedented situation for the PUWP leaders. For the first time in the history of communism in Poland, the party was actually supported by the masses, an experience which was clearly unsettling for some of its veterans. As Edward Ochab admitted in his speech to the plenum, he suddenly:

> observed a phenomenon, which to a certain extent formed the background to our conversations [with the Soviet leaders], though it also constituted a problem in itself, namely the declarations of students and workers, the resolutions and the statements of many people in many gatherings throughout Poland, who wished to defend the Central Committee against the army, by which it is allegedly threatened, or even against the Soviet army. Which one of us could ever have imagined that he would find himself in such a situation that party members, that men and women, who think with inner conviction and enthusiasm of the victory of communism, would be faced with such a problem and would arrive at such despairing conclusions about the supposed threat from the army or from our friends?[49]

Considerations such as these must have weighed heavily on the minds of PUWP leaders as they searched for solution to the political crisis. Insofar as they recognized that massive popular support for Gomulka might have provided an important factor in securing Soviet acceptance of his leadership over the PUWP, they were also faced with a real prospect that future communist policies in Poland would have to be formulated with greater attention to public opinion and actual social needs rather than merely in response to external, that is Soviet, duress. If nothing else, this realization introduced a qualitative change in the political orientation of the party. Although Soviet primacy remained a function of the party's ideological commitment to socialist goals as well as its recognition of existing realities of military and political strength, actual determination of immediate policy tasks depended to an unprecedented degree on social demands and popular support.

Given the potentially volatile nature of this change, stabilization of the new relationship between the CPSU and the PUWP became the most important task of the new party leadership. In Gomulka's view, this relationship should be shaped in the future "by the principles of international working-class solidarity; should be based on mutual confidence and equality of rights; on granting assistance to each other; on mutual criticism, if such should be necessary; and on a rational solution, arising from the spirit of friendship and from the spirit of socialism, of all controversial matters."[50] Against this general background, the new party leadership was quick to point out, however, that its demands for greater autonomy would not interfere with the long-established rules of international communist politics. Thus, the final resolution of the October plenum forcefully stressed that its efforts at "democratization, socialist construction, and strengthening of the leading role of the party are linked in the closest possible way with the participation of People's Poland in the camp of socialist countries, in the international movement of socialist and progressive forces fighting for international relaxation and peaceful coexistence. Our party considers the interests of People's Poland as inseparable from the unbreakable principle of the Polish-Soviet alliance, and with the interests of the entire socialist camp."[51]

The essence of the new relationship revolved primarily around the PUWP's insistence on having the right to settle its own problems and those of internal Polish evolution by methods it considered best under Poland's domestic conditions. This claim was subsequently amplified by Gomulka, who, while stressing the guiding experience of the Soviet Union in paving the way for all socialist parties toward socialist construction, insisted that "neglect or negation of national traits and characteristics in constructing socialism amounts to a nihilistic dogmatism. . .which hinders and distorts socialist construction and as a result turns the working masses against socialism."[52]

On a practical level, Gomulka moved rapidly to eliminate some of the most obvious Soviet interference in domestic Polish matters. On October 24, while addressing a mass rally in Warsaw, Gomulka announced that from then on "all concrete matters pertaining to our internal affairs will be solved in accordance with the estimate of the party and the government. The question whether we need Soviet specialists and military advisers, and for how long we need their aid, will depend on our decision alone."[53] During the week following the October plenum, Marshal Konstantin Rokossovskiî, the prime symbol of the Stalinist pattern of Soviet domination over Poland, was given an extended leave of absence and on November 13 officially returned to the Soviet Union. While Rokossovskiî was given the post of deputy minister of defense in the Soviet government soon after his arrival in Moscow, his old position of minister of national defense in Poland was taken by Marian Spychalski, an old Gomulka associate from wartime. Rokossovskiî's departure was followed by a massive exodus of some thirty Soviet generals and several thousand officers who had held command posts in the Polish army and security formations since the end of the war.[54]

Notwithstanding the apparent political drama of these steps, they seem to have been fully accepted by the Kremlin leadership. Gomulka and Khrushchev remained in direct communication throughout the period immediately following the October plenum[55] and there is little doubt that Gomulka's decisions were at least implicitly endorsed by the CPSU. It seems that, faced with an open popular revolt against communist rule in Hungary and the possibility of a similar breakdown in Poland, Moscow opted for cooperation with the Poles in order to stabilize the political situation in Warsaw in the shortest possible time and with a minimum of political expense.

This point was fully confirmed during Gomulka's official visit to Moscow during November 14–18, 1956. According to an official communiqué issued at the conclusion of the meeting, the Soviet Union agreed to make important concessions to the Poles, including: cancellation of Poland's debts to the USSR, combined with extension of new credits; regulations on the stationing of Soviet troops on Polish territory, thereby giving Poland a certain degree of control over their movement outside the assigned stations; and repatriation of Polish citizens from the USSR to their homeland.[56] More important, the visit provided Gomulka with symbolic rewards of Soviet respect and political recognition. In his own words, it produced an understanding that the relations between the CPSU and the PUWP were firmly based on "Leninist principles of full equality, mutual respect, independence, and sovereignty."[57] If nothing else, this represented a significant strengthening of Gomulka's political position, something he desperately needed to reestablish the party's hold on public life in Poland.

Within this context, the most important item on the PUWP leadership's scale of priorities was the rebuilding of a cohesive party organization. Having experienced the trauma of de-Stalinization, the party was torn by internal dissension and factional strife. The general weakening of the organizational discipline, combined with a declining membership, severely undermined the PUWP's ability to continue its politically dominant role in Poland's politics. After the October plenum several veterans of the old Polish Socialist Party called for a revival of their former organization, independent of the PUWP. In a similar vein, some of the young communist writers from the *Po prostu* argued for complete dissolution of the PUWP in its current form and replacing it with another organization. As one of them stated, "Since the whole party was once Stalinist and we are fighting against Stalinism, would it not be best to liquidate the whole party?"[58] Even more orthodox but equally distressed party activists agreed that drastic changes within the entire organization were necessary. As one of them concluded in an article published in the official party journal, "After the October [1956], our party cannot remain what it was before—as long as we don't want the fruits of our struggle to be lost. Both in its character and in its structure as well as in the nature of its everyday activity it must become something new because its role and policy are also new."[59] At the same time, numerous other activists saw any change within the party as political and ideological anathema and were prepared to do their utmost to preserve the old Stalinist forms and operational practices.

Confronted with this situation, Gomulka adopted a two-pronged strategy of silencing the advocates of sweeping organizational changes and, once their influence in the party was drastically reduced, reforming the party to restore its internal cohesion and to assert his own control over its activities. This strategy was intended to re-establish a firm basis for political and institutional centralization of decision making within the party. Its crucial feature was Gomulka's tactic of relating his larger social support and demands to intraparty politics and, through them, shaping the character of organizational changes.

There is little doubt that Gomulka enjoyed significant popular support during and after the October plenum. To the degree that the public associated his name with the movement toward domestic de-Stalinization and national opposition to the rigid patterns of Soviet domination, Gomulka was a symbol of political change and patriotic renovation. Yet, this support was highly personalized and grounded in a massive revulsion against past communist practices. It offered, therefore, a momentarily powerful but essentially unstable basis for rule. Given this uncertainty, Gomulka initially allowed a certain degree of unrestrained public activity and concentrated all efforts on solidifying the positive attitudes into a more durable popular commitment to the system in place.

Perhaps Gomulka's most important decision was not to interfere with a largely spontaneous movement toward dissolution of collective farms. While the party policy adopted at the October plenum did not endorse the continuation of massive programs of collectivization, the PUWP leadership was obviously taken by surprise with the intensity of hostile reaction to the collective experiment. During the three months which followed the plenum, the number of collective farms decreased from 10,510 on September 30 to 1,534 on December 31.[60] The collective farms suddenly ceased to be a factor on Poland's socioeconomic scene. The party's inability to prevent this development was frankly acknowledged by one of the top PUWP leaders, Jedrychowski, who stated in 1959 that "Some people. . .believe that the retreat in developing the cooperatives and the dissolving of many of them was the result of party policy. The truth is that the retreat was caused by the pressure of anti-socialist elements at a time when the party was not strong enough to counter this pressure. The main obstacle to the cooperative movement is the low level of cooperative consciousness among the peasants, who are tied to individual farming and are not yet convinced of the superiority of large-scale cooperative farming."[61]

Similar lack of official opposition made it possible in November 1956 to legalize a network of workers' councils. They became fully recognized as autonomous representative workers' organs with extensive powers to initiate and/or approve personnel changes at the management level, to participate in factory management, and to influence the formulation of local production plans.[62] The general movement toward spontaneous reorganization affected other areas of public life as well. At the beginning of 1957, the Stalinist Union of Polish Youth was formally dissolved after several new youth organizations, some of them openly non-communist, appeared in the wake of the October plenum. There was also a massive resurgence of different social, cultural, and educational associations and groups with separate programs and autonomous aspirations.

A major factor which prevented the expansion of these activities into a political revolt against communist rule was the widespread popularity of Gomulka and the recognition that a one-party system in Poland was still a political necessity. In this respect, the developments in Hungary during November 1956 provided the Poles with a lesson which they could not ignore. While the Hungarian uprising against the communist regime was warmly supported in Poland, the Soviet military intervention clearly pointed to the limits of political experimentation. The only guarantee of preserving the post-October freedoms was self-imposed political restraint.

A concomitant factor which facilitated the maintenance of the status quo was Gomulka's deliberately moderate position. To expand the scope of his popular acceptance, Gomulka rapidly moved to establish working relations with the Catholic Church. Within a week after the October plenum, Cardinal Wyszynski was freed from detention and shortly thereafter numerous other bishops and priests were also released. By the beginning of December, a joint Church-state commission established a new platform of cooperation. This resulted in an agreement offering extensive educational privileges to the Church and in return the "representatives of the Episcopate expressed full support for the work of the government aiming at the strengthening and development of People's Poland."[63] This attitude was subsequently translated into the political realm when the Church authorities urged all Catholics to take part in the January 1957 parliamentary elections.

The elections provided the final legitimization of Gomulka's national leadership. Preceded by the introduction of relatively democratic electoral rules, elections provided the Poles with a considerable measure of choice within the existing political framework. Although the electorate was again offered a single list of candidates sponsored by the Front of National Unity, the list included not only members of the PUWP and its allies, the United Peasant Party (ZSL) and the Democratic Party (SD), but also independents and Catholics nominated by various public organizations. The number of candidates exceeded the number of available seats by about 40 percent. From the very beginning, the elections were presented as a plebiscite for Gomulka, who warned the public that to vote against him or his party's candidates would amount to "crossing out the independence of our country, crossing Poland off the map of European states."[64] As a result, the outcome was quite predictable. The party emerged with an absolute majority of seats or 237 deputies, the ZSL had 120 deputies, the SD received 39, while the nonparty candidates captured 63 seats—among them were 12 Catholic deputies (see Appendix 2). More significant, however, were percentages of votes polled by elected candidates. The nonparty candidates had 94.3 percent of the vote cast, the SD 90.8 percent, the ZSL 89.2 percent, and the PUWP trailed with 88.0 percent.[65]

Having solidified his position in the country, Gomulka turned his attention to strengthening discipline within the party. Proclaiming that organizational unity "on the basis of democratic centralism" constituted the indispensable condition for the party's survival as a politically dominant force in Poland, Gomulka openly attacked those activists and officials who, because of either excessive doctrinal orthodoxy or reformist enthusiasm, were at odds with his stability oriented measures. The main forum of the attacks was the Central Committee plenum in May 1957. Gomulka directed his criticism especially at the threat of revisionism in the party. He particularly singled out a young communist philosopher, Leszek Kolakowski, accusing him of having "lost ideological principles, lost Marxism-Leninism, lost socialism as a result of the search for new roads toward socialism. . .in reality, socialism became something foreign." But he also implied that Kolakowski was not alone in his revisionist views and condemned all trends toward drastic changes within the party as well as any arguments for its dissolution or alteration of its activities. At the same time, but in markedly less explicit language, Gomulka criticized conservative dogmatists within the party ranks for not being able to "adjust to new methods of party work."[66]

While the revisionists were not able to present their defense at the plenum, which indicated their numerical weakness at the high organizational levels of the party, the conservatives attempted a counter-attack on Gomulka's domestic policies. Several of their leading spokesmen, notably former Natolin members Kazimierz Mijal, Wiktor Klosiewicz, and Stanislaw Lapot, criticized the leadership's failure to carry out the program of agricultural collectivization and attacked its conciliatory attitude toward the Church. In light of Gomulka's previous condemnation of revisionism, however, their arguments were largely disregarded. Gomulka's hold over the party was rapidly increasing and to the majority of the Central Committee members it was obvious that his popularity in the country at large made him relatively immune to intraparty criticism. To confirm Gomulka's organizational strength, the plenum duly elected both his long-time associate and friend Zenon Kliszko as well as a more recent supporter, Politburo member Jerzy Morawski, to the party's Secretariat.

The process of internal verification of the party apparatus closely followed the May plenum. During the spring and summer months, more than 8,600 party staff members at different levels were transferred to work in state administration. Inasmuch as the professional party employees might have been suspected of harboring conservative sympathies,[67] this action was a severe blow to the power and influence of the Stalinist opposition to Gomulka. At the same time, however, an intensive campaign was launched against the communist revisionists. Its main target was the party press. In the summer of 1957 there was a series of changes in the editorial staffs of all party publications, coupled with repeated warnings that the views published in the communist journals must correspond to those of the party leadership. In September, a strict censorship was imposed on the content of all publications and in October, the youth journal *Po prostu,* which had been the most outspoken voice for reformist political change, was closed down. In explaining the new party policy toward the press, Gomulka bluntly repeated that the task of defining a direction for "socialist construction belongs to the party's leadership" and pointed out that the main requirement of journalists was that they "link their convictions, consciousness, souls, and hearts with [the cause of] socialism."[68] To assure their compliance with the party directives, permanent commissions for control of science, culture, and education within the Central Committee apparatus, which had been abolished in the fall of 1956, were re-established by the end of 1957.

Political and ideological purification was subsequently extended to the entire party. At the Central Committee plenum in late October 1957, Gomulka again reaffirmed his determination to eliminate all political "wings or [separate] groupings" within the party and re-establish monolithic centralism of its organization.[69] Consequently, the plenum decided to launch a massive campaign of internal purge. As a result, in the period between November 1957 and September 1958, more than 261,000 party members, or about 20 percent of the total membership, were removed from the PUWP ranks.[70]

Parallel to the internal party changes, intensified efforts were directed at reconsolidation of its political control over those areas of social activity which had been particularly affected by the post-October fever of spontaneity. In April 1957, a new youth organization, the Union of Socialist Youth, was established under party sponsorship to serve as a political heir of the old Stalinist youth movement. It was joined in February 1958 by another party-created youth agency, the Union of Village Youth, with a specialized program of activity among young peasants. In a concomitant development, strict party supervision was extended over the activities of the Union of Polish Students, which had emerged in the wake of PUWP's October plenum as an autonomous organization of academic youth. Finally, the operational prerogatives of the workers' councils were severely restricted by the establishment in December 1958 of the Conferences of Workers' Self-Management. These institutions were created by a governmental decree to act as the main organs of collective decision making at the enterprise levels. They united representatives of the workers' councils, the trade unions, and the local party organization as well as other social and professional groups within a single body with economic functions rather than a mandate to defend the interests of the workers. Insofar as the councils became only one organ among many operating within the conferences, their authority as representative organizations of the workers rapidly declined and the deciding influence on factory matters shifted to the party delegates.[71]

By the end of 1958, the task of political and organizational consolidation of the party appeared finally complete. At the Central Committee plenum in mid-October, almost two years after he had returned to power, Gomulka confidently proclaimed that at last "the party emerged from the tangle of internal conflicts that had been weakening it, consolidated its ranks and became ideologically stronger, matured politically and hardened organizationally."[72] This sense of confidence was further manifested by the plenum's decision to convene a much-delayed party congress at the beginning of 1959. With the apparent achievement of internal organizational stability, the locus of party political preoccupation was shifting toward defining its future tasks in the continuing process of socialist construction.

The Little Stabilization

Party congresses, frequently described as the organs of supreme authority within the organization, have never played a creative role in policy-making processes. Rather, their main function has been to provide a formal legitimization to the lines of policy already formulated by the leadership. In this respect, the third congress of the Polish United Workers' Party, which met March 10–18, 1959, in Warsaw, did not differ. It gave *post factum* approval to Gomulka's policies since the October 1956 plenum of the Central Committee and fully endorsed his efforts at internal consolidation of the party. More important, the congress provided the leadership with a platform for the definition of new party tasks and operational methods. Having successfully withstood the social and political upheavals of de-Stalinization, the party turned its attention to a lasting consolidation of its power. The essence of this orientation was in the congress' final resolution which, following Gomulka's programmatic announcement, officially proclaimed that under the changed circumstances a new political strategy was to be adopted.

> The main task of the party is to integrate, on the basis of economic achievements in the development of the country, the entire working class as well as the urban and rural working masses around the goal of constructing a new socialist system.
>
> For the working masses, the best school of socialism is their own participation in government, in management of enterprises, in village activities, in people's councils, in all sorts of social and economic oganizations.
>
> This process of socialist democratization, along with a correct economic policy, are the determining factors in directing the main efforts of the party toward strengthening of the people's state and its social foundations.
>
> The consolidation of party influence over all aspects of life is the indispensable condition for socialist democratization as well as the fundamental element in the strengthening of the people's state.[1]

This statement was important both as an enunciation of the general principle of party activity and an elaboration of the framework through which this activity was to be expressed. It signaled the adoption of an operational formula which was to serve as the basis for the relations between the party and society and was to become a crucial factor in shaping its internal organizational development.

In general, the dominant accent was on stability. By putting the focus of its policy on integration of separate groups and strata into a future socialist society, the party officially discarded the revolutionary approach toward social change. The defining characteristic of the communist revolution was an effort to completely eradicate traditional social cleavages and its main emphasis was on politically stimulated group polarization via centrally directed, intensive class struggle. Conversely, integration refers to a process whereby distinct groups are linked together in specific areas of their activity. It produces interdependence and may lead to cooperation in pursuit of common goals, but does not necessarily entail social uniformity. More important, it implies a conscious acceptance of at least a certain degree of permanency in existing patterns of differentiation. The main thrust of an integrative activity is on finding the areas for mutual accommodation among separate groups to reduce conflicts to manageable levels. As a result, however, the scope of possible social transformation becomes reduced to those aspects of change which can be adapted to the prevailing social and political realities. With the adoption of an integrative stance, therefore, the party seemed to shift toward a gradual and evolutionary approach to change. The purpose of this reorientation, however, was not to renounce the ideologically defined goals of ultimate social transformation but to develop new ways to secure their implementation without provoking mass protests and political disruptions.

Specifically, the distinguishing feature of this approach was an appeal for mass participation in the activities of existing public institutions, provided that these activities and the institutions themselves were controlled by the party. While it suggested a party attempt to broaden public involvement in government, its motive force was not a change in the structure of power but its instrumental redefinition to secure greater public compliance. The immediate political goal appeared to have been the creation of a supportive popular base for the political system, within which the party would be able not only to preserve its leading role but also to solidify its authority over social activities.

This tendency was most discernible in the party's reliance on economic factors, the likely determinants of both systemic stability and further development toward socialist goals. Just as the establishment of a socialized economy had been crucial in laying the sociopolitical foundations for the system, its further development was considered vitally important for preserving the gains of the initial transformation. Insofar as the party had led and directed the process of change, the developmental success was viewed as vital to the task of consolidating its power and influence.

To the extent that the shift from a revolutionary to an integrative approach toward social development suggested a fundamental reorientation of party policy, questions on the degree of the already-accomplished change acquired an increased importance. Given the continuing party commitment to the goal of socialist transformation—the congress affirmed that "this historical task must be achieved by our generation"[2]—the determination of its successes and failures could go a long way toward explaining the conduct of the leadership.

If we define change in terms of a quantitative social transformation, it could appear that the party had been relatively successful in altering the traditional structure of Poland's society. The expropriation of landed estates and the early nationalization of large industrial holdings led to the disappearance of the old upper classes. The subsequent drive for industrialization brought about a massive numerical expansion of workers and white-collar groups. Furthermore, by encouraging rapid upward mobility of manual workers into administrative, managerial, and similar white-collar occupations, the party made significant progress in bridging the social gap between these two groups. To be sure, there remained large areas of inequality, most obviously the income differentials between manual and non-manual workers, but their political impact was somewhat moderated by the elevation of both groups into an ideologically defined position of equal coowners of socialized property.[3] The only conspicuous failure at structural transformation was the party's inability to incorporate private farmowners into the new society. Just as they had been before the advent of revolutionary pressures, individual peasants remained a distinct social class with its own economic base, specific behavior patterns, and traditional value systems.[4]

Yet, if we try to evaluate these changes from the viewpoint of their qualitative social impact—their contribution to a lasting transformation of values, ways of thinking, and behavior of the population—the party's revolutionary success was rather doubtful. In spite of the large-scale alterations in societal structures, there remained equally large areas of sociocultural continuity which prevented the spread and acceptance of socialist influences. In part, this was due to the revolutionary manner of imposing change through a rigid set of centrally planned and forcefully implemented measures. This effectively precluded voluntary public participation in the creation of new forms of social cohesion. Furthermore, to the degree that the public saw those measures as reflecting the narrow political interests of a small revolutionary elite supported by a traditionally hostile foreign power, they produced widespread resentment and determined albeit passive opposition and thereby solidified the ground for continuing maintenance of prerevolutionary value systems. Similarly, insofar as revolutionary attempts to put socialist content into educational programs and artistic activity were seen as an effort to uproot the national cultural heritage, they not only failed to change the patterns of thinking and behavior, but also might have contributed the greater popularity of traditional ideals and values.[5]

In addition, while the revolutionary elite considered the socialization of the economy and the functioning of political institutions as essential in creating the basis for a fundamental social change, these efforts produced several unanticipated consequences that threatened to undermine the egalitarian principle of the revolution itself. Among the most important was the emergence of a new pattern of social differentiation, in which membership and office in economic and/or political institutions acquired attributes of class-like distinctiveness, comparable to traditional social divisions but based on functional rather than proprietary criteria. Commenting on the social character of this development, a prominent Polish sociologist pointed out that "the economic hierarchy in a socialized economy is a stratifying factor. . .in that it encompasses differentiated salaries and wages, requires differentiated levels of education, and—with the differentiation of professions required by the management of a socialized economy—also brings about differentiation in occupational prestige."[6] As a consequence, a kind of social boundary emerged between the specialized elites, which controlled access to the avenues of decision making, and the working masses, which were left on the outside.

In light of the above, it became clear that even if the revolutionary efforts of the party had weakened the traditional patterns of social bifurcation, they not only failed to achieve the goal of equality, as required by the ideologically defined image of a socialist society, but also developed a new basis for stratification and sociopolitical cleavages. In short, the party's apparently successful revolutionary social transformation remained limited to basic structural changes at best, and even that could be highly misleading in practice.

There is little doubt that this failure to reach the initial objectives significantly affected the PUWP's capacity to carry out a long-range program of socialist change, as well as strongly influenced its ordering of immediate policy priorities. As the social agitation during 1955–1957 made it abundantly clear, any attempts to continue the strategy of change by centralistic imposition could create the danger of popular resistance to the system itself, lead to political turmoil, and weaken the party and its leadership. To contain the threat of possible disorder, the party leadership was forced to seek accommodation with existing social and political groupings and accept more pragmatic policy formulations. As a result, the revolutionary impetus toward centrally directed social leveling and change appeared to have been partially arrested, or even reversed, since the mid-1950s. Instead, the main emphasis was on the immediate task of rebuilding and solidifying the institutional cohesion of the system.

Its fragility was clearly revealed when the initial change in party policies from Stalinist rigidity had engendered the spontaneous emergence of autonomous workers' councils, political discussion clubs, and non-communist youth movements. To arrest further political dislocations, the party intensified its efforts to restrict public activity to the existing framework of already established institutions. Opposition to any demands for greater autonomy of social and political organizations was remarkable in its thoroughness. Most of the spontaneously created public organizations were dissolved and others, including the workers' councils, became subjected to strict supervision by state authorities.

With respect to the state administrative organs, several steps were taken to eliminate the most notorious elements of the revolutionary legacy without destroying the institutional foundations of their operations. This tendency was most discernible in the reorganization of central planning and in the restructuring of the security system. Although the powerful State Commission for Economic Planning had been dissolved in 1956, its functions were assumed in the following year by the newly created Planning Commission of the Council of Ministers and its Economic Committee. Both bodies retained extensive prerogatives in plan formulation and policy coordination, respectively. Similarly, while the semi-autonomous Committee for Public Security had been abolished in early 1957, its duties were promptly absorbed by specially created departments in the Ministry of Internal Affairs. The dominant accent in these changes remained on centralistic continuity and its motive force was the return to forms of government more in consonance with the systemic traditions of political and institutional uniformity.

These tactics of apparent initiations of institutional reform and then their elimination could be illustrated by the rise and decline in the role of the Sejm. In 1956 Gomulka had promised to make the national legislature a serious forum for policy discussion, if not policy making. This led to a rather promising start, with an expansion of debate sessions and a numerical increase of specialized legislative committees. However, soon after the initial outburst of legislative activity following the elections in 1957, the importance of the Sejm gradually decreased. The number of actual days of deliberation steadily diminished from 21 in 1957 to 18 in 1958, 15 in 1959, 10 in 1960, 9 in 1961, 11 in 1962 and 1963, and an average of less than 10 between 1964 and 1968. Although this still exceeded the Bierutist norm of 4 days average between 1952 and 1955, it could hardly suggest an enhanced importance of the parliamentary debates. Similarly, the proliferation of the legislative committees, which grew from seven in early 1955 to nineteen in 1958, proved to have "very little effect" on the floor deliberations as a whole.[7]

The continuing ineffectiveness of the Sejm as a policy-debating body may be more fully appreciated in relation to the stability of political representation among its membership. The three consecutive elections in 1961, 1965, and 1969 produced identical results: in each of them the PUWP retained 255 out of 460 seats or a 55.4 percent majority, the United Peasant Party had 117 seats or 25.4 percent, and the Democratic Party received 39 seats or 8.5 percent. The nonparty deputies maintained their share of parliamentary representation with 49 seats and 10.7 percent (see Appendix 2). Clearly, the apparent relaxation of electoral laws, which had been introduced for the 1957 elections and remained unchanged ever since, did not make it much easier for the Polish electorate to choose an alternative set of representatives.

Such insistence on institutional continuity was of course related to the leadership's strategy of stabilization. However, it also created a fertile ground for serious political difficulties. They originated essentially from two sources. The first lay in the functional incompatibility between the centralistic institutional framework and the changing objectives of party policy. Formed with the explicitly stated goal of revolutionary social transformation, the institutional framework was bound to become an obstacle to rather than an instrument of effective implementation of stabilizing efforts. The second source of difficulties came from the growing social and economic differentiation within the population. The persistently unequal patterns of allocation of socioeconomic rewards, despite the party's commitment to egalitarianism, threatened to build up tension and discontent. In the absence of clearly established institutions through which different social groups could present their problems and defend their interests, the intensification of social conflicts appeared as all but inevitable. Against this background, the entire program of stability appeared fundamentally superficial. Indeed, it merely created an impression, widely shared by the party members and the public alike, that the leadership's policy represented no more than a "little stabilization,"[8] restricted in scope and of limited duration.

To the degree that the strategy of stabilization remained ambivalent on many political and operational issues, it presented severe problems of assimilation for the party itself. They included the redefinition of the party's political role within the system, the growth of internal social and functional heterogeneity of its membership related to the increasingly complex tasks of government, and the difficulty in preserving the long-established organizational patterns under changing political conditions. Absorbing the consequences of these processes was to have inevitable impact on the organizational development of the party and the methods of its political operations.

Regarding the party's political role, its relations with other organizations and society at large were given a new interpretation. During the revolutionary transformation, the essence of communist power had depended on the party having a dictatorial and coercive control over all social activities. With the adoption of a stabilizing stance, the main thrust of party activity shifted toward cooperation with other sociopolitical organizations, providing that they would accept its position as the principal leader and policy maker. The main purpose of this change, however, was not to provide greater access for other groups to policy making but rather to establish a quasi-participatory framework within which the party's directive prerogatives would be publicly acceptable and legitimate.

The political essence of this arrangement was expressed in the notion of a "hegemonic" relationship between the party and other sociopolitical groupings. According to this notion, the character of political interaction reflected the situation in which ". . .accepting the socialist order, the parties and other groupings cooperate and emphasize the directing role of one party in Poland, the Polish United Workers' Party, for the entire political system."[9] The directive prerogatives of the party, in turn, were derived from several major functions it performed within the system. They included ideological leadership, control over political recruitment, and regulation of access to the avenues of political participation at all levels of government.[10] The institutional framework for public political activity was provided by the Front of National Unity, a formal coalition of all recognized political, social, and economic groups, which had been used by the party since 1947 as an instrument for electoral and propaganda purposes. No political opposition, in the sense of organized groups capable of competing with the Front of National Unity, was allowed to exist. If nothing else, this merely reflected a long-established practice of the party having a monopoly over all policy initiatives and a requirement that all other organizations conform to its decisions.

More important for the task of redefining the party's political role within the system was the change in its relation to society. Ever since the consolidation of its power, the party had acted as an exclusive political representative of a single social group, the proletariat. The main thrust of its policies had been to weaken and eventually destroy all other strata. With the decline of revolutionary enthusiasm, the primary emphasis in party activity shifted from social polarization and class struggle toward integration of separate social groups within a broader, national community. Its political consequence was an effort to enlarge the party's representative function from a strictly class centered one into one more nationally oriented. This position was made explicit by Gomulka in his March 16, 1965, speech to the Central Committee when he stated that "Our party . . . represents not only the working class. . . [it] represents also the alliance of workers and peasants, as well as the alliance of the working class and the intelligentsia; it represents toiling masses of town and country; it represents all national interests. . .The political system of our country does not, therefore, imply a representation of particular classes and social strata by separate political parties."[11]

To a certain extent, this shift in the party's sociopolitical orientation resulted from massive structural changes which had taken place in Polish society since the end of World War II. They were said to have reflected a "process of disappearance of objective class differences within the society as well as the weakening of separate interest orientations based on a class character."[12] Consequently, the ideological requirement of a narrowly defined proletarian identification of the party appeared to have lost its practical justification. Yet the structural transformation was not the only, or even the most important, factor behind the PUWP's efforts at broadening its sociopolitical representativeness. Much more significant appears to have been the realization that the party could fulfill its self-assumed leadership responsibilities only if it gained public support for its rule and cooperation with its activities. Under those circumstances, the new definition of the party as a national rather than proletarian organization was indicative of a major effort to secure popular acceptance of its rule. Its most significant consequence was the change in the style and methods of political leadership. Persuasion and manipulation, rather than pressure and coercion, became the order of the day. The directing role of the party increasingly became a function of its ability to regulate social conflicts and to accommodate demands of various interests within the existing framework of power relations.

To the degree that this situation suggested the danger of a lasting departure from established goals and principles, it presented the party with a serious ideological and operational challenge. The inevitable loss of ideological vitality was already decried in late 1959, when a member of the Central Committee publicly warned that stabilizing and integrative policies contributed to "the fading of the ideological pulse of the party."[13] Subsequently, Gomulka himself, speaking to the Central Committee meeting in July 1963, drew attention to "the weakness of the party's ideological work" and called for a broad ideological offensive toward a "complete victory of socialist consciousness in the hearts and minds of the working class, of all working people, and of the entire nation."[14] And yet, those warnings and appeals seemed rather hollow. The ideological concepts and commitments, so far as they had been historically linked to conflict and polarization, were singularly out of place in a situation in which the most important task for the party was to secure popular acceptance, gain stability, and solidify the system in place.

On the level of practical politics, the proliferation of various interest orientations significantly affected the party's capacity for effective implementation of its tasks of political leadership. The long-term implications of this development for the party itself were clearly acknowledged and explicitly described in the following terms: "In the struggle for the goal of socialism the party finds itself entangled with various interests: class. . .strata, group, professional, regional, immediate and long-term, generational and so on. They create social situations which frequently do not correspond to the situations envisaged and planned by the party. These various interests have a definite influence upon the party, particularly upon its strategy and tactics, its composition and its authority, as well as upon other elements of its structure."[15] Thus, the extension of the party's representative functions, an important aspect of its integrative and stabilizing efforts, became a critical factor in shaping the nature of its power and the methods of its political operations.

Closely related to the modifications in the party's political role were changes in the composition and social character of its membership. Among the most obvious features of this evolution was a rapid numerical expansion of the party ranks. At the end of 1959, having gone through several massive politically oriented purges, the party had only 1,018,466 members, the lowest level of its popular appeal since 1948. Seeking to strengthen its links with society, the leadership decided both to enlarge the membership and to broaden its social base. The policy of renewed recruitment, which had been set by the third congress in March 1959 and then temporarily postponed until the exchange of membership cards was completed in September, was unveiled with great determination. During 1960 the size of the party increased by more than 136,000 or 13.4 percent and in the period of 1960–1970 the net growth averaged in excess of 7 percent per year. The resulting expansion brought more than a million new members into the party ranks (see Appendix 1).

Such an emphasis on growth clearly reflected the party's functional concern with preserving its politically dominant position in society. This concern was frankly admitted by the secretary of the Central Committee in charge of personnel, Roman Zambrowski, who in his speech to the third congress pointed out that "as a ruling party, which is responsible for everything which goes on in the country, [the PUWP] must have its organizations. . .in all important places of work, in institutions, in the organs of authority, in villages, in universities, in schools—in short, in the entire organism of the national life, wherever this life is being created and developed."[16] Through the expansion of its membership, the party sought to enhance its ability to control and influence the social, economic, and political activities of all sectors of the population. However, this effort created specific political difficulties as well, the most important being the weakening of ties between the party and the workers. Traditionally, the ideologically defined link to the workers served as a *sui generis* legitimizing basis for the party as a proletarian organization. For this reason, the party leadership always insisted on providing preferential access to the party to manual workers and poor peasants. But with the adoption of the mass recruitment policy, the party turned its attention toward attracting other social groups into the organization. As a result, the proletarian component of its membership was bound to decline, undermining the very principle of legitimacy itself.

To prevent this from happening, the leadership imposed a recruiting requirement of stable proportional representation for different social groups in the composition of party membership.[17] As a result, the ratios of workers, peasants, and white-collar employees has not changed significantly since 1959, with the proletarian groups—workers and peasants—maintaining a permanent majority (about 55 percent) among the party's rank and file (see Appendix 1).

Notwithstanding this consistency in the statistical aspects of the party evolution, frequently stressed by various Polish writers as exemplifying the PUWP's success in creating the party of social integration,[18] the membership's stability remained more apparent than real. In effect, the mass enrollment has, since 1960, created severe problems of assimilation. In the years 1959–1970 more than 500,000 members were either expelled or purged from the party. In most cases, the reasons for elimination were organizational and ideological apathy, criminal or immoral behavior, drunkenness and other disciplinary offenses. The workers and the peasants were the main victims of the process of purification. They made up almost 82 percent of the members eliminated from the party in the period between 1959–1970. By contrast, the white-collar groups maintained considerable stability within the party and made up the greatest share in membership expansion.[19]

The most consistent gains were made by educated and professionally trained employees, particularly from among the technical and vocational intelligentsia. The number of technicians, engineers, and economists within the party more than doubled in the years 1960–1970, while that of doctors, teachers, and scientists increased threefold. If projected on society at large, these figures showed that, by the end of 1969, about 40 percent of all engineers and about 44 percent of all technicians belonged to the party, while the proportion of party members among teachers reached almost 40 percent. In general, the proportion of party members among the white-collar employees reached more than 27 percent, while only 13 percent of workers and 4 percent of peasants could be found in the party ranks.[20] If nothing else, these trends seemed to indicate a process of rapid deproletarianization of the party for which the white-collar groups became the main base of social support.

These changes in the membership's social composition had inevitable consequences in shaping the style and direction of party work. The most significant factor of this evolution was the growing role of technicians and experts in the party's activist group. According to data from the early 1960s concerning large industrial plants and local administrative organs, the highest degree of party activism was found among "men whose jobs required a fairly high degree of technical skill [and] who had a relatively high level of education."[21] They provided about 25 percent of the entire activist group, which accounted in 1964 for more than 261,000 party members elected to sit on various social commissions and councils permanently attached to provincial and district committees of the party.

The militancy of the technical and professional intelligentsia was not, however, due to group organization or politically motivated actions. It resulted rather from the penetration of occupational and political functions to provide expert knowledge in decision-making activities at different levels of power. As for the technical personnel, the motives for activist involvement in party work seemed to have reflected the conviction that ". . .through participation in the work of party committees and organs [it could] realize its desire for influence over the management of the enterprise, in matters which are the subject of its professional activity."[22] With respect to the party, its increasingly managerial preoccupations, inherent in the process of political stabilization, dictated a necessity for a broad mobilization of qualified personnel to fulfill its leadership functions. The net effect of this fusion between the party activist group and the technical intelligentsia, however, was the gradual emergence of a "tendency away from politically minded, traditional and past-oriented people to managerial, rational and achievement-oriented men"[23] in political recruitment. On the operational level, this signaled an evolving trend toward more pragmatic and technologically oriented solutions in socio-economic policies, coupled with a measure of disregard for earlier revolutionary commitments.

Still, broader forms of a lasting transformation in the basic structures of decision making were precluded by strong elements in political and organizational continuity within the party. Although the trend toward managerial orientation had an undeniable impact on party evolution, a considerable residue of older and experienced Communists remained within the activist component of the organization. Concentrated in the local echelons of power, they constituted about 30–40 percent of the activist groups in small towns and less important industrial establishments.[24] Faced with growing pressure from the more pragmatic elements, they gradually developed a defensive posture and ". . .often plotted against newcomers, manifested strongly uncooperative attitudes toward new style executive power, grudgingly opposed the imminent change, and tried to organize 'old inhabitants' or 'old activists' against the newcomers and the politics they symbolized."[25] This created lasting political strains within the party itself, laying foundations for a severe organizational conflict and, in the meantime, providing a serious obstacle to the implementation of structural reforms and changes.

Another element of continuity was the long-established set of operational principles which effectively limited participation in decision making to a select group of professional party functionaries. Despite considerable political changes following the gradual abandonment of the revolutionary strategy, the party preserved a monolithic framework of essentially revolutionary organization. The distribution of power was still based on the principle of democratic centralism, which gave monopolistic authority to the central leadership. Although lip service was repeatedly paid to the importance of "intraparty democracy," its practical significance was effectively restricted by a rule that the "intraparty democracy cannot be used for purposes other than those which reflect the interest of the party, and particularly. . .[it cannot lead to] any activity of a factional or group character, any activity against the party's ideology, its general political line, or the unity of its organizational ranks."[26] In short, the organizational character of the party remained a function of its hierarchical cohesion, with the main emphasis on obedience of lower level cadres to top leadership.

Within this framework, the key political role continued to be played by party professional staff, the apparatus. Just as it had provided the institutional backbone in party efforts at revolutionary social transformation, the apparatus was given the task of stabilization and regulation of organizational work. To a large extent, such operational continuity was an inevitable consequence of the political ferment within the party, which had arisen from the initial measures of de-Stalinization. As concern grew within the top leadership over the dogmatic opposition and revisionist pressures for change, the apparatus emerged as the only element in the party capable of upholding the centralistic line. If nothing else, the professional staff's maintenance of organizational supervision over the implementation of policy decisions made it necessary for the leadership to secure its loyalty and cooperation. At the same time, several steps were taken by the top party leaders to change the character and the style of work of the apparatus to make it compatible with the new political objectives of stabilization.

Perhaps the most obvious change was the reduction of the full-time staff. After early 1957, the size of the apparatus drastically declined from about 14,500 to 7,800 in 1963. After the fourth congress of the party in June 1964, the number of political party employees stabilized at around 7,000.[27] In part, these measures were the consequence of a political strategy to eliminate those party officials who, because of either excessive doctrinal orthodoxy or reformist convictions, found themselves at odds with the stability-oriented leadership. In addition, this process of internal purification reflected the leadership's attempt to create a more efficient staff, one capable of coping with the increasingly complex problems of implementing the party program of economic development. This task was officially proclaimed fulfilled in 1964, when Politburo member Zenon Kliszko reported to the fourth congress that "At present, the employees of our party apparatus represent a much greater knowledge and a better understanding in matters of industry and agriculture than the party functionaries of the 1940s, whose interests concentrated mainly on institutional and political problems, who were primarily organizers of the revolution and the people's power, completely devoted to social activity."[28]

In spite of such assurances, the leadership's success in changing the character of the apparatus was most problematical. The main obstacles were related to the continuing qualitative weakness of the party staff and its organizational and political orthodoxy. The capacity of the apparatus to control the party's developmental activities remained doubtful. In 1964 only 17.8 percent of the full-time functionaries were university graduates, while 55.3 percent had secondary education. It is true that even that could be construed as a significant improvement from the situation in 1959, when the graduates of universities and secondary schools had amounted to merely 7 and 22.3 percent, respectively. But the fact that about one-third of all party employees had only primary schooling or less could hardly suggest that they were well equipped to direct the party, and through it the country, toward fulfillment of ambitious plans of economic and social evolution. In terms of occupational experience, about 37 percent had economic or managerial background and 15 percent specialized in social work, history, and ideology. Furthermore, there was no indication that economic experts or other professionally trained individuals were being coopted into the staff. Instead, considerable emphasis was placed on training already employed political workers. In 1964 more than half of those with diplomas in the apparatus earned them while working full-time for the organization. This practice continued throughout the 1960s.[29]

With respect to the political character of the apparatus, the entire staff was dominated by essentially traditionalist officials. In 1964 more than 70 percent of the employees (4,000) had entered the party before 1948 and 15 percent (about 1,000) had membership tenure since World War II or earlier. More than half of them had been employed in the party for five years or longer and 4 percent had held staff positions for more than fifteen years. The rigorous training acquired in the organizational ranks of the party during its revolutionary phase made most of the staff members suspicious of the possible long-range political implications of the new integrative and stabilizing strategy for their institutional position. Hence, although they had been in favor of the initial measures of de-Stalinization, particularly those that limited the power of the security organs, they strongly resisted any changes which could jeopardize the established patterns of organizational control. This resulted in the conscious and continuing effort by the party professional machine to limit the direction and the pace of the processes of social and economic change.[30]

Given this traditionalist ethos of the politically crucial segment of the party organization, actual implementation of the strategy of evolutionary change remained in doubt. Despite the growth of an internally diversified activist movement, which might have created the source for broader participation in party work and through it for elaboration of new ways of political operation, its impact on internal processes of policy formation was largely circumvented by the long-established functionaries. The working relationship between the apparatus and the activists remained firmly grounded in the principle of strict subordination of the latter to the party staff. In this manner, in spite of the reorientation of developmental tasks, the change in the political role of the party, and the increasingly heterogeneous composition of its membership, the apparatus, which had been recruited and shaped during the revolutionary phase, continued to hold controlling positions within the organization.

In trying to explain the reasons for this remarkable continuity, two sets of factors should be taken into consideration. One was related to the need for preserving a modicum of traditional organizational patterns under conditions of a rapidly changing social and political environment. The leadership's concern with the possible political implications of this change for the party was clearly shown in Kliszko's speech to the fourth congress, in which he pointed out that "the circumstantial change in party work as well as in the tasks facing the apparatus, does not mean and must not be considered as a change in the essence of party work." He then strongly stressed the necessity of preserving the "continuity of the work of the party apparatus," to be achieved only through the practice of assigning staff positions to experienced officials, who would act as socializing agents for younger functionaries. As for the new appointees, "their moral, political, and professional qualifications would be constantly verified in the process of their work."[31] The practical expression of this concern was the effort to consolidate staff work on the central level after the third party congress in 1959. Within a year, seven out of ten staff departments received new directors, all of them experienced functionaries of the Bierutist party machine.[32]

Another set of factors was related to the growing political divisiveness within the party. Seemingly, there was nothing new about the factional fragmentation of the PUWP; since the mid-1950s it had been repeatedly torn by internal dissension and strife. And yet, intraparty cleavages that developed during the 1960s appeared to have acquired a political character of their own, presenting the leadership with qualitatively different problems.

The traditional patterns of factional politics had centered on fundamental questions of rule. Thus, the main issue of dispute between the *Pulawska* and the *Natolin* groups in 1956 revolved around succession to the party leadership and the related choice between two completely different programs of political action. Similarly, the crucial problems behind the division among the dogmatic and the revisionist wings of the party, which had emerged after the October 1956 plenum, concerned basic conceptual differences on the direction and scope of a comprehensive reorganization of the entire political system. However, largely due to the fundamentalist character of these divisions, their actual importance for the party remained limited in duration, even if political scars from the bitter encounters provided grounds for lasting personal animosities among the members of the party elite. Furthermore, they had never achieved a formal organizational or institutional identification. The ascendency of Gomulka to the party's leadership, while not fully satisfying to any of the groups, put an end to the quarrels over political succession. The subsequent consolidation of his power effectively precluded continuation of the disputes over political reorganization. The influence of the principal revisionist spokesmen was rapidly curtailed and many of them were promptly removed from positions of power within the party. As for the dogmatic conservatives, most of them rejoined the mainstream of organizational activity while some, most notably several former low-ranking Stalinist luminaries such as Wiktor Klosiewicz and Kazimierz Mijal, escaped from Poland to Albania and set up there in 1966 a separate Communist Party of Poland with a strongly pro-Chinese orientation.[33]

With the adoption of the stabilizing strategy, a new pattern of intraparty divisions came to the fore. It resulted from two distinct but mutually related processes arising from the operational formula itself. The first was the change in the character of the party's sociopolitical representativeness. To the degree that the party sought to become a sole political forum within which all social interests could be expressed, it opened up possibilities of a relative pluralization of views and influences in the organization. This development acquired a special importance at the policy-making levels where ". . .those who actually hold power very often consider themselves as merely representatives of the broader groups of the population. . .[and] the inner differences with the ruling groups do not represent their own interests only. . .[but] are subject to pressures from various 'outside' groups."[34] The second was the change in the party's developmental objectives. As the leadership's attention shifted from social transformation toward integration, preoccupation with finding the most effective means of evolutionary management acquired singular importance. Some of the party's activists and leaders saw the solution in a nationalist reaffirmation of Poland's traditional values, others considered expansion of the industrial potential and modernization as the best if not the only response to developmental problems. The frequent incompatibility between those views created a major source of tension among the party groupings.

More important, the unfolding social and functional divisions within the party gradually developed structural, if not semi-institutional identities. This development was particularly significant as it indicated that, in spite of the statutory ban on factional activities, the top leadership was unable to secure lasting consolidation of its power within the party. Its politically crucial features were the extent and the forms of the organizational fragmentation. While the earlier manifestations of factional activity had either centered on top levels of the party hierarchy or developed on the fringes of its organizational structure, the disagreements over the scope and direction of stabilization cut across formal patterns of organization. They gradually produced several separate centers of aggregation, with their own internal characteristics and specific forms of political activity. Interestingly, their emergence did not entail ideological diversification within the party. The factional politics under conditions of stabilization seemed completely devoid of any doctrinal content. The main accent was on tactical, intraparty differences over methods of policy implementation, rather than its conceptual justification.

Perhaps the most important center of factional aggression was a group of so-called Partisans. The hard core of this group was composed of veterans of the wartime communist underground. By virtue of this background, they had been closely associated with Wladyslaw Gomulka since his emergence as the leader of the Polish Workers' Party. In fact, most of them had shared his disgrace during the Stalinist period and had returned to active political life only after Gomulka's comeback in 1956. In the post-October Poland they quickly rose to positions of influence and two of their most prominent leaders, Generals Mieczyslaw Moczar and Grzegorz Korczynski, were put in charge of political and military security, respectively. Both men were also members of the Central Committee of the PUWP.

By the mid-1960s, the Partisans established a firm institutional base for their activities in the Ministry of Internal Affairs and the security and political branches of the armed forces. This became particularly apparent after Moczar's appointment, in November 1964, to head the ministry. He immediately brought several of his supporters, including Colonel Franciszek Szlachcic as his deputy, to key security posts and created a true fiefdom of Partisan influence within the formal structure of government.

The political attitudes of the group were based largely on its past experiences. As native Communists who had earned their positions during underground struggles against the Germans in Poland, the Partisans professed contempt for those party leaders who had spent the war in the Soviet Union and returned with the Red Army in 1944. They had been humiliated by the Muscovites' control over the party and a thorough purge of domestic elements from political positions during the Bierut regime. Since many Muscovites were Jews, the Partisans' attitude toward them was markedly anti-Semitic. Their wartime activity provided a strong retrospective pride in Polish military achievements and left a discernible nationalistic imprint on the Partisans' political vision.

The issue of nationalism won considerable public sympathy for the Partisans, giving Moczar an opportunity to channel popular discontent to his political support. In 1964 he became the president of ZBoWiD (Union of Fighters for Freedom and Democracy), a veterans' organization formed in 1949 but completely insignificant until then. Under his leadership, it became one of the most important organizations in the country, with a membership of more than 250,000 by the end of 1967.[35] It grouped not only former communist partisans, but also a considerable number of non-communist resistance fighters who until then had been politically disaffected by the official lack of recognition for their past patriotic efforts.

This ability to capitalize on social frustrations by uniting diversified elements into a single movement became a major source of the Partisans' political strength. Although their power base centered on security apparatus, which might have been in different circumstances considered a serious liability, the deliberately nationalistic posture of their operations received a positive response from a large segment of the population. For many a Pole who had long been deprived of a voice in public matters, the Partisans provided a unique channel to participation in political life. As for the Partisans themselves, their nationalistic appeals were indicative of "a clever long-term strategy of creating a multitude of vested interests and a broad base of personal allegiance as a substitute for an attractive political platform."[36] Taken together, however, both these factors heralded the emergence of a political force which was to become a serious obstacle for the leadership's efforts at lasting stabilization of the system in place.

Another source of factional activity was provided by a much less structured, but equally influential, group of managerially oriented politicians. To a certain extent, this tendency within the party was an inevitable consequence of the continuing program of economic modernization and industrial development. The growing complexity of socioeconomic evolution, sponsored by the leadership itself, created the need for greater specialization in problem-solving activities. The gradually unfolding functional division of labor was perceived by many party officials as a signal for a new pattern in political relationships in which highly trained personnel should play a significant, if not decisive, role. Preoccupied with problems of efficiency and productivity rather than ideological motivations, they were gradually increasing pressure upon the top leadership, demanding new policies and operational methods.

The most prominent spokesman for this group was Edward Gierek, a Politburo member since March 1959 and first secretary of the provincial party committee in Silesia, the most industrialized region of Poland. The pivotal importance of this province for the country's economy provided Gierek with a special opportunity to demand and receive far-reaching political concessions from top leadership with respect to administrative and operational autonomy for himself and his local party organization. In turn, Gierek proved to be an able economic administrator. His success gave him a growing reputation for political ability in party management and control as well as an understanding of economic problems. Gierek's appeal was particularly strong among younger engineers and technicians, who had only recently joined the party and saw the Silesian leader as the only prominent politician capable of pulling the country out of its persistent economic difficulties.

In essence, the technologically bent group appeared to represent a political tendency within the party rather than an organized faction, with its political objectives seemingly limited to "ensuring for [itself] the right to run the economy without the constant interference of 'incompetent politicians'."[37] Yet, to the degree that it developed a discernible power base in the Silesian province and found an effective and powerful spokesman in Edward Gierek, its activities gradually acquired the political meaning of supplying an alternative to the leadership in place.

Along those two principal factional orientations, there were numerous other groupings and cliques operating within the party. However, in the actual process of political action, their composition could not be clearly identified and they could not be easily separated from one another. They never achieved institutional identification, even if particular characteristics were given as a reason for their association, as would be the case with hardliners or liberals, or if some political figures were considered as their heads. In a given situation or with regard to a specific policy they could cross the hypothetical lines of differentiation or recruit some *ad hoc,* temporary allies within or outside the party itself. In addition, old personal animosities and ethnic differences as well as the entire spectrum of functional, professional, and social links provided grounds for a constantly changing network of political alliances and hostilities within the decision-making organs of the party.

To a large extent, this internal fragmentation of the party resulted from political disparities inherent in Gomulka's leadership. Having gradually consolidated his power over the party, which had been torn by bitter controversies surrounding the issue of post-Stalinist reorganization, Gomulka was determined not to introduce any major changes lest a faulty move reinforce the tensions. The influence of principal advocates of political, economic, and social reforms was considerably curtailed and many of them were removed from positions of authority within the party. Among the most prominent casualties of this process were Central Committee secretaries Jerzy Albrecht, Jerzy Morawski, and Wladyslaw Matwin, who during the years 1960–1963 were transferred to less exposed posts in the state administration. Their party offices, in turn, were given to politically orthodox and organizationally experienced functionaries. In a way, these changes were indicative of Gomulka's attempt to establish himself as the only leader responsible for the definition of the party's post-Stalinist character and power. But they also heralded a regressive turnabout in his consideration of types of individuals who should occupy responsible positions in the leading party organs.

A concomitant development was the shift in Gomulka's basis of political support. When he came to power in October 1956, the main source of his authority had been overwhelming support from the entire population, which had seen in Gomulka a symbol of long-suppressed nationalistic and anti-Soviet sentiments. But his initial program for the Polish road to socialism, albeit never elaborated in great detail, gradually turned into a system of rule marked by growing authoritarianism in domestic affairs and loyal obedience to the Soviet Union in foreign relations. Failure to satisfy the expectations of the social forces which had brought him to power rapidly eroded Gomulka's popularity and gave way to spreading discontent and dissatisfaction. Gradually, the dominant element of Gomulka's political strength became his close personal relationship with top Soviet leaders.

The basis of this accommodation had been established during the Soviet-Polish negotiations in October 1956 and, following Gomulka's trip to the Soviet Union in October-November 1958, it subsequently solidified into a personal relationship between Khrushchev and Gomulka "clearly marked by mutual respect if not cordiality."[38] The essence of this rapprochement was Soviet acceptance of internal autonomy for the Polish party while the Poles unequivocally supported Moscow's leadership in foreign affairs and the international communist movement. Its political significance for the situation in the PUWP became obvious when Khrushchev, during his visit to Poland in July 1959, called Gomulka "the dear friend of the Soviet Union" and explicitly warned his potential opponents that "those who do not support the policy of the Polish United Workers' Party, the policy of Comrade Gomulka, provide grist to the mills of revisionism, although they may criticize its leadership from an ultra-leftist position and accuse it of deviation from Marxism-Leninism."[39] Khrushchev's fall in 1964 did not bring any changes in relations between Gomulka and new Soviet leaders. Gomulka's political stature was even further enhanced by Brezhnev and Kosygin, who came to Poland to explain personally the changed situation. Gomulka, in turn, once again stressed that the Polish-Soviet alliance was regarded in Warsaw as the "cornerstone of Polish foreign policy."[40]

Although those modifications in Gomulka's domestic and foreign policy orientations might have appeared antithetical to the values that he seemed to have initially professed, they remained fully consistent with his understanding of the political situation in the party as well as the appreciation of his own role within the organization. As for the situation in the party, Gomulka was certainly aware that most of the staff and important officialdom had been organizationally and politically shaped under Bierut's supervision into a firm Stalinist pattern. They had never been loyal to Gomulka himself and accepted his return to leadership mainly because he was the only major communist political figure capable of salvaging the party after the Stalinist debacle. After 1956, therefore, Gomulka remained an isolated leader within his own party, surrounded by former political enemies and critics. However, he could not dispense with his traditional antagonists without undertaking a large-scale reorganization of the party, a course of action clearly inimical to the general purpose of political stabilization itself. In this situation, the maintenance of

Soviet support, particularly in the face of a waning public allegiance, constituted a key determinant of his power and political authority within the party.

Furthermore, whether through political cautiousness or plain lack of vision, Gomulka failed to countenance the resurgence of nationalism or the rise of technocratic trends within the party organization. Instead, he adopted a highly manipulative strategy of dealing with specific factions, controlling top political appointments, and playing one faction against the other to create a subdued equilibrium among the various party forces. Thus, to neutralize the influence of innovative technocrats and in response to a sudden economic crisis in 1959, Gomulka brought back to prominence a group of former Stalinist planners and economists, including former deputy to Hilary Minc, Eugeniusz Szyr, and former Bierut staffers Julian Tokarski and Tadeusz Gede. At the same time, however, he also accepted the inclusion of Edward Gierek to the party's Politburo. Similar tactics were employed with the Partisans. Although Moczar and Korczynski were given control over security forces, they remained administratively subordinated to politically safer officials. Moczar's activity was partially neutralized by Wladyslaw Wicha, a former deputy minister in Bierut's security apparatus, who had headed the Ministry of Internal Affairs until 1964 when he was transferred to the Central Committee's secretariat in charge of internal security matters. Korczynski always remained under close supervision of Marian Spychalski, a long-time friend and associate of Gomulka, who had become minister of national defense in November 1956 and continued ever since.

Gomulka's efforts to maintain a seemingly safe pattern of political checks and balances within the party's power structure extended to the highest organ of institutionalized authority, the Politburo. The main emphasis was on continuity and stability, with gradual expansion of the membership indicating Gomulka's attempts to respond to the political demands of emerging new groups within the party. The rate of turnover in the Politburo remained very low. At the end of 1967, seven out of nine members of the original Gomulka leadership from October 1956 retained their seats. Only Jerzy Morawski and Roman Zambrowski, two prominent leaders of the former Pulawska group, resigned during the early 1960s. The process of expanding membership indicated the growing preoccupation of the leadership with economic problems. In 1959 Edward Gierek was elected as a full member and in 1964 four additional economic leaders were brought into the Politburo. They included Eugeniusz Szyr and Franciszek Waniolka as full members, and Mieczyslaw Jagielski and Piotr Jaroszewicz as deputy members. By contrast, no Partisan leaders gained entrance to the party high council, even if they reportedly maintained close contacts with Ryszard Strzelecki, a deputy member of the Politburo since 1964 and Central Committee secretary in charge of personnel.[41]

This precarious balance of tendencies within the party was possible mainly because of the special role played by Wladyslaw Gomulka in the party and the political system. His personal experience of political persecution during the Stalinist period, as well as the unique opportunity of returning to power in 1956 as the only leader acceptable to almost all factional groups, allowed him to keep an independent position within the organization. But this also contributed to the growing political isolation of Gomulka from the party's mainstream. Distrustful of other party leaders and reticent to delegate responsibility over important matters to any but a few of his oldest associates, Gomulka gradually established a highly personalized and restrictive manner of rule. Commenting on this situation, a knowledgeable Western observer pointed out that by the mid-1960s Gomulka became "regularly accessible to only a small handful of old supporters and friends, of whom the most important were the three Politburo members Kliszko, Loga-Sowinski, and Spychalski, all of whom had been disgraced with him in 1948–1949."[42] Such exclusive relationships within the party leadership were crucial in shaping the form and the direction of decision making. They led to the emergence of an informal nucleus within the party institutional elite, consisting of trusted and proven Gomulka loyalists primarily interested in preserving his power and eliminating any possibility of opposition or threat to it rather than in providing innovative ideas on change and development. As such, they were incapable of aggregating, articulating, representing, or acting on key interests and demands of those groups within the party which became increasingly concerned with the need, if not the necessity of further evolution. As for Gomulka, having consolidated institutional mastery over the political resources of the party, he was determined to enforce his own understanding of Polish internal evolution. His attitude toward factional leaders and orientations was characterized by a contemptuous paternalism. He might "allow" them to organize and agitate but in the end it was clear that his ". . .directives were unchallengeable, that. . .[he] was not to be argued with."[43]

The distinctive quality of Gomulka's leadership was the main factor shaping political life in the country at large. Paradoxically, since he had been possibly the most outspoken critic of the cult of personality outside of the Soviet Union, Gomulka's personal attributes became the most important defining elements of the political system. As Nicholas Bethell remarked, "in decision making and administration Gomulka was demanding a finger in every pie. . . his chief attribute had been stubbornness [which]. . .turned into a sort of arrogance, the self-satisfied feeling of a ruler who knows that his people cannot vote him out of office even if they want to, that barring accidents he will be able to continue as ruler for decades."[44] Just as in the case of intraparty politics, Gomulka's main approach to social and economic problems was manipulation. Although it originated in a relatively dynamic movement toward rationalization and modernization, his Polish road to socialism rapidly turned away from the initial program of reforms. But there was also no attempt to return to the political and social excesses of Stalinism. Instead, Gomulka's policy focused on perpetuating the existing system, with the pace of change reduced to a minimum and closely supervised by the essentially conservative and inert party machine. In an effort to defuse the initial, post-October political aspirations of the population, Gomulka encouraged the proliferation of numerous quasi-political organizations but then refused to grant them even a modicum of autonomy and independence. As a result, even if the political significance of coercion and police diminished considerably, the very foundations of power and influence remained the same. Gomulka's system continued as an institutional monument to stultifying centralism in decision making but without clearly defined purpose or direction and with diminished predisposition to oppression.

However, this personalized manner of stability-oriented, centralistic rule severely conflicted with existing political, social, and organizational realities of the system. Intraparty fragmentation, continuing social divisiveness, and an overriding uncertainty as to the future evolution of Poland's society and economy effectively undermined, if not prevented, actual acceptance and implementation of Gomulka's policies. His determination to maintain continuing patterns of sociopolitical checks and balances precluded the meaningful evolution of the system and exacerbated rather than solved Poland's many developmental problems. Under these conditions, dissatisfaction welled up from many sources and, while prompted by a variety of different motives, became increasingly assertive in the generalized demand for something new.

More and more, Gomulka's strategy of stabilization seemed to create a real danger of political disintegration and institutional decay. Inevitably, the spreading malaise led to a gradual erosion of his authority within the party and a growth of opposition to his policies as well as the manner of his rule. By the late 1960s, the very concept of stabilization advocated by Gomulka came under attack. As Gierek pointed out in an article which, appearing in early 1968, was ostensibly concerned with economic management but clearly aimed at the entire style of Gomulka's leadership, ". . .ill-conceived stabilization makes it possible to attach the label of a good manager or an activist on everyone. . .who 'stabilized himself' at a level achieved some years ago. What makes it even worse, if a proponent of such stabilization occupies a responsible position, he is inclined to recruit close associates from among people who think alike—who prefer stillness, who are opposed to all new proposals. Stabilization conceived in this manner is essentially nothing but stagnation and an impediment to our development."[45]

To the degree that Gierek's complaint was indicative of a mounting criticism of Gomulka's methods of rule, it became clear that the centralistic strategy of stabilization produced a political impasse. Its solution required a change in the course of action through which the direction of future evolution of the system could be determined. Until then, anything that could rally politically disaffected groups within the party might have spurred a needed impetus for change.

Years of Crisis: 1968–1971

The ultimate collapse of Gomulka's strategy of stabilization was precipitated by an outburst in early 1968 of intellectual and student protests against the party's restrictive cultural policy. The immediate cause of the protests was the official ban of a theatrical production of *Dziady* [The Forefathers' Eve], a romantic drama by nineteenth century poet Adam Mickiewicz. The play has always been considered a cultural monument of national proportions and an historical symbol of patriotism and romantic liberty. Its abrupt closing at the end of January 1968 touched off a wave of popular indignation. But the significance of the protest went beyond any specific outrage with the government's decision. Rather, to the degree that the banning of the play confirmed the party's long-established assumption that it had an undisputed right to control all cultural activities, the intellectual opposition was indicative of a growing collision between the party's leadership and a crucial segment of Polish society, and of a conflict in interpretation of the basic principles of Poland's cultural life.

In many respects, this conflict was not new. For many years the intellectual ferment had simmered under the politically passive surface. Occasionally, sporadic resistance to certain party decisions had brought the existing disagreements into the open. The most dramatic manifestation of this opposition was the "Letter of 34" sent in March 1964 by a group of prominent intellectuals to the then premier Jozef Cyrankiewicz as a protest against censorship and restriction of newsprint.[1] In subsequent demonstrations of dissent, criticism centered on the question of party control over intellectual creativity. A movement of sustained intellectual opposition began to grow at Polish universities. It was particularly noticeable at Warsaw University, where a small community of radical dissenters took shape. This movement had no organized form, consisting of a variety of separate groupings ranging from the former political militants of October 1956 to newly admitted students. Although vocal in certain university circles, they remained politically insignificant on the larger national scene. Their activity was characterized more by a desire to stimulate academic discussions on political subjects, in private gatherings and in university-sponsored clubs, than by any conspiracy against the state. The element of potential unification for the movement was provided by a common rejection of the authoritarian aspects of the existing political system.

The best known result of those debates was the much-publicized "Open Letter to the Party," a sort of political manifesto written by two teaching assistants, Jacek Kuron and Karol Modzelewski. Smuggled out of Poland in 1965, it called for an internal "revolution" to abolish the "bureaucratic power elite" and the establishment of a true "workers' democracy."[2] However, these views were not wholly representative of the dissenting students. There were several other groups with diametrically different opinions, which they manifested in a number of protest meetings and critical statements.[3]

The high point of intellectual dissent was reached at a mass meeting at Warsaw University, convened in October 1966 to mark the tenth anniversary of Gomulka's coming to power. The main speaker, Leszek Kolakowski, severely condemned the economic, social, and cultural policies of the leadership and "charged that the ruling party oligarchy continued to act in an arbitrary and authoritarian manner and paid no proper attention to the just postulates of the population." The subsequently adopted resolution urged that the people "should have the right to express publicly differing views concerning the principles of the functioning of socialist democracy in our country. These principles should also be the subject of free discussion in the press."[4]

As frequent and ambitious as it was, the intellectual dissent was never able to affect the direction of policy making. The activity of the principal critics of the party remained dependent upon reactions and decisions of the leadership. Kuron and Modzelewski were promptly arrested after their "Letter" was made public, while Kolakowski and several of his supporters were punished by expulsion from the party ranks. Indeed, the party's interference in cultural life only intensified during 1967. By the end of that year, a prominent Catholic writer and politician, Stanislaw Stomma, pointed in a parliamentary speech to an alarming "tendency to silence discussions and to forbid all expression of other views" and he warned that "there is an attempt here to control the minds."[5]

Given this growth in restrictive trends, the closing down of *Dziady,* followed by a ban on several other plays, constituted a virtual provocation for the intellectual community. Its inevitable consequence was a further escalation of protest and dissent. Indicative of this trend was an extraordinary meeting of the Polish Writers Union, held in Warsaw at the end of February to discuss the *Dziady* affair. Much of the discussion was taken up with a condemnation of the tactics used in the removal of the play. But behind the opposition to this particular decision lay a more general criticism of the pattern of political rule in Poland. The cultural policy of the party was compared to a "dictatorship of ignoramuses" and the Polish system was said to have "nothing in common with socialism and Marxism." The final resolution strongly attacked the official policy.[6]

Meanwhile, the developments at Warsaw University indicated a constant growth of political tension. A petition condemning the ban on *Dziady* was sent to the Sejm on February 16 with more than 3,000 signatures. University authorities retorted by expelling two students accused of organizing the demonstration. This decision prompted a mass protest meeting on March 8 at the university. Although originally planned as a peaceful display of student dissatisfaction, it turned into a riot after the sudden intrusion of police and armed vigilantes. As a result of the ensuing fighting, several hundred students were arrested. Many of them were immediately tried and sentenced on charges of "hooliganism and insulting the police."[7]

The brutality with which the student meeting was suppressed provoked a wave of protests in other Warsaw schools and quickly spread to almost all provincial universities. This resulted in a series of violent confrontations between police and students throughout the country. In time, a gradual subsidence of street violence gave way to an all-national student sit-in strike. This phase of the protest movement concluded at the end of March, when the last demonstrators left the buildings of the Warsaw Polytechnic Institute.

The political significance of the student protests was considerable. For the first time since October 1956, large segments of the student population throughout the country publicly manifested their grievances. However, this sudden activism did not result from the popularity of radical political causes. Rather, it was instigated by the brutality of state intervention in university affairs. Whatever had been the role of the dissenting activists in initiating the disturbances, the leadership of the student movement quickly passed into the hands of politically moderate elements. This change was evident, since the majority of well-known dissenters were arrested either before the March 8 demonstration or immediately afterwards. In this situation, the bulk of the demands voiced by the protesters was concentrated on purely academic and educational grievances which, significantly, were never presented as an open challenge to the system. Indeed, they were purposely kept within the limits of existing legal and ideological principles. Moderation and restraint were clearly expressed in the final declaration issued in Warsaw on March 28, 1968, which summed up the demands of the students in appealing for the establishment of "a student political organization which will truly express the aims of academic circles." While stressing that such an organization "ought to be assured freedom of political action," the declaration also promised that "in view of the ideological and undeniably socialist character of the student movement, this freedom will be used within those limits which the socialist character of our state creates."[8]

This limited scope of student demands definitely precluded any extension of academic dissent into other segments of society. Support of the non-student population for the demonstrators remained restricted to passive sympathy with some rare and sporadic signs of active participation. At the same time, the extent and spontaneity of demonstrations indicated that a mood of frustration with leadership policies was spreading all over the country. Although momentarily confined to certain selected groups, this trend could become contagious for others. In view of this possibility, the intellectual unrest provided a catalyst for intensifying the already-existing conflicts within the party.

The initial party response to the student demonstrations, as distinct from police attacks, was presented by first secretary of the Warsaw committee, Jozef Kepa. In his speech, delivered on March 11 to a conference of the local activists, Kepa implied the existence of an ideologically motivated conspiracy behind the unrest. The real culprits, Kepa maintained, were "bankrupt politicians," such as Stefan Staszewski and Roman Zambrowski, both former Stalinist leaders of the party, and intellectuals affiliated with "foreign and domestic revisionists." Having selectively listed several student demonstrators, Kepa hinted that the dissenters were primarily of Jewish origin, prone to "Zionist propaganda and activity." He then extended direct responsibility for the university demonstrations to parents of the students. Complaining that many of them were children of important state officials and that until now the party authorities were too "lenient in handling this problem," Kepa announced that "decisions have already been taken to apply administrative measures in relation to those parents who occupy directing positions but whose children actively participated in the organization of recent disturbances."[9]

While Kepa's speech officially launched a propaganda campaign against the real and potential dissenters, subsequent intervention by Edward Gierek gave a major impetus to hard-line political tactics. In his address to a mass rally in Katowice on March 14, Gierek put the blame for the intellectual opposition on a small group of "old political speculators, people who wanted to enter the scene through the backdoor." He implied that the group consisted, along with former Stalinist Jewish leaders Zambrowski and Staszewski, of several non-communist writers and scientists. In reiterating Kepa's contention of the existence of an ideological conspiracy, Gierek accused these men of seeking to use the youth for the benefits of foreign interests. He also pointed out that their activity had been rooted in the initial post-Stalinist changes by explicitly observing that "the dirty scum which floated on the vortex of the October events of eleven years ago has not completely been removed from the tide of our life." In the face of such persistence from politically unreliable elements, Gierek called for a more decisive purifying action. However, this tough attitude was not without some important nuances. Thus, while demanding that "the central authorities properly punish the organizers of the [Warsaw] events," he also stressed that Silesia was calm and united in its support for the local party leadership. To keep the calm and order, Gierek vowed to "break the bones of all remnants of the old regime, revisionists, Zionists, and imperialist lackeys" who could dare to interfere in the affairs of his Silesian political base.[10] Paradoxically, on the next day, March 15, there was a massive youth demonstration in Katowice. Several hundred police troops used dogs and water guns to disperse the crowd.[11]

With this speech, Gierek gave a semiofficial blessing to the campaign of purge and intimidation that was to spread throughout the country. His personal popularity among technocratically oriented groups in the party and society, as well as his powerful position as a leader representing the industrial center of the country, provided the necessary weight to his remarks. In addition, the fact that he was the first Politburo member to speak about the political unrest placed him, in a sense, at the head of the party counterattack. Whether this resulted from a conscious acceptance of the hard-line attitude or was a calculated tactic to improve his political position within the organization, remains a matter of speculation. But whatever his motives, his political appeal was considerably enhanced. Gierek's initiative was immediately taken up by other provincial secretaries, who repeated the seemingly established pattern of charges and accusations. Indeed, a massive propaganda campaign was well on its way when Wladyslaw Gomulka decided to intervene.

On March 19, in a speech to the Warsaw party activists, Gomulka publicly confirmed that the propaganda campaign had not been of his making. Yet, while directly criticizing its extent and direction, Gomulka stopped short of an outright condemnation of its existence. Rather, his intervention was an attempt to regulate and channel the political agitation so it could be controlled by the leadership. To this end, Gomulka attempted to shift the responsibility for instigating the youth unrest away from people associated with either the party or the state and put the blame on "reactionary troublemakers." Among these, he selectively listed several writers, certain professors at Warsaw University, and a small group of radical student leaders. Although he did not dismiss completely the idea of an ideological conspiracy against the party and communism, Gomulka narrowed its applicability to this nucleus of nonconformist and liberal intellectuals.

While favorably inclined toward a centrally administered punishment for the "troublemakers," Gomulka rejected those aspects of purification that could not be fully controlled by the leadership. Thus he stressed that "the working class, filled with just indignation against the reactionary instigators and organizers of the street riots, should reject. . .all unconfirmed reports which are born out of imagination and gossip, or even the subversive political activity of the enemy. . .Before any public charge is made against anybody, it should be checked first with the proper party authority. We will not spare the guilty, we will defend the innocent."

In particular, Gomulka appeared to be concerned with "the slogan of struggle against Zionism, a slogan that was sometimes misrepresented in the course of the recent events." Accordingly, he declared that "it would be misunderstanding if we saw in Zionism a danger to socialism in Poland, for its sociopolitical system." In contrast to the widespread propaganda campaign, Gomulka did not accuse the Zionists or the discredited former Stalinists of having instigated the intellectual unrest. He even declared that "regardless of what feelings Polish citizens of Jewish origin may have, our party is decidedly against all manifestations having features of anti-Semitism." But then he also admitted that "we are combating Zionism as a political program, as Jewish nationalism, and this is right."[12] If nothing else, this provided a political opening that the proponents of the purge were waiting for.

Gomulka's statement represented a relatively moderate position in the rapidly unfolding political turbulence. But this moderation was a sign of weakness rather than of political strength. It constituted an effort to save the system associated with his name, but at the same time Gomulka opened the door for those forces within the party which seemed determined to change it. To many an activist his speech must have been just another example of the inertia and the half-measures that characterized Gomulka's rule. Their reaction was immediate. Gomulka's speech was continuously interrupted by the PUWP militants, who openly demanded more aggressive and decisive actions. For the first time in the history of the party, its first secretary was forced to listen to an audience of the faithful chanting, in front of the television cameras, the name of another member of the Politburo, Edward Gierek.[13] To neutralize the political impact of this demonstration, it was subsequently announced that Gomulka's speech represented a consensus of the Politburo.[14] But this did not affect the already-advanced course of political evolution. After a short pause, and in open defiance of Gomulka's appeals, the propaganda campaign was revived in full force.

The nationwide turbulence did not end with the collapse of the student movement. On the contrary, the growing restlessness, produced by long-existing strains in public life, only crystallized around current events, finding in them a convenient rallying point. In this process of political aggregation, the student unrest triggered a powerful countermovement that rapidly developed a momentum of its own, threatening a profound alteration of the established structures of power.

The main themes of the rising movement were fully expounded by Kazimierz Kakol, a noted journalist and known party activist. Writing a few days after Gomulka's intervention, Kakol justified the growth of militancy as a defensive reaction against "threat of a coup d'état. A group of conspirators, connected with Zionist centers, attempted, in an organized way, to lead, with the aid of patriotic and democratic slogans, such a height of demonstrations and street riots which could open to question the. . .continuation of our rule itself." But he then turned toward a penetrating criticism of the existing political system, pointing out that the crisis had been brewing for a long time, nourished by institutional decay and operational inefficiency:

> The taste of post-October freedom, the atmosphere of openness and the practice of openness, the respect of legality had been blocked by incompetence and inertia. This led to a failure in halting the growth of the tumor of bureaucracy; it did not offer the desired and necessary flexibility in economic and technical progress; it did not help in a rational selection of cadres, in ensuring the natural selection of the best forces available; it did not facilitate the implementation of the proclaimed principles of socialist democracy, especially in economy. In a definite and harmful way, we lost the differentiation between political guidance and management, the areas of jurisdiction and responsibility became unclear.
>
> In the understanding of all of us, the ripening and introduction of changes was too small, the concepts of improvement vague and inconsistent.

In conclusion, while refraining from presenting specific proposals for change—they were to evolve in the process of a "national discussion"— Kakol openly challenged Gomulka and top party leadership to "offer the answer as to the further prospects of development."[15]

Kakol's exposition could not be dismissed as just another example of intellectual criticism aimed at the party's elite. As a political activist with an established position within the party, he maintained close links with some of the powerful groups and forces operating on the political scene. In a sense, his article reflected the views of a larger coalition of groupings, inside as well as outside the party, which found a common denominator in an activist revolt against the stagnation of Gomulka's rule.

This emerging political alignment cut across formal patterns of organization and established a goal of a drastic developmental reform based on principles of efficiency and decisiveness and strong party control. Its immediate objective, however, was a comprehensive restructuring of the institutional hierarchies of influence and power. In this respect, the intellectual and student demonstrations provided a long-awaited opportunity for prompt and often violent action. The dismissal on March 13 of three government officials charged with responsibility for their children's participation in the student riots, opened the way for a prolonged purge which eventually reached into every segment of the political, administrative, and cultural establishment. During the first three months of 1968 more than 8,300 persons were expelled from the party. At the government level, 80 officials lost their jobs, including 14 with ministerial rank, 12 department directors, and 30 "ideological activists."[16] The direction of the purge indicated a systematically executed action aimed at elimination of all potential or real opponents of the authoritarian movement from position of influence in political life.

A particularly violent attack was centered on Jews, for tactical reasons presented as Zionists and hence supposedly alien and insensitive to Polish national interests. This anti-Semitic pattern was clearly established from the moment of the initial response to the intellectual and student dissent. Several Jewish professors and students were singled out as "politically frustrated, alienated and embittered" instigators of the protest movement.[17] Most of them were subsequently dismissed from positions at Warsaw University. But the anti-Semitic campaign only intensified in the aftermath of the student protests, rapidly emerging as a major issue in the authoritarian drive at political purification of the state and party organs. Typical of this trend was a resolution adopted by a local party unit in the Ministry of Foreign Trade, which demanded that ". . .our authorities stop tolerating the activity of reactionary Zionist elements in the political, social, economic, and cultural life of our country and that the mass media—the press, radio, and television—become at least instruments against political and ideological sabotage."[18] Such appeals, incessantly repeated in countless workers' resolutions and press articles and presented as examples of the overpowering wrath of the masses, had a powerful impact on the entire system. They became potent tools for social intimidation and discrimination, providing the ground for an almost indiscriminate persecution of all Jews. This, in turn, resulted in a mass exodus of Jews from Poland in the ensuing years.[19]

The scope and intensity of the anti-Semitic campaign were truly astounding, particularly considering the numerical and political weakness of this ethnic group in post-Stalinist Poland. According to generally acceptable estimates, the number of Jews ranged between 25,000 and 30,000 in the mid-1960s, constituting less than 0.1 percent of a total population of more than 31 million.[20] The Jewish component of the PUWP must have been, of course, much smaller and, since 1964, only two Jewish Communists held high positions in the party's leadership organs. They were economic expert and Politburo member Eugeniusz Szyr and a Central Committee secretary in charge of press matters, Artur Starewicz. Their influence over policy making was doubtful at best, and their functions were to execute decisions rather than to formulate them.

To a certain extent, the motivations for the attack could be traced to long-existing anti-Semitic trends in communist politics in Poland. This was particularly discernible in an authoritative exposé of the Jewish influence over the party's policies presented by a Central Committee member and leading communist ideologist, Andrzej Werblan. Justifying the virulence of the campaign as an attempt to solve an historical problem of political incompatibility between Jewish "cosmopolitanism" and Polish "patriotism" in the communist movement in Poland, Werblan suggested that the initial dominance of Jewish revolutionaries over the party and their activities had been at the roots of political failures and difficulties throughout its history.[21] Thus, he accused the Jewish Communists of having been responsible for the party's weakness in the interwar period, of engineering the fall of Gomulka in 1948, and, last but not least, of instigating the growth of revisionist trends in the aftermath of post-Stalinist changes. In the absence of a rebuttal to Werblan's thesis, it clearly acquired the status of an official party statement.

An additional factor that might have fueled anti-Semitic sentiment within the party was the leadership's resentment of the allegedly pro-Israeli inclination of Polish Jewry. Following the Israeli victory over the Arabs in June 1967, Gomulka complained that "the Israeli aggression against the Arab countries was received with applause within Zionist circles of Jewish-Polish citizens" and warned that "we do not want a fifth column to be created in our country."[22] Insofar as the Polish government had identified itself with the Arab side, any support, however innocent, of the Israeli side became synonymous, in his eyes, with political betrayal.

But to reach a fuller explanation of the political meaning of the campaign, one should add two other factors. First, the official anti-Semitism involved an effort to use the Jews as scapegoats for the particularly odious aspects of the communist past by putting the main responsibility for initial revolutionary hardships and persecutions on their shoulders. This became clearly evident after a widely publicized interview with Moczar, published on the occasion of a month of remembrance declared on ZBoWiD's initiative in April 1968. Moczar pointedly decried the postwar "arrival in our country. . .of certain politicians dressed in officers' uniforms, who later were of the opinion that it was only they—the Zambrowskis, the Radkiewiczes, and the Bermans—who had the right to leadership, a monopoly on deciding what was right for the Polish nation" and accused "the men [of this] type" of "later persecuting spokesmen of the wide, patriotic, national front."[23] In this attack on selected Jewish members of the Muscovite group, Moczar seemed to imply that had the power in 1948 been left in the hands of native, or at least ethnically Polish Communists, Stalinist excesses might have been avoided. Aside from the obvious fallacy of such an implication, the fact that it was made by a former high official of the notorious security organs added a peculiarly sinister note to the statement.

Equally important was the generalizing character of the purge campaign. Although initially centered on selected Jewish intellectuals and former politicians, it rapidly extended to include their potential non-Jewish sympathizers and supporters. In effect, the main purpose of the purge seemed to be a complete renovation of personnel in the state administration, the mass media, and in public organizations, in order to make them compatible with the long-range political aspirations of the authoritarian movement. The leadership of the campaign was firmly in hands of the second-level party activists, who had clearly defined attitudes toward the society and its future evolution. Their unifying platform was acceptance of the structural forms which characterized the system, namely the leading role of the party in political life. In their call for change, the activists sought to establish a loyal political base which would be socially and politically cohesive as well as potentially different from that which had supported Gomulka's regime since 1956.

While pretending to act in the name of the central party leadership, the purge campaign was undermining the very foundations of Gomulka's rule, raising a direct challenge to the highest party authorities. An example of such tactics was an attack on Politburo member and Minister of National Defense Marian Spychalski. In an attempt to remove Spychalski from military responsibilities, his opponents launched a rumor campaign replete with insinuations of his pro-Israeli sympathies.[24] Similar accusations were made against several other top party leaders, including Politburo members Ochab, Rapacki, and Szyr. Paradoxically, the first secretary himself was never attacked directly. Rather, through constant criticism of his associates, the activist rebels seemed to aim at seizing some or most of Gomulka's power, leaving him as a figurehead acceptable to all.

This attitude reflected the internal disparity of views among the authoritarian forces. In spite of the apparent uniformity of its immediate goals, namely administrative reform based on greater developmental decisiveness, their movement had never formed an institutional, social, or ideological entity. Having achieved a decisive breakthrough with the launching of the purge campaign, it rapidly split into separate and mutually antagonistic cliques and factional groups. The increasingly vociferous debate within the authoritarian movement centered around the question of the future pattern of political development, and particularly on the meaning of nationalism as contrasted with strictly economic reformism, as the two main orientations in policy making.

In this respect, Edward Gierek's views acquired a special importance. While his early speech had provided a legitimizing incentive to the purge campaign, the subsequently established line of the Silesian party organization indicated Gierek's growing criticism of nationalistic sentiments. This tendency was developed in an article in Gierek's house organ, *Trybuna robotnicza,* belittling the ardent nationalist propaganda by implying that it was clearly out of step with the necessities of economic modernization. The article stressed that ". . .good, selfless work is the most important factor of patriotism in the socialist order. . .Poland's name was glorified, not because of the fame of her arms and heroic deeds on the battlefields, but because of her world-renowned successes in scientific research [and] achievement in technology and engineering."[25] This declaration rapidly found an echo in several other papers, prompting calls for greater selectivity in purges, for "knowledgeable separation of the uncertain from the hostile," and for recognition of the "technicians' and engineers' work. . .as a source of inspirations and new concepts valid. . .not only in the sphere of production but also in the sociopolitical area."[26]

On the other hand, those calls also prompted an immediate negative response. Writing in the official party organ, *Trybuna ludu,* a leading exponent of the continuing purge, Wieslaw Myslek, strongly condemned the technocratic position: "Making the manager a positive hero. . . and banking on improvements which are, in fact, merely organizational, limited to a narrow sphere of economic productivity, is bound to lead one to profess a socialism typical of the mentality of a market economist. . .The idea of equality is replaced by the idea of an elite and the postulate for social stratification."[27] The theme of commercialized socialism as a vehicle for increasing social inequality rapidly emerged as the main point in the attack on the technocratic elements within the party. Indicative of this attitude was an attempt to portray the efficiency-oriented economic reforms as a source of a political tendency to weaken the party itself. Particular criticism centered on the proposals for the introduction of some measures of managerial decentralization. They were viewed as creating the foundations for "a centralism of the economic type. . . With this type of centralism, real power would have to pass in the hands of ever smaller groups of economic experts; the leading role of the party would be reduced to a minimum, and self-management would, in practice, be overcome. . .[d]ecentralization need not mean democratization; it may be an attempt to free oneself from party and workers' control."[28]

At the same time, the arguments in defense of a nationalistic line in party activities reached a clearly polemical character. Speaking on this point, Moczar officially proclaimed that "everything that our nation did during the years of the last war must be remembered and conveyed to the young generation. . . These problems must be dealt with by people who understand it, who feel the breath of the nation."[29] When contrasted with the narrow interpretation of patriotism by Gierek, it signified an assertion by the Partisans' leader of a claim to political representation of national interest in Poland. Indeed, Moczar's platform provided him with significant support from important segments of society, including numerous activists of other sociopolitical organizations, authoritarian Catholics from PAX—an organization which had politically separated itself from the Catholic Church and proclaimed its allegiance to the communist system[30]—as well as some intellectuals. In part, this support might have resulted from sheer opportunism; but it also seemed to indicate that frustration with the existing system reached the stage where any change, regardless of its political motivation, would be better than the prevailing stagnation.

There was little doubt that the top leadership was shaken by the violence of the authoritarian campaign. Faced with the prospect of an open split within the party, Gomulka was forced to take some conciliatory measures to appease the activist critics. The first step involved several important changes in the composition of the highest level state leadership. During the Sejm session in April, Edward Ochab stepped down from the chairmanship of the Council of State. Although ostensibly motivated by reasons of declining health, Ochab's resignation was reportedly prompted by his daughter's support for dissenting students.[31] His replacement as a head of state was Marian Spychalski. However, this titular promotion of one of Gomulka's closest associates hardly signified a political success. The largely ceremonial nature of the chairman's post suggested that Spychalski's removal from the active command of the army constituted a veiled maneuver to appease his opponents. On the other hand, Spychalski's continued presence in state leadership showed that Gomulka was still in a position to manipulate political realignments, despite the pressure of the authoritarian forces. The new minister of defense was Wojciech Jaruzelski, a professional officer who had served since 1960 as head of the military department in the central party apparatus.

The pattern that emerged from these personnel decisions indicated a growing tendency toward a political compromise, a solution pointing to the weakened position of Gomulka, who was forced to put up with the demands of the internal opposition. In order to mitigate its pressure, the party secretary might have been helped by those elements, inside and outside the party, which could be susceptible to the growth of nationalism, particularly in the armed forces. As if to confirm this hypothesis, three new deputy ministers of defense were also appointed from among experienced and Soviet-trained officers.[32] Shortly after the government changes were announced, Soviet ambassador to Warsaw, A. Aristov, explicitly gave his support to Gomulka, calling him in a widely publicized speech "the favorite son of Poland."[33]

Such appeasing efforts notwithstanding, internal controversies within the party continued unabated, although the purge campaign lost some of its dynamism. The conflicts broke into the open during the Central Committee meeting that, after several postponements, was held July 8–9. The debate centered on two issues: the evaluation of post-March political activity and the role of the central party apparatus in policy formulation and its implementation.

On the first point, the discussion demonstrated a widespread dissatisfaction with the pattern of Gomulka's rule. In a virtual show of unanimity, all 35 speakers who took the floor expressed a desire for change. This found official recognition in the statement by Kliszko who, speaking on behalf of the central leadership, admitted the mistake of tolerating "certain revisionist elements" in the past and almost apologized for "timidity in not having drawn any organizational conclusions" from their activity.[34] There was, however, considerable disagreement as to the direction and the scope of change. Partic-

ular attention was devoted to the question of growing nationalism and its impact on policy formulation. Several leaders, among them Politburo member
Stefan Jedrychowski, warned that "nationalism in the conditions of socialist
countries inevitably leads to anti-Soviet feelings."[35] On the other hand, numerous speakers openly praised the patriotic accents in political activity while
Wladyslaw Kruczek, a provincial secretary from Rzeszow, stressed that "today one cannot accuse the Polish nation and the party of being nationalistic."[36]

On the problem of the party's political role, the debate opened with an
important declaration by Gierek. Using the example of his local organization,
Gierek suggested specific solutions to the crisis facing the party. Thus, he
pointed out that "assuming that in the nation's opinion the party is responsible for everything. . .wrongly interpreted, the principle of total party responsibility often leads. . .to replacing the chain of state and economic administration by the party [apparatus]. Consequently, this diminishes its principal
role of inspiring and controlling." He then stressed that "times are changing,
the methods of operation of the party apparatus at all levels as well as the
methods and forms of action of the state organs of authority must change and
will have to change accordingly. These methods and forms will be [character-
ized by] a decline in practical management and will be based upon human
consciousness and the ideological involvement of society reflecting belief and
trust in large masses of working people, in their link with the idea and practice
of socialism."[37]

Gierek's call for a functional redefinition of the party's operations was
joined by several other secretaries from the more industrialized regions.
Thus, Jozef Spychalski of Lodz pointed to the positive aspects in "further experimentation in giving more independence to particular enterprises or specialized industrial complexes,"[38] while Gdansk leader Stanislaw Kociolek
openly admonished the party apparatus in saying that "party organizations
will fulfill their statutory role more effectively by developing the function of
inspiration and control instead of trying to replace professional administrators."[39]

Others, however, attacked the cult of expertise allegedly promulgated by
intellectuals and the technical intelligentsia. They received considerable support from several members of the central party organs, especially from Boleslaw Jaszczuk who, while stressing the importance of effective economic
management, condemned tendencies toward functional decentralization as
"directed primarily at undermining confidence in the leading force of the socialist society, the working class party."[40]

In light of the continuing differences within the party, no new policy could
be adopted. At the same time, several personnel changes in the top leadership, approved by the meeting, indicated the growing influence of the activist

movement. The Politburo place left vacant by the departure of the ex-chairman of the Council of State, Edward Ochab, was filled by the Central Committee secretary, Boleslaw Jaszczuk, who took charge of planning and economic affairs. In another shift, Mieczyslaw Moczar was elected to deputy membership of the Politburo as well as to the secretariat, where he took responsibility for overall supervision of security activities. Insofar as Moczar's advancement was an important success of the nationalistic and anti-Semitic Partisans, the appointment of Jaszczuk implied an effort by Gomulka to keep in check the technocratically oriented elements led by Gierek.

More important, the meeting clearly confirmed a trend toward devolution of power from the central organs to the provincial leaders. Their increased stature in the party was especially evident in the often-repeated stress on the "collective work of the provincial directing party *actif*" in the preparation of the draft theses for the forthcoming party congress. During the discussion, the majority of the speakers were heads of the provincial party committees. In terms of political issues facing the party, they constituted a dynamic group demanding changes in party policies and methods of operation. While politically significant, this development could hardly suggest an expansion of inner-party democratization or a broadening of political decentralization. Rather, it was symptomatic of a rapidly intensifying trend toward "parcellation of centralism," in which the authority of the central organs diminished, the power of the local units increased, but the essence of decision making, which limits participation in policy formation to selected party officials, remained unchanged.[41] Its immediate impact on the organization was the limitation of Gomulka's personal power and authority. The open polemics and disagreements within the party, as manifested at the Central Committee meeting, only confirmed that Gomulka was either unwilling or incapable of reestablishing his previous status of an undisputed leader. It became clear that future development would depend on the combination of factors and forces external to the top leadership rather than on its institutional authority alone.

Particularly important for the evolution of internal conflicts in the party were the developments in neighboring Czechoslovakia and the resulting changes in the international situation among the East European communist states. The Czechoslovak experiment in socialist democratization, with its inherent elements of economic reformism and political liberalization, constituted an apogee of developmental tendencies which had been long simmering in all communist countries of Eastern Europe. To the degree that it served as a source of inspiration for the liberal dissenters in Poland, the Czechoslovak model of "socialism with a human face" considerably affected the Polish political situation.[42]

There was little doubt that something akin to a community of interest existed between Czechoslovak and Polish liberal dissenters. During the March demonstrations, the Czechoslovak pattern of development was hailed in numerous student resolutions as leading to greater political freedom as well as economic and social progress. In return, the Polish intellectual dissent was met with sympathetic reactions from the Czechoslovak press and academic community. There is also no doubt that such reactions created a serious concern in Warsaw. On May 6, the Polish government officially protested the "anti-Polish campaign in Czechoslovakia" in a note delivered to the Czechoslovak party and government.[43] A day later, the PUWP leadership issued an internal party instruction on the Czechoslovak question. Containing a political interpretation of the situation in Prague, it portrayed the Czechoslovak party as torn by crisis and factional divisions. It also attacked "anti-socialist forces" which, operating outside the party, "create both underground and legal centers and demand legalization of bourgeois parties." The instruction envisaged the inevitability of a decisive action regarding Czechoslovakia, pointing out that "it is clear that the events in Czechoslovakia constitute more than an internal affair of the fraternal country. . .[T]hese developments have a principal importance for the security of Poland, the GDR [East Germany] and other socialist countries. . .We cannot, under any condition, allow the counter-revolution to take over in Czechoslovakia. The Soviet Union and other member-states of the Warsaw Pact cannot accept it either."[44] On May 8, a meeting of East European communist leaders convened in Moscow, with the significant exception of Czechoslovakia and Rumania, for the purpose of "exchanging information and views on the current problems of the international situation and in the respective countries." Simultaneously, Czechoslovak programs of internal reform were attacked in the Polish press, which linked them to "anti-socialist trends which undermine the leading role of the working class party, tend to liquidate the people's power, and set Czechoslovakia at variance with fraternal socialist countries."[45]

Perhaps the most important event to stir up political opposition among the leaders of the Warsaw Pact countries toward Czechoslovakia was the publication in Prague of the famous "Two Thousand Word Statement."[46] This article, written by novelist Ludvik Vaculik but endorsed by numerous prominent Czechoslovak personalities, constituted a liberal manifesto for political change. It called for a complete reorganization of the power structure and increased participation in political processes. Although addressed exclusively to the Czechoslovak public, this liberal *cri de guerre* had a major impact on the attitudes of communist leaders in other countries. To the degree that it projected a new conception of socialist politics based on an implicit recognition of the demands of social groups as well as suggesting the need for a more pluralistic style of leadership, the "statement" was a direct challenge to the established patterns of communist rule.

The reaction from other parties was swift. A protest letter was sent to the

Prague leaders by a Soviet-centered coalition of East European leaders meeting at a hastily convened conference in Warsaw July 14–15. It constituted, in effect, an ultimatum to the Czechoslovaks to arrest their program of democratization. The letter made clear that the primary reason for the Warsaw Pact countries' agitation over the Prague situation stemmed from fear of a collapse of communist rule in Czechoslovakia and its potential repercussions for political stability in other communist states. Indicative of this attitude were accusations that Prague forgot about "the Leninist principles of democratic centralism" and allowed the "forces of reaction" to work openly toward "undermining the socialist system and pitting Czechoslovakia against the other socialist countries."[47]

The pattern of communist unity established at the Warsaw conference injected a new element into the internal conflicts in Poland. For the authoritarian forces, the Czechoslovak development had always been inseparable from the internal trends of reform and liberalization. Therefore, they were inclined to link their criticism of the Prague situation with a parallel offensive at home. Gomulka, although equally opposed to the Czechoslovak experiment, considered the solution of this problem primarily in the perspective of international communist politics. This implied a limited action in the domestic arena but a concerted effort by the entire socialist community in securing the final solution. Given this tendency toward operational unity centered on the Soviet Union, the stabilizing impact of the Warsaw conference significantly reinforced Gomulka's political position while reducing the potential influence of the nationalistically oriented forces upon decision making. On the other hand, Gomulka's reliance on Soviet guidance increased his domestic vulnerability in case of a change in Moscow's Czechoslovak policy.

In these circumstances, the tentative compromise between the Russians and the Czechoslovaks, reached at Cierna July 29–August 1, was received in Poland with mixed emotions. Following the ratification of the agreement in Bratislava on August 4, Gomulka was said to have confronted the Soviet leaders with a prediction of "serious consequences for the whole socialist camp" which would result from their soft stand.[48]

As for the impact on Polish internal politics, the sudden appeasement of the Czechoslovak crisis appeared detrimental to Gomulka's authority. The imminent danger of a revival of factional controversies was signaled by a sudden increase in the activity of his potential opponents. Following a massive patriotic celebration of the twenty-fourth anniversary of the Warsaw uprising of August 1, 1944, Moczar reportedly described the Cierna compromise as a "decisive defeat of Gomulka's line."[49] Gierek, speaking at a meeting of the Silesian *actif* on August 15, called for rejuvenation of the policy-making personnel and stressed that "we must eradicate everything from our party line which closes the lips of honest people. . .in the fear that somebody will be 'offended',. . .that this somebody—usually placed higher in the social hierarchy—will say: by criticizing me you criticize the party and socialism."[50]

This situation changed dramatically with the August 21 invasion of Czechoslovakia by the Warsaw Pact forces, including some Polish troops. The immediate political effect on the domestic situation was the reinforcement of Gomulka's weakened authority. As a result, the factional controversies within the party were partially abandoned or modified to the requirements of political circumstances. On September 15, Moczar praised Gomulka's handling of the situation in the face of the "difficult but unfortunately necessary decision to send troops to Czechoslovakia."[51] On the other side of the political spectrum, the emerging trend toward political and operational stabilization seriously undermined Gierek's modernizing tendencies. This was reflected in a report to his provincial party conference on October 7, when he admitted that "the general line of the party was and is correct, that the plans prepared by the party were and are accurate" and merely stressed the continuing necessity to "isolate revisionist elements" in the party work.[52]

Gomulka was quick to reassert his authority. Speaking to the Warsaw party conference in late October, he condemned the "nationalistic approach to the problem of nationalities" and attacked the proponents of anti-Semitic themes by stating that "these views are voiced by those to whom the ideology of the party is alien or who do not know what Marxism-Leninism is. In our party nobody is allowed to evaluate people by their national origin. Such a position would be extremely damaging, contrary to party interests and pushing the party in an improper, false direction."[53] This admonition was supported by a call for strengthening of democratic centralism and the leading role of the party.

In light of this change, it became obvious that the Czechoslovak crisis had contributed in several important ways to the appeasement of internal party conflicts. Paradoxically, if one takes into consideration the extent of international turmoil following the Soviet-led intervention in Czechoslovakia, it provided a crucial stabilizing factor in Polish evolution. This was particularly significant on the level of national leadership. After the internal struggles and revolts, the position of established top leaders—Gomulka and his closest associates—again reached the status of unquestioned power. Having been forced to take a defensive position on domestic issues, Gomulka regained lost ground when the party faced a larger international crisis. Under the new conditions, he proved to be the only leader who had access to the means of power, the Soviet decision makers. The Soviet international intervention provided an ultimate factor in domestic stabilization, and this became decisive for the reconsolidation of Gomulka's power and authority. As if to confirm this development, Gomulka received additional Soviet support during the party congress in Warsaw during November 11–16, 1968. In a speech that indicated Moscow's preference for Gomulka's continuing leadership, Leonid Brezhnev praised him as "the faithful son of the Polish working class and leading activist of the international communist movement" while strongly implying that Poland's success in furthering internal development depended on Gomulka's activity.[54]

Notwithstanding Gomulka's regained strength, positions of respective political groupings within the party were not significantly affected. Composition of the party's top organs remained remarkably stable. Among the twelve-member Politburo, three leaders were not re-elected by the congress. They included Adam Rapacki, the long-time foreign minister who, since 1948, had been active in the highest party councils; Eugeniusz Szyr, an economic expert of Jewish origin; and Franciszek Waniolka, deputy premier in charge of heavy industry since 1962. Both Szyr and Waniolka had been criticized since March for failures in economic management and planning. Despite their political demotion, however, they preserved their seats in the new Central Committee and Szyr continued as deputy prime minister in charge of economic planning.

In their place, the congress elected Stanislaw Kociolek, Wladyslaw Kruczek, and Jozef Tejchma. While Kruczek, a province secretary of the agricultural Rzeszow region, had been close to the authoritarian Partisans, both Kociolek and Tejchma were young and pragmatically oriented members of the party apparatus. The number of deputy members of the Politburo was increased to four by inclusion of Jan Szydlak, who joined Mieczyslaw Moczar, Mieczyslaw Jagielski, and Piotr Jaroszewicz. Szydlak was also elected to the Secretariat and put in charge of propaganda and agitation. Another man elected to the Secretariat was Stefan Olszowski. He took over the party press bureau from Artur Starewicz, who, in spite of his Jewish origin, retained his seat in the party executive organ, assuming responsibility over relations with foreign communist parties.

Despite those changes, the party leadership remained in a state of flux. The continuing presence of such faithful Gomulkaists as Kliszko, Loga-Sowinski, Spychalski, and Strzelecki in the Politburo signified that Gomulka was clearly capable of stopping any attempts to remove his long-time supporters from positions of authority. Concurrently both Gierek and Moczar, the undeclared leaders of the principal factions within the party, retained their seats. While temporarily subdued, they remained in the background as potential contenders for power in the event of any future leadership crisis.

Much greater change took place in the composition and character of the Central Committee elected by the congress. Among its 91 members, 25 entered the high party organ for the first time. Of the deputy members, whose number was also set at 91, only 33 had been previously elected and the rest were totally new. Particularly important was the growth in influence of the provincial party leaders within the Central Committee. All 22 of them were elected, including 3—Gierek, Kruczek and Kociolek—who became members of the Politburo. The simultaneous introduction of numerous lower party officials and local activists into the Central Committee, many of whom were linked politically to their territorially determined patrons, provided another sign of the importance of the provincial organizations. This only confirmed that the shift in the balance of power away from the center and toward the provinces, which had manifested itself throughout the year-long crisis, was not only unaffected by the political reconsolidation but seemed to have acquired a quasi-permanent character.[55] And yet, even if those changes carried important consequences in further undermining the organizational authority of the central organs, there were no changes adopted in the party statute or formal organization. Indeed, speaking to the congress on behalf of the central leadership, Politburo member Strzelecki flatly declared that "the present statute of the party corresponds to its current tasks and internal needs, hence there is no need to introduce any important modifications."[56]

Perhaps the most significant substantive decisions, as distinct from organizational changes, were made in the area of economic policy. Just as the weakness of economic management and planning had been a focal point in the earlier propaganda campaign, the congress implicitly recognized the failure of the central leadership to develop a satisfactory program of economic evolution. The final resolution listed a number of separate phenomena which, taken together, illustrated the continuing state of economic stagnation. Among them were such symptoms as export difficulties resulting from the low quality of industrial production, disparity between the product mix of industrial output and effective industrial and consumer demand, overemployment and low productivity, overinvestment of scarce capital goods which left many unfinished products, investment projects where original cost estimates were grossly exceeded, and a continuing failure to develop accurate cost accounting methods. Faced with the real prospect of a serious economic breakdown, the party declared itself in favor of more "intensive" methods in promoting economic growth. Although the resolution did not offer any specific framework of reform, it called for a general change in planning and management. It required that immediate steps be taken toward "creation of appropriate conditions for the reconstruction of the national economy in the next five years."[57]

The first attempts at redefining economic policy were made soon after the congress. At the Central Committee meeting in April 1969, Gomulka announced a partial decentralization of planning procedures in which the local production units would prepare the working blueprints of economic targets to be coordinated later by the central planning organs. In subsequent months and through a series of authoritative statements from top party leaders, a new pattern of economic activity was elaborated, based on a "controlled utilization of market forces" and increased emphasis on "profitability and industrial efficiency."[58]

To a large extent, these efforts at formulating a new operational model resulted from the realization of an urgent need for a drastic overhaul of the entire economic system. Having gone through a period of severe criticism of their performances, top members of the party elite appeared to have concluded that the roots of decay and developmental stagnation were due to technological backwardness and bureaucratic inefficiency. As a consequence, they became determined to adjust to new technological imperatives. This sense of urgency was further compounded by several political considerations, with the drive to unite diverse elements of the party around the central leadership most important. Inasmuch as Gomulka's effectiveness had been impaired by the activist revolt, he sought to regain the lost ground by sponsoring a program of economic reorganization which would considerably reinforce the role of the central organs. Furthermore, by adopting a reform mantle himself, Gomulka might have hoped to seize the initiative from his critics, preempt their activities, and, ultimately, subject them to his political control.

The manner in which the reform program was being prepared seemed to confirm this motivation. Policy formulation was restricted to a small group of top, centrally placed party officials and their advisors. The local party organizations and the state administration were kept at the level of passive executors, and the public was simply ignored. As for Gomulka, it was subsequently said that his attitude toward other members of the leadership had been indicative of a tendency to "concentrate in his hands increasingly autocratic power." The meetings of the entire membership of the Politburo and the Secretariat became limited to only "a few times per year" while "the possibilities of discussion and confrontations of positions diminished every year; as a result the unanimity of decisions in the Politburo of the Central Committee became increasingly formal and illusory."[59] Instead, Gomulka restricted participation in policy making to only a few trusted associates. The most effective of these were Kliszko as a general political advisor, Strzelecki, in charge of the party organization, and Jaszczuk, who emerged as the key economic reformer responsible for the coordination and supervision of the entire strategy of economic change.

The most important operational measure introduced as a part of the evolving developmental model was the reform of the industrial wage system, tied to the increase in efficiency and productivity. As proposed by Jaszczuk and adopted by the Central Committee in May 1970, it envisaged the imposition of a stable wage structure, to be changed every five years with the introduction of large-scale economic plans, and the creation of separate bonus funds for white- and blue-collar industrial employees. The white-collar bonus fund was to be made up of savings gained by lowering production costs and was conceived as a direct financial incentive for the managerial and technical staffs to stimulate efficiency in their enterprises. Any increases in the workers' compensation were to be correlated with those of the white-collar employees; hence they were to depend on satisfactory fulfillment of production targets by the management, with additional funds made available by the decrease in actual blue-collar employment.[60]

The acceptance of the reform, which was to be implemented at the beginning of 1971, carried serious political implications for the party and its leadership. By adopting the narrowly defined criteria of efficiency and productivity as the determinants of social rewards, the leadership embraced an essentially technocratic approach to economic and social problems. Its practical consequence was a departure from the traditional insistence on full employment. The evolving policy aimed at forcing greater productivity through the threat of unemployment and economic deprivation. Commenting later on Gomulka's plan to create a pool of about 500,000 unemployed workers by the end of 1975, his critics pointed out that ". . .the maintenance of partial unemployment was to produce a feeling of industriousness, high productivity, respect for work, and discipline. Such an imposed atmosphere of 'good work' was to be a stimulus to intensify and improve economic results."[61]

Having accepted the view that economic success depends on the performance of managerial and technical groups, the party openly allied itself with their interests, thus abandoning its ideologically defined role of guardian of proletarian destiny. This functional reorientation tended to introduce profound changes in the style of party work. Writing about a sociopolitical dilemma resulting from this development, a respected party commentator complained that ". . .technical-economic slang sometimes replaces the party's dialogue with the masses; indices helpful in estimating production are useless in keeping an eye on social tempers."[62] This concern with the changing character of the party in leading the process of economic change led to the inevitable isolation of the leadership from the working masses, whose anxiety at the prospect of unemployment and economic scarcity would result in growing sharpening of political tension.

The event that brought the tension into the open was the announcement on December 12, 1970, of a government decision to impose immediately a 15 to 30 percent increase in the price of food and fuels. Endorsed two days later by the plenary meeting of the Central Committee as both a remedy to the shortage of meats and grains resulting from two consecutive years of bad harvests and an instrument to impose a change in consumption patterns from foodstuffs to manufactured goods, it triggered an outburst of workers' protests. The government's attempted suppression of the protesters by force set off a chain reaction of demonstrations and strikes which provoked a national political crisis, forced a gradual repeal of the reform program, and culminated, in mid-February 1971, in a revocation of the food price increases.[63]

The crisis developed in two stages. The first stage was characterized by mass street demonstrations, rebellious turmoil, and violent confrontations between the workers and the police supported by military units. Its main battlefields were the industrial centers of northern Poland, particularly the coastal cities of Gdansk, Gdynia, and Szczecin, where spontaneous demonstrations of workers' discontent turned into major riots after repeated government attempts to suppress the crowds.

The driving force behind this enforced pacification was the central leadership of the party, which chose the means to deal with the situation and then actively carried them through. On December 15 orders were issued for the troops to use weapons against the demonstrators and it was decided to impose a limited state of emergency in the coastal region. This took place at a special meeting of the leadership chaired by Gomulka and attended by Politburo members Cyrankiewicz, Jaszczuk, Spychalski, and Strzelecki, CC secretaries Moczar and Starewicz, Defense Minister Wojciech Jaruzelski, Internal Affairs Minister Kazimierz Switala, police chief Tadeusz Pietrzak, and the director of the CC Administrative Department, Stanislaw Kania, who was responsible for security in the party apparatus. The measures were said to have been proposed by Gomulka and Cyrankiewicz, but none of the others "questioned the proposals, which was equivalent to their acceptance."[64]

Operational control over military and police activities in the Gdansk area was assumed by a hastily created "staff" consisting of Politburo members Kliszko, Loga-Sowinski, and Kociolek and Deputy Defense Minister Grzegorz Korczynski. In Szczecin, where street demonstrations started on December 17, a similar role was played by Deputy Defense Minister Tadeusz Tuczapski and Deputy Internal Affairs Minister Ryszard Matejewski. The justification of the attempt to suppress the workers' protests by force, which led to the death of several hundred people and the wounding of thousands more, was the official view, openly stated by Kliszko but supported by Gomulka and others, that the workers' unrest was indicative of a "counter-revolutionary attack" against the party and the socialist system.[65]

The brutality of repressive actions provoked a wave of protests in other coastal cities and quickly spread to industrial centers throughout the country. The abortive governmental attempt to impose a nationwide state of emergency on December 18, 1970—the first action of this kind in the history of communist rule in Poland—created a clear danger of generalized revolt. Confronted with such a possibility, the party officialdom, including several members of the Politburo and numerous party notables in the Central Committee, came out in opposition to Gomulka's leadership. The seeds of a potential internal revolt against the party's first secretary were evident during the Central

Committee meeting on December 14 when the price changes had been approved. As described by one of the participants, the meeting was characterized "by two concurrently held debates: one, an official discussion under the supervision of the presidium, another, in the corridors, searching for contact with the tragic reality of events just unfolding on the streets of Gdansk, to be continued further and further . . ."[66] The growing split within the party hierarchy came into the open when Gomulka suffered a sudden heart attack on December 19. In his absence, the hastily convened meeting of the Politburo decided after seven hours of deliberations to ask Gomulka to resign from both the Politburo and the Secretariat. On the following day, December 20, 1970, a plenary meeting of the Central Committee undertook the task of "electing new leadership of the party."[67]

Following the resignation of Gomulka, leadership of the party went to its new first secretary, Edward Gierek. Among the twelve members of the Politburo, seven—Cyrankiewicz, Gierek, Jedrychowski, Kociolek, Kruczek, Loga-Sowinski, Tejchma—were confirmed in their posts, three—Jaroszewicz, Moczar, and Szydlak—were promoted from deputy status, and two—Edward Babiuch and Stefan Olszowski—were newly elected. Four deputy members of the Politburo were also elected: Henryk Jablonski, Mieczyslaw Jagielski, Wojciech Jaruzelski, and Jozef Kepa. The composition of the Secretariat was set at eight members, two of whom, Babiuch and Kazimierz Barcikowski, were the newcomers. Of the old-time Gomulka associates, only one, Loga-Sowinski, preserved his seat in the leading party organs. Others, such as Jaszczuk, Kliszko, Spychalski, and Strzelecki were voted out of their positions. The Gomulka era in the history of the party was over.

While these personnel changes provided a partial release of long-existing tensions within the party, they did not end the movement of workers' discontent. Rather, Gomulka's dismissal and the subsequent criticism of his leadership by the new incumbents seem to have appeared to the workers as an explicit recognition of the failure of the entire program of centrally directed economic change and a symbolic rejection of authoritarian methods in dealing with social protests. For once, popular agitation seemed to produce political results. This gave the workers a new determination to press for a reversal of all those decisions, including the price increases and the reforms of the wage system, which they considered detrimental to their interests. By contrast, Gomulka's departure was, for the new party leaders, merely a long-awaited culmination of factional struggles for which the workers' unrest might have only provided a convenient stimulus. While critical of Gomulka's operational tactics, they had never opposed the principle of centrally imposed economic programs of change as exemplified by his policies. Once in power, they attacked the "voluntarism of the former leading group, which formulated, according to its 'whims,' incorrect methods of implementing the correct program assumptions"[68] and were determined to carry them out. Simultaneously, they accepted certain appeasement oriented measures such as an immediate distribution of allowances to low-income families and a promise to revise some of the more rigid stipulations of the impending wage reform.

The essential ambiguity of party responses to the workers' demands, in which Gierek's initial pledge to "always maintain a close bond with the working class and the whole nation and never lose a common language with the working people"[69] was rapidly countermanded by repeated official declarations in defense of both the principles behind the new wage system and the "price regulations,"[70] profoundly affected the scope and direction of the workers' movement of discontent. After a hiatus of several weeks, a new wave of protests spread all over the country, but under different conditions and with different tactics. The street demonstrations and violent confrontations with police gave way to a series of occupation strikes. Perhaps the most significant in this stage of the protest movement was its political character. Of course, the economic issues, in particular the demand for revocation of the food price increase, occupied the primary place in the workers' activities. In time, however, these pressures for change expanded to include an implicit criticism of the political system. Among the most striking elements of this process were growing calls for independent and truly representative workers' organizations, for punishment of the officials judged responsible for repressive actions, and for a reform of administrative procedures regarding protest demonstrations.[71]

More important, the workers' strike movement rapidly developed discernible, albeit still rudimentary, forms of self-organization. These trends were particularly noticeable in the shipbuilding industry of Gdansk and Szczecin, the two largest coastal cities, where the workers set up permanent, democratically elected strike committees. They promptly established channels of communication with other factories throughout the country and successfully forced direct negotiations with top party and government officials.[72] There were numerous indications that this movement toward occupational self-representation could gather political momentum. Although the organizational dynamics of this movement will probably never be adequately described due to the existing political circumstances, there is every reason to believe that there was no large city or important industry left unaffected by work stoppages, protest meetings, or other manifestations of workers' discontent.

Confronted with the prospect of continuing workers' unrest, the new party leadership was forced gradually to yield to their demands. The most important concession was a revocation, on January 25, 1971, of the wage reforms and a return to the policy of full employment. This was combined with further increases in subsidies for the lowest paid employees and the extension of retirement programs. Finally, on February 15, faced with a threat of massive strikes in the textile industry, the government decided to reduce food prices to the pre-December levels and preclude any subsequent changes for the next two years.

The fulfillment of its economic goals was, without a doubt, the most obvious success of the workers' protest movement. To emphasize the economic aspects alone, however, would distort its potential political significance. Coming on the heels of the earlier manifestations of intellectual and student dissent and prolonged anti-Zionist purges, the worker protests testified to a persistent systemic inability to integrate separate social groups into a socialist society. The crucial issue which emerged through the evolution of seemingly constant internal crises was that the party could not cope with the task of solving the problem of permanent social tension. Its impact on the party was drastic in that it undermined its organizational cohesiveness and destroyed the traditional, ideologically defined bases of its moral authority. In the words of the Politburo report to the Central Committee meeting in early February 1971, "the crisis of confidence pervaded intra-party relations on several levels: the basic mass of party members, subjected, on the one side, to the pressure of worsening moods, and on the other side to political decisions made by the leading authorities, about whose rightness it was not fully convinced, was losing arguments indispensable for maintaining its ideological defensive spirit. The crisis of confidence was constantly widening the rift between the *actif* and the party apparatus, on the one hand, and the leading authorities on the other."[73]

In light of this assessment of the political situation within the party, it was obvious that a drastic change in the methods and style of running the organization was all but necessary as was a change in the relation of the party to society at large.

CHAPTER 8

The Evolutionary Style

Insofar as the appeasement of the workers' protests resulted from a circumstantial alteration of specific policy decisions, it alone could not provide a lasting solution to existing social, economic, and political problems. Both the tension within the power structure and the strains between the party and the society had been of such intensity and long standing that this element alone could not mitigate them for long. To contain a real threat of further political and social disruptions, the party leadership developed a wide-ranging strategy of stabilization. Its crucial feature was a centrally coordinated effort to promote economic growth and modernization. This was to be accomplished largely by redefining the party's organizational and political activities for managing economic development. This effort was intended to establish a firm basis for economic expansion and improvement in the standard of living, both considered key determinants of a successful restoration of sociopolitical stability. Implicit in this approach, however, was the return to forms of rule more in consonance with the systemic traditions of political and institutional centralism.

More specifically, this strategy produced a two-pronged action: first, the consolidation of leadership's control over all political activities and validation of its special role within the party as the sole organ of policy making; second, the adoption of new policies aimed at improvement in material conditions for the population at large with a view toward regaining social support for the party and its leadership.

With respect to the first type of action, the experience of the Polish United Workers' Party with internal crises between 1968 and 1970 provided an obvious reminder of the possible negative effects an internal factional fragmentation could have on leadership's ability to conduct and enforce its policies. Having actively participated in bringing down Gomulka's leadership, Gierek, upon coming to power, immediately undertook several measures to secure for himself the political status that would allow him to perform the leadership functions without the threat of intrusion from other members of the party elite.[1]

The first of these measures was the elimination of Gierek's potential and real opponents from positions of authority and power within the party and government. The initial brunt of this action was directed against former Gomulka associates. Following the removal of his closest friends from the inner leadership group in December 1970, the purge of old Gomulka supporters was carried out in piecemeal fashion throughout 1971. At the February 1971 meeting of the Central Committee, Ignacy Loga-Sowinski and Stanislaw Kociolek, who had held sensitive posts in Gomulka's regime controlling the trade union movement and the Gdansk party organization, respectively, were removed from the Politburo. In June, the last holdover from Gomulka's days in the Secretariat, Artur Starewicz, was dropped from the party executive body. Concurrently, sweeping changes were made in the composition of state government organs. Perhaps the most important was the removal of Jozef Cyrankiewicz, who had long occupied the position of prime minister, from executive control over the administration and his transfer to the largely ceremonial post of chairman of the Council of State on December 21, 1970. The most comprehensive personnel change took place in the economic administration. Almost all incumbents, including titular head of planning sector Stefan Jedrychowski, were replaced by new Gierek nominees.

Gradually, this process of elimination extended to supporters of factional groupings that had long operated within the party. Especially thorough was Gierek's effort to destroy the Partisan group and to completely eradicate the sources of its political influence. Although there is little doubt that the Partisans' support had been instrumental in securing Gierek's initial political success, their influence over party activities rapidly diminished. One of the main Partisan leaders, Grzegorz Korczynski, was relieved of his control over military security services in December 1970, after having been accused of orchestrating the abortive attempt at suppressing the workers' revolt by force. Subsequently, Korczynski was transferred to the foreign service and sent abroad as Poland's ambassador to Algeria. A similar fate awaited Moczar. Having reached the pinnacle of power within the party by combining his membership in the Politburo and the Secretariat in December 1970, Moczar saw his influence gradually declining during the following months. At the Central Committee meeting in June 1971, after having been appointed to the politically insignificant post of chairman of the Supreme Control Chamber, Moczar resigned his position in the party Secretariat. Control over the internal security service passed into the hands of the new Secretary of the Central Committee, Stanislaw Kania, a close Gierek supporter, who immediately launched a comprehensive purge of Moczar's appointees and supporters from the entire security apparatus. In May 1972, Moczar lost his last remaining political base when he was removed from the chairmanship of ZBoWiD, a veterans' organization that was changed into just another social service agency subject to the close supervision of the party leadership.

This process of political consolidation of the top leadership around Gierek's group culminated at the sixth party congress, which met in Warsaw on December 6–11, 1971. Among the significant personnel changes decided at the gathering was the removal of the remaining representatives of the Gomulka era, Jozef Cyrankiewicz and Stefan Jedrychowski, as well as Moczar himself from the Politburo. In addition, Cyrankiewicz was dropped from the Council of State, while Jedrychowski was transferred from the foreign ministry to the less politically sensitive post of finance minister. Their departure marked an almost complete break with the past pattern of political continuity in the top party organs; with the exception of Gierek and Tejchma, no other member of either the Politburo or the Secretariat had a tenure in each of these units going beyond the year 1968.

The process of political purification of the party rapidly extended to the entire organization. Following the Politburo decision of April 1971 to eliminate "unfortunate phenomena accompanying party evolution during the past years," a mass campaign of verification of the party membership in terms of past and present commitments to the organization was undertaken. It resulted in the removal of more than 140,000 members from the party ranks by the end of 1971, of which more than 13,000 were expelled for organizational and political abuses of party discipline. As a consequence of this purge, the greatest since 1958, the membership of the party declined by about 3.5 percent in comparison with the previous year, reversing a ten-year-long pattern of continuing growth.[2] Subsequently, the influx of new members into the party resumed at a slow pace and under the markedly tightened control of the central party organs. Indicative of this trend to solidifying centrally executed supervision over membership recruitment was the resolution of the sixth congress, imposing a requirement of annual individual interviews with at least a third of the current membership, to be conducted by professional party staffers and specially appointed representatives of the central organs.[3] In September 1972, this requirement was further amplified by a directive issued by the central party Secretariat, pointing to the need of a constant qualitative strengthening of the party through a purge of those members whose behavior could "adversely affect the policy as well as statutory rules of the party, and especially [might] weaken the principles of democratic centralism."[4]

In another consolidating measure, Gierek sought to create a new political cadre that would be politically attuned to the new developmental tasks and personally owed its loyalty to the central leadership. This tendency was, of course, most noticeable at the level of the party elite, but also extended to lower organizational organs.

Having established himself before December 1970 as a pragmatic and efficient party administrator, Gierek subsequently demonstrated a clear preference in his choice of associates for officials with management training and experience. Among nineteen members of the Politburo and the Secretariat who were elected at the sixth congress of the party in 1971, sixteen had completed university level studies and all had long years of administrative experience by having served as provincial party secretaries, officials in the party apparatus, or as leaders in communist youth organizations.[5] The importance of leadership administrative training was endorsed from the highest party level for the entire organization. The main accent was put on improving the quality of the party's professional staff, in which the full-time positions were reserved "mainly for people with at least a secondary school diploma and with prospect of improving their professional skills."[6] At the Central Committee meeting in September 1972 Prime Minister Jaroszewicz, speaking on behalf of the Politburo, officially proclaimed that all secretaries of local committees should have higher education. Less than a month later the Politburo established a Management Training Center operating under the direct supervision of the Central Committee's organizational staff.[7] Its explicitly formulated function was to raise the qualifications of both the economic administrators and the local party apparatus.

Generally speaking, this stress on educational and managerial improvement was indicative of the leadership's desire to deal more effectively with problems of economic and administrative change. At the same time, however, it was not free of certain ideological and political ambiguities. In particular, by veering toward a more realistic perception of societal needs, the leadership appeared to discard some elements of the traditional communist outlook and to embrace clearly pragmatic notions. The crucial point here was not so much an outright rejection of the ideological principles, never clearly renounced or abandoned, but rather an attempt to recast them in terms of current developmental needs. This was sufficient, nonetheless, to create grounds for potential difficulties and problems. Commenting on the implication of new personnel policy for the party, a well-known communist writer pointed out that "educated and professionally trained employees of the party apparatus find it easier to communicate with plant managers, engineers, economists, and other experts than with the workers. . .No wonder that sometimes we boast of the large number of educated men in the party cadre and then carefully point out the number of representatives of workers and peasants in party offices. And it is not hard to perceive that these two criteria—emphasized in turn—are mutually contradictory."[8]

To contain any narrow technocratic tendencies that might be spawned in managerial retraining, considerable emphasis was placed on expanding and tightening ideological preparation for party activists and staff members. Several schools closed during Gomulka's rule were reopened and the number of students completing ideological courses during 1972–1975 exceeded 30,000.[9] Viewed against the background of the party's political experiences during the previous ten years or so, this renewed emphasis on ideological preparedness testified to a centrally directed attempt to forge a specific framework of doctrinal cohesiveness.

Regarding the political aspect of this process, the motive force behind Gierek's creation of a new party operational cadre was to reassert the primacy of the centralized leadership, within which he was a clearly dominant figure, over the organization, which had long suffered from internal disorganization and fragmentation of power. Within this context, the centrally imposed requirement of high educational achievement for party office might be viewed as providing, along with the development of party managerial capacities, a potent weapon against the frequently unwieldy and rarely well-educated, established, local functionaries. The replacement of 12 out of 22 provincial secretaries during the first year of Gierek's rule, as well as a massive program of rotation of local officials at the province and district levels, was a telling indication of the internal shifts within the organization.[10]

An important factor which greatly facilitated the implementation of Gierek's centralizing tactics was the political and organizational homogeneity of the leadership group itself. In many respects the political background and experience, policy orientation, and operational preferences of all the elite members formed a congruent pattern which has contributed to the establishment of a deeply rooted sense of identity and solidarity. While some of its members had belonged to the wartime underground movements (Franciszek Szlachcic and Ryszard Frelek) and others had served in communist organizations abroad either in the Soviet Union (Piotr Jaroszewicz, Wladyslaw Kruczek, and Andrzej Werblan) or in Western Europe (Edward Gierek and Zdzislaw Grudzien) such early experiences left little discernible effect on their political activities. This was largely because their participation in those organizations had been too insignificant to establish a lasting identification with specific, historically defined groupings. Rather, the distinguishing quality of the entire group was its common experience of having gone, as relatively junior staff members, through a thorough organizational training in the ranks of the old Bierut apparatus or its youth appendages.

Having witnessed the decay of Stalinist revolutionary enthusiasm, they lost whatever ideological beliefs they might have originally had and developed their own highly pragmatic attitudes toward the political system, the society, and the nature of its future evolution. Their main concern was to preserve the existing institutional framework within which the party could continue its leading and directing political role. When faced with a threat to the stability of the system, such as a massive workers' strike movement in early 1971, they rallied to its defense through intensified efforts at promoting political unification and organizational cohesion. In some respects, such a response was not new, since political unity and organizational streamlining had

figured prominently as basic operational concepts during the earlier revolutionary phase. Under current conditions, while the policy objectives had
changed from revolution to mere administration of its results, they were again
accorded a prominent place in an effort to consolidate the party so it could
fulfill its self-proclaimed role.

Within such a conceptually unified group, a special position was occupied
by leaders with direct personal or political links to Silesia and Gierek. Of six
members with the Silesian background, four (Gierek, Babiuch, Szlachcic,
and Szydlak) held seats in both the Politburo and the Secretariat and this
group constituted a political nucleus of the leadership. In this way personal
ties, associated with mutual trust and dependence, provided the basis for the
leadership consolidation around Gierek, the central figure in the hierarchy of
power.

Closely related to Gierek's effort to create a cohesive political cadre was
his attempt to permanently restructure the entire party organization. The
main accent of this process was on a guarded, gradual, and indirect approach
to change. There was no attempt to alter the statutory rules of the party, which
had been declared at the sixth congress as "needing no change, providing sufficient ground for strengthening of the leading role of the party, serving well
[as the basis for] ideological, political, and organizational unity of its ranks,
solidifying the inner party democracy but also discipline for the realization of
its tasks."[11] Instead, the organizational change was linked to a comprehensive
modification of the state territorial administration, ostensibly designed to introduce a uniform system of management at all levels of local government.
The first step, implemented in January 1973, consolidated about 4,300 rural
communities (*gromada*) into 2,381 larger communes (*gmina*) into which were
fused all towns of less than 5,000 inhabitants. By the end of 1977, the number
of communes had declined to about 2,000. The second step, introduced in
May 1975 and immediately implemented, eliminated 314 districts (*powiat*)
and increased the number of provinces (*wojewodztwo*) from 22 to 49, of
which 3 represented large, administratively separate cities.

Parallel to the changes in the state territorial administration, the party organizational structure was substantially transformed. In 1972 a new, systematically prepared network of communal and town committees was formed,
charged with the task of "securing conformity between the resolution of localized problems and the fulfillment of communal duties consequent to the general program of socialist construction."[12] The 1975 reform led to a complete
elimination of all district committees, while the number of provincial party
units more than doubled. The political essence of these changes was two-fold:
first, the reforms provided the ground for a massive renovation of the party
administrative personnel; second, they significantly altered the distribution
of power within the organization through enhancing the controlling capabilities of the central leadership.

By creating a separate network of communal and town committees, the central organs of the party were in a position to channel some of the activists away from the influence of the long-established district and provincial units and to introduce new people into the local apparatus. To prepare a new cadre of communal party secretaries and make it compatible with the style and expectations of the central leadership, more than 2,300 specially selected activists were trained in courses organized by the Secretariat of the Central Committee.[13] The subsequent elimination of the district committees, combined with the numerical expansion of the provincial units, dealt a hard blow to the power of local leaders and organs through both the geographical limitation of their responsibilities and an effective cut in their political patronage. It also opened up the opportunity for a sweeping relocation of the administrative personnel and appointment to the newly created posts of people owing allegiance to the central leadership.

Along with those efforts at political and organizational consolidation of its position within the party, the Gierek leadership launched a program of massive economic recovery aimed at comprehensive improvement in the standard of living and lasting advancement in industrial modernization. The main emphasis was put on the rapid increase in mass consumption, with expanded imports and foreign credits as the primary stimulants of domestic development.[14]

Officially unveiled at the sixth congress in December 1971, this policy produced impressive economic results during subsequent years. At the end of 1975, the gross national product had increased by 59 percent over 1970 and industrial employment rose 14.8 percent, with the rate of industrial production going up by 44.3 percent. Aided by the continuing freeze on food prices from January 1971 until the end of 1974, real wages in 1975 were up by 40.9 percent over 1970 for an average annual growth rate of 8 percent, a major change from the average of 1.9 percent during the whole previous decade. The industrial boom provided new jobs, brought higher income, and created the foundations for an emerging feeling of material security among the population. There was no doubt about the rise in the standard of living, and the growing investments—147.3 percent in capital goods and 75.3 percent in consumer industries since 1970—reinforced expectations for further progress.[15]

Economic success furnished the basis for political stability, with a considerable degree of popular support for the leadership. Anxious to solidify these positive attitudes into a more durable public commitment to the system in place, Gierek rapidly moved to improve the relationship between the party and the society. Proclaimed officially as indicative of the emerging "new style and methods of political work,"[16] this effort found its practical expression in a number of areas.

In early 1971 numerous nonparty experts and social scientists were invited by the Politburo to join a newly created party and government commission to suggest ways of modernizing the state economic and administrative machinery. Concurrently, restrictions imposed on several intellectuals who had fallen into disgrace after the 1968 protests were lifted, and they were allowed to resume publication. In another development, several student leaders imprisoned in 1969 were released in 1971 and some emigré scholars were invited to return to Poland from the West.

Inasmuch as those conciliatory gestures showed the leadership's intention to placate the intellectual community and pacify its most vocal groups, similar measures of reconciliation were undertaken toward the workers. The most important was the introduction of new comprehensive labor legislation, the Labor Code, which, after a lengthy process of discussion and elaboration, went into effect in January 1975. Its major provisions included the abolition of any differentiation between white-collar employees and manual workers with regard to their respective rights and obligations of employment, the expansion of benefits for working women, and the codification of rules related to employment contracts, work discipline, and termination procedures. Another measure aimed at creating an atmosphere of cooperation between the party leadership and the workers was the highly publicized practice of periodic mass meetings with top party leaders in large industrial plants. These were to provide a specific forum for an ongoing process of popular consultations, which would help the leaders formulate social and economic policies while providing the workers a sense of participation in decision making.

Yet, if one assumed that these efforts to increase popular involvement in public affairs would produce a degree of democratization of political life, such expectations failed to materialize. Rather, acting on the basis of newly found social support for its economic policies, the Gierek leadership turned toward a decisive reconsolidation of the party's political control over social activities. Underlying this tendency was the leadership's determined opposition to any form of sociopolitical activity that might have developed independently of the party's direct supervision. The manner with which the authorities treated the former leaders of the 1971 workers' strikes illustrated this attitude. Although the strike committees had spontaneously dissolved following the change in government economic policy, considerable effort was subsequently mounted to undermine the popularity of the former strike activists and to sever their links with other workers. The measures taken against them included dismissal from shop-floor jobs through transfer to other duties, cooptation into established agencies of workers' representation with a view toward political resocialization, and, in some cases, direct political persecution.[17] The right to strike itself, while not explicitly denied, was never officially acknowledged. Instead, the problem was conveniently circumvented through an official and frequently repeated assertion that in the communist system in Poland "there are not and cannot be any antagonistic conflicts between the workers' organization and the economic and state administration."[18]

But this subtle form of repression was only one of the leadership's tactics. More important was a series of political reforms for lasting institutionalization of the party's leading and directing role within the system. The first step in this direction was the unification of party and state offices in one individual at all administrative levels. Following the local elections in December 1973, the first secretary of each province, district, and commune committee was to be a chairman of the corresponding people's council. The officially proclaimed motivation behind this reform was to streamline the political work aimed at "securing accelerated social and economic development of regional and local communities." But its essence lay in the "enhancement of the party's capabilities to solidify social control over administration."[19] Writing about the long-term effects of this development on the political system, a knowledgeable Western observer pointed out that it was inevitably leading to "insulating local government from local pressures, providing a single point of contact with the administration, and formally delivering governmental authority into the hands of the party."[20]

The second step was the legal recognition of the party's directing prerogatives over state and public organizations. Although the PUWP had long exercised an effective control over all sociopolitical activities in the country, its supervisory functions derived from the reality of political life rather than the official laws and statutes. In late 1975 the party leadership announced its intention to amend the constitution and, through an inclusion of the party's directing functions into the country's basic charter, to establish a legal basis of legitimacy for its rule. After a prolonged public debate and in spite of considerable opposition to this proposal, the amendment acknowledging the communist organization as a "leading political force in society at the time of socialist construction" was approved by the Sejm on February 10, 1976.[21] But the success of this constitutional change in achieving the legitimizing goal remains highly questionable. In light of the party's perpetual domination of the parliamentary body, the passage of the amendment was clearly ritualized into a mere formality.

Along with this emphasis on legalization of the party's political role and expansion of its administrative prerogatives, the leadership launched a systematically executed drive for consolidation of its influence over the existing social and professional organizations. The main targets of this drive were mass public organizations such as trade unions or youth movements which, after having long been used for transmissional purposes by the party leadership, might have been affected by recent manifestations of public unrest. Despite numerous demands for the expansion of the trade unions' responsibilities and organizational autonomy, voiced by various advocates of institutional reforms in the wake of the 1970–1971 strikes,[22] the party not only failed to heed those calls but in fact augmented the prerogatives of different economic and administrative agencies representing state interests. Thus a new government body, the Ministry of Labor, Wages, and Social Affairs, was created in 1972, with the explicit task of controlling all matters pertaining to employment, salaries, work organization, and working conditions. Subsequently, several government decrees further expanded the rights of management and central administration in decisions regulating wage increases and employment needs. Finally, the Labor Code of 1975 restricted the functions of trade unions and other worker organizations to "cooperation with the appropriate state bodies in preparing and implementing labor legislation."[23]

Similar treatment was extended to several organizations within the party-directed youth movement. In order to "immunize the younger generation against alien influences and alien aspirations and to shape the activities of the young in combatting hostile ideologies,"[24] the Central Committee called in November 1972 for a comprehensive restructuring of the movement, bringing it into line with party policies. This led to the establishment in April 1973 of the Federation of the Socialist Unions of Polish Youth, an administrative body that was to coordinate the activities of various separate organizations. The process of unification culminated in the formation, in April 1976, of a single youth movement under the name of the Union of Socialist Polish Youth. In a manner reminiscent of the early centralizing processes of the late 1940s, this movement became the main operational agency for formulation of uniform programs for youth activities and recruitment of prospective political and organizational activists.

To some extent, these consolidating measures might have been rooted in the exigencies of economic and organizational efficiency; their net political effect, however, was the decline in institutionalized public participation in economic and social policy making. Control over the flow of organized social activity became firmly re-established in the hands of top party officials.

Yet the party leadership did more than successfully resist any tendency toward decentralization of power or greater political autonomy for separate social groups emerging in the wake of prolonged intraparty crises and public manifestations of discontent. While stressing the cause of economic advancement for all social groups as the overriding justification for its actions, it also developed a vigorous campaign of ideological mobilization for unifying the entire society behind its program and policies. It included an expansion of party propaganda activities designed to inculcate the population with its socioeconomic objectives, a massive dissemination of slogans propounding the values of good and efficient work, and the introduction of a system of rewards for productive achievements.[25] Paradoxically, this massive attempt at social unification was singularly devoid of any traditional notions of either revolutionary or evolutionary egalitarianism. Rather, it seemed to be predicated on the single priority of economic development regulating politics in the entire community. Faced with this priority, all separate social groups had to put aside their particularistic interests lest they jeopardize the common interest. Furthermore, to the degree that the formulation of this priority originated from the party leadership, which was also in charge of its full implementation, all disagreements with its policies had to cease because they, directly or indirectly, were opposed to the good of all.

The major element behind Gierek's success in political and organizational consolidation of his power was the significant support granted him by the Soviet party and its leaders. Moscow's attitude toward Gierek's policies was from the moment of his ascendancy to the top of the party hierarchy, characterized by cautious approval. In part, this initially seems to have been prompted by the recognition that the excessively autocratic pattern of rule which had marked Gomulka's activity since the 1968 upheavals, was a failure in neutralizing social tensions. The resulting outburst of workers' dissatisfaction not only upset the operations of the domestic political system but also had important repercussions throughout the communist bloc. The very real possibility of similar workers' demonstrations in other countries led some of the communist governments subsequently to adopt administrative measures for improving the economic conditions of the people. Needless to say, such osmotic reactions left the Soviet leaders deeply uneasy about the possible effects of future popular upheavals on the political stability of the communist systems.

Against this background, Edward Gierek's replacement of Gomulka must have been viewed in Moscow as a much-needed remedy to an exceedingly difficult situation. Although the Soviet leaders could have been initially concerned over Gierek's ability to control the striking workers, his constantly repeated emphasis on the need to preserve the leading role of the party in all aspects of social and political life was strong assurance that the appeasement-oriented measures would stop short of giving away even a modicum of real power. This, plus Gierek's immediate and frequently reiterated promise of maintaining and further expanding "fraternal and cordial cooperation" with the Soviet Union[26] led to Moscow's decision in mid-February 1971 to extend to Poland a loan of 100 million dollars combined with other forms of economic aid.[27]

Besides these measures of economic help, which had made it possible for Gierek to avoid a major political catastrophe in the form of a possible armed confrontation with the striking workers, the continuing Soviet support provided him with an opportunity to strengthen the party's role and his own position since internal party purification and the subsequent political and organizational stabilization required concentration rather than fragmentation of power on the elite level. By establishing a good working rapport with Gierek, the Soviet leaders greatly contributed to his ability to initiate and control the process of internal party purification and the subsequent political and organizational consolidation. A related aspect of the evolving relationship between Gierek and the Soviet leadership was the political and ideological identity of his internal opponents. While the old Gomulka associates had been immediately pushed out of the main arena of party infighting, the main group of Gierek's potential antagonists consisted of Moczar's Partisans and their nationalistically oriented allies. By throwing their support behind Gierek and his group of technocratic party apparatchiks, Moscow appeared to have sought lasting neutralization of the potentially nationalistic trends in the Polish party.

Equally important seems to have been Moscow's appreciation of Gierek's abilities as an economic administrator and efficient modernizer. Although the Soviet Union has usually been prepared, for reasons of maintaining political control, to periodically supply economic help to Poland, Moscow grew increasingly eager to minimize such economic burdens.[28] Soviet support for Gierek was a logical consequence of such considerations. On the one hand, his long-standing insistence on the need to streamline economic and administrative performance made him potentially capable, or at least willing, to tackle the perennial problems of Poland's economy. On the other hand, Gierek's long tenure in the party apparatus as well as his growing political indebtedness to Moscow guaranteed his continuing loyalty to the communist cause and obedience to Soviet command.

This confidence in Gierek's managerial capabilities and political loyalty seems to have provided the foundation for the Soviet willingness to tolerate his policy of increased economic cooperation with the West. In effect, since Gierek's ascendancy to power, a determined effort was mounted to expand close contacts and cooperative relations with both West European countries and the United States. The dominant accent in this policy was on greatly accelerated trade exchanges, with imports and foreign credits constituting the bulk of all transactions. To the degree that this development enhanced the stabilizing trends in Poland, it corresponded to Soviet interests. Also, since the Soviet Union continued to be the main recipient of Polish exports, the fruits of Poland's internal economic modernization and development were bound to benefit the Soviet economy itself.

At the same time, however, there were a number of indications that the Soviet policy toward Poland went beyond simple political support and acceptance of the Polish changes. Although the extent and form of the Soviet role in Poland's politics have remained impossible to estimate, there has been little doubt that Moscow exercised considerable influence over the direction of PUWP policies. Thus, in launching the program of internal party purges in April 1971, Gierek explicitly linked this policy to Soviet prodding by explaining that "the Soviet comrades are motivated by the correct principle that for a Leninist party, anarchistic weakening [of internal discipline], which is nothing but a parody of democracy, is just as harmful as bureaucratic centralization, paralyzing the development of party organizations, and of initiative and activity among Communists."[29] Similarly, when unveiling the party-sponsored economic reforms in late 1972, Prime Minister Jaroszewicz gave a special emphasis to "the inspiration provided to us by the experiences of the Soviet Union and the other socialist countries."[30]

Indicative of the growing conformity of the PUWP's role and policies to Soviet guidance was an abortive attempt by the party leadership to formalize "the unshakable fraternal bond with the Soviet Union" through an amendment to the constitution.[31] However, following a wave of spontaneous but massive public protests in the form of open letters to the Sejm sent by hundreds of individuals and groups, the proposed change in the country's basic legal statute was restricted to a simple reminder that one of Poland's political goals is to "strengthen its friendship and cooperation with the Soviet Union and other socialist states."[32] The ensuing, bitter attack by Gierek against the opponents of the constitutional change led to a series of revealing statements from his critics on the role of the Soviet party and its leaders in Poland's politics. Thus, long-time Communist and prominent economist Edward Lipinski pointed out in an open letter to the party leader that "we have continued to cling desperately to the Soviet political system for the sake of the consolidation of power, and perhaps above all because of the pressure of the Soviet Union." He then accused the party leadership of "servility" in their attitude toward Moscow and complained that "the imposition of the Soviet-style system [on Poland] caused grave damage to our social and moral life. It was a great disaster in our national history. We are obliged to go along completely and unconditionally with Soviet foreign policy; we are no longer an independent element in world politics, and that is often against our interests."[33] In a similar vein, former Gomulka associate Wladyslaw Bienkowski denounced the Soviet ambassador in Poland for his constant, direct interferences into Polish political and cultural life, implying that such activity "closely resembles the situation of two centuries ago, when, in a still independent Poland, the representative of the Russian Empress acted as a *de facto* governor and with the assistance of corrupted elements and the support of the Russian army. . .suppressed any attempt at renewal in the country."[34]

In spite of the growth of domestic opposition to the pervasive Soviet influence over government policies, there was little doubt that the symbiotic relationship between the PUWP and the CPSU would continue unaffected. This found its full confirmation in the final resolution of the seventh party congress, which met in Warsaw during December 8–12, 1975. It proclaimed the principle of "socialist patriotism" as a guiding notion in the party's activity, "linked integrally with internationalism, with the solidification in social consciousness of a feeling of idealistic unity, friendship, and brotherhood with the Soviet Union and other states of the socialist commonwealth." It also adopted as the major political objective the goal of "impressing upon the social awareness that the realization of all Polish national aims is permanently related to socialism, to the brotherly alliance between Poland and the Soviet Union, to the membership of our country in the socialist community of states and nations."[35] As for the Soviet reaction to this pledge, CPSU leader Brezhnev made it clear in his address to the congress that he considered Gierek "an outstanding figure of People's Poland, the socialist community, and the international communist movement" while the PUWP became, under Gierek's leadership, "cohesive and confident in its strength."[36]

Judging from the course of congressional debates and the subsequent re-election of the leadership group, Brezhnev's assertion on party internal cohesion included a great deal of truth. Following two large-scale organizational reforms carried out since 1972, Gierek seemed to have re-established undisputed control over the party apparatus in all sections of the party. None of the carefully picked 1,811 delegates to the congress questioned the political and economic program submitted by the Politburo for their approval.[37] Gierek's leadership was explicitly praised by numerous speakers and his performance since the 1971 congress was unanimously endorsed.

With regard to the leadership composition, the dominant accent was on continuity. With the size of the party elite, consisting of members of the Politburo and the Secretariat, gradually expanded from 19 at the time of the 1971 congress to 22, only one member of the original Gierek team, Franciszek Szlachcic, failed to win re-election. Szlachcic's political eclipse, however, had begun already in 1974, when his personal ambitions might have put him at odds with the increasingly personalized style of Gierek's rule. Since that time he rapidly lost influence within the party and his removal from the Politburo merely confirmed his political downfall. Thus, in the wake of the congress, the party leadership became more politically homogeneous than ever before, with Gierek emerging as the indisputably dominant figure with no discernible factional groups capable of challenging his authority.

Yet, in spite of the apparent unification of the party and the political consolidation of its leadership, the prospect of a lasting stabilization of Polish sociopolitical life appeared increasingly problematical. The main problems resulted from the collapse of the leadership's strategy of rapid economic growth. The first signs of economic difficulties appeared in 1974 and then rapidly intensified. To some extent, they were brought on by a series of unintended consequences of Poland's reliance on foreign aid for stimulating domestic expansion. A deteriorating international economic situation, resulting from the worldwide oil crisis, drastically affected the government's ability to continue its program of development. The cumulative effect of growing foreign indebtedness, which reached levels of 8 to 9 billion dollars by the end of

1975,[38] and rising prices for imported goods made it necessary to expand the export of domestic products, primarily food, while imposing limitations on consumption at home.

More fundamentally, at the root of the difficulties had been the leadership's failure to develop appropriate forms of organization and management capable of coordinating economic processes, introducing innovation, and facilitating adaptability. This of course was merely a consequence of the leadership's strategy of stabilization itself, in which the main purpose had always been to preserve and strengthen the existing institutionalized framework of party and state structures and relationships rather than to promote lasting socioeconomic advancement. As a result, persistent management inefficiencies, largely due to administrative centralization, were only further magnified by the developmental boom, producing widespread overinvestment, overemployment, and inflationary growth of wages. In essence, therefore, the leadership's emphasis on maintenance of traditional forms and methods of political organization and activity contradicted the requirements of economic and social development. Under rapidly deteriorating economic conditions, such a policy was bound to produce an increase in social tension which, if unchecked, would seriously undermine the stabilizing efforts themselves.

Indicative of the burgeoning social dissatisfaction with the state and party economic performance was a series of localized strikes and protests which, since mid-1974, took place in different parts of the country. Among the more important of these were slowdown strikes in several coastal cities during the summer of 1974 against government attempts to introduce a new wage system tied to the level of productivity.[39] Later that year, there were also manifestations of discontent among the miners in Silesia protesting the shortage of food and consumer goods. Finally, in the spring of 1975 a group of women in Warsaw demolished several grocery stores, demonstrating their frustration with the persistent shortages of meat products.[40]

Regarding the capacity of the leadership to develop an effective policy for comprehensive regulation of those conflicts, the pattern of official response suggested a relatively small appreciation of the potential importance and implications for political stability of the social protests. Although localized conflicts were successfully contained through immediate measures of appeasement, there was no attempt to introduce general and lasting adjustments into social and economic policies. Instead, the dominant accent in the leadership's approach to domestic problems was on both institutional and operational continuity. Within this context, a considerable effort was mounted to present the past economic accomplishments in terms of a consistently elaborated strategy of growth, leading to further advances in the future, while current difficulties were minimized as essentially temporary impediments characteristic of the developmental processes themselves.[41] As such, they were to be dealt with primarily through administrative means, regardless of a possible public resentment of such measures.

The announcement on June 24, 1976, by Prime Minister Piotr Jaroszewicz of a drastic food price increase—ranging from a 69 percent average for meat products to 50 percent for butter and 100 percent for sugar—was a clear illustration of that attitude. In many respects, this decision at first appeared to be perfectly rational. It had been obvious for some time that the rapid growth of inflationary pressures both at home and abroad, combined with shortages of consumer products on the market, made the price increases inevitable. Furthermore, the urgent need for some form of regulation between the demand for agricultural products, especially meat, and their supply on the market had frequently been signaled by high party officials.[42] And yet, both the manner in which the change was introduced and the magnitude of the price increase had a profound effect upon the population. Perhaps most striking was the sudden and abrupt nature of the process. There was no attempt to prepare the public or secure its cooperation. Instead, the price increase was imposed arbitrarily from the top for immediate implementation. In a sense, the entire operation was reminiscent of the earlier centralistic attempt at price regulation in December 1970. As then, participation in decision making was again restricted to a small group of top party officials and their advisors, while the public was simply ignored.

But, just as it had done in 1970, the party policy provoked an immediate outburst of popular dissatisfaction. Its most important feature once again was a massive protest by industrial workers. Within a few hours after the announcement, there were strikes and work stoppages all across the country. Although unlike the situation in 1970 these protests remained essentially peaceful, there was a real danger that the workers could become violent if the price decision were to stand unchanged. Some instances of vandalism and looting took place in the Warsaw region, while in the city of Radom the local party headquarters was set on fire.[43] Faced with a prospect of a nationwide rebellion by workers and mindful that the last workers' revolt in December 1970 had led to a drastic change in the composition of the leadership, the government was forced to reverse its policy. On June 25, less than 24 hours after the original announcement, the food price increases were rescinded.

CHAPTER 9

The Drift to Nowhere

The workers' success in June 1976 in forcing the reversal of an announced government economic decision was a major political development. It was significant for two reasons. First, it exposed the authorities' inability to enforce public compliance with unpopular policies. Second, it showed the population, particularly the workers, that they were an element to be reckoned with in decision making. Both these factors were important, because they demonstrated that the authorities' efforts to ensure control over public life, efforts that had been the essence of the party leadership's strategy of political stabilization, had failed. The workers' success repeated a similar experience in 1971, confirming the government's continuing vulnerability to public pressure; this point was certainly not lost on either the authorities or the public as a whole.

The party and government leaders were obviously aware that the way in which the attempt to increase food prices had been made and the failure to carry it through had damaged their standing with the public. This was apparent from the nationwide propaganda campaign staged immediately after the revocation of the price increases in an attempt to convince the population of the leadership's good faith. Despite their protestations to the contrary, however, their actions were ambiguous and almost contradictory, concentrating on preventing further decline rather than introducing changes.

The official response to the workers' protests was typical of this approach. On the one hand, it appeared to be conciliatory. Promises were repeatedly made, for example, to consult the public—and particularly the industrial workers—before any policies were settled in the future, although exactly how this was to be done was never specified. On the other hand, the authorities moved quickly to avenge their humiliation by the workers. Immediately after the strikes ended, the government moved against selected groups of workers from those towns in which there had been limited violence. Several hundred workers were arrested, many lost their jobs, and an indeterminate number of people were sentenced in trials during the summer and fall of 1976. None of this was likely to strengthen public trust in the authorities.

Major problems also emerged in other areas. This was particularly evident in the economic realm. There was no further attempt to increase prices, but then neither was any apparent effort made to prepare alternative policies. During August and September 1976, rationing of coal and sugar was introduced, although this was a temporary measure and not a policy decision. Instead, to prevent further economic decline, the authorities sought and obtained substantial aid from the Soviet Union. Approved by Moscow in November, this aid consisted of a loan of about $1.3 billion worth of food, raw materials, and consumer products. It was clear, however, that since the Soviet help was primarily intended to provide immediate relief in a disastrous situation, it could hardly be regarded as a permanent solution to Poland's problems.

It was only in December 1976, at a plenum of the party's Central Committee, that an attempt was made to formulate an approach to the economic difficulties. Described by Edward Gierek, who delivered the main address at the plenum, as a "new economic maneuver," this approach envisaged the introduction of a series of operational adjustments to the existing economic programs; these adjustments were to be implemented gradually over several years.[1] The objectives were threefold: first, to impose a measure of austerity through a reduction in investments, primarily in heavy industry; second, to encourage food production by greater support for the entire agricultural sector, including private farmers; and third, to stimulate production of consumer goods by increasing investment in light industry, construction, and consumer services. This was subsequently coupled with promises of support for small private businesses, such as crafts, services, and retail trade outlets. The motive force behind these promises was pragmatic and reflected an "attempt to awaken the private initiative [of the population], without which it is impossible to resolve the current economic difficulties."[2]

Under other circumstances, these modifications in the economy might have met with a positive response from the population. However, given a situation in which the credibility and authority of the leadership had been severely undermined as a result of its abortive attempt to raise food prices, this was not the case. For many people, the leadership's proposals were nothing but more promises and, in light of previous unfulfilled pledges to change the economic system, they were not enough to dissipate popular doubts about the sincerity of the authorities' intentions.

These doubts were justified. None of the provisions were fully and effectively implemented.[3] In subsequent years, the rate of investments remained relatively stable, oscillating around 30 percent of the national income, and in some areas of heavy industry it even increased. The intended shift in support toward light industry was never sufficient to provide a significant, overall increase in consumer products. Official support for small-scale, private industry proved negligible, and the limited measures to encourage the expansion of crafts and services, principally through lowering taxes and providing some access to tools and machinery from state-owned enterprises, produced few results. As for agriculture, it continued to be the most troublesome sector of the economy, incapable of producing a sufficient amount of food to satisfy public demand.

In some respects, the deteriorating economic situation was independent of the leadership's policies. It became clear, for example, that any substantial cut in investments, particularly those earmarked for heavy industry, would adversely affect the economy as a whole. Furthermore, although several industrial projects were abandoned, this failed to release sufficient funds for the expansion of light industry. In addition, official assumptions about the growth in agricultural production were thwarted by a series of climatic difficulties as the country was hit—especially in 1977 and 1979—by massive flooding and drought.

A more fundamental obstacle to resolving the economic difficulties, however, was the attitude of the leadership itself. One aspect of this was its persistent attachment to the strategy of growth and development, which had been successful during the early 1970s and which the leadership was clearly hesitant to abandon or modify. The top party leaders, including Gierek himself, seemed to regard the difficulties of production and supply as temporary phenomena rather than new factors of economic life. They therefore also conceived their actions as temporary, geared to the requirements of the moment and specific problems. For them, the "new economic maneuver" was no more than a tactical adjustment within the continuing strategy of growth. As a result, the leadership never developed a comprehensive economic policy, relying instead on ad hoc, inconsistent measures.

Another feature of the leadership's approach was its reluctance to accept any permanent modification of the economy's administrative structure. This reluctance was mainly to preserve centralization, but it also reflected the existence of well-developed vested interests on the part of various economic institutions and bodies, which, having profited from the development boom of earlier years, exerted considerable pressure on decision makers to refrain from any real reform. Either because of weakness or through lack of foresight, the party leadership did little to resist this pressure.

An even more important influence on economic policy was the leadership's concern that any further price increases might provoke another outburst of public dissatisfaction and protest. Despite rapidly dwindling supplies, food prices had been artificially maintained at 1975 levels. This alone necessitated a huge program of government subsidies; in 1978 these subsidies amounted to about 61 percent more than in 1975.[4] In an attempt to neutralize the growing burden of this expenditure, the government adopted a tactic of concealed price increases by, for example, putting different labels on the same products and expanding the network of so-called "commercial shops," which offered food and consumer products that were either unavailable or difficult to obtain elsewhere at premium prices. By the end of 1979 the number of such shops exceeded 500, which was five times as many as in 1977.[5]

In this situation, the government was forced to rely on foreign aid. This was not new. Credits from abroad, particularly from the West, had already provided the impetus to the leadership's initial strategy of growth and development. Now, further credits became necessary to ride out the difficulties. In the long run, such a policy was bound to create serious problems, although the authorities had made considerable efforts since 1976 to reduce their foreign debts, particularly through the drastic curtailment of imports of consumer goods and some industrial products. Yet massive borrowing continued, reflecting the need both to guarantee the operation of industrial plants and to maintain a level of agricultural production that could contribute to satisfying public demand. By mid-1980 the country's debts to the West alone had reached $23 billion, a more than twofold increase over about $10 billion in 1976.[6]

The political effects of the economic decline were drastic, in that they produced widespread public disillusionment with the leadership's performance. Above all, this created a widespread feeling that the leadership was drifting without any sense of purpose. This fed opposition to its method of government. The emergence of organized dissent was initially prompted by the government's punitive measures against workers who had taken part in the June strikes. Criticism of the authorities' disregard of appeals for leniency for the strikers developed into active opposition to what was regarded by many as an official policy of repression.

Public opposition evolved gradually and involved the emergence of several groups.[7] It began with the establishment in September 1976 of the Committee for the Defense of Workers (KOR). Set up by a small group of prominent intellectuals, the committee's main task was to provide legal and financial help to the families of imprisoned workers and to campaign for their release. Its goals and activities received a significant response at home and abroad. Especially important was the KOR's ability to collect substantial funds to aid needy workers. By September 1977 several hundred workers' families were being provided with financial and medical help.[8]

Largely as a result of the KOR's success, new opposition groups began to appear. In March 1977 the establishment of the Movement for the Defense of Human and Civil Rights (ROPCO) was announced. At about the same time a Polish chapter of Amnesty International was formed. In the summer of 1977 several Student Solidarity Committees (SKS) were founded at various universities as an eventual alternative to the official, party-controlled organization. In the fall of 1977 the SKS network created the so-called Flying University, a series of public, university-level lectures offered by well-known intellectuals on subjects that were either not included in the curriculum of established state schools or were taught there only along the lines of the state-approved interpretation. This initiative quickly received support from other dissident organizations. At the beginning of 1978 it was named the Association of Educational Courses and continued to operate outside the control of the authorities.

In early 1978 the first unofficial workers' organizations, the Free Trade Unions, were established in the mining and shipping industries. A few months later, during the summer of 1978, several Peasants' Self-Defense Committees were founded in various rural communities. In addition, during 1978–1979 a number of other groups appeared—such as anti-abortion leagues, committees for the defense of religion and opposed to discrimination against believers, and teams for independent research—thereby announcing their determination to defend their own specific causes.

Most of these groups insisted on the principle of openness in their organization and activity. The precedent for this was set by the KOR, which announced its establishment in a letter to the speaker of the Sejm.[9] This eventually became standard practice in the dissident movement: particular groups provided formal notification of their statutes to the proper state bodies, periodically published lists of their members, and publicly announced plans of their activities. Alongside such openly operating groups there were also several clandestine organizations. The best known was the so-called Polish Independence Accord (PPN), which brought together several intellectual currents in a patriotic platform calling for the gradual transformation of Poland into an independent and democratically organized state. Yet the main emphasis in dissident activities was, from the beginning, on the public character of the organizations and their observance of the law, in turn justifying their claim to the right to monitor violations of officially prescribed human and civil rights.

The defense of human rights was, in fact, the most important issue behind dissident activities: there was a constant flow of appeals, petitions, and protests addressed to Polish government agencies, to various international organizations, or to the general public. Since these appeals and publications were free of government censorship and outside of official control, they served to break the state's monopoly over communications. By the end of 1979 there were more than twenty underground periodicals circulating in the country and several underground publishing houses capable of producing full-length novels as well as political and even scientific literature.

Thus, the emergence of dissident groups and their activities created an atmosphere of continuing political ferment. This in itself did not imply a rejection of the entire communist system or preparations to revolutionize it. It did, however, herald an attempt to broaden the framework of politics to allow greater participation by various groups under conditions in which they could maintain their own organizational identities.

Underlying this was the increasingly widespread conviction that the Communist Party leadership was incapable of effectively managing public affairs by itself. Under these circumstances, demands for open and recognized public participation in political life were conceived not so much as an attack on the party or its policies, but rather as a means of confronting problems faced by the nation as a whole.

The dissidents refrained from any consciously formulated challenges to the party's role or programs. Neither did they attempt to establish links with potential critics of the leadership's policies within the party itself. Indeed, internal party matters were viewed by the dissidents with a certain measure of disregard. Their main interest was in affecting the public as a whole. Commenting on this situation, a Western observer noted that dissident actions were

> not merely, or even primarily, directed at effecting a dialogue with the party, or with its reformist elements. Nor were they an attempt to work within the existing system of power, or to manipulate or mold it by utilizing its own mechanisms to bring about a change in the character of that system. [They were], instead, an endeavor to talk with, guide, direct, and appeal to society itself, to those on the outside.[10]

The authorities' response to political dissent was ambiguous, mostly antagonistic but also tolerant. Initially, in the apparent hope of containing the spread of opposition groups, the government adopted a series of restrictive measures ranging from press and institutional harassment to police intimidation and arrests of dissident leaders. The most dramatic incident occurred on May 7, 1977, in the city of Krakow, where a young KOR supporter was found dead in rather obscure circumstances. A protest by the KOR against the lack of an official investigation into his death resulted in the arrest of several prominent representatives of the dissident group. The government's attempt to silence its critics only prompted a counter-reaction, however: ten KOR members and sympathizers went on a week-long hunger strike in a Warsaw church to publicize their demands for the release of those arrested and of several still-imprisoned workers. This resulted in a renewed press campaign of vilification against opposition groups, complete with accusations of collaboration with foreign intelligence agencies.[11] Finally, a general amnesty in July freed all arrested protesters and workers, and their cases were officially closed.

This attempt to ease political tension by meeting the dissidents' demands failed to end the momentum of opposition activities. The release of the workers was seen by the dissidents as evidence of their growing strength rather than as an indication of the party leadership's desire for reconciliation. They were now determined to expand their work and establish themselves as a quasi-organized movement of opposition to the party and the government.[12] In September 1977 the KOR changed its name to the Committee for Social Self-Defense (KSS-KOR), which indicated the extension of its goals from the defense of a specific social group—the workers—to human rights in general. Similarly, ROPCO opened a network of offices throughout the country to collect and publicize information about official violations of individual freedom. There was no reaction from the authorities.

This restraint in dealing with the opposition was a direct consequence of the leadership's efforts to secure peace or, at least, to avoid public disturbances. It is also possible that the PUWP leaders' contacts with Western governments restricted their behavior and policy. They became particularly vulnerable to Western influence following the two-year Conference on Security and Cooperation in Europe, which culminated in the signing of the Helsinki Accords in August 1975 and created at least a formal obligation for the party leadership to respect basic human rights and individual freedom. There is little doubt that the humanitarian provisions of the accords had some impact on the leadership's activities, exposing them to international criticism while providing dissident groups with a legitimizing incentive for action. An equally important conditioning factor was the leadership's increasing dependence on Western economic support.

What was more important, the party leadership clearly did not regard the dissidents' activities as a serious challenge either to its power or its policies. In fact, the dissident groups, vocal and active as they were, were neither willing nor capable of competing for power with the institutional establishment. It is even possible that the leadership regarded the existence of open political dissent, as long as it affected a relatively small section of the population, as constructive, providing as it did an outlet for releasing tension.

The main thrust of the leadership's activities was instead concentrated on maintaining its hold over the party organization. In this area, the leadership appeared successful. Although there was considerable speculation that the June 1976 debacle would lead to a resurrection of factional infighting or would prompt changes in the composition of the highest party bodies, Gierek and his associates managed to preserve a reasonable level of organizational cohesion and discipline. No factions appeared and no changes were made.

A particular effort was made to appease industrial workers. Most of the workers imprisoned after the June 1976 strikes were freed early in January 1977 and a conditional pardon for those who "showed repentance" was announced the following month.[13] There was also a concerted recruitment drive to attract workers into the party. By the end of May 1977, the percentage of workers in the party had risen from 40.6 percent at the time of the seventh congress in 1975 to 45.6 percent, the highest since 1954. Conversely, white-collar membership declined from 42.9 to 34.3 percent, and that of peasants dropped from 9.9 to 9.3 percent (see Appendix 1).[14]

This success in managing the party was not affected by sporadic signs of internal dissatisfaction with aspects of the leadership's policies—for example, the discussion of the value of the economic and administrative centralization of the party-controlled press at the end of 1977.[15] The debate, which had developed clearly antagonistic undertones and involved several ranking party propagandists, ended abruptly and inconclusively. Another sign of possible criticism of the leadership's policies from within the party surfaced at the beginning of 1978, when an open letter to Gierek from a group of older party personalities, including former first party secretary Edward Ochab and several other past secretaries of the Central Committee, was leaked to the Western press. It contained strong criticism of Gierek's style of government and his policies and demanded the public discussion of social and economic problems. The signatories to the letter demanded drastic internal reforms, charging that "the source of our principal difficulties and failures is largely political, including undemocratic forms of government and, above all, a lack of democratic discussion to determine objectives and choose methods for solving social and political problems."[16]

Although these discussions and complaints might suggest a degree of concern within the party over the leadership's policies, they made no impact on policy making. They seemed merely to reflect the sentiments of a small portion of the membership, the great majority of which appeared solidly united behind the leadership. Such a pattern of organizational compliance strongly suggested that Gierek was still able to preserve internal conformity to his authority. This was particularly remarkable, considering that the focus of political activity in the country as a whole was noticeably shifting away from the party's control.

This development was signaled by the emergence of dissident organizations and was reinforced by the growth of the Catholic Church's activism. During the years that followed the PUWP's break with Stalinist revolutionary traditions, the Church and the party managed to establish a modus vivendi. The Church implicitly accepted the realities of power that gave the party a decisive voice in policy making and concentrated its efforts on securing the necessary conditions for its work. The party quickly discovered that it needed at least tacit cooperation from the Church to ensure public acceptance of its policies, especially at times of political crisis. This became particularly apparent during the upheavals of 1956 and 1971. In both instances Church leaders urged the population to preserve the peace.

Beneath this surface of coexistence, relations between the Church and the party remained tense. Although the party had abandoned its direct persecution of Church officials and its brutal attacks on religion, it preserved its ultimate objective of eradicating the Church's influence on society. The fundamental issue that had fueled tension in Church-party relations was the party's insistence on its prerogative to define the form and direction of organized public activities. The Church was critical of any emphasis of Marxism-Leninism in social and cultural life.

During the early years of Gierek's rule, between 1971 and 1975, Church-party relations were relatively uneventful. Although the officially supported campaign against religion continued unabated, prompting periodic statements from the Church that denounced any attempt to reduce religious influence in public life, the level of mutual recriminations remained restrained. The party leadership, it seems, consciously avoided any specific confrontation with the Church, apparently convinced that its strategy of stabilization through economic expansion would eventually weaken the influence of religion in a society bent on consumption and leisure. That much was suggested by Minister of Religious Affairs Kazimierz Kakol, who told a gathering of party activists in 1974 that "the best battlefield for defeating the Church is at the cultural level of an easier and more comfortable way of life. With a consumer society, we shall acquire the conditions, analogous to those in the West, for rapidly making the Church out of date."[17]

The latent tension in Church-party relations came into the open following the adoption in February 1976 of a constitutional amendment that formalized the party's leading role. The Church leaders decried the measure as creating the danger of dividing "citizens into two categories [party and nonparty members] and of subjecting the whole of our life to a materialistic outlook, which would be unacceptable to believers."[18] The authorities ignored the protest.

The conflict sharpened in the aftermath of the events of June 1976. In August the episcopate issued a pastoral letter protesting the official mistreatment of workers who had taken part in the demonstrations. Subsequently, several important Church leaders, including the primate, Stefan Cardinal Wyszynski, and Karol Cardinal Wojtyla, criticized in their sermons the government's civil-rights policies. More important still, there emerged something akin to an alliance between the Church and the dissident groups in their common concern over human rights. Catholic priests, in fact, were among the founders and activists of some of the opposition groups, and various dissident gatherings took place in churches. The dissidents were quick to express their appreciation of the Church's position and called for continuing cooperation.[19]

There was no official reaction to these activities, and the links between the Church and the dissidents were generally ignored. Indeed, steps were even taken by the party leadership to meet some of the Church's long-standing grievances. In May 1977, for example, after twenty years of procrastination, the authorities permitted the completion of a church in Nowa Huta, the largest "socialist town" in Poland, which had about 200,000 inhabitants and no place of worship. Permits were later issued for other churches. In another gesture indicating the party's apparent willingness to come to terms with the Church, Gierek met with Cardinal Wyszynski in October 1977 to confer on "the most important problems of the nation and the Church, which are of great significance for the unity of the Poles in their work of shaping the prosperity of Poland."[20] Nothing was said about the nature of those "problems," but on December 1 Gierek succeeded, with the openly acknowledged assistance of Wyszynski, in securing an audience with Pope Paul VI.

During that audience the Pope told Gierek that, while the Church in Poland "was not asking for privileges, it had the right to be itself and to carry out its mission unimpeded."[21] In response, Gierek promised to "do our best to establish, in the spirit of traditional Polish tolerance, a state of affairs in which there is no conflict between the Church and the state. We have the will to cooperate in the implementation of great national purposes."[22]

The conflict only intensified, however, as both sides rapidly moved to make their respective positions public. The Church's stand, expressed in various statements and pastoral letters, took the form of specific demands. They included the lifting of censorship and more newsprint for the Catholic press; television and radio broadcasts of religious services; the right to form independent Catholic associations; and, above all, the full recognition by the state of the Church's legal status as a public institution. The communist government had, in fact, withdrawn formal recognition of the Church as a legal entity in 1945, following its unilateral renunciation of a concordat with the Vatican.[23] Since then the Church has been deprived of any legal standing within the state, although the government provided in a ministerial instruction for the provisional recognition of the legal status of specific religious bodies, such as parishes and dioceses as well as religious orders and seminaries in order to facilitate their administration. The Church leaders insisted on regularizing this situation.

This insistence was justified by the Church's historical role as custodian of the nation's religious and cultural values and by the need for institutional guarantees for the preservation of political and social equality between Catholics and nonbelievers, within the framework of a militantly atheistic state. This concern that Catholics must not be deprived of their essential civil rights was expressed by Cardinal Wojtyla, the Archbishop of Krakow, in a Corpus Christi sermon in June 1978:

Being such a vast community, a community almost as great as the nation itself, we cannot be outside the law. Definition of the legal status of the Church is at the same time definition of our place, all our rights, everything that originates in the concept of the freedom of religion, recognized throughout the world and declared in international documents.[24]

These were sensitive issues, with potentially serious ideological and political repercussions for the party and the political system. This was fully understood by the Church leaders, who were careful not to present them as challenges to the party. Cardinal Wyszynski made this point explicitly in a sermon in January 1978, when he said that "the Church does not reach for power. Neither does it want. . .to create a state within the state. . .when we advocate recognition of the legal status of the Church, we do not want to make the Church an institution of political importance."[25] Even so, these demands clearly ran counter to the party's policies and its vision of the socialist state. For the party was, in fact, determined to reduce the Church's public role to the fulfillment of only those functions that would support its own leading position.

Gierek was clear on that point. Speaking at a Sejm session in January 1978, he said:

> The basic assumption of our party's policy is that socialist Poland is being built by the whole nation, that is, party members and citizens not affiliated with the party, who are united by love of the homeland and acceptance of a socialist path of development. The Polish United Workers' Party. . .is the driving force behind the nation's cause. . .This also applies to religious relations, which are being shaped by the people's government in a spirit of national unity and on the basis of the constitutional principles of freedom of conscience and religion, tolerance, and mutual respect. The common efforts of the nation leave room for cooperation between the Church and the state. This cooperation should encompass everything that serves the development of Poland and the strengthening of her security and position in the world as well as everything that is conducive to the family, the progress of culture, and the shaping of social discipline and civic responsibility.[26]

Whereas Gierek's statement focused on general aspects of the party's policy toward the Church, subsequent comments on his speech in the party press justified official refusal of the Church's specific demands. In *Polityka,* a journal regarded as close to the leadership, it was said that the Church's demands would be "impossible to satisfy because they imply violation of the principle of separation of the Church and the state. . .[which is] one of the foundations of our political system."[27] The article went on to state that "it would be illogical if the authorities, given their historical mission on behalf of the nation, were to show understanding for activities that make the fulfillment of that mission more difficult."

Even more explicit in its insistence on the dominance of the party over the Church was another comment in *Polityka.* Its author argued that "the most important demands of the Church, those concerned with the greater participation of believers in public life. . .could only be considered in connection with the further progress of socialist democracy and civic activity." He then warned that, so long as the Church refrained from "a real involvement in support of state policies," the question of the increased participation of Christians in public life would depend more on relations between "nonparty citizens and the state" than on "relations between the Church and the state." Within the state, "party members occupy a special position. . .[because] they are members of the ruling party. . .They impart character to the state, are its driving force, and through them the party implements its policy. . .That is why the scope of possible influence of the state over sociopolitical matters must not be restricted and must not be limited in any way."[28]

Here the matter appears to have rested, at least until the election of Karol Cardinal Wojtyla as Pope on October 16, 1978. His election had two immediate effects on Polish politics. First, it considerably strengthened the prestige of the Church among the Polish people. Secondly, it produced new and widespread interest in the international press, and through it, among world public opinion, about the Church in Poland. This naturally tended to strengthen the Church's role in the country's life and, by implication, weaken the party's position.

This was certainly not lost on the party. To be sure, there were no immediate concessions; instead, the authorities' position appears to have hardened. This was indicated by an article in *Polityka* that, in the absence of official statements on Church-party relations, seemed designed to restate the main aspects of the leadership's stance. Published in March 1979, the article said that "Poland will remain a lay state, and Marxists will actively work toward the preservation and the strengthening of exactly that characteristic of the people's state. Any change from that position would not be acceptable as it would be contrary to the established interests of the socialist state and the nation."[29] The article went on to say that

> The Catholic Church, by the very nature of its mission, [already] has considerable possibilities for influencing the minds of believers and to shape moral and patriotic attitudes compatible with the national interests of Poland. The realization of these tasks neither requires giving the Church any new rights nor [justifies] any interference by the Church hierarchy in those areas of social, economic, and other policies that are the sole domain of the state.

On June 2, 1979, Pope John Paul II arrived in Poland for a nine-day visit. The visit was triumphal.[30] During his travels the Pope saw and was seen by millions of enthusiastic people, delivered some 30 addresses and sermons, and projected for listeners in Poland and elsewhere—many parts of the visit were televised and broadcast in various countries—a dynamic and activist image of the Church under his pontificate. It was to be a Church openly participating in all the major events of public life and fully involved in the main issues of contemporary society. Yet it was also not to be an omnipotent Church but rather one that would draw its strength from the attitudes of the people themselves, providing that they espoused the fundamental values of Christianity.

Although the visit was, above all, a religious event, it also had other facets. It was a joyous event, as the vast majority of the population suddenly found itself united in a common euphoria of pride and satisfaction. It was a profoundly moral experience, prompting humanitarian feelings and ideas. It was also a political development, providing a serious though indirect challenge to the communist system.

This was particularly apparent in Pope John Paul II's insistence on the inalienable rights of man, including the right to religious liberty, as the basis for all public activity. It was also reflected in the discipline that the Church organizers were able to demand from the public. It suggested that the Church was not only able to mobilize considerable public support for, but also to secure mass cooperation in, the realization of its plans. That alone was a reminder of the Church's real influence over the population, a factor that was difficult for the party to ignore.

Even so, Church-party relations did not appreciably change as a result of the papal visit. Official restrictions on Catholic publications continued unabated, no permission was given for the establishment of new Catholic organizations, and there was no movement toward fulfillment of any of the Church's other demands. The leadership's policy continued to reflect an unflinching determination to oppose any form of Catholic activity that might develop independently of official supervision.

There appeared, however, signs of mounting restlessness in society generally. This was noticeable in the dissident activities. Such groups as KSS-KOR, ROPCO, the SKSs, and the Free Trade Unions periodically organized meetings and demonstrations in many cities and their unofficially published books and bulletins reached large numbers of readers throughout the country. In September 1979 a group of ROPCO members established a self-proclaimed "political party," the Confederation for Independent Poland (KPN), with an explicitly anti-communist and nationalistic program.[31]

The restlessness spread to other sectors of the population. In November 1978 a group of journalists and intellectuals, most of them active party members, set up a public discussion club called Experience and the Future (DiP). It had its inaugural meeting in Warsaw on November 14, when the organizers invited some 100 prominent scholars, writers, economists, and artists to take part in a debate on current problems. Among those present were several PUWP Central Committee members as well as some well-known Catholic activists and journalists. Alarmed by the critical tenor of the debate, the authorities expressly forbade a follow-up meeting, scheduled for January 1979.

Under any other circumstances, this would have been sufficient to put an end to the club's activities. It was not the case this time, however, although the authorities' action forced the club to modify its plans. Its founders, under the leadership of the well-known journalist and party member Stefan Bratkowski, undertook to compile a report on the views of all participants in the inaugural gathering as well as those of other selected intellectuals, some 200 people in all, on the main problems of Polish life.

The "Report on the State of the Republic and the Methods of Its Reform" eventually appeared in mid-May 1979. It reflected the views of some 50 prominent scholars and intellectuals, who anonymously answered a questionnaire on the major economic, social, and political problems facing Poland. The report was sent to the country's top political and religious leaders, such as PUWP first secretary Edward Gierek and Stefan Cardinal Wyszynski, as well as selected members of the intellectual establishment. The text was eventually published by a dissident publishing house.

The report's main contentions were that the country was undergoing a severe, deep, and multifaceted crisis and that this crisis had arisen from factors inherent "in the way of conducting policy and exercising power."[32] More specifically, the report said:

> [This] crisis affects many fundamental aspects of the community's life. It creates, therefore, a situation which is both deeply alarming and gradually, but inevitably, deteriorating. There is no longer any hope that, with the passage of time, the symptoms of the crisis will disappear as processes of internal adoptation set in and methods of government and management improve. The deterioration in the situation results, on the one hand, from the increasing incompatibility between [the country's] growing requirements—created by the development of industrialization and the complexity of contemporary society—and, on the other hand, from the ineffectiveness of the entire system of social relations.

The report said that this created a widespread public conviction that "a radical change in the sociopolitical system is both absolutely necessary and completely impossible." This, in turn, was said to have prompted the emergence of two extreme and mutually contradictory orientations among the public: either total conformity and apathy, or rejection of the entire system of government. The report appealed for the speedy introduction of reforms, but it also warned that "no reforms even if they were to be formulated with the best of intentions, can succeed without support from society."

There was no reaction to the DiP report from either the party's leadership or its rank and file, although there were various indications that the authorities' inertia was provoking objections within the ruling establishment itself. In November 1978 Mieczyslaw Moczar—the former leader of an authoritarian faction within the party, who, having lost his top leadership functions in 1971, had a relatively obscure job as chairman of the Supreme Chamber of Control—complained in a national magazine about administrative corruption and disarray. In particular, Moczar attacked the practice of preparing fraudulent statistical reports on the economy, blamed senior political and economic administrators for abetting such abuses, and called for a "decisive purge from managerial posts of those people who are dishonest, incapable, and negligent in their responsibilities and, therefore, have no moral right to exercise such functions."[33]

Even more explicit criticism of the leadership's policies was made by Tadeusz Grabski, a provincial party secretary known for his authoritarian views but also his interest in economic problems. Speaking at a Central Committee meeting in December 1978, Grabski deplored the "unrealistically prepared economic plans [leading to] a shortage of resources, materials, and energy as well as to inefficient market supply."[34] He warned that, in the public mind, "the responsibility for all this rests with the state, with the authorities, and, above all, with our party."

With the public's increasingly frustrated economic expectations and perception of the leadership's lack of direction, these opinions were bound to find an audience both within the party and among the population in general. This was reflected, for example, in the far-ranging public discussion, which took the form of letters to the editor of the weekly *Polityka,* on the need to tighten managerial procedures in economic units.[35] Although explicitly limited to narrow economic and labor problems, the correspondence, in which the great majority of participants demanded greater managerial control of production, had obvious political overtones. It served as a warning to the authorities that an influential section of the public, mostly managerial groups, was becoming rapidly disaffected by the continuing inability to solve the economic problems.

As for the party leadership itself, there was no sign of any major change in either its policy or its methods. That the many warnings of disaffection were not missed, however, was suggested by attempts by the highest party officials to reinforce their control over the party and society alike. This was particularly noticeable in the measures taken at the party's national congress and during the months that followed it.

The eighth congress of the PUWP was held February 11–15, 1980. The gathering was attended by 1,833 delegates elected at party conferences throughout the country and representatives from 32 foreign communist parties. The tone of the debates was set in Gierek's address:

Close to 10 years ago. . .our party adopted a socioeconomic strategy oriented toward man and his needs, a strategy related to the best conceptual and moral values of socialism: a strategy of creating developed socialism in our country. This strategy, adopted at the sixth congress [of the party in 1971] and developed at the seventh congress [in 1975], aimed at better satisfying social needs on the basis of dynamic economic growth, a steady strengthening of socialist democracy, and a consolidation of socialist social relations; [it] has brought great achievements to our country. It has proved correct in practice and has received the support of our nation. We shall continue [this strategy].[36]

This determination to continue the program of stabilization affected Gierek's treatment of all other problems. Though admitting economic problems, for example, Gierek merely called for the streamlining of production, greater efficiency of work, and tighter discipline, but not for reforms. He minimized political dissent and opposition, saying that it was "provoked and fomented by outside influences," and he appealed for "national unity" centered on the public's recognition of the "leading and directing" role of the party. He declared his willingness to cooperate with the Catholic Church but only in certain aspects of social policy, that is, problems of family life and the encouragement of national unity in the name of social prosperity. He expressed his leadership's interest in "the increased participation of nonparty citizens in political, social, and economic life," but then made it clear that such participation would be controlled by the party itself. No organizational or institutional changes were proposed.

The deliberations of the congress fell into two parts. One was a plenary discussion of current policies and problems. The other was a detailed debate on "all aspects of the party and national life," conducted in numerous specialized groups. The plenary sessions were heavily publicized; the work of the specialized groups took place behind closed doors and only short summaries of the discussions were released to the public.

Some 80 speakers took the floor during the two days of open discussion at plenary sessions. None criticized the party leadership or its policies. In contrast, frequent and intense attacks were made on how party policies were implemented. Among the most virulent complaints were accusations of administrative mismanagement of available resources, corruption, the faulty execution of planning, and ineffective control of the distribution of materials and machinery. The blame for all these failures and mistakes was placed on the government.

Underlying these complaints against state officialdom was the uniform and unrestrained praise given to Edward Gierek himself. Not a single criticism of his actions or his leadership was made during the debates. Instead, Gierek was constantly lauded as a perceptive, courageous, and caring leader and as the only man capable of rescuing the country from its difficulties. At times the accolades paid to Gierek bordered on glorification. For example, a provincial secretary explained to the congress that "an involved patriot is one who really works for the party, who implements the party's policies, sacrifices all his strength and ability for the benefit of all. A model to follow is the example of the daily activities of Comrade Edward Gierek."[37] It was clear from the open debates that the main message of the congress was not so much that a search for better policies should be embarked on but rather that a concerted attempt to consolidate the ranks behind the leadership of one man, Gierek, was paramount.

This was also apparent in the leadership changes made. The congress elected a new Central Committee, which, in turn, chose from among its members the Politburo and the Secretariat. The number of full Politburo members remained the same as in 1975, fourteen, while that of the deputy members increased from three to five. Ten full members were re-elected and four were removed (Piotr Jaroszewicz, Jozef Kepa, Stefan Olszowski, and Jozef Tejchma). Among their successors were two former deputy members, CC secretary Jerzy Lukaszewicz and Tadeusz Wrzaszczyk. The other two, Alojzy Karkoszka and Andrzej Werblan, were CC secretaries. Among the deputy members, only Kazimierz Barcikowski retained his position. His four new colleagues were CC secretaries Jozef Pinkowski and Zdzislaw Zandarowski and senior government officials Tadeusz Pyka and Emil Wojtaszek. Two new secretaries, Jerzy Waszczuk and Andrzej Zabinski, were also elected, while three others, Edward Babiuch, Ryszard Frelek, and Stefan Olszowski, were released from their duties.

Jaroszewicz's departure from the party leadership, which followed his failure to win re-election to the Central Committee and was subsequently capped by his removal as prime minister, was significant. Officially explained as a personal decision to retire from active political life, the real reason for it was political. Jaroszewicz was made a scapegoat for the party's disastrous performance, particularly in the economy. The long-time prime minister (since December 1970) assumed the main responsibility for the decision to increase food prices in June 1976 as well as for its eventual revocation. The participation of others, including Gierek, in the making of that decision was disregarded. By removing Jaroszewicz, his former colleagues in the leadership shifted the burden of guilt for all the failures and mistakes away from themselves and onto the shoulders of one person alone.

Equally significant was the removal of Stefan Olszowski from both the Politburo and the Secretariat. Having been elected to the Politburo in December 1970, Olszowski served as foreign minister until 1976, when he took over responsibility for economic policies in the Secretariat. In subsequent years persistent rumors linked Olszowski with reformist trends within the party; he was said to have frequently argued for the need for economic and administrative restructuring and for changes in economic policy. Partly because of these rumors, Olszowski was sometimes regarded as a potential competitor to Gierek. His departure—he was sent as ambassador to the GDR—put an end to this speculation. Immediately after the congress, the Sejm, acting on

Gierek's recommendation, elected Edward Babiuch as prime minister. Another of Gierek's protégés, Jan Szydlak, took over as chairman of the Central Council of Trade Unions, a body controlling the entire organized labor movement.

The consolidation drive extended to elected representatives of the public as well. In the national parliamentary elections in March 1980 the candidates of the Front of National Unity, the formal coalition of officially recognized political and social organizations led by the Communist Party, received 99.52 percent of all the valid votes.[38] The result of the elections, which was derided by dissidents as fraudulent, was heralded by the official media as indicating public support for the leadership's policies.

Having passed the test, the leadership turned its attention to the much more difficult task of strengthening its authority over the public. The issue it chose to test this authority was that of food price increases. This was not accidental, as it had been one of the most important, and certainly the most sensitive, problems in Poland for more than ten years. The stability of food prices, and particularly those for meat, had long been a barometer of the public's mood. Each attempt to change prices officially, as had been done in 1970 and 1976, ignited popular dissatisfaction. The failure to overcome public protests, in turn, directly contributed to the weakening of the leadership's authority. Now, the leadership was resolved to put an end to this situation.

On July 1, 1980, the authorities increased meat prices. The decision was preceded by a long propaganda campaign in which the increases were presented as part of comprehensive changes to streamline economic performance. These preparatory measures notwithstanding, the manner in which the decision was announced, its limited economic scope, and the logistics of its implementation all testified to the leadership's continuing apprehension about the public's reactions.

The announcement was made belatedly, on July 2, and took the form of a radio and television interview with a minor government official.[39] The increase involved only 2 percent of the meat available for sale. It was to be imposed indirectly, by transferring certain categories of meat from ordinary shops to commercial shops. The higher prices were to be introduced in one area of the country at a time. The greater profits involved were to be used to improve the lot of the lowest earning groups in the population.

The announcement provoked immediate protest. On July 1 the first strike broke out in several departments of a tractor plant near Warsaw, the same plant that had been directly involved in the 1976 protests. Subsequently, spontaneous and unorganized strikes occurred throughout the country. In some places entire crews joined in, in others only some of the personnel were involved. All the protests were peaceful. They centered on the workers' demand for higher wages or benefits to compensate for the increased meat prices. There was no suggestion of rescinding the increases. After lengthy bargaining, the demands were settled on a piecemeal basis, the settlements ranging from a 5 to 10 percent increase in wages and other benefits.

Initially, the operation appeared successful from the leadership's point of view, since it had demonstrated its ability to make difficult decisions and stick by them in the face of public protests. The price increases were implemented everywhere. Difficulties arose, however, from the very tactics that the authorities used in that task. The most obvious problem resulted from the gradual introduction of the decision in different parts of the country, since it only opened the way for a protracted process of new protests and new negotiations. The bargaining precedent used in one factory, in fact, was used by other workers elsewhere to obtain the same result.

The leadership's position was complicated further by its repeated but largely abortive attempts to halt the workers' demands. Although the official media refrained from reporting either the strikes or the negotiations, ample information was provided by dissident groups and their unofficial bulletins. Particularly important in this respect was the activity of KSS-KOR, whose members and sympathizers served from the beginning of the strikes as the principal sources of information for the Western press and the Polish public.

On July 9, Gierek noted in a nationally televised speech that "any broader increases in salaries" would not be accepted, although he failed to mention that salary increases had already been negotiated in various talks between workers and management groups.[40] Predictably, the statement had no effect on the workers; the strikes and negotiations continued unabated and spread to factories throughout the country. It was only a matter of time before the workers became more militant and their demands more politicized.

On August 16 representatives of 21 enterprises from the coastal city of Gdansk and its surrounding areas decided to set up an Interfactory Strike Committee to "coordinate the demands and strike action."[41] The committee published a list of demands addressed to the authorities. This list consisted of 21 separate points related to three principal groups of problems regarded by the strikers as essential. The first set of problems, defined as fundamental, dealt with the issues of "free trade unions, which would be independent from the party and the management" as well as formal recognition of the workers' right to strike. The second set, basically political, included demands for "respect of the principle of free expression," for the release and rehabilitation of political prisoners, and for the public announcement of the establishment of the committee as well as the publication of its demands. In addition, the committee called for the public release of "full information" on the economic situation in the country and for open debate on an eventual program of reform. The third set, consisting of fifteen separate demands, focused on economic matters related to calls for an across-the-board wage increase to compensate

for the rise in prices, an increase in pensions and other benefits, and the introduction of five-day workweek.

In the following days more and more enterprises joined the continuing
strike and the committee became involved in protracted negotiations with the
government; the character of the protest shifted from a spontaneous action
into an organized endeavor to defend workers' interests. The impact of this
development on both the public and the party was drastic: it began the evolution of the public movement toward self-determination and dealt a final blow
to the leadership's remaining authority.

On August 24, at a hastily convened meeting of the party's Central Committee, Gierek declared the leadership's willingness to accept

> a genuine broadening of the public's participation in deciding on matters relat-
> ing to the workplace, towns and villages, the entire country. . .We are ready to
> discuss those issues with the public and with worker representatives elected
> during the strikes. We are ready to meet their demands halfway. We cannot,
> however, make unrealistic promises; neither can we accept proposals aimed at
> the foundations of our nation and state.[42]

This was too little and too late. On August 31, 1980, an agreement accepting all the workers' demands was signed by the government in Gdansk, following by one day a similar agreement reached in Szczecin. Both agreements
stipulated the authorities' acceptance of the workers' right to establish their
own labor unions, which would be independent from party control in their
internal organization and their activities.[43] On September 3 a similar agreement was reached between representatives of the Silesian miners and the government. Poland had entered a new political era.

The Political Collapse

This was to be the era of mass participation in politics, participation based on the principles of autonomy and self-determination. These principles had long guided dissident activity; they had also nurtured the spontaneous movement of self-organization that found expression in the ad hoc committees set up by the workers in individual factories during the wave of industrial unrest in July and August 1980. With the signing of the agreements between the strikers and the authorities, these principles became the foundation of the political process as a whole. This, at least, was how the agreements were perceived by the population, a perception that provided momentum to public activities and gave them a distinctive logic in prompting new forms of self-organization that many people regarded as the means through which the objective of participation could be achieved and implemented.[1]

The workers spearheaded this development by establishing Solidarity, their own independent and self-governing union, on September 17, 1980. They were followed by many others: peasants, journalists, intellectuals, students, and artists. They all declared their intention of setting up their own unions, or at least of changing the character of their existing organizations so as to ensure their independence from state control.

This explosion of activism was not conceived as directed against the existing system of government, its institutions, or its leaders. Efforts to set up new public organizations were not linked to demands for the elimination of the old ones, while the ferment within the established bodies was basically prompted by a desire to make their work more effective. Underlying all these processes was an attempt to make the system more responsive to the population. This inevitably implied, however, the transformation of the system itself, a prospect that was obviously not lost on the leadership, making it determined to restrain and arrest the trends toward organizational pluralism and democracy. That much was clear from numerous official statements and actions. The problem for the leadership, however, was how to do so.

Nowhere was this problem more keenly perceived than in the party itself. Its leadership had obviously underestimated the impetus and force of what had started out in a sporadic and haphazard fashion but had then turned into a public movement to be reckoned with. As a result, the party had neither the resources to deal with this new political development nor a program that could attract support. Indeed, the party itself was already experiencing troubles within its own ranks and this was rapidly contributing to a decline in discipline.

It was only on August 15, more than six weeks after the outbreak of the first strikes, that the authorities publicly acknowledged the unrest. In a nationally broadcast speech Prime Minister Edward Babiuch admitted the prevalence of "periodic work stoppages in a number of places," promised changes in economic policy, and appealed to the population to display "common sense" and refrain from further protests.[2] On August 16 the Politburo established within the CC Secretariat a special unit charged with coordinating all party activities related to the strikes; the unit was headed by Politburo member and CC secretary in charge of security matters Stanislaw Kania. On August 18 Gierek warned the nation in a television address that no demand undermining the "bases of political and social order" would be accepted by the leadership and that no one should count on the authorities' "concessions, compromises, or even hesitation"; this was reinforced by an appeal to all party members to "defend the party's policy" and implement it "under all circumstances."[3] On August 19 the CC Secretariat issued a directive to all party bodies urging them to join in a fight against the "antisocialist elements" that had "taken over the leadership of the strikes" and had been spreading slogans "relating to the creation of free labor unions, changes in the electoral system, the abolition of press censorship, and the liberation of political prisoners."[4]

On August 24, Kania reported to a plenum of the Central Committee that "despite the implementation of various measures it was impossible to arrest the dangerous trends" that had shaped the political situation.[5] He warned his listeners that acceptance of some of the strikers' demands "would amount to a move toward weakening the state's socialist character," but ruled out the use of force in dealing with the strikes, arguing that in case of a mass conflict, "the only recourse is the authority of the party, its trustworthiness, and its ability to influence the masses." Noting that the party lacked those attributes, Kania said that many in the party regarded the leadership as responsible for the loss of authority.

Kania's report was significant because it confirmed the party's inability to contain the unrest, even while its leadership realized the political danger for the system arising from the public agitation, and because it laid down the tactics to be used in dealing with the strikes. They were to be political, concentrating on manipulation and persuasion rather than force. This was possibly dictated by the difficulties involved in mobilizing resources and manpower rather than by any concern for restraint in their dealings with the public. The leadership had learned from the experience of 1971 that force in itself was not a guarantee of political success.

Most important, the report called for changes in the party itself. This was probably prompted by two factors: first, the widespread participation of party members in the strikes, which, considering that industrial action was condemned by the leadership, indicated a serious breakdown in the party's cohesion; and, second, the growing complaints about corruption within the party's higher ranks. There was nothing new in these charges themselves. Corruption in the party had been endemic to its very organizational essence, expressed in its self-asserted role as the leading and directing force in the process of social changes. More significant was that the allegations of corruption seem to have been intentionally focused on a group of officials close to the leadership, particularly those officials who were directly associated with the party's first secretary Edward Gierek. The allegations appeared to have originated in the Supreme Chamber of Control, an organization chaired by former Politburo member and CC secretary Mieczyslaw Moczar. Outmaneuvered by Gierek in 1971, Moczar had never hidden his animosity toward the party's top leader, and the "revelations" about corruption in the leadership might have been his way of getting even with his old rival. Even so, the complaints grew louder and the issue rapidly acquired wider political implications. In this situation, the party's leaders decided to act.

On August 24, at the conclusion of the Central Committee plenum, four Politburo members—Prime Minister Edward Babiuch, CC secretary in charge of propaganda Jerzy Lukaszewicz, the labor unions' leader Jan Szydlak, and the principal economic planner Tadeusz Wrzaszczyk—were relieved of their posts. Deputy Politburo member Tadeusz Pyka and the CC secretary in charge of party organization, Zdzislaw Zandarowski, met a similar fate. All six had been involved in policy formulation with respect to either the economy or the party's relations with the workers. More politically significant, all had been members of the party's inner circle of Gierek loyalists. After their departure, it was clear that Gierek's power would be severely curtailed and his authority within the party diminished. This was confirmed by the plenum's decision to bring back into the party's high council two known critics of Gierek's policies: Stefan Olszowski, who resumed his seat in the Politburo and was also appointed a CC secretary, and Tadeusz Grabski, who regained his old position as a full CC member. Babiuch's post as prime minister was taken over by Jozef Pinkowski, who was also promoted to full membership in the Politburo; Pinkowski's job as a CC secretary was given to Emil Wojtaszek.

None of these changes had any impact on the strikes. Yet the personnel reshuffle seems to have provided the leadership with an opportunity for a new departure in its policy toward the workers; in the aftermath of the plenum, the negotiations between the two sides progressed in earnest. On August 30 the Central Committee gathered again to listen to another report by Kania; no details of its content or any subsequent discussion were published. The following day the leadership's representatives signed the agreements with the strikers. On September 6 another plenum of the Central Committee removed Gierek from all executive positions in the party. He was immediately replaced by Stanislaw Kania. At the same time, the committee elected two of the negotiators with the strikers, Kazimierz Barcikowski and Andrzej Zabinski, to full membership in the party's Politburo. Until then both had been deputy members. In addition, three experienced party officials, Tadeusz Grabski, Zdzislaw Kurowski, and Jerzy Wojtecki, were elected CC secretaries.

Gierek's departure, ostensibly caused by a sudden illness, served to convey to both party members and the public that the personalized authoritarianism and bureaucratic inefficiency that had been associated with his style of government had ended. Kania's election was to signify a new beginning. "Our most important task is that of restoring public confidence in authority, the confidence of the working class, of all working people in the party," the new leader told the nation in his inaugural address, adding that the leadership was determined to "find a political solution to social conflicts" and expressing the "hope that every patriotic citizen will be involved in and have an opportunity to participate in our national affairs."[6] Kania also emphasized that the fulfillment of all these tasks and promises depended on internal unity in the party. Unity, he said, was "the great source of our strength; we should always maintain this unity."

Whether these declarations in themselves denoted a qualitative difference between Gierek and Kania is doubtful. The fact that Kania had spent almost ten years as a full-fledged member of the party leadership strongly suggested that the long-established values would continue to guide him. More important still, Gierek's replacement by Kania and the other changes made little or no impact on the country as a whole.

The public accepted the changes with indifference. It was clear that the population, having witnessed the decay of the party's authority over previous years, had lost whatever respect it might once have had for it and was unconcerned about its problems. Instead, the public was preoccupied with organizing its own representative bodies. As for the party, the change in leadership not only failed to stem the tide of internal disarray but might actually have given it added impetus. Some party members were resigning their membership, apparently disillusioned with the party's performance.[7] Others argued that the time had come for a radical reform of the organization to make it more democratic and for a fundamental change in its role in society. Still others pushed in the opposite direction, arguing for tough measures to suppress any form of public autonomy but also demanding widespread purges in the party itself. Throughout the party, demands were being made for the convocation of a party congress, although it was obvious that the various tendencies had differing expectations of such a gathering.

To contain a further decline in the party's standing and to arrest the spread of internal malaise, the leadership came up with a strategy that accepted the need for change in the party's operations but also emphasized the need to preserve continuity in both its political role and its organizational structure. This strategy was unveiled by Stanislaw Kania in an address to a plenum of the Central Committee held October 4–6. It consisted of three elements. The first was a pledge to adopt new policies and methods of government. "There is a need for a new approach to the party's tasks, to socioeconomic policy, to the development of socialist democracy, to the role of the trade-union movement, and to work among the youth; it is no longer possible to use the old methods," Kania told the committee.[8]

The second element was the insistence that the party play a leading role in the process of change. "The much-needed renewal of public life can only be a socialist renewal," Kania said, adding that "the leading force in that process will be the Polish United Workers' Party." This insistence on the party's dominance was particularly obvious when Kania spoke about the situation in the labor movement. While accepting the existence of various workers' representative organizations, he stressed that "the political unity of the workers' movement will not be undermined" and that only in that context could the party's relations with the unions be "based on constructive cooperation." The same was to apply to other forms of self-organization: none of these groups was to interfere with the leading role of the party. "Not only are social autonomy and the leading role of the party not contradictory," Kania said, "they are mutually dependent." It was clear, however, that he supported the existing institutions rather than any new public bodies; he promised the enhancement of the Sejm's role in public life, more responsibility for local administrative and elective bodies, and greater power for the youth organizations. All this was to be supervised by the party itself.

To ensure that the party could cope with these assignments, Kania called for its consolidation around the leadership. This was the third element of the new strategy, defined in very specific terms:

> The Marxist-Leninist party can fulfill its leading role. . .only when it is able to apply the principle of democratic centralism to its actions. This [principle] constitutes the basis for the united and disciplined activity of the party. Democratic centralism provides, above all, for the unity of the party's ranks, both ideological unity and unity of action in the political struggle. . .It defines how the party operates.

In emphasizing the importance of democratic centralism, which ensured the leadership's control over party work, Kania seemed to have brushed aside demands that had been made in local party bodies for greater democratization. He acknowledged their existence, of course, but also suggested that they should be considered at some future party congress. In the meantime, Kania proposed increasing the powers of the Central Committee in the formulation and implementation of party policy and strengthening the party's disciplinary bodies, such as the Central Control Commission, to assure the compliance of the rank and file and low-level officials with the party's directives. Connected with this was the affirmation of the need for a change of personnel at various levels of the party so as to facilitate the implementation of new policies. "Personnel policy is to be based on an objective and fair evaluation of performance, ideological preparedness, and qualifications," Kania said, making it clear that it was the leadership that would determine the candidate's suitability.

The Central Committee approved Kania's plan for "socialist renewal." Its resolution confirmed that the "key tasks for the party are to consolidate its ranks around the Central Committee and to rebuild its links with the masses," stressed the need for long-term changes in the running of the economy through the introduction of comprehensive "reforms" to be outlined by the government, and expressed support for the established institutions.[9] With regard to the labor movement, the committee declared itself "in favor of a renewal of the labor movement and of the development and the strengthening of both the [existing] unions and the newly emerging ones." At the same time, it said that the new unions would have to be "established on constitutional lines, on the basis of the recognition of the socialist system, our alliances, and the leading role of the party," adding that "the constant task of the party is to combat the activities of anti-socialist forces."

Several members were removed from the Central Committee. Among them were all those former members of the Politburo and the Secretariat who had lost their positions on August 24, as well as two former executives of the Committee for Radio and Television, Maciej Szczepanski and Eugeniusz Patyk. Both men had been charged with widespread financial malpractices and excessive corruption. In addition, the committee accepted the resignation of Zdzislaw Grudzien from his Politburo post. All these people had been closely associated with Gierek, the deposed party leader. The committee did not take any action against Gierek himself, but said that his case would be examined at some future date.

Two new deputy members of the Politburo were elected: Wladyslaw Kruk, a provincial party leader, and Roman Ney, a scientist. Two experienced party officials were also elected to the Secretariat: Politburo member Barcikowski and a leader of the party-controlled youth organizations, Stanislaw Gabrielski. These four men headed a long list of newly elected members and deputy members of both the Central Committee and the party's Central Control Commission.

The changes came in the wake of a long and stormy discussion within the committee on the party's role and functions in the current situation. The emphasis was on criticism of the former leadership for its "voluntarism" in policy making and for its "arrogance" and "autocratic tendencies" in the exercise of power.[10] Most speakers called for changes in policy, especially economic policy. No one, however, proposed specific remedies; the reformist fervor was confined to vague and general appeals for a new approach. The underlying theme of the entire gathering was the concern that the party was in real danger of suffering a political demise reinforced by the realization that the party had brought this situation on itself.

At the same time, the October plenum of the Central Committee opened a new era for the party. Although at this stage there was no definite program, the leadership proposed a concept of what needed to be done. This concept was to guide the activities of the leadership in the months and years to come. The immediate difficulty, however, was in ensuring its implementation.

The main obstacle was that the brunt of public activities had shifted away from the party's control as new groups, particularly the workers, developed their own independent organizations to defend their interests. This struck at the heart of the party's strategy of socialist renewal, since it inevitably meant a limitation of its authority and power. Under these circumstances, the containment of the movement toward self-organization and the eventual reimposition of control over public activities were indispensable for the successful implementation of the strategy. The leadership's efforts focused on accomplishing this.

They approached the problem in a number of ways. Perhaps the most evident was the tactic of delaying the institutional recognition of the new groups. Solidarity had to overcome a series of legal and political obstacles put in its way by the government to achieve registration as an autonomous public group. Similar difficulties were created for the independent unions of peasants and students. In each case their legal recognition came only after repeated protests, strikes, and demonstrations and was only granted provisionally, pending eventual re-examination prior to passing definitive legislation on labor unions, higher education, and so on.

To complicate matters further, the authorities openly encouraged the establishment of many other organizations. Some of them were simply the remnants of the party-sponsored trade unions, which had long been directed by a centrally appointed council but were now redrafting their statutes and drawing up new programs. Others were set up in factories, universities, and various cultural establishments. Indeed, virtually every time an independent group was legally recognized, a corresponding but more conformist organization was also registered. This was presumably done in the hope that a proliferation of groups and organizations would muddle the very issue of public self-organization and weaken the activity of those bodies that had grown out of the strikes.

In dealing with the public, the authorities employed both persuasion and toughness. Repeated appeals for peace, order, and work discipline were made by political leaders, government officials, and the loyalist media. Their main theme was the threat of impending economic disaster, but they also warned specifically about possible foreign intervention in Poland unless the public agitation, which was allegedly causing chaos and anarchy in the country, ended.

These threats and warnings had started right from the beginning of the strikes in July 1980. They became increasingly frequent in the aftermath of Solidarity's registration in mid-November 1980. The most explicit warning came from a Central Committee press spokesman, Jozef Klasa, who said on December 4 that if and when "socialism became endangered" and "power slipped from the hands of democracy into the hands of anti-socialist elements, Polish Communists would have the right and the duty to ask for assistance from the Soviet Union and other countries."[11] Klasa was quick to affirm, however, that no such eventuality was imminent.

This warning was made against the background of a major increase in tension, which was partly the result of a series of disputes between Solidarity's Warsaw chapter and the authorities over how the government was suppressing dissent and criticism and partly due to an outburst of complaints from the military establishment about the potentially adverse effects of public unrest on the country's defense capabilities in general and its relations with other Warsaw Pact armies in particular. The principal message was the need for the consolidation of public support behind the party leadership.

Even more publicized was an appeal made by General Wojciech Jaruzelski on February 12, 1981, the day after his confirmation as prime minister. He called on the population "to arrest a creeping process that has undermined the stability of the country" and accept a moratorium on protests and strikes "so we [the government] can use that time to put order into the most fundamental problems of our economy. . .to undertake the most urgent social programs. . .and to prepare for wide-ranging reforms."[12] The appeal had some success, in that some of the strikes were called off, but the authorities showed no sign of keeping their part of the bargain.

Their toughness showed itself in the frequent instances of harassment and intimidation of Solidarity activists and those involved in the work of other autonomous groups. Such cases were particularly common in small towns and localities in which it was more difficult for the public to organize itself and in which the harassment might often have been instigated by local officials.

There are grounds to believe, however, that at least some such cases were tolerated or even encouraged by the central political leadership. This was particularly so in the conflict between Solidarity and the authorities that followed an incident in the city of Bydgoszcz in March 1981, in which several worker and peasant activists were mishandled by the police. The Politburo supported the police, announcing that the "action by the forces of law and order carried out on the orders of the competent authorities was in accordance with the law."[13] Solidarity demanded an immediate investigation into the case and the punishment of those guilty. Eventually, after Solidarity had threatened a general strike and successfully staged a nationwide warning strike, the conflict ended with a compromise in which the authorities apologized for the incident and admitted that the police action had violated "the principle of solving all conflicts through political means," while Solidarity accepted the authorities' demand that it should "refrain from any action. . .that could undermine internal peace in the country."[14]

The ambiguity of the authorities' policies was not lost either on Solidarity's activists or on the public as a whole. The frustration it engendered gave rise to recurrent protests and strikes, regarded by many as the only means by which they could influence the authorities, but it also strengthened people's determination to preserve the autonomy of the new organizations. Indeed, the public's resentment of the authorities' tactics and its distrust of their intentions greatly contributed to the popularity of these groups, particularly Solidarity. Set up in mid-September 1980 and formally recognized as a public body in mid-November, Solidarity grew rapidly to comprise by mid-January 1981 about 60 percent of all those employed in the state economy and administration—that is, almost 8.5 million people—in addition to one million or so others.[15] It was the largest public organization in Poland's history.

The party was crumbling. Its membership declined month after month by tens of thousands, mostly as a result of resignations.[16] Its leadership was in apparent disarray, plagued by division and uncertainty. During the nine months that followed the August strikes 28 first secretaries and 72 other secretaries of the 49 provincial party committees were removed from their posts, as were 18 chairmen of the provincial party control commissions.[17]

There was also a considerable turnover in both the Politburo and the Secretariat of the Central Committee. At the beginning of December 1980, Politburo members Wladyslaw Kruczek, Alojzy Karkoszka, Stanislaw Kowalczyk, and Andrzej Werblan lost their posts; Werblan was also removed from the Secretariat. Their places were taken by Tadeusz Grabski and Mieczyslaw Moczar as full members and Tadeusz Fiszbach as a deputy member. Werblan was replaced as a CC secretary by Roman Ney. At the end of April the Central Committee removed Jozef Pinkowski and Emil Wojtaszek from the Politburo and Wojtecki and Zielinski from the Secretariat. It also elected two manual workers, Gerard Gabrys and Zygmunt Wronski, as full Politburo members and two local party secretaries, Jozef Masny and Kazimierz Cypry-niak, as a deputy Politburo member and a CC secretary, respectively.

Some of these changes, particularly in the central party bodies but also in several provincial committees, reflected the leadership's resolve to remove from the political limelight those individuals who had been identified in the public mind either as personally close to Gierek or as supporters of the auto-cratic style of government that the leadership clearly intended to associate with the fallen leader. Their departure was meant to suggest a change in the party's policies and methods. Other changes, however, were prompted by the leadership's realization that the incumbent personnel were neither willing nor capable of implementing the key tenets of socialist renewal in a way that would ensure both their acceptance by the public and discipline in the party.

Indeed, the very concept of socialist renewal appeared to have caused widespread confusion within the party. The reason for this was not the princi-ple of change itself, which seemed to have been accepted by the great major-ity of party members and officials, but uncertainty about the scope, direction, and timing of its implementation. This was sufficient, however, to produce serious divisions within the party, which reflected the conflicting interests of various groups in its hierarchy.

Provincial and local party officials were perhaps the most apprehensive about the new strategy. Intent on holding on to their traditional powers, which had given them considerable control over their districts, they were anx-ious lest the public activism that had found expression in the strikes and the emergence of Solidarity would erode their prerogatives and standing. They tended to regard the leadership as weak and on the defensive. At party meet-ings, including plenums of the Central Committee, they often argued for strong measures in dealing with the public and were prone to react precipi-tately to anything that might undermine their positions. Determined to de-fend their privileges, they used every opportunity to pressure the leadership into limiting the scope of the renewal and slowing its implementation.

This conservative attitude contrasted with the sentiments expressed by many of the party's rank and file, who demanded both radical changes in the organization and a thorough overhaul of its methods. Their demands were obviously influenced by the public mood generally, but they also grew out of resentment at being continually disregarded by the party leadership and forced to follow orders from above without any concern being shown for their interests or reactions. Deprived of the benefits enjoyed by ranking party of-ficials, outraged by revelations about corruption in the establishment, and in-creasingly aware of the inability of the party's leaders to improve the standard of living, the mass of ordinary members was now determined to put an end to the autocratic principle whereby anyone occupying an office within the orga-nization had the right to control the activity and behavior of its members.

The resentment was primarily directed at local officials, secretaries of provincial committees, and professional staff members employed in those committees. These were the people who had been in direct contact with the rank and file. At times, however, there were also demands for a change in how the central leadership was selected. This pressure from below was particularly evident in repeated appeals for the speedy convocation of a party congress; some of these appeals were combined with grass-roots efforts to prepare a new program for the party, to be outlined in basic party bodies in the factories and regions and presented to the congress by independently elected delegates.

Within weeks of Gierek's removal, attempts were made to start coordinating programmatic work among party bodies in factories and universities without regard to central directives and instructions. These attempts came to be known as "horizontal cooperation." They were meant to ensure "a spontaneous integration of the party from below, [conducted] with the fullest respect for [the party's] ideological principles and statutes" and were prompted by the "painful vacuum [in the party's work] created by the absence of contacts and cooperation" among the various basic bodies in the organization.[18] This "horizontal" movement started in the city of Torun at the end of October 1980 and spread rapidly throughout the country. Several attempts by established party bodies either to dismantle or to undermine it failed. Under these circumstances, the party's establishment decided to become involved in the movement itself, apparently in the hope that this would dilute any political effectiveness it might have.

This decision became apparent at the nationwide Forum for the Party Accord, which had been organized by various "horizontal" bodies and designed to give the movement a measure of organizational identity. The forum met in Torun in mid-April 1981 and involved about 750 delegates representing various party bodies from all parts of the country. The gathering was organized by rank-and-file party activists without any prior approval or sanction from the national leadership. This, in itself, was a violation of the party's fundamental principles of organizational behavior. Even so, there was no criticism from the leadership. Instead, several observers from the Central Committee and its staff attended the meeting, took part in the discussions, and even provided some of the facilities for the conference.

The forum featured lengthy debates about the need for the reform of the party but produced only relatively innocuous resolutions. These included generally formulated demands for changes in the party's top leadership, more information about grass-roots activities in the party, the convocation of a two-stage congress (the first stage to elect new leaders and the second to draft a new program), and a secret ballot to elect delegates to that congress. In addition, the participants appealed to the Central Committee to draft a letter to be sent to other communist parties informing them of the "real situation in the party and in the country."[19]

The demands were not new. They had been made repeatedly at party gatherings ever since the removal of Edward Gierek in September 1980; this suggested that many members regarded change in the party as fundamental to resolving the current difficulties. The convocation of the forum signaled that some members might be prepared to take matters into their own hands. The involvement of the leadership in the "horizontal" movement, limited though it was, meant that such a possibility had not been overlooked and that the leadership would go a long way to maintain control over changes in the party.

At the end of April 1981, the leadership announced that an extraordinary party congress would be held in mid-July. This officially opened a nationwide campaign of preparation for the event. Unofficially the preparation had been under way since February 1981, when first electoral meetings were held in some factories. Following the announcement, meetings were held in all large plants and then in towns, culminating in a succession of provisional conferences. The main purposes of the campaign were to select delegates for the congress—who were to outline a new program and choose a new national leadership—and to elect local party leaders. The party leadership guided the campaign throughout; it selected the campaign's main themes, shaped its scope, and influenced its outcome. Moreover, it used the campaign to eliminate some of its critics from the mainstream of party politics.

A key aspect of the campaign was the provision that the election of all officials and delegates be conducted by secret ballot from a large number of candidates. These were to be nominated by special electoral commissions selected by local party leaders and approved by the higher party authorities; however, all members attending an electoral conference were to have the right to nominate additional candidates, and there was no limit on the number of these additional candidates. This procedure was adopted in a Central Committee resolution, after a draft of the electoral rules had proved unacceptable to many grass-roots activists. That draft had been prepared by the committee's staff in December 1980 and envisaged no more than 50 percent of the available seats being contested by candidates nominated from the floor.[20]

The adopted resolution was a major departure from long-established practice. The electoral regulations prepared for the 1971, 1975, and 1980 party congresses had given the centrally appointed electoral commissions the right to nominate the full slate of candidates and limited the number of additional candidates proposed from the floor to only 15 percent of the seats. The 1981 change became necessary when it became known that some local party bodies were planning to elect their own officers without setting up any commissions and without waiting for the leadership's acceptance.[21]

The campaign was a stormy one for the party hierarchy, taking place as it did against a background of continuing and widespread public agitation and intense ferment in the party. It was rife with controversies between contending groups; it exposed conflicting views to public display; and it was punctuated by frequent challenges to established procedures.

Even so, the campaign did not address the leadership's strategy of socialist renewal, which suggests that the strategy may have already been accepted by most people in the party. Instead, the emphasis of the campaign was on replacing people who occupied positions of authority within the party. This became apparent during the first weeks. At electoral meetings in factories and small localities, about 50 percent of the incumbent office holders who ran for election as delegates to provincial conferences lost; this meant that they lost their jobs as well.[22] The same happened at the provincial level; about half the incumbent office holders who ran either for re-election to their positions or as delegates to the congress were defeated. When the campaign ended in early July, 75 percent of all leadership posts at local and regional levels had been taken over by newcomers, signifying the greatest personnel change in the party's history.

The central party leadership was also affected. Of 143 incumbent members of the Central Committee, only 46 won mandates, and only 28 of the 108 deputies were re-elected. Four of the nineteen Politburo and Secretariat members failed to be elected as delegates to the congress. They were Gerard Gabrys and Zygmunt Wronski, the two worker-members of the Politburo, and deputy members Jozef Masny and Jerzy Waszczuk; the latter was also a CC secretary.

None of the more prominent leaders lost their posts, and some—most notably Stanislaw Kania and Wojciech Jaruzelski—gained ground. Kania not only won a mandate for himself but was also successful in swaying several conferences to accept his choice of candidates as delegates to the congress. This was the case with two reputed conservative leaders, Andrzej Zabinski from Katowice and Stanislaw Kociolek from Warsaw, who had experienced considerable difficulty in winning mandates on their own. At the same time several activists who had been critical of Kania in the past failed to be selected.

Particularly striking was the failure of the "horizontal" movement to secure a representation for itself among the elected delegates to the congress. There were several reasons for this. First, the campaign demonstrated that although the need for change had been deeply felt in the party, it took the form of a grass-roots revolt against the incumbent establishment rather than a wish for the real reform advocated by the "horizontalists."

Second, the reformers became embroiled in disputes with several orthodox communist groups that had appeared on the political scene in 1981.[23]

These groups, known as "forums" or "discussion clubs," were actually loose associations of conservative party members who professed to being appalled by what they regarded as the growing disarray in the party and the political system, castigated those whom they held responsible, and argued for the re-imposition of discipline and rigor. Among the most publicized of those groups was the so-called Katowice Forum. In May 1981 the group issued a long manifesto that strongly criticized the political situation in the country and condemned the party leadership's inertia in dealing with both the public agitation and reformists within the party.[24] The manifesto, and other statements by the group, received considerable publicity in the Polish and foreign communist press. This, in turn, provoked protests from various party bodies in the country. The forum was eventually rebuked by the leadership and announced that it was suspending its activities; even so, it continued to issue statements on the political situation.

These groups had no noticeable support among the party's rank and file. Indeed, it is difficult to establish who and how many the members were. Instead, there was strong circumstantial evidence that their emergence and activities were encouraged by the central leadership or, at least, some of its members. It was publicly reported, for example, that Politburo member Zabinski, who was also first secretary of the Katowice provincial committee, was actively involved in both the organization and, indirectly, the activities of the forum there. His committee was said to have "provided the group with a meeting place," facilitated its publishing work, and kept abreast of its actions.[25] Another Politburo member, Stefan Olszowski, openly admitted his support for two well-known orthodox groups, the overtly anti-Semitic Grunwald Association and the doctrinaire Warsaw-80 group.[26] Other members of the leadership did nothing to constrain the groups' activities.

The election campaign was strongly influenced by criticism of the situation in the party from foreign communist groups and institutions, particularly the Soviet press and the Soviet leaders. It had, of course, been evident ever since the emergence of an independent labor movement in 1980 that the Soviet Union was both concerned about and alarmed by the developments in Poland. The situation there had been consistently presented in the Soviet media as the result of attempts by anti-socialist elements and counter-revolutionary forces to undermine the authority and power of the party and the system of government in Poland.[27]

Nevertheless, there is reason to believe that the Soviet leadership approved Kania's plans for only operational changes in the party. This was first acknowledged in a communiqué from a meeting in Moscow on October 30, 1980, between a group of Soviet officials led by Leonid Brezhnev and Stanislaw Kania. The statement conveyed to the Poles "the conviction of Soviet Communists and the working people of the Soviet Union that the Communists and the working people of fraternal Poland will be able to resolve the acute problems of political and economic development that are facing them."[28] The communiqué also expressed concern over "subversive activities against socialist Poland and [attempts] to interfere in its [internal] affairs."

Moscow's concern grew with the realization that institutional changes in the social area were beginning to affect the system itself. On December 5, 1980, a sudden meeting of Warsaw Pact leaders took place in Moscow amid rumors of possible military intervention in Poland. The meeting was attended by seven members of the Polish Politburo, led by Kania, and ended with a reminder that the "Communists and workers of Poland" would have to ensure "the further development of the country along a socialist path."[29]

It soon became obvious, however, that the public drive toward self-determination was gathering momentum and the party was falling apart. The USSR responded in two ways. First, a massive propaganda campaign was mounted against what the Soviet media called "the existence of anarchy and chaos" in Poland, a situation allegedly fostered by enemies of socialism and of the Polish working class. Second, the Soviet authorities maintained, and even expanded, their cooperation with the Polish leadership. There were more low-level political and economic visits on both sides. In mid-February 1981 the two governments reached a trade and credit agreement that envisaged additional Soviet credits to Poland, and they announced a four-year moratorium on the payment of interest on Poland's debt to the USSR. In Moscow on March 4, in the aftermath of the Twenty-sixth Congress of the CPSU, a statement was issued at the conclusion of a meeting of the top Soviet party and government leaders and a four-man delegation of the Polish leadership: Kania, Jaruzelski, Zabinski, and Wojtaszek. In this statement the Soviet leaders said they expected the Polish party "to reverse the course of events and to eliminate the peril looming over the socialist achievements of the Polish nation."[30] They went on to say that the USSR was ready to help in that task.

Subsequently, as turmoil in the party grew and demands for greater internal democracy proliferated, the Soviet authorities became directly involved in efforts to consolidate the PUWP around its leadership and to ensure discipline within its ranks. On April 23 Mikhail Suslov, the Soviet party's senior Politburo member and its ideological guardian, went to Warsaw for a brief visit and talked with Kania and other members of the Polish leadership. These talks were said to have been held "in a cordial party atmosphere."[31] On April 25, barely one day after Suslov's return to Moscow, the Soviet press charged that "revisionist elements within the ranks of the PUWP" were aiming to "paralyze the party of Polish Communists as the leading force in society."[32] The Soviet press identified these revisionists as "those demanding reforms in the PUWP, the renunciation of its present organizational structure, and the creation, under the guise of so-called horizontal structures, of various forums outside the statutes that would substitute for the leading bodies of the party."

The Soviet press propaganda against the alleged disruption in the Polish party intensified during the election campaign. Throughout the entire exercise, and particularly at the time of the provincial conferences, the Soviet press carried critical articles on Poland almost daily, gave publicity to orthodox groups in the party and their statements, and castigated reformist tendencies in the organization. Similar articles were carried by the East European press, particularly that of Czechoslovakia and the GDR. All of these articles were summarized and quoted by Polish newspapers and were mentioned daily by other media.

The most important single demonstration of Moscow's official interference in the campaign, as distinguished from the press criticism, was the widespread distribution in early June of a letter from the Soviet leaders to the members of the PUWP's Central Committee. Signed by Brezhnev himself, the letter repeated Moscow's support for the basically operational changes proposed by Kania in October 1980, but it was critical of the failure to implement them in a way that would reassert the party's leading role.[33] Moreover, the letter condemned reformist trends in the party and called on all "honest Communists" to rally together to improve the situation even before the opening of the congress. The letter implied that the party's top leaders—First Secretary Kania and Prime Minister General Jaruzelski—"as well as other Polish comrades" had failed to heed Moscow's earlier warnings about the situation. It stopped short of calling for their resignations, however, and merely emphasized that more energy was needed to find a solution to the problems.

The letter rapidly became the key issue in party politics. It furnished the basis for a stormy discussion at a special CC plenum, was read at party electoral meetings, and was published in many newspapers. Its effect on the party was undeniably strong, although it was not obvious whether the message was fully or uniformly understood.

This became apparent during a CC meeting on June 9 and 10. It provided a forum for a thorough criticism of the leadership's policies and methods, which were described by many speakers as "ineffective," "vacillating," "indecisive," and "defeatist."[34] Most of the speakers were regional officials and ranking activists, and their complaints amounted to almost open revolt when a Politburo member and CC secretary, Tadeusz Grabski, charged that "the Politburo in its present composition and under the leadership of Stanislaw Kania is unable to lead the country out of the political crisis." It is possible that Grabski's statement was prompted by his frustration over the continuing ferment and agitation in both the country and the party—Grabski had long had a reputation for autocracy—as well as by his personal ties to some of the regional leaders. In addition, he most certainly regarded the Soviet letter as an indication of the CPSU's dissatisfaction with the leadership in Poland.

Kania immediately demanded a formal vote of confidence for each member of the Politburo. This motion was rejected by a majority of 89 to 24, with 5 abstentions, following a debate in which "opinions expressing confidence in Stanislaw Kania and Wojciech Jaruzelski were clearly predominant."[35] At the conclusion of the CC meeting, Kania noted that the Soviet letter "had its purpose in our situation." Without explaining what this purpose might have been, he added that he and his associates always enjoyed Moscow's "understanding for our policy [of socialist renewal], even while this understanding has been accompanied by concern over threats to the socialist development of Poland, growing anarchy, and the counter-revolutionary forces."

Indeed, it is plausible that Soviet objectives in sending the letter and intervening in the election campaign were not so much to prompt immediate political changes in the party as to ensure that the election did not turn into a runaway victory for the reformers. This is even more probable considering that Moscow was certainly alarmed by the reformers' apparent acceptance of democratic changes that had been brought about by the emergence of autonomous public groups. The Soviet Union has never explicitly opposed changes in Poland's economic or administrative policies and methods, provided that those changes were proposed and implemented by the party itself. The leading role of the party is the political basis of the system, and Moscow's primary interest has always been to safeguard that system.

The Extraordinary Ninth Congress of the PUWP opened on July 14 in Warsaw. It was called extraordinary since it took place only seventeen months after the last ordinary congress, held in February 1980, instead of the customary five-year interval. During the next seven days, the party gathering featured long procedural disputes, was marked by spirited debates replete with contradictory statements, and offered to its participants and numerous observers moments of genuine excitement and surprise. Perhaps its most unusual aspect was diversity. None of the congress's resolutions were passed unanimously. Each of them was opposed by some delegates, and there were abstentions on every vote. This in itself was a major departure from past practice, an acknowledgement of something out of the ordinary.

The emphasis was on change in the leadership. There was an almost general resolve to put an end to the legacy of Edward Gierek. The former leader was charged with responsibility for the decline in the party's authority, found guilty of corruption and of abetting in the corruption of others, and expelled from the party; the same fate was shared by several of his former associates. This resolve influenced the voting for the Central Committee. The candidates were nominated both from a list prepared by the nominating commission and from the floor; all candidates were required to respond to questions from the delegates; and the election itself was conducted by secret ballot. The result was dramatic: only 18 of the previous 143 members of the Central Committee remained in the new 200-member body, including only 4 members of the incumbent 11-member Politburo (Barcikowski, Jaruzelski, Kania, and Ols-zowski). Major changes also took place in the composition of the Central Control Commission and the Central Auditing Commission.

The choice of the new first secretary of the party was more conventional. The congress re-elected Kania, who outpolled Barcikowski by 1,311 to 568 votes; 60 delegates voted against both candidates, and 5 votes were ruled invalid. The contest was decided by a secret ballot cast by all delegates present, which was an unprecedented move. Even so, the contest was more apparent than real. Both men were nominated as candidates for election at a special meeting of the newly elected Central Committee. The choice was unanimous after two additional candidates proposed by some members of the committee—Stefan Olszowski and Mieczyslaw Rakowski—had declined to run and declared their support for Kania. Barcikowski consented to have his candidacy presented to the congress only after the CC had determined that "the presence of at least two candidates constituted a fundamental requirement" for a democratic election.[36] Both men had closely cooperated with each other ever since the outbreak of social upheavals in August 1980.

Following Kania's re-election by the congress, the Central Committee elected the Politburo and the Secretariat. Candidates for election to those bodies—fourteen full and two deputy members of the Politburo as well as seven secretaries of the Central Committee—were proposed by Kania himself; an additional six candidates were nominated from the floor. The election was conducted by secret ballot; only those candidates proposed by Kania were elected. Kania, as the party's first secretary, became a member of the Politburo on an ex officio basis.

The new leadership consisted of relatively unknown people. Only the four incumbent Politburo members had recognized experience in national politics. These men formed the operative nucleus of the leadership. Two other Politburo members and CC secretaries, Jozef Czyrek and Miroslaw Milewski, were experienced state officials. They had served during the months preceding the congress as ministers of foreign affairs and internal affairs, respectively. Of the remaining Politburo members, some were workers (Zofia Grzyb, Jan Labecki, Jerzy Romanik, and Albin Siwak); others were local party officials (Tadeusz Czechowicz, Stanislaw Opalko, Tadeusz Porebski, and deputy member Wlodzimierz Mokrzyszczak) or intellectuals with a strong administrative bent (Hieronim Kubiak, Zbigniew Messner, and deputy member Jan Glowczyk). Two new CC secretaries, Zbigniew Michalek and Marian Wozniak, had considerable experience in the local apparatus of the party but were unknown at the national level. The determining factor in the selection of most of these individuals was Kania's personal support for their candidacy.

While the election of new party bodies clearly captivated the attention of the congress, little progress was made in preparing the party's political program. The congress merely produced a vague declaration supporting the general principle of socialist renewal as a guideline for the party's activity and left work on a long-term program in the hands of a special commission. Nor was much progress made in reforming the party itself. Although the congress had discussed—in a closed session—and accepted a draft of new statutes that would democratize party structures and operations, the final version was left to be prepared by the Central Committee and the Politburo. This and the fact that the party program was excluded from the congress deliberations and was to be eventually outlined by special commissions created serious doubts about the prospect for any real change in policy.

That, at least, was how the situation was perceived by both the party's rank and file and the public as a whole. Conceived as a turning point in party politics, the congress proved little more than a procedural diversion for many party members. Indeed, it might even have convinced people that the party was incapable of changing its political orientation and caused them to leave it; resignations continued unabated.[37]

The feeling of disappointment with the party's performance was reinforced by a drastic deterioration in relations between the political establishment and the public. In the beginning of August 1981, the government initiated talks with representatives of Solidarity about the possibility of ending the political crisis but then abruptly cut them off when it became apparent that it was impossible to force the union to accept official views about what should be done. From this moment the two sides embarked on a collision course punctuated by frequent conflicts.

The authorities repeatedly mounted propaganda attacks against Solidarity and other public autonomous groups, and the union responded with strikes, demonstrations, and protests. While neither side seemed able to prevail, both were determined to defend their positions; the result was a national downslide. This was particularly apparent in the economic area, in which declining production and sluggish management, combined with the government's unwillingness to introduce reforms, threatened catastrophe. Indeed, the standard of living was declining rapidly and there was no prospect of reversing this trend.

Correctly or not, this decline was seen by many sectors of the public as resulting from the authorities' inertia or even unwillingness to act. Under these circumstances, many groups decided to act on their own. Perhaps the most important of the many public initiatives was a proposal by several workers' groups—the so-called Network—to give complete autonomy to factory-based self-management bodies that would be elected by all employees and act as sui generis owners operating with the help of executive managers hired directly by those bodies and accountable to them.[38] This proposal had major political implications, since it envisaged control over the economy shifting away from the government into the hands of the public.

The party reacted promptly. Meeting on September 2 and 3, the Central Committee acknowledged the need for changes in economic management and supported the principle of a more effective self-management system. However, it charged that arguments that self-management bodies should have autonomy in running enterprises were "anarchistic" and nothing but attempts "to gain first economic and then political power in the state."[39] Kania told the committee at the end of the meeting that the party "cannot be pushed out to a position of marginal importance" in public life, that "the authorities would use all available means to defend socialism," and that "the party would never abandon its right to [control] recruitment" to all state posts. This conformed to the long-established views and practices of the party. Under the circumstances, however, such a position was no more than a defense of a thoroughly discredited practice based on the *nomenklatura,* a system of control through appointments.

Solidarity responded in the form of a resolution adopted by the union's national congress in which it appealed to the Sejm to organize "a nationwide referendum on self-management" before any legislative decision on the matter was taken.[40] This appeal was reinforced by a threat that failure to heed the demand would force the union to conduct a referendum in factories "using its own means." Moreover, Solidarity warned that "if a law basically different from the will of the workers is adopted, the union will have to boycott the law and take steps to ensure the unrestricted operation of genuine self-management." This amounted to an open challenge to the party and the government.

Indeed, one could argue that both the party and the government were challenged by the very convocation of Solidarity's congress, let alone by its various resolutions. The gathering, which spanned two sessions—5–10 September and 26 September–7 October—symbolized the breakdown of long-standing restrictions and authoritarian constraints.[41] The congress was a major political event, marking the institutionalization of the public movement for self-determination and setting directions for future public actions in culture, education, and the economy. Most important, it both defined and reinforced the lines separating the autonomous public organizations and the political establishment.

None of this was lost on the party leadership and its foreign supporters. On September 16, after the first session of the Solidarity congress, the Politburo condemned the gathering for "depriving the working class of its influence on and control over the [labor] organization"; it warned Solidarity that any attempt at confrontation with the authorities "would threaten bloodshed" and appealed to the public to defend "the constitutional principles of socialist statehood as well as the security of Poland."[42] Two days later the media made public a statement from the Soviet authorities expressing the "concern of the CPSU's Central Committee and the Soviet government about the growth of anti-Soviet trends in Poland, trends that have reached dangerous proportions."[43] Furthermore, it carried a warning that "further lenience shown [by the Polish authorities] to any demonstration of anti-Sovietism does immense harm to Polish-Soviet relations and is in direct contradiction to Poland's allied obligations and the vital interests of the Polish nation." The statement concluded with a reminder that the Soviet authorities expected that "the leadership of the Polish party and government [would] immediately take determined and radical steps in order to cut short the malicious anti-Soviet propaganda." Neither the Politburo statement nor the Soviet protest had any discernible effect on Solidarity or its supporters.

On October 18 Stanislaw Kania submitted his resignation as first secretary of the PUWP's Central Committee; it was accepted by a vote of 104 to 79 at a plenary session of the committee. The CC then elected General Wojciech Jaruzelski as first secretary. He was the only candidate for the position, winning 180 of the 184 votes cast. The change meant no alteration of the leadership's policy but suggested that its objectives would be pursued by different means.

This was confirmed by Jaruzelski himself, who, addressing the committee immediately after his election, announced his resolve to follow the policies prescribed by the principles of "socialist renewal."[44] Admitting a bond of continuity between himself and his predecessor, Jaruzelski said that they had "shared the same road characterized by accomplishments as well as failures" and pledged to "continue on the same general course," though he also promised "to do everything to make [this course] more effective."

The search for effectiveness appears to have been the main reason for the change in leadership. Having accepted the resignation of Kania, who had been identified in the public mind with political efforts to regain control over the general populace, the CC turned to Jaruzelski, a politically tested military officer, in the apparent hope that this would facilitate the accomplishment of that task. That alone, however, merely emphasized both the internal malaise in the party and its declining influence over society.

Indeed, in the desire to select a leader with an image of decisiveness and strength, the CC did not hesitate to break some long-established political and organizational traditions. Communists had long considered the selection of a military officer as head of the party as amounting to Bonapartist tendencies, endangering its role as a body that stood above all other institutions. It is true that in Jaruzelski's case such views may have been exaggerated. He was a very political general, having served as chief of the Main Political Administration of the Armed Forces—the military department of the Central Committee—

from 1960 to 1964 and as a member of the Politburo since December 1970. Even so, Jaruzelski was regarded by most party members and by the public as a soldier rather than a party official.

Jaruzelski's election was promptly endorsed by other communist parties. Particularly important was Leonid Brezhnev's message of congratulations, which expressed Moscow's confidence in Jaruzelski's ability to "rally the ranks of the PUWP on the basis of the principles of Marxism-Leninism, in the interest of defending the socialist gains of the Polish working class and all the working people of Poland against encroachments by counter-revolution."[45] Other communist party leaders sent similar congratulatory messages.

The leadership openly adopted a policy of firmness in dealing with public unrest. Having elected Jaruzelski, the Central Committee called on the executive leadership to conduct "a political struggle against the opponents of socialism. . .[and] concerted action by all party bodies against any form of counter-revolutionary activity."[46] Subsequently, several top party officials used strong language in making allegations about the negative impact on Poland of public autonomous activities. For example, Politburo member Kubiak talked openly about the "possibility of using force" in quelling the unrest, and Barcikowski warned that anyone who failed to recognize the "leading role" of the party was making an "unforgivable mistake."[47]

On October 23 the government announced the establishment of special military "operational groups" to streamline "the implementation of official economic policies." Three days later soldiers were sent to some two thousand rural communities and small towns to "ensure the two-way flow of supplies between the towns and the countryside." The operational groups were recalled in mid-November, only to be sent out again on November 23 to large cities and industrial plants. Again, their mission was said to be to facilitate economic and administrative operations.

On October 28 the Central Committee elected, on the recommendation of the Politburo, Deputy Minister of National Defense General Florian Siwicki as a deputy member of the Politburo. The committee also elected Wlodzimierz Mokrzyszczak, already a deputy member of the Politburo, and Marian Orzechowski as CC secretaries. A top-ranked official in the Main Political Administration of the Armed Forces, General Tadeusz Dziekan, was appointed head of the crucial department of personnel. Explaining Siwicki's and Dziekan's appointments, Jaruzelski said that they reflected "the need of the moment and [the recognition that] people have confidence in people in uniform."[48]

The element of toughness was also stressed by Barcikowski, who told the CC plenum about the "need to defend party members against hostile attacks . . .through protective legal measures."[49] He went on to say that it was particularly urgent, since "we had a decline in activity within the party and apathy following every wave of strikes."

None of these warnings or changes had any effect on the public. Instead, frustrated at what people perceived as the authorities' unwillingness to introduce and implement real economic and social changes, an increasing number of public groups became determined to take matters into their own hands. This invariably meant a deterioration in relations between the party and those groups. In fact, the party and its operations were increasingly regarded by the public as obstacles in political and economic life; demands for the "removal of party organizations from industrial enterprises," for example, had been made in many provinces, towns, and industrial areas.[50]

On November 27 and 28 the Central Committee met to assess the situation. It was told that the "principal source of the prolonged and catastrophic economic crisis is, above all, the social and political struggles. . .[and] there is still no possibility of implementing the [government] program to overcome the crisis and to stabilize the economy."[51] The official assessment of the party's standing in the system was even worse:

> There have been serious problems in maintaining political and organizational discipline as well as instances of faulty interpretation of the principle of democratic centralism. This has resulted in the internal disintegration of some sectors of the party's ranks. Certain bodies and their leaderships have become incapable of active party work. No attention has been paid to the dangerous [activities of] opponents of socialism and there has been a tendency to accept the possibility of conducting party work on bases that differ from those of Marxist-Leninist principles and major statutory regulations.

Under these circumstances, the leadership proposed, and the CC accepted, a statement that "deemed it necessary to equip the government with full means for effectively counteracting the destructive actions that are destroying the country and its economy and threatening the socialist state, law and order, and public security."[52] The statement was an admission of the party's political collapse.

At midnight on December 13, 1981, all communication lines were cut throughout the country. Tanks, police, and soliders appeared on the streets. In the morning the entire country was formally declared to be under martial law.

The Socialist Renewal

Martial law was designed to restore the party's control over the public. Its objectives were to eliminate all forms of opposition, real or potential, and to create conditions in which the party could regain its capacity to act authoritatively. It was to be a temporary measure, but its effects were intended to be permanent.[1]

The most apparent feature of the martial-law regime was the authorities' determination to destroy all vestiges of public independence. Labor unions, youth organizations, various professional groups, and religious associations were suspended and their offices were closed. Drastic penalties were imposed for any form of organized activity that could conceivably escape the direct control of the authorities.

Thousands of potential opponents of martial law were interned (that is, detained in specially prepared camps and houses without charges being made against them). They included Solidarity activists, intellectuals, workers, peasants, students, and even those party officials and activists who were presumably considered sufficiently independent in spirit and behavior to represent a threat to the new order. Hundreds of people who dared to defy the martial-law regulations were arrested and sentenced in summary proceedings. People working in factories, educational institutions, and offices were forced to sign a formal pledge of loyalty to the regime and to resign their membership in autonomous organizations; if they refused to do so, they faced the prospect of dismissal.

The imposition of martial law was carefully devised and effectively carried out, which created the impression that the operational inertia characterizing the work of the authorities during much of the preceding period was a thing of the past. A crucial element in the entire operation was the emphasis on the military's role in formulating and implementing official decisions. A new political authority, the Military Council of National Salvation, was established; it consisted of twenty military officers and was chaired by General Wojciech Jaruzelski. The council's orders were said to be binding on all other institutions. The coordination of all administrative, economic, and cultural agencies was assumed by the Committee for the Defense of the Country, which was also chaired by Jaruzelski and which maintained a network of provincial defense committees to supervise the implementation of its instructions. In addition, many administrative and economic institutions were militarized: their employees were mobilized into the armed forces and thereby made subject to military discipline. This new military involvement in public affairs was constantly and extensively publicized.

The implication was that the military had emerged as the key agent in running the country and had replaced other institutions, particularly the Communist Party and the government, in their functions. In some respects this was true, particularly so far as their institutional supervision was concerned. Military officers were appointed to head the principal civilian agencies of administrative control, such as the Ministry of Internal Affairs (General Czeslaw Kiszczak), the Ministry of Local Administration (General Tadeusz Hupalowski and General Wlodzimierz Oliwa), and eventually the Supreme Chamber of Control (General Hupalowski). A military officer was also designated to watch over the political loyalty of employees in the central administration (General Michal Janiszewski, head of the prime minister's office). The prerogatives and power of the control bodies responsible for discipline in the armed forces were enlarged to include the supervision of civilian agencies, and military officers were sporadically sent to various local organizations to monitor their operations and verify their accounts. Moreover, military officers, or commissars, were sent as special permanent representatives of the Military Council of National Salvation to administrative, economic, and cultural bodies and to large factories throughout the country to observe whether they were complying with the instructions issued by the council and the Committee for the Defense of the Country.

The military also featured prominently in propaganda. In the first weeks of martial law Poland's television viewers saw only uniformed speakers, and the public was inundated with reports about the armed forces and their activities. Eventually, the high profile of martial law was phased out and the military became less visible.

Despite all appearances to the contrary, however, there was never any doubt that the military continued to be subject to the party. This was made possible by the party's traditional and uninterrupted control of the armed forces through its thorough penetration of the officer corps. An overwhelming majority of officers were reliably reported to be party members,[2] and they were involved in various aspects of public affairs during the martial-law period. According to persistent reports in the Polish media, the military's work was directed by experienced party activists in the armed forces—the "party members in uniform."[3] These consisted of senior staff officers, party activists, and officials of the Main Political Administration of the Armed Forces, which had long functioned as a military department of the central party professional staff and was responsible to a party secretary rather than a military commander; until October 1981 it had been controlled by First Secretary Stanislaw Kania himself.[4] While a degree of organizational separateness appropriate to their own special disciplinary code and esprit de corps may well have existed, this did not put them outside the party.

Indeed, the military was a uniquely fitting instrument for the leadership in its efforts to protect the system. Traditionally popular with the public, which saw the armed forces as the principal defender of the nation, the military lent the party's policies an aura of patriotic concern and resolution, if not respectability. The characteristic deference of the armed forces to the hierarchy ensured compliance and made certain that they could be relied on to carry out orders. This was made clear in Jaruzelski's statement on December 13, 1981, when he told the nation that the military's involvement in the imposition of martial law did not signify any wish "to stage a military coup d'état or to impose a military dictatorship"; it was not intended to "replace the constitutional authorities" but rather to "protect the legal order in the state and to create operational guarantees that will make it possible to regain discipline and conformity to the law."[5]

Subsequent developments confirmed this. The emergence of the Military Council of National Salvation hardly changed the system of government. Heralded by the media as the main policy-making agency, it proved to be neither a policy-making nor an executive body. It met rarely, issued occasional statements that were exhortations rather than authoritative announcements, and generally refrained from defining any political or economic strategies for government.

Equally vague was the military's role in running the country. The implementation of policy was coordinated by the Committee for the Defense of the Country. This was not a military body, however; although its membership has never been revealed, it seems to have consisted of a large number of officials—some of whom may have been members of the military but many, if not most, of whom were civilians—headed by the prime minister. The provincial defense committees were presided over by the head of the local administrative body and included party secretaries, police commanders, and military representatives. This arrangement suggested a degree of cooperation between civilian and military officials, but it hardly implied any clear predominance of one over the other. Indeed, important areas of government activity were controlled by civilians. This was particularly striking in the case of two interministerial committees set up immediately after the imposition of martial law that dealt with all aspects of social and economic policy and were directed by deputy prime ministers Mieczyslaw F. Rakowski and Janusz Obodowski, respectively.

There was nothing vague, however, about the changes produced by these developments in both the style and the method of government. They became distinctly militaristic, emphasizing discipline, firmness, and toughness. This was combined with the centralization of decision making and the consolidation of existing institutions. Inherent in all of this was the authorities' conviction that the centrally controlled streamlining of the system was both necessary and sufficient for its maintenance.

This attitude was particularly apparent in the leadership's approach to the party. The party was weak: organizational disarray and political demoralization were evident at all levels. To rescue the PUWP from this situation, the leadership emphasized the need to return the party to "Leninist" organizational practices. The stage was set by an instruction prepared by the Central Committee's Secretariat that, after approval by the Politburo, was sent to all provincial party secretaries a few days before the imposition of martial law. Defining "the activities of the party in conditions endangering the security of the state," it drastically reduced the role of elective party bodies and imposed strict control over rank-and-file members.[6] The instruction became effective with the imposition of martial law.

Decision making became even more centralized. Local party bodies were deprived of the right to make their own decisions without prior approval from the leadership; party committees were again subordinated to their first secretaries; and the central leadership's right to overrule any decisions—including those on personnel matters—that might have been taken in the past by local party agencies, was confirmed. The very principle of the election of party officials was suspended; all changes were to be made by cooptation, by appointment, or by a centrally imposed purge. Moreover, local secretaries were given the right to dissolve or suspend any local party body or group whose activities they judged "contrary to the ideological principles defined by party rules and [incompatible with] instructions issued by party bodies at higher levels and the political line and program of the party."

The practical effects of the instruction were immediate. Numerous party bodies in factories, offices, and universities were dissolved; in many other institutions the party ceased to function altogether. Within two months of the imposition of martial law, almost 100,000 party members had been expelled from the ranks; several provincial first secretaries were replaced; 349 secretaries of provincial and town committees were removed, along with 307 secretaries of factory committees and 2,091 first secretaries of basic party organizations (particularly those in large factories and industrial plants). In addition, some 2,000 members of various town and provincial committees and large numbers of activists were purged.[7] Most of those people had been elected in 1981.

The brunt of the purges was aimed at individuals and groups that had in the past displayed tendencies to reform the party or were suspected of wavering in their compliance to centrally prescribed orders. The purpose of the campaign, which was directed by CC secretaries Kazimierz Barcikowski and Wlodzimierz Mokrzyszczak, was to effect a thorough change of personnel in various party bodies in order to make them compatible with the leadership's concept of a unified, disciplined, and efficient party. In a programmatic address to a Central Committee meeting on February 24, 1982—which was the first gathering of the party's main deliberative body since the imposition of martial law—Jaruzelski said that "it is about time to put an end to dividing the party into wings. . .We must maintain one common goal, and, while one could and should discuss how to achieve this, we must not, and we shall not, relax the rules of iron discipline in implementing our decisions."[8]

More specifically, Jaruzelski excluded the continuation of any of the "horizontal" structures that had emerged during 1980 and 1981 to promote democratizing reforms in the party; he said that to allow their further activity would "sooner or later lead to the abolition of the party." But he also excluded orthodox, hardline groups. "So-called forums or similar forms of extraparty activity have been harmful to the party," he noted, and added that "the party does not need any help from 'left-wing advisers.' "

This statement amounted to a resolution to clamp down on divisions within the party. Its main targets were orthodox groups, since the proponents of democratic reform within the party—the "abolitionists"—had already largely been rooted out from positions of any influence through purges or resignations. By contrast, the hardliners were more active than ever. Having emerged during 1981 as a numerically small but vocal group within the party whose main concern was to counter the very concept of party reform and oppose any change in traditional policies, the hardliners enthusiastically embraced the imposition of martial law as the means toward the realization of their objectives. Indeed, in leaflets and declarations they urged the leadership to adopt a tough stance toward any form of opposition, called for the tightening of bonds between Poland and the Soviet Union, and demanded that the purges be extended to include anyone whos views they regarded as different from their own; they even demanded the dismissal of some members of the leadership.[9] More important, some hardline activists took steps to provide themselves with a semblance of organizational identity.

On January 13, 1982, the nationwide Association of Clubs for Social and Political Knowledge was set up to work for "a return to true socialist practices [in public life] and a rejection of the deviations from the system that undermined socialism in Poland." The association was chaired by former Politburo member and CC secretary Tadeusz Grabski. It declared its intention to

> set up a public movement, which, through the dissemination of knowledge about the principles and mechanisms of socialist development, will act to strengthen socialism and to counter the plans of its enemies and [in so doing] to

contribute to the eradication of all those dangers that prompted the imposition of martial law.[10]

This was enough to press the leadership into quick, though indirect, action. On February 25 the Central Committee endorsed the Politburo's decision to "halt the activity of all movements, structures, forums, and seminars" within the party.[11] That alone did much to undermine the hardliners' pretensions and aspirations. It negated their privileged position as a movement within the party and put the new association and a host of other orthodox bodies—such as the openly anti-Semitic and authoritarian Grunwald Association—under the control of government administrators rather than party ideologists. Other steps followed. An orthodox journal, the Warsaw weekly *Rzeczywistosc,* which was allowed to resume publication after the initial rigors of martial law had been eased, was put under the direct control of the central party publishing cooperative; several journalists who had joined the orthodox association were removed from positions of influence in the media; and finally, Grabski himself was sent off to the GDR to take a minor post in the Polish commercial office there. In a farewell letter to his party cell, Grabski bitterly complained that, as a result of the leadership's policies, "the party is dying, losing its leading role in society and its directing role in the state."[12] The letter had no political effect and merely earned Grabski a rebuke in a specialized party publication. At the end of 1982 the Association of Clubs for Social and Political Knowledge was quietly dissolved.

This was sufficient to dissipate the threat of the emergence of an orthodox faction within the party but not to eliminate hardline sentiments in some sectors of the organization. Yet the leadership did not even attempt to restrain these sentiments; its attention focused on the containment of every form of organized activity that could escape its direct control, irrespective of the political orientation involved. Once this goal was achieved, the leadership actually encouraged the spread of orthodox ideas by supporting hardline publications and by promoting discussions in the media among opponents and proponents of orthodox trends. (For example, the Warsaw weekly *Polityka* would usually lead with critical articles about the hardline groups, and other papers—such as *Rzeczywistosc* or the Warsaw weekly *Przeglad tygodniowy*—would respond in kind about the centrist or liberal circles. All of these papers were published by the same party cooperative, which, in turn, was tightly controlled by the CC Secretariat.) Such discussions helped to focus public attention on party matters, which was a problem of considerable political importance in the circumstances of martial law.

The leniency in the treatment of orthodox trends in the party had at times been regarded as indicative of the hardliners' ability to veto any policy initiative of which they did not approve. That may indeed have been the case in some instances, but there was no evidence that any hardline group had ever attempted to force a change in the leadership's decision on any important issue. Instead, there was considerable evidence that the leadership's decisions corresponded closely with what could be regarded as traditional party values. This implied the existence of a certain political affinity with the orthodox orientation, an assumption strongly supported by the fact that most orthodox clubs and seminars had been established during 1981 with the connivance of the leadership.

In any case, there was certainly no room in the party for self-styled liberalizers or reformers, even though they might have professed loyalty to the leadership. This was demonstrated by the expulsion of Adam Schaff from the party in 1984. A known Marxist theorist and a former member of the PUWP's Central Committee, Schaff ceased his political activity in the aftermath of the 1968 anti-Semitic campaign and devoted his time to writing and to teaching at the University of Vienna. Upon his return to Poland in early 1982, Schaff repeatedly voiced his approval of martial law while calling for changes in the party that would cut down the influence of orthodox forces. These views were eventually found by the Central Control Commission to be "incompatible with the principles of the party statutes" and "harmful to the process of consolidation" within the organization.[13]

In contrast to the consolidating processes that affected the party membership and local bodies, no discernible upheavals occurred in the national leadership. Of fifteen full Politburo members elected in 1981, only three—Jan Labecki, Miroslaw Milewski, and Stefan Olszowski—resigned their posts in the following four years. Labecki, a worker from Gdansk, departed in July 1982. Milewski, who had served as the party's supervisor for security matters until November 1984, was pushed aside in May 1985 following the trial of policemen who had murdered a popular Warsaw priest, Jerzy Popieluszko. Olszowski's resignation in November 1985 was said to have been prompted by "personal considerations and plans to devote his time to writing and scholarly pursuits";[14] he was regarded by many as a potential competitor to other party leaders, including General Jaruzelski himself.

Two new full Politburo members were elected in July 1982: a worker from Poznan, Stanislaw Kalkus, and an experienced party staffer, Marian Wozniak. In addition, three deputy members were chosen: Stanislaw Bejger and General Czeslaw Kiszczak in 1982 and Marian Orzechowski in 1983.

There was more movement among the Central Committee secretaries. At the end of 1985 only three of those elected at the 1981 congress remained: Jozef Czyrek, Zbigniew Michalek, and Marian Wozniak, who had left the Secretariat in 1982 to lead the Warsaw party committee and returned in November 1985. Two former secretaries moved to other positions while preserving their high standing in the party (Barcikowski and Hieronim Kubiak); two others lost all their posts in the party (Milewski and Olszowski). Six newcomers were Politburo member Tadeusz Porebski (1983), Henryk Bednarski (1983), Jan Glowczyk (1982), Wlodzimierz Mokrzyszczak (1981), Waldemar Swirgon (1982), and General Jozef Baryla (1985).

There were almost no changes in the Central Committee itself. Of its 200 or so members elected in 1981, only a handful were removed and one fled to the West. Several new members were coopted, among them a few military officers who had served as deputy members as well as General Jozef Baryla, head of the Main Political Administration of the Armed Forces, who had failed to secure election at the congress in 1981.

The stability of the leadership was truly remarkable, considering the upheavals in the party as a whole, but hardly surprising. Many of the Politburo members had certainly been aware of the preparations for martial law. More than probably some of them, as well as several junior members of the Secretariat, had abetted the preparations and then took part in the martial-law implementation. They were also involved in its maintenance.

The Central Committee's continuity reflected an obvious shift in power and activism away from the CC and toward various executive and staff bodies. This shift became apparent in the immediate aftermath of the 1981 congress, when most of the experienced party officials failed to gain election to the committee and their places were taken by new and frequently unknown activists. The leadership made no attempt to alter that situation but held the new committee in relative disregard. This became particularly noticeable after the imposition of martial law. The Central Committee formally had the highest statutory authority in the party, yet it was neither consulted before the imposition of martial law nor formally notified once it had been introduced. The first meeting of the committee under the new conditions took place more than two months after the announcement of martial law. Even then the committee was neither asked, nor did it attempt, to adopt any programmatic statement about what should be done in the future; it merely acknowledged the event. The subsequent sessions of the committee were no different: they provided forums for the leadership's statements and featured occasional discussions, but no decisions were taken and no policies were made there.

Along with the changes in the party, the leadership imposed far-reaching transformations in the work of other institutions and in their relations with the public. This was done through government-sponsored legislation designed to provide central administrative bodies with greater powers to decide, control, and act. In 1982 alone, 57 new laws were adopted that dealt with economic, educational, and cultural administration. In addition, numerous existing laws were modified, such as those on the management of state enterprises, workers' self-management, and the financing of economic enterprises. This legislative effort continued in subsequent years, albeit at a slower pace.

The authorities also mounted a sustained campaign of purges, particularly at the levels of ranking administrators in central offices and the provinces, directors and managers in large factories, and heads of various institutes, universities, and cultural establishments. Its objective was to fill those positions with people who would be both politically loyal and compliant to orders from above. Many of the posts were given to the party's professional staff members. Indeed, between the beginning of December 1981 and June 1982, about 3,500 political employees of the party staff were moved to administrative positions in the government.[15] There is every reason to believe that such transfers continued in subsequent years.

The stated purpose of all these changes was to "create a strong and effective administration that would be capable of an efficacious performance in the service of the socialist state"[16]—that is, to strengthen the party's controlling capabilities and, above all, to minimize the chances of another outburst of public movement toward self-determination and autonomy. Nothing symbolized this better than the authorities' treatment of the labor unions.

All labor unions were officially dissolved in October 1982, when new legislation established that future workers' organizations would have to conform in their statutes and activities with "the constitution as well as with other laws."[17] More specifically, the new unions would have to indicate in their charters that they would "respect the state ownership of the means of production. . .the socialist political system. . .Poland's international alliances. . .[and] the leading role of the party" in the system. The law banned Solidarity and two other types of labor organizations: the branch unions and the autonomous unions.

Within months of the law's adoption, the first of the new labor organizations appeared in factories. By the end of 1983 branch federations had emerged, uniting individual unions in specific industrial sectors. In November 1984 the so-called Council of Trade Unions' National Agreement was created to represent all union groups. Its establishment was described by the authorities as "a higher and desirable form of integration" of the workers' movement and an important "element in the implementation of both the aims and the tasks of socialist renewal."[18] Expanding on that theme, Jaruzelski assured the council of the leadership's interest in "the strengthening of the role played by . . .the labor unions in public life" and said that the leadership "will do anything so that the labor unions are listened to and will make every effort to shape the partnership between the [state] administration and the class-based labor movement."[19] The council's chairman, Alfred Miodowicz, a veteran party activist, was appointed a member of the Council of State in 1985.

Many other public organizations were treated in a similar fashion: banned only to be replaced with more compliant and politically loyal groups. These included the peasants' independent union, the autonomous students' organization, the actors' union, the journalists' union, and the writers' union. The authorities based their actions on the need to "normalize" public life and to ensure prerogatives for themselves. All public protests against those actions, as well as against other aspects of the authorities' autocratic methods, were suppressed through the continued harassment of individuals, the intimidation of groups, detentions, and physical force. These tactics undeniably instilled fear in many people, but they hardly contributed to the political stabilization of the country.

In December 1982 the authorities announced the suspension of martial law, as though to tell the Polish public and the world that some of the conditions judged indispensable for the protection of their interests had already been achieved. The military commissars were removed from some factories and administrative agencies, censors' stamps vanished from letters, and interferences in telephone conversations, which had been used to remind people that they were being monitored, ceased. All internment camps were closed and all internees freed, although several prominent Solidarity leaders as well as a group of former KOR members were kept in prison on charges of conspiring against the state. The suspension of martial law was accompanied by the passage of laws providing the authorities with the right to reimpose it if conditions required and legalizing its rigors for the future.

On July 22, 1983, martial law was lifted. The Military Council of National Salvation was formally dissolved and an amnesty was declared for some of the imprisoned opponents of the martial-law regulations and for those who still remained in hiding. Announcing these measures, Jaruzelski warned that "anarchy will not return to Poland and any attempt to engage in anti-state activity will be treated as severely as during marital law."[20] Indeed, several laws regulating the operation of central and local government agencies and a host of special regulations for controlling public behavior in the case of any outburst of opposition were adopted as precautionary measures. The lifting of martial law was met with indifference from the population, which apparently reflected the conviction that rigors and restrictions were certain to continue, regardless of what the system called itself.

In the immediate aftermath of the imposition of martial law, it was almost commonplace to argue that this development had served to diminish the party's role in the system of government. In fact, the reverse was probably the case, since martial law created opportunities for the party to embark on a new beginning. When martial law lifted, which was authoritatively described as a "rescue phase," the party was said to have become organizationally stronger and more "ideologically united" than before.[21] It was also said to "have regained the initiative [in shaping] public life and [to have been] progressively reacquiring the confidence and support of society."

This may have been wishful thinking rather than a factual assessment. Although the party certainly became more disciplined and there were no apparent factional groups in the membership, this could hardly be regarded as demonstrating either strength or unity. It reflected the leadership's undeniable success in imposing central control over all aspects of party work, but that, in itself, guaranteed neither improvement in the membership's morale nor a political rapport with society.

In fact, the party continued to experience major problems both in recruiting new members and in maintaining an appreciable measure of activism among the rank and file and in basic cells. The membership had started to decline in mid-1980 (see Appendix 1), and the involvement of ordinary members in internal party affairs had dramatically diminished during 1981, particularly after the extraordinary congress. More significant, these trends persisted after the imposition of martial law and perhaps even intensified.

The leadership was obviously aware of these problems, but its efforts to resolve them brought no immediate results. In April 1982 the leadership held a national conference for ideological activists to launch a party debate about the very nature and program of organization. The conference produced a draft declaration—the theme of which was "What are we fighting for; where are we going?"—designed to assure the rank and file that the party still remained attached to the revolutionary principles of equality and social justice.[22] It failed to ignite any interest in the party as a whole, however, and, following a series of amendments introduced into the text by the Politburo and the Secretariat, the declaration was adopted by the National Party Conference of delegates to the 1981 congress only in March 1984.[23] In November 1985 another party ideological conference started to prepare a draft program for party activities until the year 2000. It was to be discussed by party bodies and, after approval by the Politburo, presented to the 1986 national congress.

Nevertheless, it was clear that even the best program would remain ineffective unless it received a degree of support not only from the party's membership but also from the population as a whole. Yet the relationship between the party and the public had worsened. In their attempts at normalization, the authorities had inflicted a great deal of damage and abuse on society, particularly by their efforts to suppress anything that might have suggested public autonomy or a public identity different from that of the communist state. This was obviously difficult to forgive and forget. In fact, since the imposition of martial law, neither resistance nor the public's disgust with, and distrust of, the political system disappeared or weakened. That mood might have been temporarily subdued at times, but it was visible everywhere—in factories, on farms, in cities, and in villages.

The leadership remained determined not to yield. Its policy toward society was rooted in the principle of "agreement and struggle," which had provided the guiding light for all official activities since the strikes of August 1980. In this case, the "agreement" always meant agreement by others with official policies, and the "struggle" denoted the leadership's refusal, frequently emphasized by repressive action, to accept any other view. No alternative strategy was contemplated and any attempt to suggest other approaches was either ignored or suppressed.

The leadership emphasized its quest for agreement immediately after the imposition of martial law, and it encouraged the establishment of the so-called Citizens' Committees of National Salvation, which served to unite activists of political and social organizations who were willing to support official policies. Subsequently, these committees provided the foundation for the emergence of the Patriotic Movement of National Rebirth, a nationwide body designed to provide the authorities with a formal channel for "consultations" with the public; it performed functions comparable to those of the former Front of National Unity. The political role of the movement was defined officially as "fulfilling society's hunger for active participation in political life, in the formulation of party and government policies."[24] From the very moment of the movement's establishment in September 1982, however, the party's leadership made it clear that the organization, though "spontaneously organized" by ordinary citizens, was and would be "inspired" in its work by the party itself.[25]

The authorities also made considerable efforts to reinvigorate public organizations and groups that had long maintained a record of compliance with the principles of Communist-directed political and institutional centralism. These included the two political parties—the United Peasant Party and the Democratic Party, which for decades had been allied with the PUWP—and the three traditionally pro-party Catholic groups: PAX, the Christian Social Association, and the Polish Catholic Social Union. These latter groups cooperated with the party in establishing the Patriotic Movement of National Rebirth. Also included were the officially sanctioned youth organizations: the Socialist Youth Union, the Rural Youth Union, the Socialist Union of Polish Students, and the Polish Scouts' Union. All these groups constituted the institutional expression of the "national agreement," and they formed a social basis for the political system itself, since the rest of the population was either hostile or at best ambivalent in its attitude toward the regime.[26]

Indeed, the most important problem for the authorities was their failure either to contain or silence the public. Although all autonomous public groups were outlawed in the months that followed the imposition of martial law, this merely pushed the opposition underground instead of destroying it. In time, the public resistance to official policies developed into a national movement that attracted groups and individuals from many sections of society, led to the emergence of specific organized bodies (for example, the Provisional Coordinating Commission of Solidarity and regional commissions of Solidarity), and succeeded in creating a truly remarkable publishing system capable of producing both books and papers as well as radio and video cassettes.[27]

The resistance's methods ranged from organizing demonstrations on the streets to clandestine radio broadcasts and the dissemination of papers and leaflets. There was no discernible program of action. The main issue that united all groups and tendencies was a refusal to acquiesce in the authorities' claim that the Communist Party alone could and would direct the country. In this way the resistance was effective, since it certainly made the authorities' task much more difficult.

The regime was determined to put down the resistance. Opposition members, contemptuously described by officials and the media as "fanatics" led by foreign powers and as domestic counter-revolutionaries, were constantly arrested, persecuted, and sentenced to prison terms. There was no indication, however, that such tough treatment succeeded in discouraging opposition to the party and government policies. Twice, in 1983 and 1984, the authorities offered pardons to all political offenders if they would cease their activity; neither offer produced any change in public attitudes. In 1985 the government started a program of selective releases from prison, apparently in the hope that this would encourage a measure of compliance among opposition activists. It was far from certain that this tactic would prove more effective than the previous ones.

A crucial factor undermining the authorities' effort to quash the underground was the support provided to its activists by the public as a whole. Prominent underground figures, such as Zbigniew Bujak from Warsaw, were lodged for years in private apartments at considerable risk to their owners. Unofficial journals and books were distributed by countless couriers and sellers; more important, those publications were frequently printed on paper provided from state enterprises, using equipment from state publishing houses. All this strongly suggested that the public's opposition to the system and its methods was both widespread and ongoing.

The most illustrious opposition leader was Lech Walesa, who, more than anyone else, personified in the public mind the popular longing for self-determination. He was a worker who had led the workers' team in successful negotiations with the authorities in August 1980 and then became the elected chairman of Solidarity, the largest public organization in the history of Poland. Walesa was interned after the imposition of martial law and kept in isolation until November 1982. Upon his release he resumed his public activities, although under markedly different circumstances and in spite of many restrictions. His complaints about his treatment were either ignored or ridiculed by the authorities and the official media.

In October 1983 Walesa was awarded the Nobel Peace Prize, a development that both honored the achievements of the Polish labor movement and signaled a serious setback for the authorities: it served to reinforce the public's resolve to persevere in its efforts to ensure for itself a voice in politics. The authorities tried to diminish the importance of the award, claiming that it was the result of the maneuvers of their Western enemies. There was no doubt, however, that the award made it much more difficult for the authorities to suppress their opponents.

This difficulty was compounded by the noticeable affinity between the opposition and various individuals, groups, and bodies within the Catholic Church. The Church had been deeply involved in all public developments during the months preceding the imposition of martial law. Indeed, in many people's minds, the Church—as an institution autonomous from party control—had been identified with the public rebellion against authoritarian constraints; the Church itself did not accept that identification. In fact, throughout the months of upheavals and conflicts the Church had maintained the role of mediator in the disputes between the authorities and public groups. This was particularly important at the time of severe tension between Solidarity and the authorities in March 1981, when Primate Stefan Cardinal Wyszynski succeeded in keeping the two sides talking. After Wyszynski's death in May 1981, a similar role was played by Primate Jozef Glemp, particularly during a meeting between Jaruzelski and Walesa in November 1981. Under the conditions of martial law, however, the mediating function obviously lost its justification.

Even so, the Church remained deeply involved in political and public matters. This was particularly apparent in its growing activism in areas that had an essentially secular character: work on behalf of political prisoners, the gathering and distribution of aid from abroad, and efforts to set up a foundation to provide aid to private farmers. All of these activities prompted the emergence of a diversity of views within the Church regarding its methods of social work, its scope, and, most important of all, the meaning and extent of the Church's relations with the public and with the authorities. This diversity emerged clearly in the frequently outspoken criticism of the authorities' actions by numerous local priests, which contrasted with the relatively measured pronouncements by national Church leaders. Many local priests became directly involved in organizing cultural and educational programs in their churches and parishes that had not been sanctioned by the authorities; some of those priests were harassed by the authorities.

This ferment in the Church reflected different preoccupations among particular groups. The leadership's position, as displayed in Glemp's pronouncements, was concerned with the status of the Church as a religious institution within the framework of a militantly atheistic regime. The attitude of local priests and some of their bishops was influenced largely by their sensitivity to the feelings of ordinary people, who, deprived of any forum of their own by the authorities, looked upon the Church as the only body that could and should defend their civil and public rights.

This situation did not change as a result of Pope John Paul II's visit in June 1983. The visit merely confirmed and dramatized the gap between the political system, its values, its institutions, and the populace. The Pope met with Walesa privately to acknowledge the importance of the movement of self-determination; he met with Jaruzelski officially to pay his respects to the formal authorities. No changes in the activities of either the local clergy or the national Church leadership ensued. Several months after the visit, Primate Glemp, who had been made a cardinal in the meantime, noted in an interview that the Polish Church should not be regarded as "a parliament that voted unanimously."[28] He went on to say that internal disagreements were being overcome by such factors as basic unity within the Church in matters related to religious dogma and discipline; in addition, methods of work had been developed during the last decades of coexistence between the Church and the communist government.

It was not certain, however, whether the meaning of coexistence between the Church and the communist government was understood by the two sides in the same way. The authorities' view, expressed in numerous statements and official or semiofficial declarations, focused on several points. The most important was the definition of long-range objectives that were regarded as determinants of official policy toward the Church. These objectives included an insistence that all religious activities conform with the constitution, which endowed the Communist Party with a "leading" role in public life and ensured that its Marxist-Leninist ideology provided a justification for all activities.[29] Moreover, the authorities declared themselves opposed to what they proclaimed to be "political clericalism," that is, an involvement by either Church officials or lay believers in public activities not explicitly related to religion but conducted in places of worship.

Furthermore, while the authorities proclaimed their interest in reaching some form of agreement with believers and the Church, they made clear their determination to limit the scope of the latter's involvement in public life to officially sanctioned organizations that supported the "socialist character" of the state. From their point of view, the struggle against "political clericalism" should be regarded as "a defense of the proper character of both religion and the Church."[30] Nevertheless, the authorities acknowledged that the Church should take part in some types of public activity that were not explicitly religious in character. These activities were defined in terms of "cooperation by the Church with the socialist authorities in the tasks of strengthening the family [as a social institution], of combating immorality, of inculcating in the population an understanding of the superiority of public over [private] values, and of the consolidation of society in support of the principles of the security and well-being of Poland." Finally, the authorities claimed the right to criticize all those aspects of the Church's activity that touched on the public domain, particularly those that might have "contributed to the evolution of negative national characteristics both in the past and in the present, especially with regard to the connection between the Church and the opposition."[31]

Practical steps followed. The official actions formed a pattern: the Church as a religious body was seldom condemned or criticized; instead, the thrust of the attack, conducted through statements by political leaders and media commentaries, was directed at each person or group regarded by the authorities as guilty of "political clericalism." Needless to say, the authorities themselves determined what constituted such activity. They approached the issue in a variety of ways. At times they merely ignored the Church's initiatives to improve the quality of public life; this was particularly evident in the official disregard of various proposals to give the public a greater say in politics as well as in the continuing procrastination in dealing with the project to set up a private agricultural foundation to aid private farmers. In other instances, the authorities moved in open disregard of public and Church opposition to assert their self-claimed prerogatives; this was apparent in the repeated conflicts over the official policy of removing crucifixes from public buildings. Harsh and virulent criticism was directed at priests whom the authorities accused of being involved in secular problems. Most of these priests worked in cities or industrial centers among people particularly affected by the authorities' crackdown on independent unions and other groups. The authorities conducted a systematic campaign against them, accusing them of political radicalism, threatening them with legal action, and repeatedly complaining about their work to the Church leadership. None of these steps proved effective.

In October 1984 government security agents abducted and murdered a popular Warsaw priest, Jerzy Popieluszko, who was well known for his critical views of official policies. The murderers, who were party members, were tried and sentenced to prison terms. Yet neither their motives nor the circumstances of the crime were satisfactorily explained during the public trial, which, in fact, was turned by the prosecution and the judges into an attack on the Church. The authorities described the case as a "political provocation" designed to undermine cooperation between the Church and the state. Seen against the background of recurrent conflicts and continuing problems between the two sides, this assertion was both baseless and cynical.[32] Within weeks of Popieluszko's murder, three other priests had been maltreated; the perpetrators were not apprehended.

None of these developments enhanced the authorities' prestige, respect, or standing among the public. However, it seemed to matter little to the self-proclaimed guardians of order, discipline, and hard work. They did maintain considerable power, in that they were able to enforce their decisions in spite of opposition from others. The foundations of this power were not in society or any part of it; they resulted from the support and help the authorities received from their foreign, and particularly Soviet, allies. This was the determining factor in the leadership's conduct.

Soviet support had been fundamental to the system's survival during the popular upheavals of 1980–1981; it had no doubt been crucial in bringing about the imposition of martial law; and it was instrumental in the Polish leadership's successful destruction of popular aspirations to self-determination.[33] The support ranged from much-publicized programs of economic assistance to more discreet and largely indirect means of political guidance.

The publicity surrounding Soviet economic help was not surprising: Poland was going through a major economic crisis, was heavily in debt, had no immediate prospects of obtaining credits from the West that would alleviate the situation, and was clearly incapable of solving its problems by itself. The Soviet Union has long been Poland's most important trading partner and has provided it with raw materials and energy resources (more than 90 percent of its cotton, more than 80 percent of its iron ore, and 100 percent of its natural gas and oil imports), while Poland's exports were mostly of machinery and consumer products. In the 1970s Poland had posted regular gains in its trade with the Soviet Union, but its first deficit came in 1980 and the country has been falling deeper into debt ever since. Poland repeatedly sought the postponement of the debt's payment, and the Soviet Union complied either through direct rescheduling agreements or by means of Council for Mutual Economic Assistance (CMEA) loan arrangements favorable to Poland; each such arrangement was heavily publicized. Even so, it was clear that the postponement of the repayment of Soviet debts by itself had a relatively marginal effect on the Polish economy as a whole. What was needed was a massive influx of resources, either in the form of hard currency or raw materials or both, but this the Soviet Union was unwilling or unable to provide.

More important was Moscow's political help, most noticeably expressed in the strengthening of ties between the parties, the governments, and other public bodies. Immediately after the imposition of martial law there were almost weekly visits by Soviet delegations to Poland and by Polish delegations to the Soviet Union. This exchange involved various party bodies in both countries, official government institutions, public associations, and media representatives. Jaruzelski himself made between 1982–1985 seven trips to the Soviet Union, three of which were necessitated by the funerals of Soviet leaders (Leonid Brezhnev, Yuri Andropov, and Konstantin Chernenko); all the other party leaders also made visits.

Such personal exchanges were important, inasmuch as they engendered mutual understanding and rapport between officials on both sides. It was extremely unlikely, of course, that any member of the Polish political establishment, particularly of the party or the government hierarchies, would be anti-Soviet; all of them have always acted as staunch Soviet loyalists. This attitude, perhaps more than anything else, has constituted the basic prerequisite for holding office in Poland. Even so, post–martial-law circumstances required that only the most loyal of the loyalists should be in charge of rebuilding a vital Communist Party in Poland. The exchanges served to ensure the fulfillment of that requirement.

On October 13, 1985, a new Sejm was elected in the first ballot for the national legislature since March 1980. The elections had originally been scheduled to take place in March 1984 but were postponed owing to the authorities' apparent concern about their outcome; the balloting for the local People's Councils in 1984 had, according to official figures, attracted only 75 percent of the eligible voters, while the opposition claimed a 60 percent turnout. In 1985 both sides agreed that the turnout was bigger than in 1984. The official figures showed that 78.86 percent of the registered voters had cast their ballots for candidates that had been selected by the Patriotic Movement of National Rebirth; no other candidates had been allowed to run. The opposition claimed a turnout of approximately 66 percent.

The result was sufficient for the authorities to proclaim the onset of political stability resulting from their efforts to normalize the country. On November 6, at the first session of the new Sejm, Jaruzelski formally relinquished his position as head of the government and became chairman of the Council of State, the body functioning as a collective head of state. This step was made to symbolize the fulfillment of normalizing efforts, since when Jaruzelski was appointed prime minister in February 1981 he had promised to stay in office until the situation stabilized.

Whether this was actually the case remained doubtful, however. The Sejm elections demonstrated stability, although this stability was hardly of a kind that corresponded to the authorities' expectations. It confirmed the existence of a significant number of people who continued to be openly opposed to the system, its institutions, and its methods. Irrespective of the exact figures, it was obvious that their number was substantial. More important, these people appeared to come from a wide range of social groups and from all parts of the country, particularly from the urban and industrial areas. This strongly suggested that the official policy of normalization had failed and the party's control over the public had not been restored.

The authorities were certainly aware of that, but they were determined to continue the tactics of socialist renewal. This was confirmed at the party's national congress, held from June 29 to July 3, 1986. The congress fully endorsed the leadership's policies and methods. There was only a limited reshuffle of the Politburo and the Secretariat (see Appendix 3) and the changes in the composition of both the Central Committee (its size was reduced from 270 to 230 members of whom two-thirds were new) and the Control and Auditing Commissions (which were merged into one of much smaller membership) brought to the fore a group of loyal and disciplined party officials who had already been effectively conditioned to obey without question orders from above. Whether this would be sufficient to ensure the success of socialist renewal was far from certain, however. That would require public compliance; and there was no clear prospect of the party's being able to secure it.

Conclusions

The history of the Communist Party in Poland may be divided into five phases. The first dates from the formation of the KPRP in 1918 until the dissolution of the KPP in 1938. The second starts with the revival of the party in the Soviet Union during 1941 and lasts until the establishment of the PUWP in 1948. The third encompasses the years 1949–1954, and the fourth extends until the end of 1981. The fifth phase starts with the imposition of martial law and continues until the present. This division is of course chronological, but beyond a recapitulation of the party's past, it also refers to specific political and organizational problems that the party faced during each of those stages.

During the initial period of its existence, the party was a miniscule oppositional force within an independent and anti-communist Polish state. Its main task was to secure its political and organizational survival and to perpetuate a dream of a revolutionary proletarian transformation of society. The gradual disintegration of the party, leading ultimately to its dissolution, made questionable the viability of the dream itself.

The restoration of the party was due to massive changes in the international environment, the war, and the disappearance of the Polish state rather than to a resurgence of revolutionary enthusiasm. Its main objectives were to seize power and to establish a communist state. Once in control of the government, the party concentrated on the consolidation of its political position. The emphasis in its work was on social and economic reforms with a view toward securing popular support for communist rule.

With the achievement of a political breakthrough, the basic task of the party changed from power consolidation to socioeconomic transformation. The defining characteristics of the party's activity during the third period was its concerted effort to eliminate all social, economic, and cultural traces of the prerevolutionary past and to establish a lasting institutional framework for a future communist system and a socialist society. This emphasis on a revolutionary socioeconomic breakthrough had a decisive impact on party organization, internal distribution of power, and party-society relations. The interaction between revolutionary commitment and party structure, which had been designed for the task at hand, provided a single perspective on change and defined the methods of its implementation.

A gradual dissipation of revolutionary commitment, prompted by larger international developments but intensified by adverse reactions at home, marked the beginning of the fourth developmental stage. The party's political objective shifted away from the transformation of society and toward its integration within the existing system of institutional authority. The maintenance of stability became the party's primary concern and the traditional goals of building a socialist society were consciously limited to those aspects of change that could be adapted to prevailing economic and cultural conditions.

There were no changes in the party's organization, however. It maintained a rigidly hierarchical and centralized internal structure even while it became increasingly clear that this pattern, which had been adopted to forge a disciplined and effective organization to impose revolutionary change, was simply dysfunctional and cumbersome in evolutionary conditions. This had serious consequences in the party's political appeal, the recruitment of political leaders, and the periodic outbursts of tension within the organization.

The numerical expansion of the party, which followed its ascendancy to power and became even more accentuated after the adoption of an evolutionary and integrative orientation, raised serious questions about its social and ideological definition. To the degree that membership growth was largely due to an influx of white-collar employees and professionals into the party ranks, the organization not only lost its traditional proletarian character but also acquired a distinctly "socialist bourgeois" identity. This development had inevitable consequences for the party's relations with society. The party was increasingly seen by many as a vehicle for upward social mobility as well as an instrument to maintain its members at the top of the social structure. This produced, however, a rising undercurrent of resentment from lower groups, particularly the workers, who, lacking the skills and the organization that could influence policy formation, found themselves pushed outside the political arena.

For many years this current of resentment simmered under the politically passive surface, while the party was able to control and regulate occasional outbursts of dissatisfaction. This pattern broke down during the 1970s, when two consecutive, successful workers' protests against the implementation of party decisions exposed the vulnerability of the system to social pressures. This, in turn, led to a dramatic growth of the dissident movement, which signaled that numerous groups could no longer be accommodated within the existing setup.

The party failed to respond to these challenges in a way that would ensure stability of the system. In part, its difficulties resulted from the proliferation of frequently contradictory policy preferences within the organization itself and the growing functional heterogeneity among its specialized organs. A more important reason for the failure, however, was the leadership's insistence on the maintenance of the stultifying centralization of political decision making. During the late 1960s the party had undergone internal decentralization of authority, with signs of devolution of power from central bodies to various territorially and functionally defined organizational centers. This process was reversed in the 1970s by a partial restructuring and a comprehensive purge of personnel. The political essence of this was negative, since it aimed at preventing innovative changes in the organization and denying other groups the right to meaningful political participation.

The insistence on centralization was a crucial factor in the recruitment of party leadership. The main prerequisites for selection to the party office were loyalty to the leaders and obedience to their orders rather than competence or problem-solving capacities. No efforts were made to put experts or specialists from outside into positions of power and responsibility. No mechanism of effective succession or personnel change was developed. Major political breakdowns and social rebellions remained the only means for the overhaul of the party elite and officialdom.

The workers' strikes of 1980 that gave rise to a major public rebellion against the system of government ushered in a new form of political challenge for the party in that it focused on the issue of a potential reconstitution of power within the system itself. That alone produced turmoil within the party and seriously affected its relations with the public. The crisis led to an eventual collapse of the party's traditionally self-claimed leading role in public life and was halted only through the imposition of martial law.

The subsequent developments demonstrated the preference of the party's leadership for centralization of decision making and its equal rejection of the public's right to participate in policy formulation under any circumstances and in any fashion. Indeed, the leadership's main efforts were directed at building a new legal framework that would minimize the opportunities for any form of autonomy for the public. The leadership defined its policy in terms of a socialist renewal, which could suggest its wish to return to the old traditions of autocratic control over a placid and subdued society. The fulfillment of that wish seemed doubtful.

Serious conflicts between the party and society appeared inevitable. The experiences of recent years have shown clearly that many public groups could no longer be persuaded to accept the party's control over their activities and were ready to develop their own methods of work independent of the party and irrespective of its wishes, even though they might be forced to operate underground. So long as the party fails to recognize the public's right to take part in politics, it only contributes to the preservation of a hostile environment in which discontent and protests will inevitably flourish.

Even so, the future of the party seems relatively secure. Inasmuch as social upheavals can affect the party's internal organization, its policies, and its relations with the public, its destiny depends ultimately on factors other than public acceptance of, or popular support for, its rule. Above all, continuing aid and support from the Soviet Union provides a decisive guarantee of the party's existence. Just as it supplied the party in Poland with major premises for political and organizational development in the past, the Soviet Union today vitally contributes to the preservation of its control over the country. In the end, it is still Moscow's help that constitutes the most crucial determinant of the continuation of communist power in Poland.

A P P E N D I X   1

Party in Figures

I. MEMBERSHIP AND SOCIAL COMPOSITION OF THE COMMUNIST PARTY IN POLAND

1. COMMUNIST PARTY OF POLAND (KPRP AND KPP)

Year	Number	Year	Number
1919	6,310	1929	3,504
1920	n.a.	1930	3,688
1921	875	1931	7,616
1922	4,825*	1932	8,812
1923	2,901	1933	9,327
1924	3,346	1934	7,097
1925	2,466	1935	6,911
1926	2,832	1936	7,034
1927	5,934	1937	3,927
1928	3,432	1938	n.a.

SOURCE: Franciszka Swietlikowa, "Liczebnosc okregowych organizacji KPP w latach 1919–1937," *Z pola walki,* no. 2, 1970, pp. 187–201.

*including 3,000 in the legally operating Silesian organization.

2. POLISH WORKERS' PARTY

Year	Number (in thousands)	Workers Percent	Peasants Percent	White Collar Percent	Others Percent
1942	1.5-4.0	n.a.	n.a.	n.a.	n.a.
1943	est. 8.0	n.a.	n.a.	n.a.	n.a.
1944	est. 20.0	n.a.	n.a.	n.a.	n.a.
1945	235.3	62.2	28.2	9.6	—
1946	556.0	64.7	23.2	9.3	2.8
1947	820.8	57.7	21.6	14.1	6.6
1948	955.9	57.4	22.1	17.1	3.5

SOURCES: N. Kolomejczyk, *PPR 1944–1945,* pp. 294–96; *Nowe drogi,* January 1951, pp. 235–39; Michal Sadowski, *System partyjny PRL,* p. 230; *Z pola walki,* no. 4, 1961, pp. 174–78.

3. POLISH UNITED WORKERS' PARTY

Year	Number (in thousands)	Workers Percent	Peasants Percent	White Collar Percent	Others Percent
1949	1,368.7	61.3	14.4	22.8	1.5
1950	1,240.9	54.7	14.1	28.9	2.3
1951	1,138.4	49.3	13.3	35.2	2.2
1952	1,146.9	48.2	13.4	36.2	2.2
1953	1,226.7	47.7	13.0	37.0	2.2
1954	1,293.0	48.1	13.8	36.2	2.0
1955	1,343.8	45.1	13.0	39.2	2.6
1956	n.a.	n.a.	n.a.	n.a.	n.a.
1957	1,283.0	39.9	12.8	38.8	8.5
1958	1,023.4	41.8	12.2	43.9	3.9
1959	1,018.5	40.0	11.5	43.5	5.0
1960	1,154.7	40.3	11.8	42.9	5.0
1961	1,306.2	40.1	12.0	42.9	5.0
1962	1,397.0	39.8	11.5	43.7	5.0
1963	1,494.1	39.7	11.2	43.9	5.2
1964	1,640.7	40.2	11.4	43.0	5.4
1965	1,775.0	40.1	11.7	42.7	5.5
1966	1,894.0	40.2	11.7	42.6	5.5
1967	1,931.3	39.7	11.5	43.5	5.3
1968	2,104.3	40.2	11.4	43.0	5.4
1969	2,203.6	40.2	11.4	42.8	5.6
1970	2,320.0	40.3	11.5	42.5	5.7
1971	2,254.0	39.7	10.6	43.6	6.1
1972	2,262.9	39.6	10.1	43.9	6.4
1973	2,322.5	39.4	10.2	44.0	6.4
1974	2,363.9	n.a.	n.a.	n.a.	n.a.
1975	2,436.9	40.6	9.9	42.9	6.6
1976	2,568.4	44.9	9.3	38.8	7.0
1977	2,665.6	45.6	9.3	34.3	10.8
1978	2,928.9	n.a.	n.a.	n.a.	n.a.
1979	3,079.0	46.2	9.4	33.0	11.4
1980					
(June)	3,150.0	—	—	—	—
(September)	3,088.0	—	—	—	—
1981					
(March)	2,942.4	—	—	—	—
(September)	2,770.0	—	—	—	—
(November)	2,734.0	—	—	—	—
(December)	2,692.0	—	—	—	—
1982					
(October)	2,400.0	—	—	—	—
(December)	2,372.3	—	—	—	—
1983					
(December)	2,186.0	39.4	9.1	—	—
1984					
(August)	2,158.7	—	—	—	—
(December)	2,130.0	38.8	—	—	—

3. Polish United Workers' Party *Continued*

Year	Number (in thousands)	Workers Percent	Peasants Percent	White Collar Percent	Others Percent
1985 (June)	2,112.0	—	—	—	—
1985 (December)	2,115.0	—	—	—	—

Sources: *Nowe drogi,* March 1954, pp. 68–69; June 1956, pp. 102–6; May 1961, pp. 136–44; also *Zycie partii,* October 1968, pp. 3–5; January 1978 (back cover); *Rocznik statystyczny,* Warsaw, published in respective years; *Zolnierz wolnosci,* February 10, 1980; July 9, 1981; *Glos wybrzeza,* November 18, 1981; *Trybuna ludu,* December 10, 1981; December 16, 1982; January 19, 1984; June 13, 1985; and *Zycie partii,* December 19, 1984; January 23, 1986.

II. DISTRIBUTION OF PARTY ORGANIZATIONS

Categories	1945	1950	1959	1964	1968	1975	1977	1979	1981
Primary organizations	25,000	43,000	51,000	64,100	69,500	75,200	72,000	75,000	76,976
Communal and town Committees	n.a.	n.a.	4,600	4,575	4,900	2,739	2,300	2,500	2,359
District Committees	n.a.	n.a.	314	314	314	—	—	—	—
Province Committees	17	17	19	22	22	49	49	49	49

Sources: *Nowe drogi,* July–August 1947, p. 207; January–February 1951; January 1972, pp. 47–49; January 1976, p. 36; June 1977, p. 6; also *Trybuna ludu,* June 20, 1964; *Zycie partii,* October 1968, pp. 3–5; *Zolnierz wolnosci,* February 10, 1980; July 1981; *Nowe drogi,* August 1981, pp. 59–60.

Parliamentary Representation 1947–1978

1. CONSTITUENT SEJM (PARLIAMENT), 1947

Party	Seats
Polish Workers' Party*	119
Polish Socialist Party*	119
Peasant Party*	103
Democratic Party*	43
Polish Peasant Party	28
Labor Party	15
Others	17
	444

SOURCE: *Monitor Polski,* January 28, 1947.

*Government bloc

2. UNCONTESTED ELECTIONS, 1952–1976

Party	1952	1957	1961	1965	1969	1972	1976	1980	1985
PUWP	278	237	255	255	255	255	261	261	245
	65.4%	51.7%	55.4%	55.4%	55.4%	55.4%	56.7%	56.7%	53.3%
ZSL	88	120	117	117	117	117	113	113	106
	20.7%	26.1%	25.4%	25.4%	25.4%	25.4%	24.6%	24.6%	23%
SD	26	39	39	39	39	39	37	37	35
	6.1%	8.5%	8.5%	8.5%	8.5%	8.5%	8.0%	8.0%	7.6%
Non-party	33	63	49	49	49	49	49	49	74
	7.8%	13.7%	10.7%	10.7%	10.7%	10.7%	10.7%	10.7%	16%
Total	435	459	460	460	460	460	460	460	460

SOURCES: *Rocznik statystyczny,* respective years.

Party Leadership 1986

1. POLITBURO MEMBERS (15)

Name	Date of birth	State office	Elected	Responsible for
Jaruzelski, Wojciech	1923	State Council chairman	1971 (a)	CC first secretary
Barcikowski, Kazimierz	1927	State Council deputy chairman	1980 (a)	—
Baryla, Jozef	1924	—	1986	CC secretary, (security)
Czyrek, Jozef	1928	—	1981	CC secretary (international)
Glowczyk, Jan	1927	—	1986	CC secretary (propaganda)
Kiszczak, Czeslaw	1925	Minister of Internal Affairs	1986	—
Messner, Zbigniew	1929	Premier	1981	—
Miodowicz, Alfred	1929	Trade Unions' Council Chairman	1986	—
Mokrzyszczak, Wlodzimierz	1938	—	1986	Control and audit commission
Muranski, Zygmunt	1952	—	1986	—
Orzechowski, Marian	1931	Minister of Foreign Affairs	1986	—
Porebski, Tadeusz	1931	—	1981	CC secretary (general affairs)
Siwicki, Florian	1925	Minister of National Defense	1986	—
Stepien, Zofia	1939	—	1986	—
Wozniak, Marian	1936	—	1981	CC secretary (economy)

(a) Deputy Politburo member, 1970–1971.
(b) Deputy Politburo member, 1971–1980.

2. Politburo Deputy Members (5)

Name	Date of birth	State office	Elected	Responsible for
Bejger, Stanislaw	1929	—	1982	First secretary, Gdansk
Ferensztajn, Bogumil	1934	—	1986	First secretary Katowice
Kubasiewicz, Janusz	1938	—	1986	First secretary Warsaw
Michalek, Zbigniew	1935	—	1986	CC secretary (Agriculture)
Rembisz, Gabriela	1937	—	1986	—

3. Secretariat of the Central Committee (11)

The seven listed above and:				
Bednarski, Henryk	1934	—	1983	Ideology
Ciosek, Stanislaw	1939	—	1986	Administration, Public bodies
Cypryniak, Kazimierz	1934	—	1986	Organization
Wasilewski, Andrzej	1928	—	1986	Culture

Notes

1: THE REVOLUTIONARY TEMPTATION

1. For analysis of the early history of the socialist movement in Poland see Lucjan Blit, *The Origins of Polish Socialism*; also Lidia and Adam Ciolkosz, *Zarys dziejow socjalizmu polskiego*; see also an excellent and well documented summary in M. K. Dziewanowski, *The Communist Party of Poland*; for an evaluation by a contemporary communist scholar see Tadeusz Daniszewski, *Zarys historii polskiego ruchu robotniczego, 1864–1918.*

2. As cited in the translator's preface to Rosa Luxemburg, *The Industrial Development of Poland*, p. 65.

3. For an interesting discussion of Polish underground movements, with a special emphasis on patriotic formations, see Feliks Gross, *The Revolutionary Party,* pp. 121–60.

4. Rosa Luxemburg, "Leninism or Marxism," in *The Russian Revolution and Leninism or Marxism,* p. 86.

5. Dziewanowski, *The Communist Party of Poland,* p. 38.

6. On this point see an article by one of the top SDKPiL leaders, Adolf Warski, "W sprawach partyjnych," *Nowy przeglad 1922,* p. 199.

7. See, in particular, a speech by Maria Koszutska (Wera Kostrzewa), one of the most important leaders of the PPS-Left, at the party conference in 1916, included under the title "Sytuacja polityczna i zadania partii," in her *Pisma i przemowienia,* vol. 1, pp. 170–83; also Henryk Walecki, "Zwiazki zawodowe a partie polityczne," in his *Wybor pism,* vol. 1, pp. 273–82.

8. Walentyna Najdus, *Lewica polska w kraju rad,* p. 424.

9. Rosa Luxemburg, "The Russian Revolution" in *The Russian Revolution and Marxism or Leninism,* pp. 25–80; also Maria Koszutska, "Rewolucja rosyjska a proletariat miedzynarodowy," *Pisma i przemowienia,* vol. 1, pp. 237–55.

10. For the text of the program see *KPP. Uchwaly i rezolucje,* vol. 1, pp. 41–43.

11. "Tymczasowa ustawa organizacyjna Komunistycznej Partii Robotniczej Polski," *ibid.,* pp. 50–52.

12. Franciszka Swietlikowa, *Komunistyczna Partia Robotnicza Polski,* p. 80.

13. *Ibid.,* pp. 53–72.

14. Roza Luksemburg, "Socjalpatriotyzm w Polsce" in her *Wybor pism,* vol. 1, p. 63.

15. On this point see the work of Luxemburg's close collaborator, Julian Marchlewski, "Proletaryzacja chlopow" in his *Pisma wybrane,* vol. 1, pp. 559–64.

16. Both before and after the October Revolution Lenin consistently supported the principle of self-determination for Poland. Immediately after the establishment of the Bolshevik government, a proclamation in this sense was issued by the new Soviet republic.

17. Text in *KPP. Uchwaly i rezolucje,* vol. 1, pp. 42–43.

18. For details see Swietlikowa, *Komunistyczna Partia Robotnicza Polski,* pp. 117–18.

19. *Ibid.,* pp. 123–24; also Dziewanowski, *The Communist Party of Poland,* pp. 72–73.

20. Jozef Kowalski, *Zarys historii polskiego ruchu robotniczego,* vol. 1, 111–15.

21. Henryk Walecki, "O taktyce i o stosunku do parlamentaryzmu," in his *Wybor pism,* vol. 2, pp. 25–26.

22. For a thorough discussion of Polish federalist conceptions see M. K. Dziewanowski, *Jozef Pilsudzki: A European Federalist, 1918–1922.*

23. On this point see a well documented work by Tadeusz Teslar, *Propaganda bolszewicka podczas wojny polsko-rosyjskiej 1920 roku;* for a detailed discussion of the Polish and Soviet policies see Piotr S. Wandycz, *Soviet-Polish Relations, 1917–1921;* also Norman Davies, *White Eagle-Red Star: The Polish-Soviet War 1919–1920;* for a basic outline of communist tactics in the party documents see *KPP. Uchwaly i rezolucje,* vol. 1, pp. 95–98.

24. For a discussion of the different views within the KPRP on the question of Polish-Soviet relations written by a life-long communist leader see Roman Zambrowski, "Uwagi o wojnie polsko-radzieckiej 1920 roku," *Zeszyty Historyczne* (Paris), no. 38, 1976, pp. 3–30.

25. On this point see a letter by Aleksander Litwin to *Z pola walki,* no. 4, 1959, p. 284, in which he cites archival sources indicating a direct Soviet intervention in the organization of the Provisional Revolutionary Committee.

26. Julian Marchlewski, "Rosja proletariacka a Polska burzuazyjna," in his *Pisma wybrane,* vol. 2, pp. 764–66.

27. For texts of those programmatic appeals see *Tymczasowy Komitet Rewolucyjny Polski,* pp. 88–89, 111–13, 132–36.

28. Swietlikowa, *Komunistyczna Partia Robotnicza Polski,* pp. 210–21.

2: THE FADING SPARK

1. "Uchwala o jednosci frontu," in *KPP. Uchwaly i rezolucje,* vol. 1, pp. 141–43.

2. See the records of the congress in *Z pola walki,* nos. 3–4, 1958 and 1, 3–4, 1959.

3. *Ibid.,* no. 4, 1958, p. 149.

4. *Ibid.,* p. 156.

5. *Ibid.,* p. 161.

6. Text in *Nowy przeglad 1924–1925,* pp. 238–42.

7. Maria Koszutska (Wera Kostrzewa), *Pisma i przemowienia,* vol. 2, p. 288.

8. For a subsequent article reflecting his views see Julian Lenski, "Sprawa KPRP na V Kongresie," *Nowy przeglad 1924–1925,* pp. 106–15.

9. For Koszutska's speech see her *Pisma i przemowienia,* vol. 2, pp. 285–300.

10. Polish language text is in *KPP. Uchwaly i rezolucje,* vol. 2, pp. 52–60.

11. Text in *Nowy przeglad 1924–1925,* p. 188.

12. "O bolszewizacji partii," *KPP. Uchwaly i rezolucje,* vol. 2, pp. 122–39.

13. Adolf Warski, "IV konferencja KPP," *Nowy przeglad 1926,* pp. 14–15.

14. For a thorough analysis of this transition in Polish politics see Joseph Rothschild, *Pilsudski's Coup d'Etat.*

15. M. K. Dziewanowski, *The Communist Party of Poland,* p. 118.

16. As published in *Nowy przeglad 1926,* p. 588.

17. Text in *KPP. Uchwaly i rezolucje,* vol. 2, pp. 360–76.

18. For an account of the congress' proceedings see Jan Alfred Regula, *Historja Komunistycznej Partji Polski,* pp. 199–205; for a recent communist assessment see Jozef Kowalski, *Zarys historii polskiego ruchu robotniczego w latach 1918–1939,* pp. 387–98.

19. For details see Jozef Kowalski, *Trudne lata,* pp. 97–100.

20. *KPP. Uchwaly i rezolucje,* vol. 3, pp. 111–58.

21. See, in particular, a collection of speeches and writings from the years 1934–1937 of the party's top leader, Julian Lenski, *O front ludowy w Polsce.*

22. Jozef Kowalski, *Komunistyczna Partia Polski, 1935–1938,* pp. 79–82.

23. For detailed description of the organization and activity of those parties see Adam Strapinski, *Wywrotowe partie polityczne,* pp. 60–62.

24. *Ibid.,* p. 89; also Franciszka Swietlikowa, "Liczebnosc okregowych organizacji KPP w latach 1919–1937," *Z pola walki,* no. 2, 1970, p. 185, as well as R. V. Burks, *The Dynamics of Communism in Eastern Europe,* pp. 158–61.

25. For a listing of all members of the Central Committees until 1938 see *Z pola walki,* no. 4, 1958, pp. 96–100.

26. On this point see Celia S. Heller, *On the Edge of Destruction,* esp. pp. 253–60.

27. Text in *KPP. Uchwaly i rezolucje,* vol. 1, pp. 255–62.

28. *Ibid.,* vol. 2, pp. 122–39.

29. Kowalski, *Komunistyczna Partia Polski, 1935–1938,* pp. 82–83.

30. Roman Zambrowski in *Z pola walki,* no. 4, 1958, p. 205.

31. Kowalski, *Komunistyczna Partia Polski, 1935–1938,* p. 72.

32. For details see the unpublished doctoral dissertation of Alexander J. Groth, "Parliament and the Electoral System in Poland, 1918–1935," Columbia University, 1960, pp. 134–35 and 232–33.

33. For details see Andrzej Gwizdz, "Frakcja komunistyczna w burzuazyjnych sejmach polskich, 1921–1935," *Z pola walki,* no. 4, 1958, pp. 64–95.

34. *KPP. Uchwaly i rezolucje,* vol. 1, p. 140.

35. T. Dabal, *Powstanie krakowskie* (Minsk: n.p., 1926), p. 39 as cited by Dziewanowski, *The Communist Party of Poland,* p. 106.

36. The rate of industrial unemployment ranged from a low of about 10 percent in 1930 to 43 percent in 1933, with the average for the entire decade oscillating around 30 percent. During that time there were several hundred strikes per year, with the high point reached in 1936, when some 700,000 workers took part in 2,056 strikes with nearly four million workdays lost. For details see Ferdinand Zweig, *Poland Between the Wars,* pp. 146–52.

37. *KPP. Uchwaly i rezolucje,* vol. 3, p. 394. Significantly, those documents were subsequently carefully censored to eliminate any expressions of the KPP's support for German claims to Pomerania, Upper Silesia and Gdansk.

38. As cited by J. A. Regula, *Historja Komunistycznej Partji Polski,* p. 288.

39. For details see Dziewanowski, *The Communist Party of Poland,* pp. 147–48; also Kowalski, *Trudne lata,* pp. 628–34.

40. For a partial listing of victims' names see Kowalski, *Komunistyczna Partia Polski, 1935–1938,* pp. 377–79.

41. Of the three surviving full members of the Central Committee (Alfred Lampe had died in 1943 in Moscow), Jan Izydorczyk and Szymon Zachariasz reached positions of limited responsibility in communist organizations after the war, and Zenon Nowak has been the only KPP luminary who emerged after the war as one of the most important officials in the Polish United Workers' Party.

42. I. A. Sventitskiî, "Provokatory za rabotoi," *Kommunisticheskii internatsional,*

no. 1, 1938, pp. 92–94.

43. For details see Marian Malinowski, *Geneza PPR,* pp. 31–48; also Kowalski, *Komunistyczna Partia Polski, 1935–1938,* pp. 400–34.

44. i.e., Dziewanowski, *The Communist Party of Poland,* pp. 153–54; also Hansjakob Stehle, "Polish Communism," in *Communism in Europe,* ed. William E. Griffith, vol. 1, p. 88. As for the official Polish communist historiography, it places the blame for KPP dissolution on "mistakes and deviations arising from the cult of personality." Kowalski, *Komunistyczna Partia Polski, 1935–1938,* pp. 380–83.

45. See the report of Dmitrii Manuilskii, the Comintern head in the late 1930s, to the eighteenth congress of the Soviet party as published in *World News and Views,* April 6, 1939, p. 107.

46. According to recent Polish information, the source of persistent leaks on KPP internal politics as well as Comintern secret instructions might have been Jozef Mitzenmacher, a deputy member of the KPP Central Committee elected in 1932. Mitzenmacher was said to have died in Poland in 1947. He was never discovered by Polish authorities and his activity became known only some time after his death. For details see Malinowski, *Geneza PPR,* p. 371.

3: RITES OF PASSAGE

1. For text of the agreement, and especially a secret protocol dealing with the partition of Poland, see R. J. Sontag and J. S. Beddie, eds., *Nazi-Soviet Relations, 1939–1941. Documents from the Archives of the German Foreign Office,* p. 78.

2. The number of Polish deportees was put at about 1,500,000 persons; for a comprehensive documentary presentation of Soviet policies toward the Poles see Wiktor Sukiennicki, ed., *Biala ksiega;* also Wladyslaw Pobog-Malinowski, *Najnowsza historia polityczna Polski,* vol. 3, pp. 106–12.

3. Marian Malinowski, et al, *Polski ruch robotniczy w okresie wojny i okupacji hitlerowskiej,* p. 99.

4. They included Wanda Wasilewska, Stefan Jedrychowski, and Jan Turlejski, who were elected to the Supreme Soviet of the USSR, as well as Marceli Nowotko who became a deputy in the local Soviet in Bialystok; see *ibid.,* p. 99.

5. There is considerable literature, in English and in Polish, dealing with the underground resistance in Poland during the war. For a comprehensive treatment of this problem see Pobog-Malinowski, *Najnowsza historia polityczna Polski,* vol. 3, particularly pp. 117–27, 321–419; also memoirs of former commander of the non-communist forces Tadeusz Bor-Komorowski, *Armia podziemna,* as well as those of a leader of the Peasant Party, Stefan Korbonski, *W Imieniu Rzeczypospolitej;* for an analysis by a leading communist historian see Maria Turlejska, *Sport o Polske,* pp. 67–242.

6. Georgi Dimitrov, "Voina i rabochii klass kapitalisticheskikh stran," *Kommunisticheskii internatsional,* nos. 8–9, 1939, pp. 23–26.

7. Marian Malinowski, *Geneza PPR,* p. 212.

8. *Ibid.,* p. 221.

9. *Ibid.,* pp. 189–91.

10. *Ibid.,* p. 304.

11. *Ibid.,* pp. 310–12; also Malinowski, *Polski ruch robotniczy,* pp. 136–51.

12. For text of the program see *Ksztaltowanie sie podstaw programowych PPR w latach 1942–1945. Wybor materialow i dokumentow,* pp. 11–15.

13. As cited by Malinowski, *Geneza PPR,* p. 358. Emphasis in the original.

14. For a description of the meeting see memoirs of one of the participants, Wlodzimierz Dabrowski, "Wspomnienia dzialacza PPR," *Z pola walki*, no. 4, 1961, pp. 262–63.

15. See memoirs of several party organizing agents in *ibid.*, pp. 263–77; also Jadwiga Ludwinska, "Narodziny Polskiej Partii Robotniczej," *ibid.*, pp. 299–311; Marian Spychalski, "Wspomnienia o partyjnej robocie," *Archiwum ruchu robotniczego*, vol. 2, pp. 281–86.

16. Quoted in Malinowski, *Geneza PPR*, p. 462.

17. *Ibid.*, pp. 469–73.

18. See the memoirs of Dabrowski, "Wspomnienia dzialacza PPR," pp. 269–70; also Spychalski, "Wspomnienia o partyjnej robocie," p. 282.

19. For details see Jozef Swiatlo, *Za kulisami bezpieki i partii*, pp. 27–28. Swiatlo was a former security officer in charge of party internal matters, who defected to the West in 1953.

20. *Ksztaltowanie sie podstaw programowych PPR*, p. 68.

21. For a documented report on these negotiations see Malinowski, *Polski ruch robotniczy*, pp. 261–67.

22. For a full treatment of the Katyn massacre and its political implications see Janusz Zawodny, *Death in the Forest*.

23. Malinowski, *Polski ruch robotniczy*, pp. 359–64.

24. For text of the declaration see *Ksztaltowanie sie podstaw programowych PPR*, pp. 461–68.

25. Wladyslaw Gomulka, "Polemika z 'Archiwum ruchu robotniczego'," *Zeszyty historyczne*, no. 39, 1977, p. 5.

26. Text in *Z pola walki*, no. 4, 1961, p. 174.

27. Spychalski, "Wspomnienia o partyjnej robocie," pp. 285–86.

28. Turlejska, *Spor o Polske*, pp. 232–33.

29. Paul Lendvai, "The Party and the Jews," *Commentary*, September 1968, p. 57, cites a ". . .leading Polish sociologist who spent the war in the Soviet Union" as stating that "at one point, Jews accounted for 60–70 percent of the top and medium level functionaries."

30. In a report to Dimitrov, Finder assessed the share of former KPP members in the PPR at one-third, while radical leftists accounted for one-fourth in January 1943. *Z pola walki*, no. 4, 1961, p. 178.

31. Texts in *Archiwum ruchu robotniczego*, vol. 2, pp. 35–48.

32. See minutes from a meeting of the leaders of the Union of Polish Patriots held on July 18, 1944 during which Osobka-Morawski reported on his conversations with Stalin after which "there emerged the necessity of an immediate formation of the Polish Committee of National Liberation." *Ibid.*, p. 146.

33. Text in *Rada Narodowa*, July 26, 1944.

34. For detailed descriptions of the rise and fall of the Warsaw uprising, as well as the analysis of Soviet policy toward the non-communist insurgents see Jan M. Ciechanowski, *The Warsaw Uprising of 1944;* also J. K. Zawodny, *Nothing But Honour*.

35. See a programmatic speech by Roman Zambrowski to the first PPR congress, *O masowa milionowa partie*.

36. Kliszko's speech at the same occasion, *O projekcie statutu*.

37. *PPR. Rezolucje, odezwy, instrukcje, i okolniki Komitetu Centralnego, VIII 1944–XII 1945*, p. 235.

38. For details see Norbert Kolomyjczyk, *PPR 1944–1945*, pp. 22 and table on p. 295; also pp. 162–74.

39. *Ibid.*, pp. 174–81 and table on p. 296.

40. As cited from a Central Committee resolution of May 1945, in *ibid.*, p. 224.

41. In September 1945, out of 23,230 employees of the Ministry of Public Security, there were 11,200 members of the PPR, 710 of the PPS, 462 of the Peasant Party, 61 of the Democratic Party; see *ibid.*, pp. 225–26.

42. Ignacy Blum, *Z dziejow Wojska Polskiego w latach 1945–1948*, p. 13; see also Turlejska, *Spor o Polske*, pp. 272–309.

43. For details see memoirs of Stanislaw Mikolajczyk, *The Rape of Poland.*

44. This seems to be the conclusion of a prominent communist historian, Maria Turlejska, *Zapis pierwszej dekady; 1945–1954*, pp. 65–67; for a comprehensive analysis of communist agrarian policies of that era see Andrzej Korbonski, *Politics of Socialist Agriculture in Poland: 1945–1960*, pp. 67–134.

45. For the text of the nationalization decree see *Dziennik ustaw Rzeczypospolitej Polski*, February 5, 1946.

46. For a report on the referendum by the U.S. ambassador to Poland see Arthur Bliss-Lane, *I Saw Poland Betrayed*, pp. 244–45.

47. On Western protests against the elections see *ibid.*, 272–73 and 276–87; see also a revealing criticism of the elections by Turlejska, *Zapis pierwszej dekady*, pp. 75–76.

48. Turlejska, *Zapis pierwszej dekady*, p. 122.

49. That is, Gomulka's May Day speech in 1947 in his *Artykuly i przemowienia*, vol. 2, p. 421.

50. For a thorough discussion of the Yugoslav-Soviet split, see Adam Ulam, *Titoism and the Cominform.*

51. On Gomulka's opposition to the Cominform, see Nicholas Bethell, *Gomulka*, pp. 136–39; also Zbigniew Brzezinski, *The Soviet Bloc*, pp. 53, 61–62.

52. For details see Bethell, *Gomulka*, p. 135 and *passim;* on Gomulka's agricultural policy see Korbonski, *Politics of Socialist Agriculture*, pp. 135–140.

53. Gomulka's speech was made public only in 1983, after a hiatus of almost 35 years, in *Miesiecznik Literacki*, February 1983, pp. 77–87.

54. For texts of speeches see *Nowe drogi*, September–October 1948, *passim.*

55. *Ibid.*, p. 27.

56. "Deklaracja ideowa PZPR. *Nowe drogi*, January 1949, p. 13.

4: THE CONTRIVED REVOLUTION

1. For a discussion and definition of decisive political breakthroughs see Kenneth Jowitt, *Revolutionary Breakthroughs and National Development*, pp. 7–20.

2. The term "contrived revolution" was borrowed from an article by Alfred G. Meyer, "Authority in Communist Political Systems," in *Political Leadership in Industrialized Societies*, ed. Lewis J. Edinger, p. 89, where he defined the contrived revolution as resulting more from "political and military operations outside the systems than of spontaneous developments at home."

3. On the relationship between the people's democracies in Eastern Europe and the dictatorship of the proletariat in the USSR see Zbigniew Brzezinski, *The Soviet Bloc*, pp. 71–77.

4. Roman Zambrowski and Henryk Swiatkowski, *O statucie i zadaniach organizacyjnych PZPR*, p. 10.

5. Boleslaw Bierut and Jozef Cyrankiewicz, *Podstawy ideologiczne PZPR*, p. 54.

6. For the full text of the 1952 constitution see A. Gwizdz, Z. Jarosz, Z. Pop-

kowski, eds., *Ustroj Polskiej Rzeczypospolitej Ludowej*, pp. 14–30; English translation is in Jan Triska, ed., *Constitutions of the Communist Party-States*, pp. 332–48.

7. Gwizdz, *Ustroj Polskiej Rzeczypospolitej Ludowej*, p. 120; Brzezinski, *The Soviet Bloc*, pp. 77–82.

8. See Eugeniusz Szyr, "Wspolzawodnictwo pracy i walka o wyzszy poziom planowania," *Nowe drogi*, May–June 1949, pp. 15–26.

9. Hilary Minc, "Szescioletni plan rozwoju gospodarczego i budowy socjalizmu w Polsce," *Nowe drogi*, July–August 1950, p. 11.

10. *Ibid.*, pp. 33–39; also Boleslaw Bierut, "Poland on the Road to Socialism," *Bolshevik*, no. 21, 1950, p. 23.

11. On the role of State Agricultural Farms in the process of socialization of Poland's agriculture see Andrzej Korbonski, *Politics of Socialist Agriculture in Poland, 1945–1960*, p. 179.

12. Renata Siemienska, *Nowe zycie w nowym miescie* (Warsaw: PWN, 1969), p. 18, as cited by George Kolankiewicz, "The Polish Industrial Manual Working Class," in *Social Groups in Polish Society*, eds. David Lane and George Kolankiewicz, p. 94.

13. See a series of reports from several party conferences on cultural affairs in *Nowe drogi*, July–August 1949, pp. 129–42.

14. For details see Jozef Kowalczyk, "Aktualne zagadnienia naszej polityki oswiatowej," *Nowe drogi*, January–February 1950, pp. 25–39.

15. On the subsequent critical evaluation of the work of the Polish Academy of Sciences in restraining the development of Polish science see Jozef Chalasinski, "Drogi i drozki socjalizmu w nauce polskiej, 1949–1954," *Kultura i spoleczenstwo*, no. 1, 1957.

16. As quoted by George Gömöri, "The Cultural Intelligentsia: The Writers," in eds., Lane and Kolankiewicz, *Social Groups in Polish Society*, p. 163.

17. Zambrowski and Swiatkowski, *O statucie*, p. 79; also Edward Ochab, *O niektorych zadaniach organizacyjnych i zmianach w statucie partii*, p. 35.

18. On the relations between the Church and the PUWP during the 1950s see M. K. Dziewanowski, *The Communist Party of Poland*, pp. 241–51; also Richard F. Staar, *Poland 1944–1962*, pp. 241–50.

19. Franciszek Jozwiak-Witold, "O stalinowska linie w polityce kadr," *Nowe drogi*, November–December 1949, pp. 163–64.

20. Brzezinski, *The Soviet Bloc*, p. 89; also Maria Turlejska, *Zapis pierwszej dekady, 1945–1954*, p. 183.

21. See the report by Franciszek Jozwiak-Witold to the second PUWP congress in March 1954, *Nowe drogi*, March 1954, pp. 252–54.

22. Julian Tokarski, "Na marginesie pierwszych doswiadczen realizacji wytycznych IV Plenum," *Nowe drogi*, May–June 1950, p. 64.

23. Boleslaw Bierut, *Zadania partii w walce o czujnosc rewolucyjna na tle sytuacji obecnej*, p. 58.

24. Boleslaw Bierut, "Walka narodu polskiego o pokoj i Plan Szescioletni," *Nowe drogi*, January-February 1951, pp. 38–39.

25. See the evaluation of the PUWP administrative and managerial performance in the economy by George Kolankiewicz, "The Technical Intelligentsia," in *Social Groups in Polish Society*, ed. D. Lane and Kolankiewicz, pp. 183–90.

26. Bierut, *Zadania partii*, pp. 24–27; 71–79; also Nicholas Bethell, *Gomulka*, pp. 163–69.

27. For a comprehensive elaboration of the massive purge campaign see Francis-

zek Jozwiak-Witold, "Podstawowe zadania w pracy Centralnej Komisji Kontroli Partyjnej," *Nowe drogi,* March–April 1950, pp. 83–99.

28. On these points see Brzezinski, *The Soviet Bloc,* pp. 96–97; also Bethell, *Gomulka,* pp. 184–87; as well as Jakub Berman's speech to the PUWP's Central Committee plenum on October 21, 1956, *Nowe drogi,* October 1956, pp. 85–95.

29. Bierut, "Zadania partii w walce o nowe kadry na tle sytuacji ogolnej," *Nowe drogi,* March–April 1950, p. 44.

30. *Ibid.,* pp. 45–50.

31. Jerzy J. Wiatr and Krzysztof Ostrowski, "Political Leadership: What Kind of Professionalism?," in *Studies in the Polish Political System,* ed. J. J. Wiatr, p. 155.

32. Seweryn Ajzner, "O demokracji wewnatrzpartyjnej," *Nowe drogi,* May 1952, p. 112.

33. Boleslaw Bierut's report to the second PUWP congress in March 1954, *Nowe drogi,* March 1954, p. 72.

34. Wladyslaw Gomulka's speech to the October 1956 plenum of the PUWP's Central Committee, *Nowe drogi,* October 1956, pp. 39–40.

35. *Khrushchev Remembers: The Last Testament,* translated and edited by Strobe Talbot, p. 172.

36. For a glimpse at Soviet control within the PUWP apparatus see Seweryn Bialer, *Wybralem prawde.* Bialer was a former staff member of the PUWP Central Committee who defected to the West in 1955.

37. Jerzy Morawski, "III Plenum KC PZPR," *Nowe drogi,* February 1955, p. 6.

38. For an implicit criticism of pervasive bureaucratization of the party apparatus see Helena Kozlowska, "Uwagi o stylu pracy naszego aparatu partyjnego," *Nowe drogi,* January 1955, pp. 72–84; for a more direct critical assessment see J. Bogusz, "W sprawie aparatu partyjnego," *Trybuna ludu,* November 1, 1956.

39. For details of the interal organization of the Ministry of Public Security as well as discussion of its links with the Soviet police networks see Jozef Swiatlo, *Za kulisami bezpieki i partii,* a Radio Free Europe pamphlet written by a former high official in the Ministry who escaped to the West in 1953.

40. Feliks Gross, *The Revolutionary Party,* p. 70.

41. *Nowe drogi,* August–September 1948, p. 36.

42. On this point see a remarkable book by Czeslaw Milosz, *The Captive Mind.*

43. For an interesting discussion of the "heroic" concept in the communist propaganda and its subsequent implications for the party organization see Paul Neuberg, *The Hero's Children,* particularly parts I and II.

44. Alex Inkeles, "The Totalitarian Mystique" in *Totalitarianism,* Carl J. Friedrich, ed., esp. pp. 105–07.

5: TEST OF RETREAT

1. Richard Hiscocks, *Poland: Bridge for the Abyss?*, pp. 170–71.

2. See the reprints of Soviet articles on the political and organizational importance of "collective leadership" in *Nowe drogi,* June 1953, pp. 27–42 and August 1953, pp. 69–81.

3. "O przyswojenie nauk plynacych z 50-lecia KPZR," *Nowe drogi,* August 1953, p. 9.

4. See Hilary Minc's speech to the plenum, *Nowe drogi,* October 1953, pp. 135–44.

5. For details, see Jozef Swiatlo, *Za kulisami bezpieki i partii,* pp. 21–22.

6. Brzezinski, *The Soviet Bloc,* p. 165.

7. *Nowe drogi,* March 1954, pp. 7–82.

8. *Ibid.,* pp. 97–128.

9. For the text of PUWP's statut, see Edward Ochab, *O niektorych zadaniach organizacyjnych i zmianach w statucie partii,* pp. 45–58.

10. Bierut's report to the congress, *Nowe drogi,* March 1954, p. 68.

11. *Ibid.,* p. 471.

12. *Ibid.,* p. 59.

13. For details, see Bialer, *Wybralem wolnosc,* p. 12 as cited by Brzezinski, *The Soviet Bloc,* p. 167.

14. Swiatlo, *Za kulisami,* passim.

15. Bialer, *Wybralem prawde,* pp. 10–13.

16. Ochab's speech to the Central Committee plenum on October 21, 1956, *Nowe drogi,* October 1956, p. 115.

17. Jerzy Morawski, "III Plenum KC PZPR," *Nowe drogi,* February 1955, pp. 10–11.

18. For a detailed history of the club's activities, see Witold Jedlicki, *Klub Krzywego Kola.*

19. Brzezinski, *The Soviet Bloc,* p. 243.

20. For the English translation of the "Poem," see *National Communism and Popular Revolt in Eastern Europe,* ed. Paul E. Zinner, pp. 40–48.

21. This is an official evaluation of the Union's activities by the PUWP Central Committee's staff member as cited by Bogdan Hillebrandt, "PZPR i socjalistyczne wychowanie mlodziezy (1948–1957)," *Z pola walki,* no. 2, 1977, p. 197.

22. For a discussion of *Po prostu's* history, see Konstanty Jelenski, "The Rise and Fall of *Po prostu,*" *The New Leader,* December 2, 1957.

23. Brzezinski, *The Soviet Bloc,* p. 245.

24. Jerzy Morawski, "Nauki XX Zjazdu KPZR," *Nowe drogi,* March 1956, p. 30.

25. R. Hiscocks, *Poland,* p. 183.

26. For the trend-setting article, see editorial "O kulcie jednostki i jego konsekwencjach," *Trybuna ludu,* March 10, 1956.

27. The best discussion of the workers' revolt in Poznan is by Ewa Wacowska, "Poznan 1956," in *Poznan 1956–Grudzien 1970,* pp. 153–216.

28. Roman Jurys, "Niektore problemy naszej partii," *Nowe drogi,* February 1957, p. 70.

29. For text of Ochab's speech, see *Nowe drogi,* July–August 1956, pp. 138–166.

30. *Ibid.,* pp. 198–99.

31. Wladyslaw Gomulka, *O naszej partii,* pp. 223–25.

32. For a thorough discussion of factional divisions within the PUWP in the period preceding October 1956, see Witold Jedlicki, *Klub Krzywego Kola,* especially chapter I.

33. For details, see R. V. Burks, *The Dynamics of Communism in Eastern Europe,* p. 169.

34. See Jedlicki, *Klub,* pp. 30–32; also Paul Lendvai, "Poland: The Party and the Jews," *Commentary,* September 1968, p. 58.

35. For a discussion of the beginning of workers' councils in Poland, see George Kolankiewicz, "The Polish Industrial Manual Working Class," in *Social Groups in Polish Society,* ed. David Lane and George Kolankiewicz, pp. 103–13.

36. Probably the best discussion of Poland's trade unions in the 1950s and beyond is by Georges-H. Mond, "Pologne" in *Le Syndicalisme en Europe de l'Est; La Docu-*

mentation Française, Paris, September 29, 1972, pp. 46–68.

37. "Co robic," *Po prostu* (Warsaw), April 8, 1956.

38. Leszek Kolakowski, "Intelektualisci a ruch komunistyczny," *Nowe drogi,* September 1956, p. 31.

39. For example, Oskar Lange in *Zycie gospodarcze,* July 16, 1956, and Edward Lipinski in *Nowa kultura* (Warsaw), September 9, 1956.

40. Julian Hochfeld in *Zycie Warszawy,* September 24, 1956, as cited by Hiscocks, *Poland,* p. 204.

41. The best and most thorough analysis of Soviet attitudes toward Gomulka is by Brzezinski, *The Soviet Bloc,* pp. 248–68.

42. *Nowe drogi,* October 1956, p. 17.

43. Ochab's speech, *ibid.,* p. 113.

44. *Khrushchev Remembers,* p. 200.

45. For text of the speech, see *Nowe drogi,* October 1956, pp. 21–46.

46. *Ibid.,* p. 3.

47. Brzezinski, *The Soviet Bloc,* p. 255.

48. Wladyslaw Bienkowski, *Rewolucji ciag dalszy,* pp. 11–12.

49. *Nowe drogi,* October 1956, p. 113.

50. *Ibid.,* p. 39.

51. *Ibid.,* p. 12.

52. Gomulka, *O naszej partii,* pp. 272–73.

53. *Trybuna ludu,* October 25, 1956.

54. M. K. Dziewanowski, *The Communist Party of Poland,* pp. 283–84.

55. Brzezinski, *The Soviet Bloc,* p. 262; also Hiscocks, *Poland,* pp. 223–28.

56. The full text in English is in *National Communism,* ed. P. E. Zinner, pp. 306–14.

57. Gomulka, *Przemowienia 1957–1958,* p. 112.

58. Roman Zimand, "Pare zwyklych dni we Wroclawiu," *Po prostu,* December 9, 1956, as cited by Adam Bromke, *Poland's Politics,* p. 179.

59. Roman Jurys, "Niektore problemy naszej partii," *Nowe drogi,* February 1957, p. 71.

60. *Rocznik statystyczny 1957,* p. 138.

61. Stefan Jedrychowski in *World Marxist Review,* May 1959, p. 63.

62. The law giving the workers' councils full autonomy was passed by the Sejm on November 19, 1956.

63. Cited by Dziewanowski, *The Communist Party of Poland,* p. 279.

64. As quoted by Hiscocks, *Poland,* p. 240.

65. *Ibid.,* p. 241.

66. Gomulka, *O naszej partii,* pp. 314–30.

67. For an example of such accusations directed at lower ranks of the party apparatus see Roman Werfel, "Mysli w sprawie aktywu," *Nowe drogi,* August 1957, esp. pp. 60–62.

68. Gomulka, *O naszej partii,* pp. 351–54. This was the speech delivered on October 5, 1957, to party press editors and newsmen.

69. *Ibid.,* pp. 367–68.

70. Walenty Titkow, "Niektore problemy rozwoju partii," *Nowe drogi,* December 1958, p. 87.

71. For a discussion of the post-1958 fate of the workers' councils, supported by well documented evidence, see Kolankiewicz's article in *Social Groups in Polish Society,* ed. Lane and Kolankiewicz, pp. 118–20; 137–49.

72. Gomulka, *O naszej partii,* p. 423.

6: THE LITTLE STABILIZATION

1. *Nowe drogi,* April 1959, p. 653.

2. *Ibid.,* p. 663.

3. There is considerable Polish sociological and economic literature dealing with quantitative change in Poland's society. In a representative sample one could include: Adam Sarapata, ed., *Przemiany spoleczne w Polsce Ludowej*; Wlodzimierz Wesolowski, *Klasy, warstwy i wladza*; Stanislaw Widerszpil, *Sklad polskiej klasy robotniczej.*

4. On this point see Branislaw Galeski, *Socjologia wsi;* also by the same author *Spoleczna struktura wsi.*

5. For a thorough discussion of this problem see an excellent book by Joseph R. Fiszman, *Revolution and Tradition in People's Poland.*

6. Jan Szczepanski, *Polish Society,* p. 141.

7. Vincent Chrypinski, "Legislative Committees in Polish Lawmaking," *Slavic Review,* vol. 25, no. 2, June 1966, pp. 247–58.

8. This expression was greatly popularized by Polish playwright Tadeusz Rozewicz through a play published in *Dialog,* May 1962.

9. Jerzy J. Wiatr, "Elements of Pluralism in the Polish Political System," *Polish Sociological Bulletin,* no. 1, 1966, p. 23.

10. Wladyslaw Gomulka, *O naszej partii,* p. 455; also Jerzy J. Wiatr, "The Hegemonic Party System in Poland," in *Studies in the Polish Political System,* ed. J. J. Wiatr, pp. 117–20.

11. Gomulka, *O naszej partii,* pp. 629–30.

12. Michal Sadowski, *Przemiany spoleczne a system partyjny PRL,* p. 194.

13. Romana Granas, "Gdzie jest szkola komunizmu," *Polityka,* September 26, 1959.

14. Gomulka, *O naszej partii,* pp. 565 and 573.

15. A Dobieszewski, "Struktura i zasady dzialania partii," *Nowe drogi,* June 1971, p. 66.

16. *Nowe drogi,* April 1959, p. 160.

17. As confirmed by Politburo member Edward Babiuch, "O niektorych problemach rozwoju i umacniania partii," *Nowe drogi,* September 1971, pp. 9–10.

18. See, for example, Andrzej Kurz, *Spoleczna rola PZPR*; also Sadowski, *Przemiany spoleczne a system partyjny PRL.*

19. For details see Jan B. de Weydenthal, "Party Development in Contemporary Poland," *East European Quarterly,* vol. 11, no. 3, 1977, esp. pp. 344–47.

20. M. Sadowski, *Przemiany spoleczne a system partyjny PRL,* p. 202.

21. Zygmunt Bauman, "Social Structure of the Party Organization in Industrial Works," in *Studies in the Polish Political System,* ed. Wiatr, p. 174.

22. J. Burzynski, "Mentalnosc Inzynierow," *Polityka,* December 4, 1965.

23. Zygmunt Bauman, "Economic Growth and Social Structure: the Case of Poland," in *Studies in the Polish Political System,* ed. Wiatr, p. 32.

24. Aleksandra Jasinska, "Socio-Psychological Characteristics of Local Leaders," *ibid.,* pp. 233–34.

25. Zygmunt Bauman, "Economic Growth and Social Structure: the Case of Poland," *ibid.,* pp. 31–32.

26. "Statut PZPR," art. 22 in *Nowe drogi,* April 1959, p. 752.

27. de Weydenthal, "Party Development in Contemporary Poland," p. 350.

28. Zenon Kliszko, "Zmiany w statucie PZPR i niektore problemy polityczno-organizacyjne partii," *Nowe drogi,* July 1964, p. 133.

29. Mieczyslaw Marzec, "Z problemow pracy partyjnej," *Nowe drogi,* April 1964, pp. 107–08; also J. J. Wiatr and Krzysztof Ostrowski, "Political Leadership—What Kind of Professionalism," in *Studies in the Polish Political System,* ed. Wiatr, pp. 148–55.

30. On this point see a perceptive analysis of the Polish party apparatus by Wladyslaw Bienkowski, *Socjologia Kleski,* pp. 36–51; for a short but comprehensive discussion of the apparatchiks' position in East European politics see Jan F. Triska, "The Party Apparatchiks at Bay," *East Europe,* December 1967, pp. 2–8.

31. *Nowe drogi,* July 1964, p. 134.

32. For details see Richard F. Staar, *Poland 1944–1962,* pp. 195–203.

33. For the program of Mijal's party see "Pod sztandarem Marksizmu-Leninizmu do walki o socjalizm," in *Schizmy,* pp. 42–60.

34. Wiatr and Przeworski, "Control without Opposition," in *Studies in the Polish Political System,* ed. Wiatr, p. 131.

35. *Trybuna Ludu,* January 6, 1968.

36. Michael Gamarnikow, "Poland: Political Pluralism in a One-Party State," *Problems of Communism,* July–August 1967, p. 10.

37. *Ibid.,* p. 11.

38. Adam Bromke, *Poland's Politics,* p. 137; also Brzezinski, *The Soviet Bloc,* pp. 359–66.

39. *Trybuna Ludu,* July 22, 1959.

40. Wladyslaw Gomulka, *Przemowienia 1964–1966,* p. 237.

41. For details see J. F. Brown, *The New Eastern Europe,* pp. 57–58.

42. *Ibid.,* p. 53.

43. *Ibid.,* pp. 53–60; also Nicholas Bethell, *Gomulka,* p. 250.

44. Bethell, *Gomulka,* p. 250.

45. *Trybuna robotnicza,* February 11, 1968.

7: YEARS OF CRISIS: 1968–1971

1. The English text is in *Poland since 1956,* ed. Tadeusz N. Cieplak, p. 130; see also Gaston de Cerezay, "Gomulka and the Intellectuals," *East Europe,* December 1964, pp. 22–30.

2. Jacek Kuron and Karol Modzelewski, *List otwarty do partii,* pp. 12–95.

3. For details see A. Ross Johnson, "Warsaw: Politics and the Intellectuals," *East Europe,* July 1967, pp. 14–16; also Jan B. de Weydenthal, "Academic Dissent as a Catalyst for Political Crisis in a Communist System," *Polish Review,* vol. 19, no. 1, 1974, pp. 23–24.

4. As cited by Michael Gamarnikow, "Poland: Political Pluralism in a One Party State," *Problems of Communism,* July–August 1967, pp. 7–8.

5. *Le Monde,* December 22, 1967.

6. For text of the resolution and excerpts from the discussion see "Polish Writers Meeting," *Survey,* July 1968, pp. 102–08; also "Zebranie warszawskich literatow," *Kultura* (Paris), April 1968, pp. 104–05.

7. *The New York Times,* March 11, 1968.

8. *Survey,* July 1968, p. 100; for similar resolutions and statements see *Wydarzenia marcowe 1968,* Paris 1969, pp. 31–63 as well as *Polskie przedwiosnie,* pp. 44–54.

9. *Trybuna ludu,* March 12, 1968.

10. *Ibid.,* March 15, 1968.

11. *The New York Times,* March 18, 1968.

12. W. Gomulka, *O naszej partii,* pp. 633–76.

13. *The New York Times,* March 24, 1968.

14. *Trybuna ludu,* March 21, 1968.

15. Kazimierz Kakol, "Sprawy i ludzie," *Prawo i zycie,* March 24, 1968.

16. *Trybuna ludu,* April 19, 1968; for a tentatively established list of some of the victims see *East Europe,* June 1968, pp. 50–51.

17. i.e., Henryk Jablonski, "Zaburzenia studenckie w marcu 1968," *Nowe drogi,* May 1968, pp. 189–93; Wladyslaw Machejek, "Zaczelo sie od 'Dziadow'?," *Zycie literackie,* March 24, 1968.

18. *Trybuna ludu,* March 13, 1968.

19. For a detailed and well-documented analysis of the anti-Semitic campaign see Paul Lendvai, *Anti-Semitism without Jews,* esp. pp. 89–239; also Wlodzimierz Rozenbaum, "The Jewish Question in Poland since 1964," in *Nationalism in the USSR and Eastern Europe in the Era of Brezhnev and Kosygin,* ed. George W. Simmonds, pp. 335–43.

20. Lendvai, *Anti-Semitism,* p. 25.

21. Andrzej Werblan, "Przyczynek de genezy konfliktu," *Miesiecznik literacki,* June 1968, pp. 61–71.

22. The English text is in *Radio Free Europe Situation Report,* June 22, 1968.

23. *Trybuna ludu,* April 13–15, 1968.

24. For details see Wladyslaw Bienkowski, *Motory i hamulce socjalizmu,* pp. 48–49.

25. Maciej Szczepanski, "Patriotyzmu ksztalt wspolczesny," *Trybuna robotnicza,* March 23–24, 1968.

26. Mieczyslaw Rakowski, "Ludzie i socjalizm," *Polityka,* March 30, 1968.

27. "Jaki socjalizm i jacy ludzie," *Trybuna ludu,* April 10, 1968.

28. Mieczyslaw Krajewski, "Demokracja socjalistyczna a 'socjalizm rynkowy," *Trybuna ludu,* March 29, 1968.

29. *Trybuna ludu,* April 13–15, 1968.

30. For a comprehensive analysis of PAX activities see Lucjan Blit, *The Eastern Pretender*; also Adam Bromke, *Poland's Politics,* pp. 213–28. By contrast, the Catholic Church openly condemned propaganda excesses of the activist movement, while the Catholic parliamentary group "Znak" sent a written interpellation to the government demanding explanation and justification of its tolerant attitude toward the propaganda attacks.

31. A. Ross Johnson, "The End of the post-October Era," *Survey,* July 1968, p. 88.

32. On this point see J. B. de Weydenthal, "The Military Factor in Polish Politics," *East Europe,* September 1972, pp. 2–6.

33. *Trybuna ludu,* April 21, 1968.

34. *Nowe drogi,* August 1968, pp. 13–16.

35. *Ibid.,* p. 127.

36. *Ibid.,* p. 28.

37. *Ibid.,* p. 11.

38. *Ibid.,* p. 35.

39. *Ibid.,* p. 63.

40. *Ibid.,* p. 46.

41. For a perceptive discussion of this development see W. Bienkowski, *Socjologia kleski,* pp. 44–51.

42. For a detailed analysis of Czechoslovakia influence on Polish politics see J. B. de Weydenthal, "Polish Politics and the Czechoslovak Crisis in 1968," *Canadian Slavonic Papers,* vol. 14, Spring 1972, pp. 31–56.

43. *Trybuna ludu,* May 7, 1968.

44. Text in *Polskie przedwiosnie,* pp. 126–28.

45. *Trybuna ludu,* May 9, 1968.

46. Text in *Winter in Prague,* ed. Robin A. Remington, pp. 196–202.

47. *Ibid.,* pp. 225–31.

48. *The New York Times,* October 31, 1968.

49. *Le Monde,* August 22, 1968.

50. *Trybuna ludu,* August 16, 1968.

51. *Ibid.,* September 16, 1968.

52. *Ibid.,* October 8, 1968.

53. *Ibid.,* October 26, 1968.

54. *Ibid.,* November 13, 1968.

55. For a detailed analysis of personnel changes decided at the fifth congress of the party see Jerzy Ptakowski, "The Fifth Polish Party Congress," *East Europe,* January 1969, pp. 3–8; also "The New Central Committee of the PUWP," *Radio Free Europe Research Report,* December 16, 1968.

56. *Zycie partii,* December 1968, p. 10.

57. Text of the resolution is in *Nowe drogi,* December 1968, pp. 89–124.

58. Michael Gamarnikow, "Poland Returns to Economic Reform," *East Europe,* November–December 1969, pp. 11–18.

59. See a Politburo report to the Central Committee meeting on February 6–7, 1971, later published in a restricted edition of *Nowe drogi,* undated, as translated by *Radio Free Europe, Polish Press Survey,* no. 2313, 1971, pp. 8–14.

60. *Trybuna ludu,* May 25, 1970.

61. *Polish Press Agency Reports* (English Edition), March 15, 1971; also see discussion of Gomulka's economic policy by Henryk Krol, "Rozwoj intenzywny a zatrudnienie," *Trybuna ludu,* February 15, 1971, and Antoni Rajkiewicz, "Wezlowe problemy polityki zatrudnienia," *Ekonomista,* no. 2, 1971, p. 198.

62. Wieslawa Grochala, "Kadra," *Polityka,* April 24, 1971.

63. For a comprehensive discussion of the workers' revolt and an analysis of the workers' role in Polish politics see J. B. de Weydenthal, "The Workers' Dilemma in Polish Politics," *East European Quarterly,* vol. 13, no. 1, 1979, pp. 95–119.

64. See the Central Committee report on "The Causes, the Character, and the Consequences of Social Crises in the History of the Polish People's Republic." The initial text of the report was leaked in Warsaw and was eventually published in *Zeszyty historyczne* in Paris. The final and censored version was published in *Nowe drogi.* See also Zygmunt Korybutowicz, *Grudzien 1970,* and, for an official assessment of the 1970 events, Mieczyslaw F. Rakowski, *Przesilenie grudniowe.*

65. Barbara Seidler, "Gdansk-Gdynia: Grudzien-Luty," *Zycie literackie,* February 21, 1971.

66. Wladyslaw Machejek, "Refleksje na temat VIII plenum KC PZPR," *Zycie literackie,* February 14, 1971.

67. For a detailed analysis of political circumstances surrounding Gomulka's resignation see Zbigniew A. Pelczynski, "The Downfall of Gomulka," in *Gierek's Poland,* ed. Adam Bromke and John W. Strong, pp. 1–23.

68. Maciej Szczepanski in *Trybuna robotnicza,* January 27, 1971.

69. *Trybuna ludu,* December 21, 1970.

70. i.e., Stanislaw Kociolek's speech in Gdansk on January 7, 1971, as reported in *Glos wybrzeza*, January 9–10, 1971.

71. For texts of specific workers' demands as well as the detailed chronology of the protests see *Poznan–1956–Grudzien 1970*, pp. 19–65, 217–18; also *Rewolta szczecinska i jej znaczenie*, pp. 196–99, 238–46.

72. On this point see a remarkable transcript of the meeting between Gierek and the striking workers in Szczecin on January 24, 1971, a unique event in the history of the East European communist systems, in *Rewolta szczecinska i jej znaczenie*, pp. 25–147; also a report by former chairman of the strike committee in Szczecin, Edmund Baluka, *Na antenie*, September and October 1973, pp. 22–25 and 15–17 respectively.

73. *RFE Polish Press Survey*, no. 2313, p. 14.

8: THE EVOLUTIONARY STYLE

1. For evaluation of Gierek's early policies see Michael Costello, "Political Prospects," *Survey*, Summer 1971, pp. 51–73; Adam Bromke, "Poland under Gierek: A New Political Style," *Problems of Communism*, September–October 1972, pp. 1–19; A. Ross Johnson, "Polish Perspectives, Past and Present," *Problems of Communism*, July–August 1971, pp. 59–72; Richard F. Staar, "Poland: Old Wine in New Bottles?," *Current History*, May 1973, pp. 197–201, 226–27.

2. Wlodzimierz Wiszniewski, "Niektore uwagi o tendencjach rozwojowych PZPR," *Zycie partii*, May 1972, pp. 4–6; also Edward Babiuch, "O niektorych problemach rozwoju i umacniania partii," *Nowe drogi*, September 1971, pp. 9–10.

3. See the text in *Zycie partii*, January 1972, p. 32.

4. *Zycie partii*, October 1972, p. 24.

5. For biographies of the leadership members see *Zycie partii*, January 1972, pp. 1–8.

6. Wieslawa Grochola, "Kadra," *Polityka*, April 24, 1971.

7. For Jaroszewicz's speech see *Trybuna ludu*, September 28, 1972; also "Modernization of Management and Administration: A Progress Report," *Radio Free Europe: Polish Situation Report*, July 1975.

8. Grochola, "Kadra."

9. *Nowe drogi*, January 1976, p. 42.

10. See a series of interviews with newly appointed local party officials in Wieslawa Grochola, "Partia blizej ludzi," *Polityka*, September 22, 1973.

11. *Zycie partii*, January 1972, p. 15, Babiuch's speech to the sixth congress.

12. Babiuch's speech to the Central Committee meeting on September 27, 1972, in *Trybuna ludu*, September 28, 1972.

13. *Ibid.*; see also an interview with Central Committee secretary Barcikowski, in *Zycie partii*, September 1972, p. 6.

14. For a comprehensive discussion of Gierek's economic policies see Michael Gamarnikow, "Poland under Gierek: A New Economic Approach," *Problems of Communism*, September–October 1972, pp. 20–30; also Zbigniew M. Fallenbuchl, "The Strategy of Development and Gierek's Economic Maneuver," in *Gierek's Poland*, ed. Adam Bromke and John Strong, pp. 52–70.

15. All data from *Maly rocznik statystyczny 1976*, Warsaw, 1976.

16. See an interview with Politburo member Stefan Olszowski in *Polityka*, September 25, 1971.

17. For details see Boleslaw Sulik, "Robotnicy," *Kultura* (Paris), October 1976, pp. 65–77.

18. See the speech by Politburo member and chairman of the Central Council of Trade Unions, Wladyslaw Kruczek, to the seventh congress of trade unions in *Trybuna ludu*, November 14, 1972, as well as his speech to the eighth congress in *Trybuna ludu*, December 7, 1976.

19. *Zycie partii*, December 1973, pp. 4–5.

20. Robert W. Dean, "Gierek's Three Years: Retrenchment and Reform," *Survey*, Spring–Summer 1974, p. 61.

21. For the text of the amendments see *Trybuna ludu*, January 27, 1976.

22. For a selection of articles dealing with different aspects of proposed changes in the nature of trade union activity see a booklet *Propozycje* (Warsaw: CRZZ, 1972) published under the auspices of the Central Council of Trade Unions.

23. See the published project of the Labor Code, *Kodeks pracy oraz przepisy wprowadzajace* (Warsaw: CRZZ, 1974), art. 19.

24. *Trybuna ludu*, November 30, 1972.

25. For an authoritative presentation of the objectives and scope of the mobilization campaign by a Central Committee secretary in charge of ideological questions see Jerzy Lukaszewicz, "Niektore problemy frontu ideologicznego partii," *Nowe drogi*, April 1973, pp. 5–16.

26. See Gierek's inaugural speech in *Trybuna ludu*, December 21, 1970.

27. For details see Gamarnikow, "Poland under Gierek," p. 23.

28. On this point see Paul Marer, "Has Eastern Europe Become a Liability to the Soviet Union?," in *The International Politics of Eastern Europe*, ed. Charles Gati, pp. 59–81.

29. Gierek's speech to a Central Committee meeting in April 1971 in *Trybuna ludu*, April 17, 1971.

30. *Trybuna ludu*, December 16, 1972.

31. Babiuch's speech to the Sejm on December 19, 1975, in *Trybuna ludu*, December 20, 1975.

32. *Trybuna ludu*, January 27, 1976.

33. The English text is in *Survey*, Spring 1976, pp. 194–203.

34. As cited by Adam Bromke, "A New Juncture in Poland," *Problems of Communism*, September–October 1976, p. 14.

35. *Zycie partii*, January 1976, p. 33.

36. *Trybuna ludu*, December 10, 1975.

37. For the report on deliberations and excerpts of speeches see *Trybuna ludu*, December 9–13, 1975.

38. For details see Roman Stefanowski, "Poland's Indebtedness in the West," *Radio Free Europe, Background Report*, October 19, 1976.

39. *The Financial Times* (London), August 29, 1974.

40. See a discussion of severe economic difficulties during February 1975 in Zygmunt Szeliga, "Mieso—klopoty i perspektywa," *Polityka*, March 15, 1975.

41. i.e., Gierek's speech to the seventh congress in *Trybuna ludu*, December 9, 1975.

42. *Ibid.*; see also Richard F. Staar, "Poland: The Price of Stability," *Current History*, March 1976, esp. pp. 101–03.

43. Peter Osnos in the *Washington Post*, June 30, 1976; also *The New York Times*, June 28, 1976.

9: THE DRIFT TO NOWHERE

1. *Trybuna ludu*, December 2, 1976.

2. Radio Warsaw on November 9, 1977, as quoted in *Radio Free Europe Research (RFER), Polish Situation Report,* December 3, 1977.

3. For a comprehensive analysis of the Gierek leadership's economic policies see Jan B. de Weydenthal, *Poland: Communism Adrift,* pp. 32–48.

4. *Trybuna ludu,* April 18, 1978.

5. *RFER, Polish Situation Report,* July 9, 1980.

6. Marian Krzak, "Indebtedness and Consumption," *Polityka-Export-Import* (a supplement to the weekly *Polityka*), October 25, 1980.

7. For an analysis of the dissident movement, see de Weydenthal, *Poland,* pp. 49–63; and Adam Bromke, "The Opposition in Poland, *Problems of Communism,* September–October 1978.

8. A detailed report by the KOR was published in *Kultura* (Paris), November 1977.

9. For details see Peter Raina, *Political Opposition in Poland, 1954–1977,* pp. 280–316.

10. William F. Robinson, "Whither Dissent in Poland," *RFER, Background Report,* May 26, 1978.

11. For example, see "To Consider," *Polityka,* May 28, 1977, and a series of articles in *Zycie Warszawy* by Bohdan Rolinski and Anna Klodzinska that were reprinted throughout the country.

12. See, for example, the article by Adam Michnik in *Le Monde,* October 25, 1977.

13. *The New York Times,* February 5, 1977.

14. Edward Babiuch, "The Working Class Party—the Party of the Nation as a Whole," *Nowe drogi,* June 1977, p. 9, and *Zycie partii,* January 1978 (back cover).

15. See Mieczyslaw F. Rakowski, "The Limits of Centralization," *Polityka,* November 5, 1977; Wladyslaw Ratynski, "For the Democratic Centralism," *Zycie Warszawy,* November 9, 1977; and Henryk Chadzynski, "Which Centralization, Which Decentralization," *Zycie Warszawy,* November 11, 1977.

16. See the text of the letter in *Der Spiegel* (Hamburg), January 16, 1978, pp. 94–97.

17. The speech was published in *Documentation Catholique* (Paris), August 15, 1976.

18. The text is in Raina, *Political Opposition,* pp. 224–28.

19. See, in particular, a book by one of the KOR leaders, Adam Michnik, *Kosciol, lewica, dialog.*

20. *Polish Press Agency,* October 29, 1977.

21. *Trybuna ludu,* December 2, 1977.

22. *Ibid.*

23. For details see J. B. de Weydenthal, "Church-State Relations in Poland: A Matter of Status," *RFER, Background Report,* June 30, 1980.

24. As quoted in *ibid.*

25. *Tygodnik powszechny,* February 12, 1978.

26. As quoted by William F. Robinson, "Church and State in Poland: From Dialogue to Cooperation," *RFER, Background Report,* July 12, 1978.

27. Mieczyslaw F. Rakowski, "The Basis for Cooperation and Dialogue," *Polityka,* March 25, 1978.

28. Jan Bijak, "The Most Important Is the Direction," *Polityka,* May 20, 1978.

29. Mieczyslaw F. Rakowski, "The Supreme Interest," *Polityka,* March 10, 1978.

30. For an analysis of the visit see de Weydenthal, *Poland,* pp. 77–82.

31. The KPN's program was based on a book, *Rewolucja bez revolucji,* by its founder Leszek Moczulski. The book was issued in a mimeographed form in mid-1979 in the underground.

32. The English-language text of the report is in *Poland: The State of the Republic.*
33. Mieczyslaw Moczar, "The Supreme Chamber of Control," *Zycie literackie,* November 19, 1978.
34. As quoted by de Weydenthal, *Poland,* pp. 41–42.
35. See October and November 1978 issues of *Polityka.*
36. *Trybuna ludu,* February 12, 1980.
37. *Ibid.,* February 15, 1980.
38. *Polish Press Agency,* March 24, 1980.
39. For details see Jan B. de Weydenthal, "Workers and Party in Poland," *Problems of Communism,* November–December 1980, pp. 1–22.
40. Radio Warsaw, July 9, 1980.
41. *Strajkowy biuletyn informacyjny,* August 16 and 19, 1980.
42. *Trybuna ludu,* August 25, 1980.
43. For the text of the agreements see *Zycie Warszawy,* September 2, 1980, and *Glos pracy,* September 6–7, 1980; for the English-language translation, see Jan B. de Weydenthal et al., *August 1980: The Strikes in Poland,* pp. 416–43.

10: THE POLITICAL COLLAPSE

1. There is considerable English-language literature dealing with developments in Poland in the aftermath of the August–September 1980 agreements. Among the most important books are Timothy Garton Ash, *The Polish Revolution: Solidarity 1980–1982*; Jan B. de Weydenthal, Bruce D. Porter, and Kevin Devlin, *The Polish Drama: 1980–1982*; Dennis MacShane, *Solidarity: Poland's Independent Trade Union*; Alain Touraine et al, *Solidarity: The Analysis of a Social Movement: Poland 1980–1981*; and Lawrence Weschler, *Solidarity: Poland in the Season of Its Passion.* The most comprehensive Polish-language book is Jerzy Holzer, *Solidarnosc 1980– 1981*; see also *Sisyphus: Sociological Studies,* a journal of the Polish Academy of Sciences, especially vol. III, *Crises and Conflicts: The Case of Poland 1980–1981,* Warsaw, 1982.
2. Radio Warsaw, August 15, 1980.
3. *Ibid.,* August 18, 1980.
4. The text of the directive was published in *Solidarnosc,* a daily bulletin issued at the Gdansk shipyard; English-language translation is in de Weydenthal et al., *August 1980,* pp. 343–344.
5. *Nowe drogi,* September 1980, pp. 18–22.
6. *Ibid.,* pp. 69–73.
7. For early description of this development see Witold Pawlowski, "Weryfikacja" in *Polityka,* November 8, 1980; see also Mieczyslaw F. Rakowski, "Porozmawiajmy o partii," *ibid.,* November 29, 1980. For a general discussion about the situation in the party during 1980–1981 by a relatively sympathetic observer, see George Sanford, *Polish Cummunism in Crisis.*
8. *Nowe drogi,* October–November 1980, pp. 9–32.
9. *Ibid.,* pp. 33–36.
10. *Ibid.,* pp. 59–399.
11. As reported from Warsaw by AP, Reuter, UPI, December 4, 1980.
12. Radio Warsaw, February 12, 1981.
13. *Trybuna ludu,* March 23, 1981.
14. *Ibid.,* March 31, 1981.
15. *Polityka,* January 31, 1981; see also Jacek Kurczewski's report on public opinion surveys as published in *Kultura* (Warsaw), March 1, 1981.

16. For details see Jerzy Olbrycht, "Raport o stanie partii," *Zolnierz wolnosci,* July 9, 1981; see also Appendix 1.3.

17. See Tadeusz Kolodziejczyk, "Nad przemianami w aparacie," *Zycie partii,* September 2, 1981; see also *Nowe drogi,* August 1981, pp. 60–61.

18. Lech Witkowski in *Polityka,* February 7, 1981; Witkowski was the party's first secretary at Torun University. See also Stanislaw Swiatek, "Uwaga: struktura!," *Nowosci* (Torun), May 13, 1981, and Zygmunt Simbierowicz, "W pionie i w poziomie," *Kultura* (Warsaw), May 10, 1981.

19. Marta Wesolowska i Piotr Moszynski, "Zyc wlasnym zyciem," *Polityka,* April 25, 1981; also *Nowosci,* April 16, 1981.

20. *Trybuna ludu,* April 30, 1981.

21. Instances of such insubordination were reported in *Zycie Warszawy,* March 13, 1981; *Glos wybrzeza,* March 16, 1981, and other papers; see also Piotr Moszynski in *Polityka,* March 7, 1981, and Ernest Skalski, "Notatki z Gdanska," *ibid.,* April 11, 1981.

22. See Kolodziejczyk in *Zycie partii,* September 2, 1981, esp. pp. 47–48.

23. For a partial listing of those groups see *Glos wybrzeza,* July 9, 1981.

24. The text appeared first in *Sztandar mlodych,* May 28, 1981; for a report about the Katowice Forum group see Jacek Maziarski, "Do tylu," *Kultura* (Warsaw), June 14, 1981.

25. See *Glos wybrzeza,* June 1, 1981.

26. See Marta Wesolowska's report from a party meeting in Warsaw in *Polityka,* April 11, 1981.

27. For a comprehensive discussion of the Soviet Union's policy toward Poland in 1980–1982, see de Weydenthal et al., *The Polish Drama,* esp. pp. 101–43, 283–98; for a detailed analysis of the Soviet press reports about Polish developments, especially during the last months of 1980, see Ricardo Estarriol, *The Soviet Approach to the Polish Crisis.*

28. *Tass,* October 30, 1980.

29. *Ibid.,* December 5, 1980.

30. *Polish Press Agency,* March 4, 1981.

31. *Tass,* April 23, 1981; *Polish Press Agency,* April 24, 1981.

32. *Ibid.,* April 25, 1981.

33. The letter was first published in *Trybuna ludu,* June 11, 1981.

34. See the July 1981 issue of *Nowe drogi,* which includes Kania's speech as well as texts of the discussion and resolutions.

35. *Ibid.,* p. 6.

36. *Ibid.,* August 1981, p. 8; this entire issue was devoted to congressional documents.

37. See Appendix 1.3.

38. See de Weydenthal et al., *The Polish Drama,* p. 83.

39. *Trybuna ludu,* September 3, 1981.

40. *Tygodnik Solidarnosc,* September 11, 1981.

41. For an analysis of Solidarity's congress see de Weydenthal et al., *The Polish Drama,* pp. 85–88.

42. *Trybuna ludu,* September 17, 1981.

43. *Polish Press Agency,* September 18, 1981.

44. The text of Jaruzelski's speech is in *Nowe drogi,* November 1981, pp. 52–54.

45. *Trybuna ludu,* October 20, 1981.

46. See the text in *Nowe drogi,* November 1981, pp. 40–44.

47. See *The Guardian* (London), October 23, 1981, for Kubiak's statement and

Radio Warsaw, October 24, 1981, for Barcikowski's speech to a group of party activists in Poznan.

48. *Nowe drogi,* November 1981, p. 233.
49. *Ibid.*
50. *Ibid.,* pp. 234–39.
51. *Ibid.,* December 1981, pp. 8, 22.
52. *Ibid.,* p. 28.

11: THE SOCIALIST RENEWAL

1. For a discussion of the martial-law developments and their impact on Poland's public life, see de Weydenthal et al., *The Polish Drama,* pp. 237–81.
2. See A. Ross Johnson, Robert W. Dean, and Alexander Alexiev, *East European Military Establishments,* p. 201; see also George C. Malcher, *Poland's Politicized Army,* p. 44, and J. B. de Weydenthal, "Martial Law and the Reliability of the Polish Military," in D. N. Nelson (ed.), *Soviet Allies: The Warsaw Pact and the Issue of Reliability,* pp. 225–49.
3. *Trybuna ludu,* January 23–24, 1982.
4. *Zycie partii,* February 1981, p. 22, and *Polityka,* August 15, 1981.
5. *Trybuna robotnicza,* December 14, 1981.
6. See an article by Jozef Cegla in *Polityka,* March 6, 1982.
7. *Zycie partii,* March 3, 1982. For specific examples of those streamlining tactics, see articles by a former CC staff member, Michal Jagiello, and former provincial first secretary from Poznan, Edward Skrzypczak, published in the Warsaw underground quarterly *Krytyka,* no. 18, 1984, pp. 106–19 and 120–49, respectively.
8. *Nowe drogi,* March 1982, pp. 28–29.
9. See articles by Dan Fisher in *The Los Angeles Times,* February 15, 1982, and Bradley Graham in *The Washington Post,* February 17, 1982.
10. *Rzeczywistosc,* May 23, 1982.
11. *Nowe drogi,* March 1982, p. 37.
12. As quoted in *Zycie partii,* December 22, 1982.
13. *Trybuna ludu,* July 2, 1984.
14. *Zycie partii,* December 4, 1985.
15. *Zycie Warszawy,* June 25, 1982.
16. *Rzeczpospolita,* February 15, 1982.
17. *Zycie Warszawy,* October 9–10, 1982.
18. Speech by M. F. Rakowski, cited in *Trybuna ludu,* November 26, 1984.
19. *Ibid.,* November 27, 1984.
20. *Ibid.,* July 22, 1983.
21. *Ibid.,* June 1, 1983.
22. The text of the first draft appeared in *Nowe drogi,* March 1982, pp. 39–50.
23. *Trybuna ludu,* March 21, 1984.
24. *Gazeta robotnicza,* July 26, 1982.
25. *Zycie partii,* September 1982, p. 3.
26. That was implicitly admitted by Politburo member Kazimierz Barcikowski in an interview published in *Polityka,* March 3, 1984.
27. For a description of underground bodies and operations, see a book of remarkable interviews with several top underground leaders: M. Lopinski, M. Moskit, and M. Wilk, *Konspira.*
28. *Niedziela,* March 4, 1984.
29. *Nowe drogi,* April 1983, p. 18.

30. *Ibid.,* p. 36.
31. See *Polityka,* September 24, 1983.
32. For a perceptive analysis of the Popieluszko case, including a full transcript of the trial, see P. Michel and G. Mink, *Mort d'un Pretre.*
33. de Weydenthal et al., *The Polish Drama,* pp. 101–43, 283–98.

Selected Bibliography

PRIMARY SOURCES: MEMOIRS,
DOCUMENTS, SPEECHES

Archiwum ruchu robotniczego. 2 vols. Warsaw: Ksiazka i Wiedza, 1975.

Bialer, Seweryn. *Wybralem prawde*. New York: Free Europe Committee, Inc., 1955.

Bierut, Boleslaw. *O partii*. Warsaw: Ksiazka i Wiedza, 1952.

————. *Zadania partii w walce o czujnosc rewolucyjna na tle sytuacji obecnej*. Warsaw: Ksiazka i Wiedza, 1949.

————, and Cyrankiewicz, Jozef. *Podstawy ideologiczne PZPR*. Warsaw: Ksiazka i Wiedza, 1952.

Bliss-Lane, Arthur. *I Saw Poland Betrayed*. Indianapolis: Bobbs-Merrill, 1948.

Gomulka, Wladyslaw. *Artykuly i przemowienia*. 2 vols. Warsaw: Ksiazka i Wiedza, 1962 and 1964.

————. *O naszej partii*. Warsaw: Ksiazka i Wiedza, 1968.

————. *Przemowienia*. 1956–1968. 11 vols. Warsaw: Ksiazka i Wiedza, 1957–1969.

KPP. *Uchwaly i rezolucje*. 3 vols. Warsaw: Ksiazka i Wiedza, 1953–1956.

Khrushchev, Nikita S. *Khrushchev Remembers: The Last Testament*. Trans. and ed. Strobe Talbot. Boston: Little, Brown, 1974.

Kliszko, Zenon. *O projekcie statutu*. Warsaw: Ksiazka, 1946.

Korbonski, Stefan. *W imieniu Rzeczypospolitej*. Paris: Instytut Literacki, 1954.

Koszutska, Maria (Kostrzewa, Wera). *Pisma i przemowienia*. 3 vols. Warsaw: Ksiazka i Wiedza, 1961–1962.

Ksztaltowanie sie podstaw programowych PPR w latach 1942–1945. Wybor materialow i dokumentow. Warsaw: Ksiazka i Wiedza, 1958.

Lenski, Julian (Leszczynski, Julian). *O front ludowy w Polsce, 1934–1937*. Warsaw: Ksiazka i Wiedza, 1956.

Luksemburg, Roza. *Wybor pism*. 2 vols. Warsaw: Ksiazka i Wiedza, 1959.

Luxemburg, Rosa. *The Industrial Development of Poland*. New York: Campaigner Publications, Inc., 1977.

————. *The Russian Revolution and Leninism or Marxism*. Ed. by Bertram D. Wolfe. Ann Arbor, Mich.: The University of Michigan Press, 1961.

Marchlewski, Julian. *Pisma wybrane*. 2 vols. Warsaw: Ksiazka i Wiedza, 1952, 1956.

Mikolajczyk, Stanislaw. *The Rape of Poland: Pattern of Soviet Aggression*. New York: McGraw-Hill, 1948.

Nowy przeglad. 1922–1929. 6 vols. (re-edition). Warsaw: Ksiazka i Wiedza, 1957–1966.

Ochab, Edward. *O niektorych zadaniach organizacyjnych i zmianach w statucie partii*. Ksiazka i Wiedza, 1954.

Poland: The State of the Republic. London: Pluto, 1981.

Polskie przedwiosnie. Wybor dokumentow. Paris: Instytut Literacki, 1969.

Poznan 1956—Grudzien 1970. Paris: Instytut Literacki, 1971.

PPR. Rezolucje, odezwy, instrukcje i okolniki Komitetu Centralnego PPR, VIII 1944–XII 1945. Warsaw: Ksiazka i Wiedza, 1959.

———. *Statut PPR uchwalony na I zjezdzie PPR.* Lodz: Ksiazka, 1948.

PZPR. Deklaracja ideowa i statut PZPR. Warsaw: Ksiazka i Wiedza, 1949.

Rewolta szczecinska i jej znaczenie. Paris: Instytut Literacki, 1971.

Schizmy. Paris: Instytut Literacki, 1966.

Sontag, R. J. and Beddie. J. S., eds. *Nazi-Soviet Relations, 1939–1941. Documents from the Archives of the German Foreign Office.* Washington, D.C.: U.S. Department of State, 1948.

Sukiennicki, Wiktor, ed. *Biala Ksiega.* Paris: Instytut Literacki, 1964.

Swiatlo, Jozef. *Za kulisami bezpieki i partii.* New York: Free Europe Committee, Inc., n.d.

Toranska, Teresa., ed. *Oni.* London: Aneks, 1985.

Tymczasowy Komitet Revolucyjny Polski. Warsaw: Ksiazka i Wiedza, 1955.

Walecki, Henryk (Horwitz, Maksymilian). *Wybor pism.* 2 vols. Warsaw: Ksiazka i Wiedza, 1967.

Warski, Adolf (Warszawski, Adolf). *Wybor pism i przemowien.* 2 vols. Warsaw: Ksiazka i Wiedza, 1958.

Who is Who and What is What in Solidarnosc. Gdansk: BIPS, 1981.

Wydarzenia marcowe, 1968. Wybor dokumentow. Paris: Instytut Literacki, 1969.

Zambrowski, Roman. *O masowa milionowa partie.* Katowice: Trybuna robotnicza, 1945.

———, and Swiatkowski, Henryk. *O statucie i zadaniach organizacyjnych PZPR.* Warsaw: Ksiazka i Wiedza, 1949.

SECONDARY SOURCES

Andrews, Nicholas G. *Poland 1980–1981.* Washington: National Defense University Press, 1985.

Ash, Timothy Garton. *The Polish Revolution: Solidarity 1980–1982.* London: J. Cape, 1983.

Asherson, Neal. *The Polish August: The Self-Limiting Revolution.* London: Penguin, 1981.

Beck, Carl et al. *Comparative Communist Political Leadership.* New York: David McKay, 1973.

Bethell, Nicholas. *Gomulka.* London: Penguin Books, 1972.

Bienkowski, Wladyslaw. *Motory i hamulce socjalizmu.* Paris: Instytut Literacki, 1969.

———. *Rewolucji ciag dalszy.* Warsaw: Ksiazka i Wiedza, 1957.

———. *Socjologia kleski.* Paris: Instytut Literacki, 1971.

Blit, Lucjan. *The Eastern Pretender.* London: Hutchison, 1965.

———. *The Origins of Polish Socialism: The History and Ideas of the First Polish Socialist Party,* 1878–1886. Cambridge University Press, 1971.

Blum, Ignacy. *Z dziejow Wojska Polskiego w latach 1945–1948.* Warsaw: Ministerstwo Obrony Narodowej, 1960.

Bromke, Adam. *Poland's Politics: Idealism vs. Realism.* Cambridge, Mass.: Harvard University Press, 1967.

———, and Strong, John W., eds. *Gierek's Poland.* New York: Praeger, 1973.

Brown, J. F. *The New Eastern Europe.* New York: Praeger, 1966.

Brumberg, Abraham, ed. *Poland: Genesis of the Revolution.* New York: Random House, 1983.

Brzezinski, Zbigniew K. *The Soviet Bloc: Unity and Conflict.* Cambridge, Mass.: Harvard University Press, 1967.

Burks, R. V. *The Dynamics of Communism in Eastern Europe.* Princeton, N.J.: Princeton University Press, 1961.

Ciechanowski, Jan M. *The Warsaw Uprising of 1944.* New York: Cambridge University Press, 1974.

Cieplak, Tadeusz N., ed. *Poland since 1956.* New York: Twayne Publishers, 1972.

Ciolkosz, Lidia and Adam. *Zarys dziejow socjalizmu polskiego.* London: Gryf Publishers, 1966.

Curry, Jane L., ed. *The Black Book of Polish Censorship.* New York: Vintage, 1984.

Daniszewski, Tadeusz, ed. *Zarys historii polskiego ruchu robotniczego, 1864–1918.* Warsaw: Ksiazka i Wiedza, 1961.

Davies, Norman. *White Eagle—Red Star: The Polish-Soviet War, 1919–1920.* London: McDonald, 1972.

de Weydenthal, Jan B. *Poland: Communism Adrift.* The Washington Paper no. 72. Beverly Hills and London: Sage, 1979.

——— et al. *August 1980: The Strikes in Poland.* Munich: Radio Free Europe Research, 1980.

———, Porter, Bruce D., and Devlin, Kevin. *The Polish Drama: 1980–1982.* Lexington and Toronto: Lexington Press, 1983.

Dziewanowski, M. K. *Jozef Pilsudski: A European Federalist, 1918–1922.* Stanford, Calif.: Hoover Institution Press, 1969.

———. *The Communist Party of Poland.* Cambridge, Mass.: Harvard University Press, 1976.

Edinger, Lewis, ed. *Political Leadership in Industrialized Societies.* New York: Wiley, 1967.

Estarriol, Ricardo. *The Soviet Approach to the Polish Crisis; Mimeograph.* Cambridge, Mass.: Harvard University Russian Research Center, 1982.

Farrell, R. Barry, ed. *Political Leadership in Eastern Europe and the Soviet Union.* Chicago: Aldine, 1970.

Fischer-Galati, Stephen, ed. *Eastern Europe in The Sixties.* New York: Praeger, 1963.

Fiszman, Joseph R. *Revolution and Tradition in People's Poland.* Princeton, N.J.: Princeton University Press, 1972.

Friedrich, Carl J., ed. *Totalitarianism.* Cambridge, Mass.: Harvard University Press, 1954.

———, and Brzezinski, Zbigniew K. *Totalitarian Dictatorship and Autocracy.* New York: Praeger, 1966.

Galeski, Bronislaw. *Socjologia wsi.* Warsaw: Panstwowe Wydawnictwo Naukowe, 1966.

———. *Spoleczna struktura wsi*. Warsaw: Panstwowe Wydawnictwo Naukowe, 1962.

Gamarnikow, Michael. *Economic Reforms in Eastern Europe*. Detroit: Wayne State University Press, 1968.

Gati, Charles, ed. *The International Politics of Eastern Europe*. New York: Praeger, 1976.

———, ed. *The Politics of Modernization in Eastern Europe*. New York: Praeger, 1974.

Gibney, Frank. *The Frozen Revolution in Poland: A Study in Communist Decay*. New York: Farrar, Straus and Cudahy, 1959.

Granas, Romana. *O statucie PZPR*. Warsaw: Ksiazka i Wiedza, 1950.

Griffith, William E., ed. *Communism in Europe*. Vol. I. Cambridge, Mass.: The M.I.T. Press, 1964.

Gross, Feliks. *The Revolutionary Party*. Westport, Conn.: Greenwood Press, 1974.

———. *The Seizure of Political Power*. New York: Philosophical Library, 1958.

Gwizdz, A., Jarosz, Z., and Popkowski, W., eds. *Ustroj Polskiej Rzeczypospolitej Ludowej. Wybor materialow*. Warsaw: Panstwowe Zaklady Wydawnictwo Szkolnych, 1967.

Gyorgy, Andrew, ed. *Issues of World Communism*. Princeton, NJ.: Princeton University Press, 1966.

Heller, Celia S. *On the Edge of Destruction: Jews of Poland Between the Two World Wars*. New York: Columbia University Press, 1977.

Hiscocks, Richard. *Poland: Bridge for the Abyss?* New York: Oxford University Press, 1963.

Holzer, Jerzy. *Solidarnosc 1980–1981*. Paris: Instytut Literacki, 1984.

Hough, Jerry F. *The Polish Crisis: American Policy Options*. Washington, D.C.: Brookings Institution, 1982.

Huntington, Samuel P. and Moore, Clement H., eds. *Authoritarian Politics in Modern Society: The Dynamics of Established One-Party Systems*. New York: Basic Books, 1970.

Ionescu, Ghita. *The Politics of the East European Communist States*. New York: Praeger, 1967.

Jedlicki, Witold. *Klub Krzywego Kola*. Instytut Literacki, 1963.

Johnson, A. Ross; Dean, Robert W.; and Alexiev, Alexander. *East European Military Establishments*. New York: Crane Russak, 1982.

Johnson, Chalmers, ed. *Change in Communist Systems*. Stanford, Calif.: Stanford University Press, 1970.

Jowitt, Kenneth. *Revolutionary Breakthroughs and National Development: The Case of Romania, 1944–1965*. Berkeley, Calif.: University of California Press, 1972.

Kertesz, Stephen D., ed. *The Fate of East Central Europe*. Notre Dame, Ind.: University of Notre Dame Press, 1956.

Kolomyjczyk, Norbert. *PPR 1944–1945*. Warsaw: Ksiazka i Wiedza, 1965.

Kolakowski, Leszek. *Toward a Marxist Humanism*. New York: Grove Press, 1968.

Komorowski, Tadeusz (Bor). *Armia Podziemna*. London: Veritas, 1951.

Korbonski, Andrzej. *Politics of Socialist Agriculture in Poland, 1945–1960*. New York: Columbia University Press, 1965.

Korybutowicz, Zygmunt. *Grudzien 1970*. Paris: Instytut Literacki, 1983.

Kowalski, Jozef. *Komunistyczna Partia Polski, 1935–1938*. Warsaw: Ksiazka i Wiedza, 1975.

———. *Trudne lata*. Warsaw: Ksiazka i Wiedza, 1966.

———. *Zarys historii polskiego ruchu robotniczego w latach 1918–1939*. Warsaw: Ksiazka i Wiedza, 1962.

Kuron, Jacek and Modzelewski, Karol. *List otwarty do partii*. Paris: Instytut Literacki, 1966.

Kurz, Andrzej. *Spoleczna rola PZPR*. Warsaw: Ksiazka i Wiedza, 1967.

Lane, David and Kolankiewicz, George, eds. *Social Groups in Polish Society*. New York: Columbia University Press, 1973.

Lendvai, Paul. *Anti-Semitism Without Jews*. New York: Doubleday, 1971.

Lewis, Flora. *A Case History of Hope: The Story of Poland's Peaceful Revolution*. New York: Doubleday, 1958.

Lopinski, Maciej, Moskit, Marcin, and Wilk, Mariusz. *Konspira*. Paris: Editions Spotkania, 1984.

MacShane, Dennis. *Solidarity: Poland's Independent Trade Union*. Nottingham: Spokesman, 1981.

Malcher, George C. *Poland's Politicized Army*. New York: Praeger, 1984.

Malinowski, Marian. *Geneza PPR*. Warsaw: Ksiazka i Wiedza, 1972.

———, et al. *Polski ruch robotniczy w okresie okupacji hitlerowskiej*. Warsaw: Ksiazka i Wiedza, 1964.

Masa-Lago, Carmelo and Beck, Carl, eds. *Comparative Socialist Systems: Essays on Politics and Economics*. Pittsburgh, Pa.: University of Pittsburgh Center for International Studies, 1975.

Michel, Patrick, and Mink, Georges. *Mort d'un Pretre*. Paris: Fayard, 1985.

Michnik, Adam. *Kosciol, lewica, dialog*. Paris: Instytut Literacki, 1977.

Mieroszewski, Juliusz. *Ewolucjonizm*. Paris: Instytut Literacki, 1964.

Milosz, Czeslaw. *The Captive Mind*. London: Secker and Warburg, 1953.

Najdus, Walentyna. *Lewica polska w kraju rad*. Warsaw: Ksiazka i Wiedza, 1971.

Nelson, D. N., ed. *Soviet Allies: The Warsaw Pact and the Issue of Reliability*. Boulder and London: Westview, 1984.

Neuburg, Paul. *The Hero's Children: The Post-war Generation in Eastern Europe*. New York: William Morrow, 1973.

Pobog-Malinowski, Wladyslaw. *Najnowsza historia Polski*. 3 vols. London: Gryf Publishers, 1956–1960.

Raina, Peter. *Wladyslaw Gomulka*. London: Polonia, 1969.

———. *Political Opposition in Poland, 1954–1977*. London: Poets and Printers, 1978.

Rakowski, Mieczyslaw F. *Przesilenie grudniowe*. Warsaw: PIW, 1981.

Regula, Jan Alfred (pseud.) *Historja Komunistycznej Partji Polski*. Warsaw: Drukprasa, 1934.

Remington, Robin A., ed. *Winter in Prague*. Cambridge, Mass.: The M.I.T. Press, 1969.

Rocznik Statystyczny (annual publication). Warsaw: Glowny Urzad Statystyczny.

Rothschild, Joseph. *Pilsudski's Coup d'Etat*. New York: Columbia University Press, 1966.

Sadowski, Michal. *Przemiany spoleczne a system partyjny PRL*. Warsaw: Ksiazka i Wiedza, 1969.

———. *System partyjny PRL*. Warsaw: Ksiazka i Wiedza, 1971.

Sanford, George. *Polish Communism in Crisis*. New York: St. Martin's Press, 1983.

Sarapata, Adam, ed. *Przemiany spoleczne w Polsce Ludowej,* Warsaw: Panstwowe Wydawnictwo Naukowe, 1965.

Selznick, Philip. *The Organizational Weapon*. Glencoe, Ill.: Free Press, 1960.

Seton-Watson, Hugh. *The East European Revolution*. London: Methuen, 1952.

Shneiderman, S. L. *The Warsaw Heresy*. New York: Horizon Press, 1959.

Sinanian, Sylvia, et al., eds. *Eastern Europe in the 1970s*. New York: Praeger, 1970.

Skilling, H. Gordon. *The Governments of Communist East Europe*. New York: Crowell, 1966.

———. *Czechoslovakia's Interrupted Revolution*. Princeton, N.J.: Princeton University Press, 1976.

Simmonds, George W., ed. *Nationalism in the USSR and Eastern Europe in the Era of Brezhnev and Kosygin*. Detroit: University of Detroit Press, 1977.

Staar, Richard F. *Communist Regimes in Eastern Europe*. Stanford, Calif.: Hoover Institution Press, 1977.

———. *Poland 1944–1962: The Sovietization of a Captive People*. Westport, Conn.: Greenwood Press, 1975.

———, ed. *Aspects of Modern Communism*. Columbia, S.C.: University of South Carolina Press, 1968.

———, ed. *1969–1982 Yearbook on International Communist Affairs*. Stanford, Calif.: Hoover Institution Press, 1969–1982.

Stehle, Hansjakob. *The Independent Satellite*. New York: Praeger, 1965.

Strapinski, Adam. *Wywrotowe partie polityczne*. Warsaw: Instytut Naukowy Badania Komunizmu, 1933.

Swietlikowa, Franciszka. *Komunistyczna Partia Robotnicza Polski, 1918–1923*. Warsaw: Ksiazka i Wiedza, 1968.

Syrop, Konrad. *Spring in October: The Story of the Polish Revolution in October 1956*. London: Weidenfeld and Nicolson, 1957.

Szczepanski, Jan. *Polish Society*. New York: Random House, 1970.

Teslar, Tadeusz. *Propaganda bolszewicka podczas wojny polsko–rosyjskiej 1920 roku*. Warsaw: Wojskowy Instytut naukowo–oswiatowy, 1938.

Toma, Peter A., ed. *The Changing Face of Communism in Eastern Europe*. Tucson: University of Arizona Press, 1970.

Touraine, Alain et al. *Solidarity: The Analysis of a Social Movement: Poland 1980–1981*. Cambridge: Cambridge University Press, 1983.

Triska, Jan, ed. *Constitutions of the Communist Party-States*. Stanford, Calif.: Hoover Institution Press, 1968.

————, and Cocks, Paul, eds. *Political Development in Eastern Europe*. New York: Praeger, 1977.

Turlejska, Maria. *Spor o Polske*. Warsaw: Czytelnik, 1972.

————. *Zapis pierwszej dekady, 1945–1954*. Warsaw: Ksiazka i Wiedza, 1972.

Ulam, Adam. *Titoism and the Cominform*. Cambridge, Mass.: Harvard University Press, 1952.

Wandycz, Piotr S. *Soviet-Polish Relations, 1917–1921*. Cambridge, Mass.: Harvard University Press, 1969.

Weschler, Lawrence. *Solidarity: Poland in the Season of Its Passion*. New York: Simon and Schuster, 1982.

Wesolowski, Wlodzimierz. *Klasy, warstwy i wladza*. Warsaw: Panstwowe Wydawnictwo Naukowe, 1966.

Index